2005

ANTECEDENTS TO MODERN RWANDA

AFRICA AND THE DIASPORA
History, Politics, Culture

SERIES EDITORS

Thomas Spear
David Henige
Michael Schatzberg

ANTECEDENTS TO MODERN RWANDA

THE NYIGINYA KINGDOM

Jan Vansina
Translated by the author

THE UNIVERSITY OF WISCONSIN PRESS

The University of Wisconsin Press
1930 Monroe Street
Madison, Wisconsin 53711

www.wisc.edu/wisconsinpress/

3 Henrietta Street
London WC2E 8LU, England

1   3   5   4   2

Printed in the United States of America

Library of Congress Cataloging-in-Publication Data
Vansina, Jan.
[Rwanda ancien. English]
Antecedents to modern Rwanda : the Nyiginya Kingdom / Jan Vansina.
p.   cm. — (Africa and the diaspora)
Translation of: Rwanda ancien, with an update to the chronology
between 1876 and 1885.
Includes bibliographical references and index.
ISBN 0-299-20120-1 (alk. paper)
ISBN 0-299-20124-4 (pbk. : alk. paper)
1.   Rwanda—Kings and rulers.   2. Rwanda—History.
I. Title.   II. Series.
DT450.34.V3813   2004
967.571′01 — dc22   2004007798

967.571
V 279

CONTENTS

MAPS

PREFACE

This book is an introduction to the history of Rwanda before 1900 and in particular of the kingdom that forms its core. It has not been written for specialists only, but for all those who are interested, Rwandans and others, whether their goal be to better understand the present through a better knowledge of the past, a past that stretches back over several centuries, or whether they are attracted to the history of the kingdom itself. Indeed I am convinced that the substance of this history is not merely interesting in and for itself, but also as a topic for fruitful thought for those who focus on contemporary issues and problems. Hence I include an occasional note here and there with a brief reminder to a parallel situation in the present.

In consideration of the audience for which I am writing, I chose to write a rather straightforward and nonpolemical exposition from which issues that are mainly of interest to specialists—such as historiographical debates, arguments about the value of particular sources, and detailed chronological issues—have been excluded. Yet since every reader must also be kept informed of the sources that support each of the statements made in this book, that information is given in the notes. Moreover, many notes include references to other authors whose opinions often diverge strongly from my own; these references provide a further reading list for the reader who would like to further explore the various questions that the notes raise.

Since we are dealing here with a book aimed at a rather wide range of readers I have presented the unfolding of the political history in a straightforward fashion and in chronological order, almost as if a tale was being told. But the social history that undergirds the political dynamic requires a less narrative-oriented approach and more of an analytical one. In consequence, I decided to alternate between analytical chapters dealing with social history and more detailed narrative chapters covering political developments for the same period. The subject is thus presented in paired chapters, one century after the other, the only exception being the last chapter, which deals with the end of the nine-teenth century. One can therefore read only the narrative chapters and skip the others or the reverse—but that would be a bad idea. For while social history is the essential backdrop for an understanding of the nar-rative detail that focuses on the political dynamics in the narrow sense, the more generalized character of this social history must of necessity be embedded in the framework of the more concrete details of the nar-rative chapters. Hence like all authors, I strongly encourage my readers to read the whole book!

Since the publication of *Le Rwanda ancien: le royaume nyiginya*, it has been pointed out to me that an influential group of interested readers does not read French and would wish to see this book translated into English. Here it is then, nearly identical to the original, although I used a bit of new evidence in Appendix 1 to fine-tune the chronology between 1876 and 1885.

Madison, August 2003

ACKNOWLEDGMENTS

To a large degree this work is a product of research pursued in Rwanda between 1957 and 1962 as part of a large-scale endeavor to collect together the genre of historical tales known as *ibitéekerezo*. The research was carried out under the auspices of IRSAC (the Institute for Scientific Research in Central Africa). I therefore not only want to thank hundreds of storytellers for their participation in this project and to commemorate the role of the institute in this project, but also to recall the memory and the devotion to their task of those Rwandans who were members of this research team. Among them Alexis Mumvaneza stands out especially since one of his contributions was to report the set of archaeological sites around Dahwe that have proved to be of such importance for the early history of the country.

This study has benefited from the assistance of several of my colleagues. Pride of place goes here to Catherine and David Newbury for their valuable, detailed commentaries on a first draft of this text and for the copy of the inquiries of Ivan Reisdorff that they gave me. I also particularly appreciate the input of Michele Wagner who read and annotated a good part of the text despite her heavy workload. As for David Henige, that virtuoso in the study of the rules of evidence, he became more than once the laboratory where I could try out various interpretations of rather slender data. In addition he took great pains to locate various publications for me. Other colleagues have also helped me to find documents and given their opinion on specific issues. René Lemarchand asked me some challenging questions, drew attention to several important documents, and sent me a copy of an important report by Léon Classe. Beatrix Heintze encouraged me and mailed me copies of several rare publications. I must also thank Gerda Rossel, Alain Froment, and Henri Médart for their advice and texts. Although I have not always made the opinions proffered by these scholars my own, still sometimes they did change my own views and they have always helped me in presenting my ideas in a more convincing manner. To all of you, heartfelt thanks!

NOTE ON SPELLING

In general we follow the usual spelling for Kinyarwanda, the language of Rwanda. We do not indicate suprasegmentary segments (vowel length, tones) except when a linguistic argument requires it. The letter sequence "li" is always written "ri," which is the canonical variant. Hence we always have Cyirima, for instance, never Cyilima. Ordinary substantives in Kinyarwanda are cited with their prefixes and augments (or pre-prefixes), although these elements change from singular to plural. Thus one has *"umugaragu"* for "client herder" in the singular and *"abagaragu"* for "client herders" in the plural, or *"umuryango"* for " great lineage" in the singular and *"imiryango"* for "great lineages" in the plural. But in more complex cases—for instance, when the invariable part of the word begins with a vowel—one cites the singular, followed by "sing.," only when a plural is cited. For example, *"abami"* for "kings" (*"umwami"* for "king," sing.), *"amooko"* for "species" or "kinds" (*"ubwoko"* for "species" or "kind," sing.) Place names and names of persons are written in the official Rwandan spelling, except for the official sequence "li." But with regard to the names of ethnic or other human groups—for example, clans—we follow the international convention according to which all initial elements are deleted. Hence we have the Rwanda for the people of the country, not the Abanya-rwanda, the Ngwe, not the Abene-ngwe, the Nyiginya, not the Abanyiginya, and the Ega, not the Abega.

Historical regions of central Rwanda

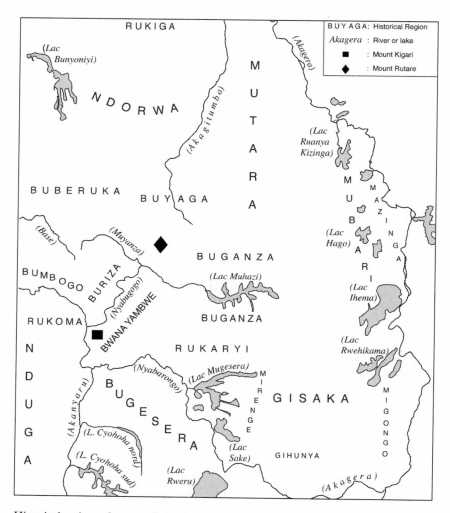

Historical regions of eastern Rwanda

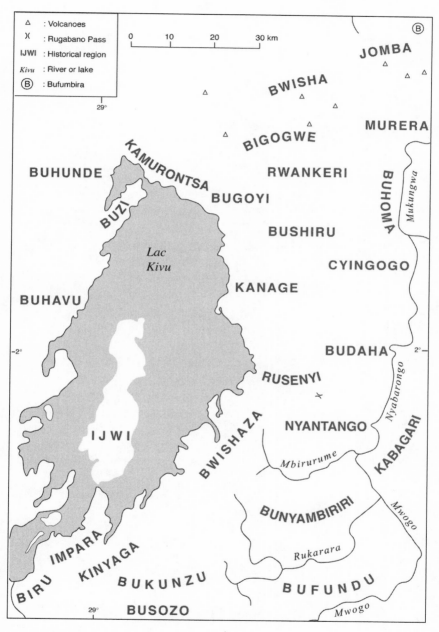

Historical regions of western Rwanda

ANTECEDENTS TO MODERN RWANDA

Introduction

Interest in the history of Rwanda before 1900 has been reawakened today by recent events and the topic has become embroiled in a good deal of controversy linked to contemporary political, social, and cultural issues that confront the Republic of Rwanda. It is essential to know the early history of Rwanda, and in particular the history of the former Nyiginya kingdom, if one is to understand the history of the country in the twentieth century, for modern Rwanda was built on the economic, social, and political foundations encountered by the first colonials. Indeed, when the first German military administrator arrived in the country, the Nyiginya kingdom had already had a checkered career spanning two centuries. Moreover, this earlier history is not just of considerable interest to Rwandans today, but it is also valuable for comparative studies of the kingdoms of the region because it reveals certain peculiar features that turned it into an extraordinary kingdom, "the greatest and the most complex" in the Great Lakes region and one that differed from all the others.[1]

Furthermore, a plethora of information about this kingdom is available, stemming from a varied and very rich corpus of oral traditions.[2] These sources constitute the main foundation of its historiography. Still, we should not forget that these are oral sources. They absolutely cannot be handled just like written sources, which is what most historiographers have unfortunately been inclined to do. For while an original written source is the same now as the day it was written, oral sources are evanescent and one must therefore apply appropriate rules of evidence to them before using them. To a large extent it is the oral character of the sources that has fostered historiographic controversies as well as a number of myths that have been propagated about the history of this kingdom. All too often recent authors have used one or another isolated oral utterance without worrying about its representativeness or its intrinsic reliability and that is also the major weakness of the older syntheses. Still, the historical critique of oral traditions has made considerable

progress over nearly half a century and now allows for a better informed use of these data.[3] That has encouraged me to write this history,
even though in spite of all my best efforts this monograph cannot resolve all the controversies, if only because the temptation to pick out a
stray oral utterance to "prove" a favorite thesis will no doubt often remain irresistible. But I may hope that my readers will accept the need
for a critical approach so that, even if they end up rejecting this or that
proposition made here, they will do so as a result of applying the rules of
evidence. That by itself would be a nice achievement!

So far no published book deals with the history of the Nyiginya kingdom in a satisfactory way. Yes, several histories of Rwanda have recently
been published, but they all focus on the history of the immediate past.[4]
When it comes to times before 1900 one can reproach them that, rather
than study all the available sources anew, they are content to faithfully
reproduce the by-now older syntheses produced by that great collector
of traditions and oral literature, Abbé Alexis Kagame,[5] adorned by some
further considerations about the Rwandan way of life toward the end
of the nineteenth century. Yet the syntheses of this scholar essentially
consist in providing a chronicle of the doings of the kings. I have been
disappointed by this surrender to the old views by recent authors and
it was this in the end that finally pushed me to write a history of the
Nyiginya kingdom, one that to my mind seems to be very different
from those of Kagame and his epigones.

The legacy of Kagame should not be underestimated, for even
today it is still rooted in the general historical consciousness of Rwandans and it still dominates the perception of Rwanda's history, even that
of his most virulent critics.[6] This situation results just as much from the
profusion of oral information that Kagame deploys as from the fact
that his *Abrégés* were and still are textbooks used in many schools. Moreover, his vision of the past is not his own, nor is it the vision of the colonial historiographers—mostly missionaries or administrators—who
preceded him. The essence of his vision comes from the royal court and
more precisely from a handful of courtiers who were official ideologues
in charge of giving a meaning to history and of elaborating the official
version of its details. It was their task to set it forth, to hold it, to defend
it against heresy, to elaborate on it, and to apply it to all the historical
genres practiced at the court. They were that "corporate intelligentsia"[7]
that produced the essential data used by all the authors. Thus almost
the whole written historiography merely reproduces the royal ideology
as it existed around 1900. Such was the formal character and the

thoroughness of the hold of the Nyiginya court over the production of history that no author, perhaps with the exception of Kagame, has been aware of its full extent. They thought that they were interrogating the best "informants," they believed that they were obtaining "independent" information, but they did not escape from the hold of the court ideologues. And as the researchers did not expect to meet any institution in charge of controlling the production of history and of its representation, let alone an institution of such a wide reach and such a degree of subtlety, they have all been caught in its cognitive glue.[8]

To a large extent Kagame's *Abrégés* are mainly the written precipitate of this official vision and it is against this vision that this book rebels, especially on the following points, among others: that the Nyiginya kingdom is not equivalent to Rwanda as a whole; that a history of the kings is not a complete History in general, indeed, not even a complete political history; that the kingdom has not existed since hoary antiquity but is a relatively recent creation; that its kings were neither autocratic nor omnipotent; that its politics were not planned; that its centralization was peculiar and not founded on a homogeneous territorial administration; that its military was not always victorious; and that its upper class was not more intelligent or better able to command than any of the other classes were.

The Oral Sources

It is self-evident that treatment and critique of the oral sources is of crucial importance to the construction of any history of the Nyiginya kingdom and it is fitting to say something more about them.[9] The oral traditions can clearly be divided into a set of official sources transmitted and controlled by the court and a set of popular sources. The first include a very large number of traditions, rendered in a much wider fan of genres than has been common in other African kingdoms. Merely to draw attention to this fact is already to underline how exceptional the role of history has been in the ideology of Nyiginya royalty.

Samples of most of the literary genres in which these official sources were composed have been published and certain genres have benefited from general critical analysis.[10] Yet useful as it is, such a critique of the different types of sources tends to obscure a fundamental truth, to wit, that all these sources belong to but a single reservoir of information that circulated throughout a single social network at the court. Hence information stemming from one genre of sources, especially those of a narrative nature, was easily used to enrich or even to construct a tradition in any other genre. Thus one cannot really privilege any literary genre above any other. Kagame did privilege three categories of sources because they were learned by rote and because great care was taken with their transmission owing to the exceptional ideological or ritual importance of their content. He believed that their uttering had not been altered by a single sound since their composition, which virtually turned such sources into written texts and rendered them more credible than others, in particular more credible than ordinary historical tales whose precise rendering varied with each performance. He did accept that the date to be assigned to the testimony of ordinary traditions must be the date of their collection, always after 1900, but claimed that the text itself of his privileged categories dated to the time of their composition so that certain texts would date to the seventeenth century. The three genres to which he accorded privileged status are the liturgy of the rites of kingship (utterances and practices),[11] dynastic poems,[12] and the list of the dynastic succession.[13]

It has been demonstrated, however, that even within those three genres certain utterances have been altered by interpolation, deletion, or substitution. The texts recorded on paper do therefore not date to the moment of their first composition. Moreover, both the dynastic poems and the liturgy are allusive. They do not include a straightforward setting out of historical events and their allusions cannot be understood without glosses.[14] Since those glosses or narrative commentaries are not learned by rote they should in any case be handled as if they were merely ordinary historical tales. At the most one might argue that an allusion in an old poem "proves" what one also finds in an historical tale but even that is not safe. For the tale could well only be the narrative development of a speculative gloss aiming to account for an allusion that could not be understood. Moreover, we should never forget that the performances of these three genres of sources were always closely and directly monitored by the court because they were crucial to the legitimacy of both king and political regime and also served to justify political actions taken by the court. This role evidently did favor their being remodeled according to the taste of the moment—for instance after a coup d'état—or their being used to justify a political innovation in search of precedents. In the final analysis there is no reason to privilege any genre over any other since they all draw from the same reservoir of information.[15] At the most one might accept that in certain cases where there is no suspicion of a later interpolation, historical allusions made in certain dynastic poems do refer to the narrative historical traditions about the king to whom the poem was addressed.[16] These traditions could then safely be assumed to have existed during the lifetime of that monarch.

By 1907 at the latest Europeans began to record some popular traditions.[17] But the specialists at the court, the Abacurabwenge, still refused to give any information. Ten years later that stance had changed, for in 1917 de Briey obtained the first official list of dynastic succession dictated by the "Bachurabwenga."[18] Then Pagès mentioned these "official historians" in 1927, but unfortunately he did not name the one who had been his informant.[19] Soon a single set (and always the same set) of Rwandans began to serve as major collaborators—the expression is Schumacher's—and transmitted their version of Nyiginya history to Schumacher, Delmas, and the young A. Kagame.[20] Thanks to Schumacher's synthesis we know what the state of knowledge was in 1936, the year he left the country.[21] As it happened Kagame began his research in the same year. At the outset he obtained a general overview of the official traditions from Sekarama, official performer and dynastic poet, who had been one of Schumacher's collaborators. But soon the number of his interlocutors grew so as to progressively include nearly all the competent officials at the court, whose data he used to further enrich the already established framework. Kagame published his first synthesis in 1943 and again in 1947.[22]

Because Schumacher's synthesis had been written in German and remained unpublished it found no echo, whereas Kagame's, written in the Rwandan language and published locally, was avidly read all over the country. It became the "true" version for the leaders of Rwanda, for its official historians, and for a good many popular storytellers as well. His second synthesis, the *Abrégés*, essentially maintained both the framework and the overall interpretation from his earlier *Inganji Karinga*, but was enriched by a great mass of details.

The gist of the single reservoir of traditions was thus written down between 1910 and 1936 and stemmed from a handful of specialists at the court. Schumacher in particular based his work on the testimony of four main collaborators, two of whom also appear in Delmas and three of whom appear in Kagame.[23] The crucial persons among these were Rwanyange, the official keeper of the official list of dynastic succession,[24] Sezibera, chief of the guild of dynastic drummers,[25] Kayijuka, a senior chief and ritualist,[26] and Sekarama,[27] official performer and composer of dynastic poetry as well as a great expert of the traditional tales. In the last analysis, then, these four people, all trained at the court of Rwabugiri, have imposed their views on the whole historiography.[28]

Yet one must still account for the differences found in the traditions as presented by various authors. According to Pagès, for instance, the King Ruganzu Bwimba campaigned against Burundi or Bugesera, not Gisaka as later authors claim, and Ruganzu Ndori raided Karagwe, an unimaginable situation for Kagame who claims that a pact of eternal peace existed between Rwanda and Karagwe.[29] Researchers have usually accounted for such differences by claiming that the first historiographers were not very knowledgeable and often misunderstood what they were told or alternatively obtained only bits and pieces from incompetent persons. Therefore, the reasoning has gone, one should rather rely on more recent information and especially on what Kagame tells us, since he himself was both a Rwandan and a ritualist. Although this explanation is clearly valid with regard to the very early and hasty collections— especially with respect to the official list of dynastic succession—it does not hold for the later historiography beginning with Pagès. Actually Schumacher's synthesis is particularly valuable because it gives us a detailed state of the question on the eve of Kagame's research. A comparison of his work with the syntheses of Kagame allows one to see how much the latter owes to the framework of Sekarama and his colleagues as well as to verify a series of detailed assertions made by Kagame, but by no one else, and to place these in the context of the whole traditional body of evidence.

Bearing in mind that there was only a single official reservoir of information at the court, irrespective of literary genre, that the information given by a few historians, who were the recognized official experts at the court of Musinga, was asserted to be authoritative, and that these experts knew each other, as did the historiographers they informed, it becomes clear that one must have recourse to another dynamic to account for the divergence of information among authors of different dates. Yes, the historiographers drew their knowledge from conversations and interviews with the historiologists (oral historians) who were their collaborators. But little by little the latter discovered that different versions existed from the one they knew and they saw the need to account for the existence of these different versions. For any divergence among different versions only becomes glaringly apparent when a text is written down, an action that freezes it and allows for detailed comparison with other versions. Therefore the foremost historiologists consulted with each other and used their authority to impose one version and eliminate the others. They sometimes did so by invoking still secret esoteric commentaries and explanations *(intekerezo)*.[30] Secondly the historiologists took note of the questions and the objections lodged by the historiographers during their meetings and invented answers to these that were then incorporated into later performances. Finally the historiologists also adopted new elements introduced by the historiographers, who had found them in writings about neighboring countries.

Thus the history of the kingdom took shape step by step as the result of the dialogue between historiographers and historiologists. The clearest example of this process is the harmonization of the chronologies of Burundi and Rwanda. Schumacher and his collaborators went to visit the literate chief Pierre Baranyanka to exchange data and to set up a common chronology.[31] Later on Kagame, who was not happy with the results of this encounter (which Sekarama had told him about), renewed the dialogue with Baranyanka until he reached satisfactory results, which later on became the received truth.[32]

To sum up: the active official traditions in Rwanda began to be standardized in 1917, thanks to a collaboration between historiologists and historiographers, and by around 1936 a permanent and definitive version of Rwandan history had been arrived at. Hence the divergent versions of yore were not the product of misunderstood information or even incompetence, but represent variants that were accepted before standardization, at a time when for certain Rwandans, Ruganzu Bwimba had indeed campaigned against Bugesera and Ruganzu Ndori against Karagwe.

Faced with these now-standardized traditions, what can a historian do to recover the content of the traditions before 1920? A very severe critic will conclude that they cannot be recovered since most of them were not written down, that we have no idea as to how variable or how credible they were, and that it is therefore futile to attempt to write a history of the Nyiginya kingdom. That is too much! After all, the standardized version is not sheer invention. It is based on older versions. Should we not then after all privilege the dynastic poems and the liturgy of the royal rituals since they were learned by rote? For even if they were not totally invariable and even if they were subject to interpolations and deletions, the bulk of their content as written down certainly is mainly what it was by the end of the nineteenth century. Moreover, one readily finds numerous passages that were altered as the result of the dramatic events of 1895–96. But still, one must keep in mind that most of the historical information of the poems and liturgy stems from explanatory

oral glosses, glosses that drew on the general reservoir of oral information, that is, when they were not a product of speculation pure and simple. Hence they too did probably not escape the overall standardization.

Actually, the historical narratives remain the keystone of any reconstruction and to establish their value one must find their variants. To do
so one can, on the one hand, compare the versions of Pagès and Schumacher with the canonical version established by Kagame, and, on the
other, compare Kagame with the more popular versions gathered after
1943, even those of storytellers who were somewhat influenced by
Kagame. This has turned out to be a fruitful approach. In most cases
one finds a variant in each narrative, and the magnitude of the difference from the other versions gives a good idea of the relative credence
one can accord to any given narrative. On the other hand, the total absence of variants does not inspire confidence. In those cases one can
only arrive at an opinion about reliability by both focusing on internal
criteria and by observing how well the tradition fits into the context of
all other known data. For to write a history, one must arrive at an evalua-
tion. Hence the reconstruction that follows in this book will be the one I,
keeping the imperfection of the sources in mind, since in the last resort
none of them are really beyond suspicion, judge to be the most credible.

How did these oral traditions envisage the past? For them the history
of the kingdom is that of its kings. They begin by telling us how the first
King Kigwa ("fallen") descended from heaven and organized the aristocracy. They continue by giving a series of names of successors that
stops at Gihanga ("creator"), the cultural hero who founded the first
empire, which he left to his children, one of whom was Kanyarwanda,
an eponym for the country. Then follows a new series of royal names
until RUGANZU[33] Bwimba is reached. He is the first monarch about
whom historical tales are told. From then on the list of dynastic succession constitutes the framework around which the whole body of oral
traditions has been organized.

DYNASTIC LIST FROM RUGANZU BWIMBA TO YUHI MUSINGA[34]

RUGANZU Bwimba
CYIRIMA Rugwe
KIGERI Mukobanya
MIBAMBWE Sekarongoro Mutabazi
YUHI Gahima
NDAHIRO Cyamatare

RUGANZU Ndori
MUTARA Semugeshi alias (and?) NSORO Muyenzi
KIGERI Nyamuheshera
MIBAMBWE Sekarongoro Gisanura
YUHI Mazimpaka
KAREMERA Rwaka, not officially acknowledged as legitimate king.
CYIRIMA Rujugira
KIGERI Ndabarasa
MIBAMBWE Sentabyo
YUHI Gahindiro
MUTARA Rwogera
KIGERI RWABUGIRI, died in the fall of 1895.
MIBAMBWE Rutarindwa, not officially acknowledged as
    a legitimate king.
YUHI Musinga, February 1897–1931

Under Bwimba and his successors the small domain of Gasabo increased in size to ultimately encompass most of central Rwanda. But after the death of YUHI Gahima, a civil war tore the country into two parts. The legitimate King NDAHIRO Cyamatare who ruled over the southern part, Nduga, was then attacked by barbarians from the west and died during the hostilities. His kingdom was invaded and disappeared.

But RUGANZU Ndori, son of Cyamatare, who had been sent to neighboring Karagwe as a child, claimed his royal inheritance, reconquered the whole country, and added new provinces to it on nearly all its borders. His successors maintained this legacy until the reign of CYIRIMA Rujugira. This king, who had been unjustly denied his place in the line of succession by his father, succeeded nevertheless to seize the throne and was a great warrior just like KIGERI Ndabarasa, his son and successor. They foiled the plots of all the great kingdoms that surrounded the Nyiginya realm and annexed parts of them, while at the same time regaining control of all the lands between central Rwanda and Lake Kivu. The death of Ndabarasa was followed by a struggle for the throne that ended with the recognition of a baby as king. A series of powerful rulers followed, culminating with KIGERI Rwabugiri who further increased the size of the kingdom. When Rwabugiri died in 1895, the country included not merely the whole territory of the present Republic of Rwanda but also other districts that today form part of Uganda and the Democratic Republic of the Congo. In December 1896 a coup d'état resulted in the overthrow of his successor and the installation of

Musinga as king, a mere three months before the arrival of the first German colonial officer.

So much for a summary of the standardized history. The analysis of the whole corpus of narrative traditions reveals that it consists of different bodies.[35] A first batch includes two series of Genesis myths, one focused on Kigwa and the other on Gihanga. These speculative accounts yield above all information concerning the perception of the ideology of kingship and that of the social categories around 1900.[36] A second set includes the tales attributed to the kings from Bwimba to Gahima. It turns out that most of these narratives are not historical in origin and hence they are discussed in the second appendix to this book. This set is followed by a cycle of tales about the foundation of the kingdom by Ndori that will be form a basis for our second chapter. A fourth body includes all sorts of traditions starting with Gisanura for some, but with Mazimpaka for most. The data become more and more numerous, detailed, and credible as one approaches the present.[37] The following five chapters of this book are built on these data. Two of these close in 1796 with the eruption of a long civil war. They are followed by a chapter that deals with the social transformations during the nineteenth century and another that discusses political history during the first two-thirds of that century, when power fell into the hands of the elite at the court while the country continued to expand. The last chapter is devoted to the reign of Rwabugiri and its immediate consequences.

In writing this book I have as much as possible relied on the sources themselves, but I also have used information cited by other authors when the sources they used were not available.[38] This is especially the case with the sources Kagame used for his studies, which deal with the history of the armies and of the official herds.[39] With the exception of a few tales about an army, these sources stem in fact from various family remembrances and it is rare to find traces of them elsewhere.[40] I use them and, following standard historical practice, then cite the author as a source. So there is no need to take offense as certain researchers, who are not historians, did "that author X is being treated like a vulgar informant."[41] On the other hand I have refused to accept information solely on the grounds that it was labeled esoteric, since esoteric data are precisely those that are most easily manipulated. I also have refused to accept any unsupported affirmations such as the one that Nyamuheshera added Mount Kigari to the kingdom[42] since the author does not indicate the source of his information and no trace of it can be found elsewhere. Finally I do not cite secondary authors, that is authors who are not familiar with the sources, unless they propose an interpretation that has turned out to be fruitful. As this book is destined to all the readers who are interested in the early history of Rwanda, its aim is to limit itself to the essentials. Hence it does not indulge in detail, does not discuss in each case why one particular source merits more credence than another one, and it avoids polemics, although the footnotes give access to such details, sources, and polemics.

1

Central Rwanda on the Eve of the Emergence of the Kingdom

The main theater in which the Nyiginya kingdom emerged and where its history was played out is central Rwanda. But it did not appear in a total void. It was built on the economic, social, and cultural practices that its founder encountered there. Hence any history of the kingdom must begin with the situation in the country on the eve of its creation, which is what we attempt to do in this chapter. We will therefore successively sketch the physical nature of the country, its settlement, its economic occupations, its social habits, and its political entities at the time. We cannot trust oral traditions in undertaking this sketch as they are too much tainted by anachronisms, nor can we rely on ethnographic descriptions since they are only valid for the end of the nineteenth century. Moreover, as the extant archeological data tell us only relatively little, our main source of information must come from a prudent use of historical linguistics, and especially of comparative semantics, which yields a relative chronology.[1]

The Country and Its Inhabitants

Central Rwanda is a natural space that is clearly delimited for the most part. It is the country located to the east of the mountains of the Congo-Nile crest, that is, to the east of the upper Nyabarongo and Mwogo Rivers, and south of the highlands of the current prefecture of Byumba. To the east and the south its limits are the Akanyaru River, which separates it from Burundi and Bugesera. Toward the east its border is less clear-cut. Here the former province of Buganza[2] constitutes a transition to the regions of today's eastern Rwanda.[3] The internal ecology of central Rwanda remains quite varied even though the country is thus separated as a natural region from the ones that surround it. The landscape consists of hills surrounded for the most part by rivers and marshes. Most of

their ridges are flat but windy and rather infertile for lack of enough surface soil. Their slopes are usually gentle and rich in various soils, while
their numerous low-lying lands are marshy and unhealthy but essential
nevertheless during the dry season. Each hill thus forms a well delimited
geographical unit, with its inhabitants often isolated from each other
since the marshes are difficult to cross. The hill was the fundamental
unit of settlement and its inhabitants considered themselves as constituting a neighborhood set apart from all others.[4] Moreover, each hill aligns
several natural environments forming not only a catena from its summit
to its base, but laterally as well, since the different folds of its slopes contain in their concavities and convexities different soils that also greatly
differ in fertility. Yet this description is only valid for the central part of
the country to the south of the middle Nyabarongo. North of that river
the relief becomes more clear-cut and the climate becomes rather different. To the west of the upper Nyabarongo on the highest ridges of the
historical provinces of Marangara and especially of Ndiza the floral
conditions are also clearly different, while further east, toward the lower
Akanyaru, the province of Mayaga is less hilly and more marshy.

The altitude of central Rwanda is lower than two thousand meters, an altitude that is a significant boundary for both farming and
health.[5] As the monsoon winds usually blow from the southeast, hitting
the high mountains, rainfall increases from east to west. Eastern Rwanda
is therefore drier than central Rwanda while the mountainous regions
of the north and the west receive the most rainfall. Usually central
Rwanda can count on between twelve hundred millimeters of rain and
a little less than eleven hundred millimeters per year going from west to
east. The rains are seasonal. If one omits a few local variations one can
state that in general the dry season runs from June to September with a
mere 10–12 percent of the annual rainfall occurring during this period.
The dry season is followed by an intermediary season that runs from
October to January, during which 31–38 percent of the annual rainfall
occurs. That season is followed in turn by the main rainy season. This
season runs from February to May and over 52 percent of the annual
rainfall occurs during it. This pattern raises the problem of how to fill
the gap in the availability of food between the two harvests in the rainy
seasons. One must set up food reserves and/or cultivate the marshes
during the dry season.[6] But as the annual variability of the rainfall is
fairly considerable, one always has had to take into account the possibility of droughts or of inundations capable of triggering a famine. Given
the wind direction these risks are greater toward the east and the south

than toward the north and the west. They are much less so in the mountains. This explains the reputation as rainmakers of the leaders of communities in the mountains such as Busigi to the north or Suti and Nzaratsi to the west.

The vegetation map for the early first millennium CE and later allows one to distinguish between the wooded savannas of the central plateau and the less fertile and less well watered savannas with acacias that are located at a lower altitude. Thus Mayaga, Bwanacyambwe, and Buganza are not considered part of the savannas of the central plateau. In central Rwanda, Marangara[7] and Ndiza are less fertile than Nduga or Busanza while Bumbogo is blessed with the best farming conditions in the whole region.[8] To the north and the west, land covered with rain forests borders on the central plateau. These were uninhabited before 1600 except for foragers. To the west the border of these forests correspond almost everywhere with the isohyetal line of 1900 meters. A good deal of the forest north of the middle Nyabarongo, however, had already been or was being cleared during the seventeenth century. At that time, a piedmont transition separated the great mountain forests from the savannas of the central plateau. While farmers were also settled there, this transition zone was especially important to cattle breeders, since they sent their cattle to pasture there during every dry season.[9]

Nearly every hill of central Rwanda was probably inhabited in the seventeenth century and the population must have been rather well distributed, except for a few nodes of higher density. At least this is what the distribution and the frequency of the archeological sites suggest.[10] The inhabitants spoke the Rwandan language and most toponyms in central Rwanda have a clear meaning in that language. Among those that frequently recur are, for instance, "Rutare" meaning "rock," "Butare" meaning "iron ore," "Remera" meaning "heavy wild prune tree,"[11] "Rubona" meaning "panorama," "Gisozi" meaning "big hill," and "Muyaga" meaning "windy." Moreover, the same toponyms recur also in Burundi and even beyond Rwanda toward the north, which suggests that human settlements in this region took place over a considerable period of time. They also imply a considerable stability in the bulk of the population since very remote times.

The archeological data confirm this. The first known settlement of central Rwanda is at least tens of thousands years old, for one encounters abundant traces of Stone Age industries since at least the Sangoan-Lupembian.[12] But no doubt this settlement remained fairly sporadic. A denser pattern of settlement was created by the first farmers who

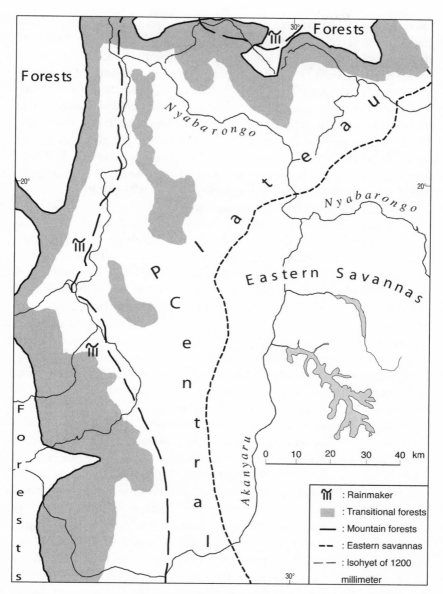

Vegetation on the central plateau in early CE times

appeared with Urewe ceramics in the Early Iron Age during the first millennium BCE.[13] The excavations tell us that these people cultivated sorghum and finger millet (eleusine), smelted iron, and owned at least some bovid cattle.[14] This Early Iron Age ended around 600–650 CE. A first Later Iron Age followed from 700 or 800 CE onward.[15] Its ceramics, labeled W, were quite different and are associated with another type of iron-smelting furnace. Despite the pronounced differences between these types of ceramics and an apparent hiatus in the dating, no such hiatus did occur between Urewe and W, for another ceramic labeled C, whose decor marks a transition between Urewe and W, shows up in the eighth century[16] (though Desmedt concludes, "We think that the W group was introduced by a new population"[17]).

Some twenty odd W sites have been located in central Rwanda. Their inhabitants were farmers still, since one finds seeds of sorghum, finger millet, and of one legume, pits, which probably were used as granaries, grinding stones, and hoes. On certain sites to the north of central Rwanda shards of W ceramics are also associated with some bones of game and domestic animals, including chickens, sheep or goats, and bovid cattle.[18] One also finds iron objects (including spear points) and it is believed that the great hoes (a single type) and the heavy, round hammers/anvils (two types) that have been found by accident in the whole region should be associated with these ceramics. But this supposition must remain unproven as long as such hoes or hammers are not found in direct association with W ceramic shards.[19]

The W ceramic disappeared around 1300 CE or later. It was followed, during a second Later Iron Age, by a utilitarian ceramic, labeled X, which, apart from its decor, is very similar to W ceramic. Sometimes a fine luxury ware labeled Y accompanies it. Later, pipe bowls would also be associated with it. This X/Y ceramic is dated from circa 1600 onward and persists until the twentieth century.[20] Once again the chronological hiatus (1300–1600) between W and X/Y is illusory and entirely due to the fact that only a few dates are available. In fact, W and X ceramics follow each other without any break on several sites. This is particularly evident at Muyaga where the pits contain a lower layer of W shards, followed by a layer of mixed W and X/Y shards and then a layer that only contains X/Y shards with fragments of pipes in its upper part.[21] In central Rwanda there are four unquestionable old X/Y sites among which Dahwe (c. 1655 +/- 85) is the oldest and Gaseke (c. 1700 +/- 90) the most recent. But we assume that there are many more, as it is rare to find a hill where isolated shards stemming from unrecovered

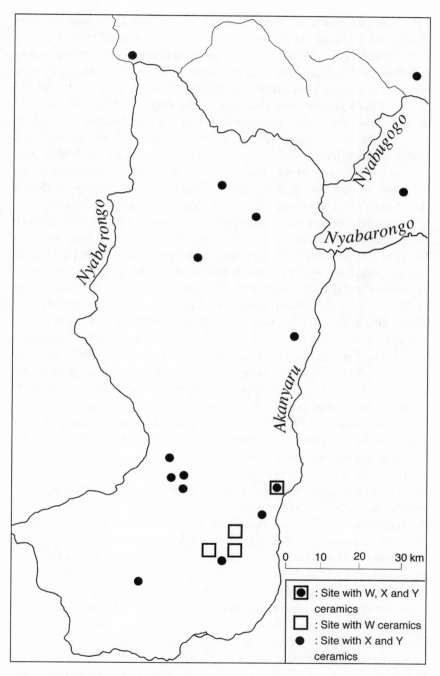

The later Iron Age in central Rwanda

sites do not turn up in the fields. X and Y shards have been found in close association with grinding stones, cereals, and some small iron objects.[22] In general they do not suggest any important change in the economy before the introduction of the smoking pipes that date from the eighteenth century. Let us keep in mind, though, that the replacement of W ceramic by X/Y pottery would still have been ongoing in central Rwanda during the seventeenth century. It has been suggested that the change in ceramic style was accompanied by a parallel change in the types of hoes and hammers that now become "modern." But at least one hammer of the old type was kept at the Nyiginya court. It was supposed to stem from the reign of the son of King Ndori, which amounts to saying that it dated from the seventeenth century, perhaps even as late as 1700.[23]

What can be concluded from all of this? Desmedt draws attention to the incontrovertible fact that the X and Y styles spread from western Uganda and postulates a emigration from there into central Rwanda as well as into Buhaya and countries further south. Moreover, on the basis of certain oral traditions she supposes that this documents the invasion of Bunyoro by the Nilotic Bito and their subsequent expansion into Nkore and Buhaya. In my judgment this goes much too far. After all, we are talking only of minor changes in pottery decor, essentially a change in fashion. No need to postulate a migration accompanied by potters. Rather, because fashions change with the taste of princes, it could be supposed either that older elites in central Rwanda began to imitate their northern neighbors or that a new elite emigrated from the north. The most important point in all of this is that a luxury ceramic (Y) appears for the first time, which thus directly attests to the emergence of a true elite during the seventeenth century.

It is certainly tempting to link the appearance of luxury vessels and the decor change in utilitarian pottery to the creation of a kingdom in central Rwanda by a group coming from the north that did not disturb the bulk of the population. But a new set of very careful and well dated digs will be required before this idea can be better evaluated. For, if the good taste of the masters can explain the changes in decor, it does not explain the technical changes that affected the hoe and the smiths' hammer. Those changes essentially consist in less metal per hoe or hammer being used and yet these tools becoming technically better. The size of the hoe diminished by about a third and its blade acquired a central rib that reinforced it. Thus the hoe becomes lighter and stronger. As to the hammers, they went through an intermediate stage by also being made lighter and then were given a hitting surface better adapted to their function.[24] If one is to believe a tradition that ascribes the ownership of an intermediary model to a son of Ndori, some old-style hoes and hammers were still in use during the seventeenth century but were being replaced. Should one really link this technical evolution to the creation of a new kingdom? Can one, as one author suggests, tie the spread of various techniques for the construction of smelting furnaces to the territorial expansion of various kingdoms?[25] I don't believe so. Rather these techniques spread from place to place thanks to their superiority or simply because they represented a new fashion. But they followed the axes of communication at that time and, as we shall later see, the borders between kingdoms were not an important obstacle to the movement of populations. It is therefore just as probable that even the luxury ceramic Y spread by imitation from center to center without any migration, not even by new political leaders.

This brief overview of the archeological data indicates that after the Early Iron Age there may *perhaps* have been a certain migration at the time the W ceramic appeared, but not since then. What is in fact most striking is the astonishing stability of settlement for at least the last two thousand years. One only has to look at the small region east of Butare to be convinced of it, for all the periods are represented here on numerous sites and on the same hills. This wealth of known sites clearly is the fruit of intensive research in the region over a long time period, but that does not alter the conclusion. No doubt equally intensive research in other sectors of central Rwanda will uncover a similar pattern.[26]

The data do not yet allow us to calculate population densities for the seventeenth century or to establish a map of their distribution.[27] In central Rwanda archeological remnants are common on hills of medium height south of the Nyabarongo and perhaps most common in Rukoma and in Bwanamukari[28] where nodes of higher densities of population may have existed. The great "empty" forest—which was in fact inhabited by a few bands of foragers—still covered the whole mountain mass of Ndiza at the time and covered all the hills west of the upper Nyabarongo and Mwogo Rivers.[29] As to the regions that surrounded central Rwanda in the seventeenth century, Bugesera, for one, certainly had a very low population density.[30] To the north, a population cluster was probably already settled on the fertile lava soils along the Mukungwa River.[31] To the east densities would have been very low except for some well settled parts of Gisaka.[32]

This fundamental stability of settlement in no way prevented a rather high mobility among people, especially among herders and later among elites, as is suggested by data that become available by the end of the eighteenth century. In the seventeenth and eighteenth centuries, herders were no doubt forced to move from one region to another often as the result of political or environmental pressures, whereas farmers were not quick to move, except along the great forests where they still frequently hunted. Usually this mobility affected only a few persons at once, that is, an infinitesimal fraction of the inhabitants in each sector.[33] Otherwise farmers left their hills only to escape a severe famine or insoluble local conflicts over arable land. In the last case especially, they went into the forests to clear out new domains there. Although a severe climatic crisis might chase away whole populations, most such runaways seem to have returned to their native land as soon as the crisis was over.[34] Paradoxically the most stable population of all may have been that of the foragers in the forests: Yes, these people did constantly move over a sizeable area, but they did not easily abandon their usual hunting grounds and stubbornly defended their lands against the incursions of sedentary settlers.[35]

The fact that settlements were extremely stable, and migrations minuscule and often peristaltic, flagrantly and massively contradicts the conviction, be it to account for the spatial distribution of clans or to explain the presence of great blocks of population practicing different economies, that one finds strewn throughout the literature of ever so many massive great migrations.[36] All these conjectures must be radically rejected, not only for the period we are considering here but also for the whole Later Iron Age, at the very least since the introduction of W ware, and probably well before that period.

Actually, central Rwanda was a privileged habitat compared to other tropical habitats. Neither malaria nor trypanosomiasis was found here. The most frequent serious diseases were amebiases, helminthiases, lung diseases, a sort of diphtheria, yaws, a variant bubonic plague, and TB (tuberculosis).[37] Yet infant mortality was probably quite high[38] while the average life expectancy of the adult population can be estimated to have been around forty years or less, as was usual before the industrial revolution elsewhere. The demographic movement of the population alternated rapidly between high peaks and deep chasms. Normally, natality was higher than mortality and the population grew. But from time to time a great famine produced a hecatomb. Witness, for instance, a laconic report by Kandt about Bugoyi in 1898: "One saw it in Ruanda, at the time when many corpses of the starved [slaves] who had not found any buyers were strewn on the banks of the lake."[39] Yet the population probably did increase over the long run. In principle, the increase of the herds occurred faster than that of people, but was affected by epizootic diseases and droughts.[40] Still, one is left with the impression that over the long haul the natural increase of the herds occurred faster than that of people. However, raiding was much more responsible for the multiplication of cattle herds in central Rwanda than natural increase.

Fields and Herds: Subsistence Activities

The people of central Rwanda engaged in three different sorts of subsistence activities during the seventeenth century, even though most people were farmers, many of whom also kept one or two head of cattle. But a minority of sedentary cattle herders lived alongside them. They became sedentary because they only kept herds of a moderate size, which was certainly due to the lack of extensive pastures. No masses of cattle bones have been found here as are commonly found on sites that were occupied by shepherds with large herds and extensive pastures, such as in Bweru or at Bweyorere in Uganda or at Ryamurari in Ndorwa.[41] Besides farmers and herders there were small groups of nomadic foragers in the mountain forests and on the banks of the great marshes along the main rivers.[42] In order to better focus on the agricultural and herding economies we will not consider them further here.

Let us start with farming, since its products were essential for the whole population. The Rwandans were so well aware of this that they chose the hoe as the symbol to stand for the unity of the country in the royal rituals, rather than the royal bull, despite the attraction and the political importance of cattle at the time.[43] The farmers were settled on the poor soils of the flat ridges of the hills. They constituted neighborhoods there in which each house was built at a distance from the others but always on the same hill. They hoed fields and fallows on the slopes and during the dry season they cultivated some crops on the low-lying lands at the bottom of the hills.[44] They practiced a form of intricate and already rather intensive agriculture, based on crop rotation, the intercalary association of different plants, and manuring, but probably as yet without irrigation.[45] After cleaning it with a sickle and burning it during the dry season, the farmers prepared the field by hoeing,[46] manuring, and composting. Then the cereals were sown and the legumes and tubers planted, each in its proper season. This was followed by several rounds of weeding, the harvest, the first threshing, and storage in a granary. Later the cereals were threshed a second time, winnowed, and stored in the granary for cereals. Banana plantations with a few other associated plants were set outside the fields and around the houses, while small, dry-season fields were exploited on the margins of the marshes for the cultivation of tubers (water yam, taro). Agricultural products required no additional transformations before cooking, but did so for the brewing of different beers (cereal beer, banana beer, and mead).[47]

The main crops during the seventeenth century were sorghum, finger millet,[48] the small *inkori* beans (*Vigna sinensis* Endl.),[49] taro,[50] water yam,[51] African yams,[52] gourds,[53] calabashes,[54] *Coleus kilimamanschare*,[55] and, later, bananas.[56] With the exception of sugarcane, the plants used as ancillary crops are little known except for some "spinach" such as *isugi (Papilionacea: Mucuna stanz), isogi (Gynandropsis gynandra* L.), and *urusogi (Solanum nigrum L.)*.

This list might leave one with the false impression that the farmers were not interested in trying new crops and agricultural techniques. To the contrary, the agricultural system was wide open to innovations. In the seventeenth century the light resistant hoe had just displaced the heavy hoe of the preceding period, and the wooden two-pronged fork,[57] *isuka n'isando* (a small fork used to dig, weed, and rake), was perhaps not yet totally obsolete. Finally, the first introduction of bananas seems to date from this century and with the crop came a whole new farming technique. Moreover, the relative importance of various crops has also changed quite a deal over time. Many more yams were probably cultivated in the seventeenth century than in the nineteenth, but even then they had already lost much of their importance in favor of taro and perhaps water yams. And even though peas *(Pisum sativum)* had not yet been cultivated in central Rwanda, they were on the rare fields that farmers had established at altitudes above two thousand meters.

Besides these crops, one must also mention tree plantations, especially fig trees cultivated for bark cloth, and acacias and *umusave (Markhamia platycalix Sprague; M Luthea-spathodea nilotica Stem)* for wood for building.[58] Complementary domestic stock mostly consisted in goats but many families also owned one or a few head of bovid cattle.[59] And let us not forget beekeeping.[60] Gathering was relatively unimportant, except in the vicinity of the forests. There it yielded wood, game, skins, furs, and above all honey. These products were major resources of the Twa who seem to have exchanged game and honey for agricultural produce.

The division of labor by gender was not absolutely rigid. In general, men and women collaborated on major tasks such as the clearing of fields, working with the hoe, harvesting, and perhaps threshing. But certain tasks belonged to one gender or the other. Men sowed cereals and women planted, men burned the fields and took care of the banana groves, and women weeded, winnowed, stored the produce in granaries, prepared food, and brewed. Women were also mistresses in their house and its compound.[61] But, on the other hand, they could not hold claim over any land and their personal status was mostly determined by the fact that they were always dependent on a man, whether as daughters, spouses, or mothers.

Among herders the economic unit was the herd *(ubushyo)*, which contained roughly between thirty and fifty head of cattle in the nineteenth century.[62] Several of these herds might constitute a larger whole called *umutwe* ("head") but each herd of that whole was managed separately. The extent of the available uninterrupted tracts of pastureland dictated this relatively small herd size much more than did the limit imposed by the extent of male labor available in the family of the owner.[63] As the population density of central Rwanda at that time was much less than what it is today, the number of cattle per herd was often fifty or a little more, but without reaching seventy as was found in the forest or in Bigogwe around 1900. But even fifty was only half of the standard herd of one hundred cattle, which was the norm among nomadic Hima herders in Uganda and in the region of Mutara.[64] Moreover, over there *imitwe* counted thousands of head rather than the few hundred in central Rwanda. Herders were ubiquitous in central and eastern Rwanda but not only there. It is quite probable that they could already also be found on the southern slopes of the volcanoes, such as in Bigogwe, to the north of the volcanoes and in Bufumbira, Jomba, and perhaps in small groups in Bwishaza near the banks of Lake Kivu.

Herders also built their houses and cattle pens on the ridge of the hills but not in the immediate vicinity of the farmers. Their pasturelands were located on the slopes and they had built watering places for the daily needs of the cattle on the low-lying terrain at the foot of the hills. But at the very least once a year they had to lead their herds sometimes rather far away to salty wells, while in the dry season they had, if possible, to pasture their herds in the mountain meadows. And herders could not merely lead their herds to the watering places, the salty wells, and the mountain meadows; they also needed rights of free passage to these places.[65]

Cattle rearing itself required a precise daily routine. In the rainy season this began early in the morning when a fire was lit in the cattle pen. Then came milking, watering, and leading the beasts to pasture, a second watering, a return to the pasture, then the return home and the second milking. The routine for calves differed because they needed protection from the midday heat. Meanwhile, other tasks also had to be performed, such as cleaning the cattle pen, cutting fresh grass for the night, cleaning the milk pots, and churning and storing the butter. Then there was a seasonal routine as well. At regular intervals the drinking troughs near the house had to be cleaned and during each of the two dry seasons the watering places had to be repaired. Usually once a week or once a month, according to the distance to be traveled, the herd was brought to the salty wells *(imbuga)*. The long dry season was a tricky period because of a lack of grass on the pastures. June and July were particularly difficult until such time as the herd could begin to graze the stubble after the cereal harvest. After this one took the herd to far-away pastures on the forested heights where grass was still growing profusely thanks to the more abundant rains and the residual humidity.[66] This transhumance was quite important and it explains why cattle breeders were always on the lookout for pastureland not far from high land. If no transhumance was possible the herd would graze near the marshes until September, a month that constituted a second season of scarcity for the cattle. Finally, the reproduction of the herd was managed by regulating the access of the bull of the herd to its cows.

Cattle rearing also included the preparation of the pastures. It was at least necessary to burn the meadows during the long dry season and again, but on a more modest scale, during the short dry season. Moreover, the land in the forests, in the bush, or near the marshes was cleared according to need. Finally, pastures were rotated. Cattle grazed in different meadows according to a given schedule and the pastures that were held in reserve had to be protected from the ravages of goats and the attempts of farmers to cultivate them.[67]

Cattle rearing was more labor intensive than farming, at least if measured in terms of the yield in food per person and per unit of land. Three or four herders or more were needed to pasture a herd and protect it against the attacks of the great carnivores or cattle rustlers,[68] while additional men and women were required for the tasks at the cattle pen. The herders formed a team composed of the young men of the family unit, who managed the herd; this team joined forces with neighbors for the transhumance during the long dry season. At that time, the herders constituted a little closed community of their own within which great solidarity reigned, but that could be aggressive toward the outside world.[69] No doubt the great demand for labor explains why already at this time free servants were supplemented with slaves, especially with raided women.[70]

The division of labor by gender was sharp, although the most menial female work was sometimes assigned to male servants. Women were not directly involved in caring for the herd and were absolutely forbidden from milking the cows. But they tended the fire in the cattle pen and mucked it out. They also cleaned and maintained the houses, which included, for instance, manufacturing the houses' woven screens, took care of the milk containers, which had to be kept in pristine condition, stored the milk needed to feed the calves, churned the butter, and exchanged the butter for honey. This is how the consequences of the negligence of one of these women—and hence also her importance—are described:

> The straw for the cattle lies wet in the enclosure, the calves have been left outside, the milk pots have not been washed. . . . My cows spent all day long in the cattle pen, the calves stayed within the enclosure. My daughter does not go out. My wife did nothing at all, and even though that [situation] only lasted a single day . . . when I came in the evening I found my cattle ill-treated and my household dirty.[71]

As one sees, within the enclosure, the wife of the leader of the family was also the mistress who directed all the tasks, assisted by the female members of the household, and, in well-to-do households, by slave maids.[72]

The fact that the agricultural and herding economies were interwoven on the hills, without, however, being integrated with each other, required a certain coordination between herders and farmers—for instance, with regard to the annual burning of the vegetation, and the designation of a certain authority to decide every year how to use the land. Beyond the issue of burning, the daily points of contact between the agricultural and herding economies were as follows. Cow dung was appreciated by the farmers as manure for the fields and the practice of letting the herd graze on the stubble in the fields after the harvest benefited both economies.[73] Certain soils were richer and better adapted to farming while others, often on the same hill slope, were less rich but offered good grazing.

But as soon as the population was so dense that it became necessary to use all available land on a hill, points of friction multiplied. The first and least serious nuisance related to the rights of passage for the cattle and the question of the damage such a passage might ultimately cause to the crops. The second trouble was more serious. During the dry season the margins of the low-lying marshes were essential for both groups: farmers planted some taro or yams there as a crop to assist during the annual period of scarcity and herders pastured their herd there before the new growth of nutritive grasses.

The third conflict produced by far the most serious tensions. Herding required more land per unit of production than farming—each head of cattle required an amount of land that was nearly twice what was necessary to support a family of farmers.[74] The natural growth of a herd occurs faster than that of people but depends in the first place on the amount of pastures available, and so herders were often intent on occupying new tracts of land. The farmers did not object to the herders doing so as long as the population density remained low, but as soon as the population increased, they resisted the overtaking of their lands and conflicts thus became nearly inevitable. This situation explains why, even in central Rwanda during the seventeenth century, one could no longer find tracts of pasture large enough to keep herds of more than thirty to fifty cattle.

Moreover, the issue could not be resolved by partitioning the available lands once and for all into farmland and pastureland. First, it was rare to find plots of land that were unsuitable as pastures but useable as fields (the slopes were overly steep and some folds in the terrain were infertile) or unsuitable for fields but good for pastures (poor soils existed side-by-side with rich soils). But the main headache was caused by the need in both farming and herding for soil rotation. Every year or every few years certain fields had to be left fallow in order to be regenerated, while other tracts or pastures then in fallow were cultivated. Even though herders could use fallows as supplementary pastureland, these tracts were naturally poor and could only be used for a short period of time. The main pastures had to be located on exactly the same sort of land that the farmers coveted for new fields and, just like fields, such tracts also needed to lay idle from time to time to allow the grass to regenerate.

Given these rotation demands one could not base any land tenure on a permanent partition of the land when the population was fairly dense. The situation, then, required cooperation every year with regard to the use of the available lands and the annual burning of the bush in addition to precise rules governing access to watering places and marshes as well as the passage of a herd in transhumance. But above all it required a new allocation of the lands every year. Each community had to make concessions but the upshot was determined by the relative power of both local communities. Therefore, in a densely inhabited district, the political structures dictated the way the land was exploited and hence exercised considerable influence even at the lowest level. Indeed, this inordinate local influence of the prevailing political regimes sets Rwanda and Burundi apart from nearly all other African political regimes.

Usually herders needed farmers more than the reverse. Farmers were relatively independent from the herders because their diet included few or no milk products. On the other hand, the menu of seventeenth-century herders certainly also included a porridge of sorghum flour as well as beans, despite their insistence that they only lived on milk, beer from sorghum or other cereals or honey, and roast beef.[75] Yet in times of famine the situation was reversed for farmers suffered far more rapidly from it than herders did. The herding economy was much more mobile than the agricultural one, which, in a country with such a high degree of ecological diversity, allowed herders to escape the rather frequent local famines. For from time to time, perhaps once a decade or so, a more or less localized scarcity erupted. These famines were due to the failure of the harvest and a lack of grass, triggered by drought, locusts, overly abundant rains, or rains out of season. After having exhausted their reserves the farmers could still subsist for some time on famine foods such as drought-resistant weeds in the fields and plants in the marshes. At the same time they would also try to obtain food from elsewhere by barter. If the famine was local and of short duration, they could manage to overcome it in this way. Herders, on the other hand, were willing to go relatively far in search of pastures, especially in the forests, returning only after the famine was over.[76] But sometimes a generalized famine erupted and persisted for two or three years. These disasters were always provoked by droughts, the effects of which were usually exacerbated by military operations that either had prevented farmers from cultivating in good time or had destroyed the harvests.[77] When such a disaster occurred the whole social framework gave way—all those healthy enough to do so began to wander around in search of food, and people died by the thousands and sometimes by the tens of thousands. The survivors ended up finding refuge, by choice or by force, in regions that had not been struck.[78] After such a catastrophe, a farmer, whether he returned to his old haunts or elsewhere, needed to amass a reserve of food and to find sowing stocks before he could begin to clear land again. As to the herders who were trying to reconstitute their herds, they were often aided by loans from their colleagues.

Besides the occupations already mentioned there existed a few specialties that were practically hereditary, mainly metallurgy, potting, tanning, woodcarving, and the manufacture of bark cloth. Sometimes such specialists worked on demand, either at home or in the customer's compound (the latter would always be the case if the customer was a member of the court). The master iron smelters did not wait for any orders but produced such quantities of iron as they estimated could be sold as hoes. Sometimes the blacksmiths and the potters did the same and then went to peddle their wares from door-to-door, for there was very little trade.[79] Neighbors exchanged goods by barter. Hunters, farmers, and herders exchanged game, leather goods, honey, sorghum, beans, milk, and butter, among other things. Iron objects and hoes above all were preferably exchanged for goats and if possible cattle, but sometimes also for the goods we have just enumerated. Indeed, the hoe was probably already the standard of value as it was in the nineteenth century.[80] There probably were no markets in central Rwanda and it is not known whether the commercial circuit that existed north of Lake Kivu during the nineteenth century was already in place or not.[81] It is also possible that from time to time a fabulous, rare, and exotic piece of jewelry appeared in the region, such as a copper object from central Africa, or a few cowries, conus shells, or glass beads from the East Coast.[82]

Kinship and Society

The basic social unit was the localized and exogamic patrilineage called *inzu* ("the house"), which included three generations: grandparents, their married sons, and their grandchildren all living in the same compound or nearby.[83] In everyday life, but not for rituals, the local group also included spouses and sometimes servants. The lineage leader practiced rites of worship of the male ancestors of the lineage from the immediately preceding generation as far back as its founder, regulated marriages, paid or received ransoms, and held collective title to a landed domain or to a herd. Moreover, the *inzu* was the smallest unit concerned with vendetta or collective vengeance.[84] The duty to avenge had priority over all others for members of the wronged lineage, even over a royal order to mobilize in times of war.[85] A vendetta was not only waged against the murderer but also against any captured member of his *inzu*. The notion of vengeance was so closely linked to that of lineage that a father could disown his son in the following terms:

Listen my children, it is I who am your father and the father of Rwiihiimba: I no longer want Rwiihiimba among you, I throw him out of the family. If one of my children kills someone, revenge will not be taken on Rwiihiimba. If Rwiihiimba kills someone, none of my children will be liable to the vendetta; I banish him from the community of my children.[86]

As new generations were added, for instance when grandchildren married, new *inzu* lineages grew. But on the basis of their common gene-alogy they still considered themselves as belonging to a single major lin-eage, the *umuryango* ("the gate to the compound"),[87] and often still inhab-ited the same neighborhood on the same hill. This exogamic group was in the first place responsible for the security of its members and were ex-pected to practice vendettas against the lineages *(inzu* or *umuryango)* who had killed one of their members or rustled their cattle. Its membership consisted of all those who were held to vengeance in the case of a mur-der. This duty resulted from the worship owed to the ancestor who had been murdered.[88] When an *umuryango* became too large—roughly, when it encompassed more than twenty families or so—quarrels erupted and the lineage split. A new *umuryango* was created, received the name of its founder, and spirit worship no longer included any ancestors antecedent to that founder.[89]

Social status within kin groups was determined first by age and then by gender. Only the older married men, who had lost their parents and belonged to an older generation, were really independent. They were the leaders of *inzu* and its representatives to the outer world. All others, men and women, were their dependents. The social position of women was complex and variable.[90] In principle they were inferior to one man—this was most evident in the case of women married to farmers since women could not control any land, but it was also apparent among herders despite women's right to own cattle. Usually their status derived from that of their fathers, husbands, or sons. The royal status of a queen mother, which stemmed from that of her son, is the most strik-ing example of this. Yet age and personality were of considerable im-portance as well. At least that is the picture, valid for the twentieth cen-tury, painted for us by tales of fiction and historical narratives. In their capacity as future spouses young girls had the potential to seal an alli-ance and to bring in bridewealth, and as a result they enjoyed some re-gard and considerable freedom of action.[91] But once they were young brides, still childless and strangers to the *inzu* in which they lived, they

remained under the thumb of the other women in the household, at
least until the birth of a son. Later in life married women were set up in
their own houses with their children and exercised considerable authority over the tasks of the household, even over all its men, including their
husbands. The nature and the quantity of labor that was thought to be
womanly in a given community strongly influenced the regard in which
a woman was held. One has the impression that among herders women
enjoyed more personal authority than among farmers, even before the
introduction of new crops of beans and sweet potatoes overworked
them. Another source of consideration stemmed from feminine healing
or mystical talents. Oral literature often underlines the mystical power
inherent in femininity and human fecundity. Some women became
famous as magicians or healers, and above all as prophets. Thus they
played a key role in the propagation of the Ryangombe cult.[92] On the
other hand, however, this same supposedly inborn female quality also
justified the attribution of all household tasks to women, from cooking
to educating small children, to dispensing everyday medical care. And
because slaves were mostly used for household work, nearly all slaves
were women.[93]

Even if society in the seventeenth century was no doubt more egalitarian than it would be in later centuries, there were differences among
living standards and there were different social classes. The presence of
luxury wares (Y ceramics) among the ceramics found in the ground directly testifies to the presence of elites *(imfura)* whose style of living was
somewhat more opulent than that of the bulk of the population. This
quality of life certainly derived in part from the political authority such
elites possessed, and from the size of their lineage, but in part also from
the amount of wealth such a group had at its command.[94] In terms of
goods, rich and poor differed by the quantity of land they held, the size
of their food stocks, and the number of their cattle. These were the
trumps that dictated how many people a leader could attract to his place
and whom he could order about. In the seventeenth century, wealth was
mainly counted in cattle since all social payments, such as, for instance,
bridewealth, fines, debt, or dues, were due in cattle and by default only
in goats or hoes.[95] Yet iron still retained some value as an item of wealth,
especially among farmers, and hoes were used everywhere as a medium
of exchange. A calculation in terms of head of cattle was especially significant in measuring the difference in wealth among different lineages
of herders. That difference was probably already great[96] at the time and

had probably led to the subordination of poor families who had to enter into the service of rich lineages by securing one or another contract of servitude from a patron. Among these, *ubugabire* was the most important. It consisted in the loan of any good, but especially of cattle. After a client solicited him the patron would entrust him with one or several cows. In return, the client would return one calf of the first calving to his patron and some more calves later on at regular intervals. But he was expected above all to aid his patron and come to work for him when the need arose. This contract created a relation of inequality, but its duration was not unlimited and either party could end it, particularly after the death of the first cow that had been given.[97]

At the time, central Rwandan society acknowledged the existence of some large groups that exceeded kinship groups proper. Several *imiryango* were grouped in a larger social group, the clan. This only appeared to be a kinship group. It consisted really in an alliance between equal *imiryango* and it is significant that, contrary to the lineages, the names of most clans were not those of common ancestors. The clan was *ubwoko*, "race, species, family, order."[98] In this case one translates the word as "clan" but when applied to human beings the term did not only designate this institution, but also other human aggregates, such as, for instance, the whole of all royals, the fraction of a clan, or even the social categories Tutsi, Hutu, and Twa.[99] The twenty-odd clans that are actually known within the territory of the Republic of Rwanda are found everywhere mixed one with the other, a situation that is the product of an historical evolution.[100] In the recent past the clan was chiefless, was neither exo- nor endogamic, and its constituent *imiryango* never acted together. The clan became significant when two individuals met who were not otherwise related to each other, a situation that arose above at all the royal court and in the case of travelers such as hawkers. If both individuals bore the same clan name, they were supposed to act like kinsfolk and expected to aid and protect each other. Moreover, in any given region up to three clans were supposed to be autochthons, or *abasangwa butaka*, "those found on the ground." In various specified circumstances, such as at the initial clearing of a field, the building of a house, and the cessation of mourning, among others, those involved in the activity in question had to be ritually assisted by a "godfather" *(umuse)* who was a member of one of the locally recognized autochthon clans. In other circumstances, such as, for instance, when cattle had been raided, the intercession of the godfather was discretionary.[101] Many scholars hold that the clan had lost its genuine function in the nineteenth century but that in a remote past it had once represented a more efficient social aggregate; one may, however, doubt even that.

To begin with, a clan is not an unchanging entity that has always existed.[102] We will see that the Nyiginya clan developed from a group of Ndori's kinsfolk that dates its emergence to the late seventeenth century. The known genealogies show how starting at that time all sorts of descent groups snowballed into a clan by attaching themselves to the ruling lineage.[103] This example and the case of the autochthon clans lead one to suspect that far from being groups of hoary antiquity that survived all later changes even though they were gradually stripped of their functions, clans are in fact phenomena that derive from the political arena. This is why Nyagahene, following others, finds ties between most of the clans known today and the precolonial kingdoms, both real and imagined.[104] Because he does consider them to be true descent groups, he imagines multiple migrations from illustrious cradles that then lead to the hodgepodge of clans observed today. Not so. Being alliances rather than descent groups, clans were mutable and every *umuryango* leader could always abandon his clan name and its food taboo to form an affiliation with another one.[105] In fact the number of lineages composing a clan has constantly varied over time according to the political adventures of the great families within the region. This also explains why traditions of all types use clan names to designate what were in fact specific *imiryango* and even *inzu* with considerable political weight. The size of a clan today and the distribution of its units merely reflects the result of this historical movement. The political character of the clan is also evident in the very notion of "autochthon clan." All the lineages that were believed to have been established in early times and that were met by an immigrating lineage were all collapsed into a single entity by the latter, whatever their true origins had been. The immigrants united them all together into a single "autochthon clan" without any further ado. They needed an autochthon clan because a "godfather" was required for all the rituals involving land.[106]

What, then, was the situation in seventeenth-century central Rwanda? It seems both that there were already clans by then, probably more than the fifteen or so found there in the recent past, and that they were also much smaller. A certain number of these clans were later absorbed by others.[107] The Singa were perhaps the oldest autochthon clan, but the two others known in the region, the Zigaba and Gesera, were probably at the time still ruling clans in one principality or another.

Originally, the clan was an alliance between *imiryango* created to promote their common security, be it at the level of common defense, including that of their tenure of land, or at the level of relations between herders and farmers. But in seventeenth-century central Rwanda that role had already been taken over long ago by monocephalic political institutions. By then, the affiliation of *imiryango* with one clan or another certainly reflected in large part the balance of power among the small principalities of the period.

Making distinctions among clans was not the only way the population of central Rwanda differentiated itself. A variety of ethnonyms testifies to this. These names belong to two categories: those bestowed on the whole population of a given territory and those bestowed on a subgroup of such a population. Let us consider the territorial ethnonyms first. Traditions name two of these: "Rwanda" and "Renge." "Renge," or "the mountain people," designated a population that was different from the one in which the traditions were handed down, a population that was settled near the forests of the piedmont toward the west, but which is said to have dominated Nduga around the beginning of the century and to have still been dominant in Bungwe in Ndori's time.[108] The same traditions imply that all the other inhabitants of central Rwanda belonged to one other ethnic group. But its ethnonym remains unknown. For the word "Rwanda" literally means "the surface occupied by a swarm or a scattering"; hence its semantic derivation is "a large space," and it was always used with a qualifier of locality. Thus "the scattering of Kamonyi" indicates the space occupied by people who had scattered from Kamonyi.[109] In the historical tales one hears kings talk of "my Rwanda," or when they are addressed by others, "your Rwanda," to designate the territory of the people who obey them. The whole of all those who belong to a single swarm are the Abanyarwanda of X. But without this X the term is not an ethnonym. The word was so little tied to the Nyiginya kingdom that in a tale one hears Ndori tell his troops during a campaign against his enemy Nzira, king of Bugara: "Spread out in the Rwanda of Nzira."[110] Here "Rwanda" refers to the country of the enemy. One concludes from all of this that before Ndori's arrival the only known territorial ethnonyms referred to the small principalities to which they were linked, either by the use of Abanyarwanda +X, or by the use of a toponym such as Abariza (meaning "people of Buriza") or Abanyanduga (meaning "people of Nduga"). No ethnonym is found to designate all the inhabitants of central Rwanda in opposition to the mountain people of the north and the west.

Nonterritorial ethnonyms were "Twa," "Hima," and "Tutsi." To-gether they established an opposition between the bulk of the farming population and smaller groups that did not farm. The terminology sug-gests that an agricultural way of life was perceived as the normal condi-tion of the inhabitants, from whom one had to distinguish "different" people who practiced another way of life. Among these small groups "Twa" was the name given to the foragers who lived in the forests and near the great marshes on the borders and also to a few communities of potters. Mutual hostility was the rule between the Twa of the great for-ests in the west and the north of central Rwanda and their neighbors, especially farmers who were liable to clear the forests, thus restricting the land left to the hunters. Avoidance and scorn, which was perhaps mutual, characterized the relations between the Twa and all other in-habitants. Not only did Twa and others never intermarry, but they did not even drink from the same beer pot for fear of social pollution.[111] De-spite this, however, some symbiosis did exist between Twa and the other inhabitants, for the products of the forest—above all, honey, game, skins, and furs—were swapped for agricultural products. This bartering, which still occurs today across all of central Africa, certainly occurred in the seventeenth century.

The names "Hima" and "Tutsi" have been recorded in the literature of the Great Lakes region ever since the nineteenth century. Both are ethnonyms accepted by the populations they designate and whose ety-mology remains unknown.[112] At that time, the label "Hima" was ap-plied to all the herders of southern Uganda and northern Buhaya, to certain herders in Karagwe, and also to certain herders only in Rwanda and Burundi. The label "Tutsi" had the same meaning, and was found in Rwanda, Karagwe, Burundi, Buha, southern Buhaya, and beyond, in northern Tanzania as far as Tabora.[113] Where both terms coexisted (Rwanda, Burundi, Karagwe), "Tutsi" referred to an elite among the herders and "Hima" to the commoners. Thus the 1924 dictionary de-fines "Hima" as "inferior race of Tutsi."[114] The spatial distribution of the two words suggests that the word "Hima" spread from the north and "Tutsi" from the south. It also suggests that the exact meaning of both ethnonyms evolved from a term used to label certain groups of owners of herds and that it was still changing around 1900. It is evident, moreover, that the meaning of the term "Tutsi" evolved with the growth of those kingdoms in which herders formed part of the political elite. Therefore, one may well ask if herders outside of central Rwanda, and especially those in Bwishaza, Bigogwe, Bufumbira, and in the neighboring regions of Congo, considered themselves to be Tutsi in the seventeenth century like those of central Rwanda or not. And what about herding elites in the regions to the southeast and the south? To apply the label "Tutsi" to all those populations could well constitute an indefensible anachronism.

What was the case in seventeenth-century central Rwanda before Ndori? Was the word "Tutsi" applied to all herders at that time, whatever their presumed origin, or did it only designate one category among herders whose origin was deemed to be southern and different from that of the Hima, or was the term applied above all to a political elite among the herders? No known data allow us to give a definitive answer to this query. Most likely "Tutsi" then referred mostly to a social class among herders, a political elite, as was still the case in Burundi before 1960 and in Karagwe before 1858. Moreover, since farmers and herders were even then already completely imbricated on the ground in central Rwanda, it is likely that the herders, whatever their origin, often called themselves "Tutsi." The fact that the Nyiginya dynasty did abandon its label as "Hima" in favor of that of "Tutsi" is an indication of this. Later on, the growth in prestige of the term "Tutsi" went hand in hand with the growth of the Nyiginya kingdom. Gradually all nontranshumant herders in the kingdom claimed this designation even if their social condition was but modest. "Hima" came to be a label reserved for the seminomadic herders of Mutara, a tem used scornfully by the elites to designate their less-favored brethren. We shall later see how the ruling class toward the end of the nineteenth century ended up labeling all herders "Tutsi" in implicit opposition to all subjects who were farmers.

In the nineteenth century, a pattern of avoidance similar to that which separated the Twa from all other people also obtained between the Tutsi and all others on the level of both commensalism and marriage.[115] Around 1900 Rwandan society was therefore divided into a hierarchy of three social categories.[116] In the seventeenth century the situation was probably not as clear-cut since later Tutsi behavior toward the bulk of the population was probably to a large extent only an imitation of the behavior and the ideas of the then-ruling elites. It appears that in the seventeenth century people divided the population in general into a hazy hierarchy of "good" and "less good" or "bad" families by comparing some *imiryango* with others, as was still the case in Burundi around 1900.

That an extensive endogamy has obtained for a very long time within the Twa and elite Tutsi groups is nearly certain, given the genetic diversity of the Rwandans. There is no doubt that present-day Rwandans really encompass three different biological "populations" and that whichever scenario is adopted to account for this fact, the differences among the groups run so deep that they must extend back millennia rather than centuries.[117]

Polities

From a political point of view, seventeenth-century central Rwanda was divided into a number of small countries *(ibihugu)* ruled by kings *(umwami / abami*, pl.) who shared their authority with their queen mothers *(umugabekazi)*.[118] The kings and their dynastic drums were the incarnation of these territorial political entities in the collective imagination. Moreover, royal power was made concrete in its emblems, the most important of which besides the drum were a smith's hammer, a musical instrument like an ocarina, and, among the herders, a dynastic bull with his herd of cows.

The government of the king was above all spiritual. It guaranteed prosperity by its very existence and by the execution of rituals destined to ensure the fertility of the land, the fecundity of the cattle, and that of his subjects. He was aided in achieving this by specialized ritualists[119] who were in charge of performing the necessary rituals, within each of which a more or less prominent role was set aside for the king. Certain rituals, such as those dealing with enthronement and royal burial, concerned the king personally. Others managed the fertility of the country. Among these the agrarian rituals of the first fruits *(gicurasi* and *umuganura)*[120] were the main ones, for each year they reemphasized the essential role of the king in maintaining the prosperity of his subjects.[121] Moreover, the king surrounded himself with diviners who studied omens, prepared amulets, and recommended appropriate ritual action to prevent calamities or to remedy them. When need be the king also called upon other specialists, such as the *abavubyi* who were able to regulate the rains, the *abavumyi* who could prevent invasions by locust swarms, those who knew how to curse calamities, and many others, among whom specialists in war magic were certainly not absent.[122] Still, it is remarkable that the kings themselves were seen having abilities in every area of this domain, including as *abahinza*, "masters of agriculture," and as tamers of all scourges.[123] Many of the kings of yore are described as talented diviners and celebrated magicians in the traditional stories that dwell on those long-gone times.[124] In any case, the ritual role of kingship was the keystone of that institution because it legitimized the authority of the king in the eyes of his subjects. Of fundamental importance in this context was the belief that the king owned a supernatural power, acquired during the rituals of succession. Every year the sumptuous performance of the ritual of first fruits *(umuganura)* unified the whole population around the king through the participation of many people from all over the country.[125]

Nevertheless, the king was more than a manager of the supernatural; he also was a secular leader. At the outset of the seventeenth century most political entities were still small and often encompassed but a few hills. Hence one hesitates to call them "kingdoms." The hill, a well delimited natural entity in the landscape, was the smallest political unit no matter what the political regime. Its importance appears in the cult of Ryangombe. This cult emerged in the Gitara region of Bunyoro and seems to have spread to Rwanda a short while before the coming of Ndori. It was adopted by everyone, farmers as well as hunters and herders.[126] The cult was territorial since each agglomeration had its own congregation in which the "mysteries" of the cult were celebrated.[127] Moreover, it explicitly celebrated the superiority of the territorial community over the lineage by claiming precedence over the ancestor cult. The initiates implored the assistance of the companions of Ryangombe to force their own aggressive ancestors to stop tormenting the living and to procure favors for them.[128] Moreover, and in contrast to the rite of ancestor worship that was practiced by an elder in his compound in the name of all the members of his *inzu*, the rite of the cult of Ryangombe was practiced by initiates who individually chose to join a territorial congregation. Further, the practice of the rites of the cult was egalitarian within each congregation and the usual social hierarchy did not obtain during the sessions since all were equally inferior to the supernatural hunterking. Contrary to life within the lineage, women played a leading role here because of their mystical ties with fecundity.[129] But one must underline that in the nineteenth century, and probably much earlier, no equality was recognized any longer among congregations, for by then the wealthy and the political elite had constituted separate congregations.

Despite the presence everywhere of the same basic cell, the community of those who lived on the same hill, territorial entities did not share the same structure since two types of political entities existed, lineage territory and principality.[130] In the first, power rested on an alliance of lineages. The "kings" were supposed to be the direct descendants within the lineage of those who had come first and cleared the land. Members of other lineages, named *"abagererwa,"* meaning "land-tenure clients," descended from later immigrants who had been given land by the first settlers, recognized its leader as their king, sealed marriages with the founding lineage, and sometimes linked themselves to its leader, the king, by a blood pact. Thus emerged a single social community based on two different statuses.[131]

Land tenure was thus the crucial foundation of the political structure. It rested on the rights stemming from clearing the land, rights that were called *ubukonde*. Whomever cleared a plot of land became its owner because the arable land was the fruit of his labor. Since clearing was a collective endeavor by the men of a whole *umuryango,* property rights were vested in the *umuryango* as a whole, something that also contributed to the internal cohesion of this group.[132] From a secular point of view, the king of such an entity was the leader because his lineage had been the first to clear the land of his whole country. As to the *abagererwa* lineages, they held the hills they occupied by a grant from the founding *umuryango*. The hereditary leaders of the lineages who held land in this capacity were considered to be territorial chiefs *(abatware)* of the king. They probably provided him with some corvée labor and a few dues that were essential for the maintenance of the royal residence in return for royal protection. In essence, such an entity consisted then in a coalition among lineages, its territorial center being the residence of the royal lineage. In such an entity there was no permanent militia but when war broke out all men who could fight were called upon to defend the country.

At that time the boundary of the great western forests was still located well to the east of the upper Nyabarongo and there still was plenty of wasteland in Ndiza and in northern Bumbogo. It was in these surroundings, on hills that farmers had only recently cleared, that political entities of the lineage type flourished. Still, one could probably find other entities of this type on certain tracts that had long since been cleared elsewhere in central Rwanda. Among the "kingdoms" that appear in the traditions, Bugara to the northwest of central Rwanda and the polity of Murinda in Rukoma, which was located on land that had by then long been tilled, seem to have been lineage entities and yet powerful in military terms.[133]

In the principality, power rested in the hands of a group of herders. Territorially, such entity was divided into more or less large units governed by hereditary chiefs or *abatware* who were not linked by kinship to any of their farmer subjects. The size of these territorial entities varied between three and seven hills to the north of the middle Nyabarongo and from five to twenty south of the river.[134] These chiefs claimed ownership of the land. They guaranteed tenure of the tilled land to the farmers and access to the pastures to the herders. Their power rested on the military force of their guard, which consisted of young men from their kin group and from those of the Tutsi or Hima families in their chiefdoms, a group whose makeup was analogous to that of the standard team of herdsmen during transhumance. But these young men were military professionals and hence a few of them were enough to intimidate the whole population.[135] The chiefs accepted the precedence of a lord-king to whom they moreover sent one or more of their sons to be enrolled as "pages" in the royal guard and to be educated at his court. Their families married into the royal family, paid an annual tribute, and sent corvée labor to do porterage or to work for the court.

Under this type of political regime, the court was a little more organized internally than in the politics based on lineage. One found three sorts of corporations there, all inspired by the model of the teams of herdsmen in the domestic economy. One corporation entrusted to a designated *inzu* lineage care for the herd linked to the cult of the royal ancestors, the so-called dynastic herd, and also supplied foodstuffs to the court. A second sort of corporation consisted in a team of probably hereditary servants of the court who were in charge of corvée labor and of gathering the tribute necessary to its operation.[136] The third corporation was military. It was the permanent royal guard, composed of professional warriors and the sons of chiefs. One can estimate its size in the largest territories at this time at about 100 to 150 men, a number barely higher than that of the guard of the chiefs.[137] When the need arose, the troops of the chiefs joined this guard. This corporation was the only one that was not based on a descent group. Each king recruited a new guard from among the sons of his chiefs, which made it an agency for centralization because the soldiers came from every part of the realm. A striking image of life at such a court has been preserved in the Ryangombe myths.[138] In these, Ryangombe is the king and the hero. They represent him in action, rather like a King Arthur and his faithful companions roving from adventure to adventure in search of battles, hunts, and cattle to raid.

The emergence of principalities only became possible by the forceful seizure of all the lands.[139] Lands here had been cleared long ago, all available land was occupied, and it was becoming obvious that there was an increasing land deficit in each district. The lack of land was caused in the first place by an increase in the need for pasture, a need that grew in proportion to the growth of the herds.[140] In the seventeenth century, pastureland and arable land were already inextricably mixed, not only because of the nature of the soil on the slopes of the hills, which often varied from one terrain fold to another, but above all as the result of cohabitation on the same hill, which meant, as we have seen, that the tiller of the soil and the herder always needed the same lands. This situation required a single managing authority for all. This figure emerged in the form of the strongest of the herder lords who could call on a permanent military force. From then on the land belonged to the political chiefs who guaranteed tenure of the tracts of tenured land, called *isambu,* "fallow." This word especially designated a tract of land belonging to a farmer, and originally its counterpart in herding would have been *ubwatsi,* "grass," or *umukenke,* "the pasture." The political chief maintained ownership but allowed land to be farmed by those who were already settled in his domain in return for payments and corvée labor. He granted rights to tracts called *ingobyi,* "cradles," but only to *inzu* of farmers, not to whole *imiryango.*[141] Once such a right had been granted it became nearly inalienable although the amount of land included in the *ingobyi* was subject to change. Moreover, the chief maintained a large portion of the domain in collective pastures for the local herders. But as the same lands had to take part in the flow of the single agricultural and herding cycle, certain tracts of *ingobyi* land had to be regularly re-assigned as pastureland and vice versa. When *inzu* of agriculturalists split, which frequently occurred, or when new farmers wanted to settle in the domain of the political chief, the latter created new *ingobyi* and in order to do so he then often took back a portion of the *ingobyi* lands he had previously ceded.[142]

Because the principality was based on the threat of coercion, most of the inhabitants of the principality were forced to pay exactions. An annual payment in foodstuffs and/or in manufactured objects and some corvée labor for the chief were certainly part of the rent due in return for tenure. Moreover, and as was still customary around 1900, the usufructuary of a new *ingobyi* most probably had to cultivate a field for his chief during the first farming season if only because of the symbolic value of such a tithe. But the imposed rents and corvées must have remained rather light, for as long as farmers could easily immigrate to other more lenient domains, the means of coercion of their master remained limited. To require too much would deprive a chief of his people to the benefit of a rival, precisely at a time when small chiefdoms competed with each other in order to attract subjects. Crushing tributes and corvées would only appear once the population density increased to the point that it henceforth prevented any migration of the local farmers.

In spite of its ideology, in spite of its royal guard, and in spite of the territorial extent of the greatest among them, the principality, while centered on a king, still remained a coalition among chiefs whose domains were small. The model of the land of Ryangombe, which dates perhaps from this period, is that of a kingship based on an alliance of herding comrades. During the seventeenth century a good handful of these small principalities flourished both south and north of the middle Nyabarongo, although several of the largest coalitions rapidly dissolved. Thus the old principality of Nduga disappeared south of the Nyabarongo, while north of that river the disaffection of many chiefs shrank the domains of another self-proclaimed royal lineage almost to vanishing point. At this juncture Ndori appeared.

2

The Rwanda of Ndori

RUGANZU Ndori founded the Nyiginya kingdom. That statement contradicts all of Rwanda's historians and most of the oral traditions about the country's history. And yet, it is so, since the so-called kings of the preceding era are purely imaginary. Their whole history has been cobbled together from a collection of fictitious tales in order to legitimize the Nyiginya dynasty and to exalt its majesty by claiming a past more hoary than any one else's. Hence a discussion of this imaginative patch-work is relegated to an appendix in order to truly underline that this alleged prehistory is *not* in fact relevant to the foundation of the Nyiginya kingdom.

The Foundation of the Kingdom

The Nyiginya kingdom was founded by Ndori, some time in the 1600s. Who was this Ndori? Above all he is the protagonist in an epic story, the hero of a great cycle of marvelous tales, some of which are endowed with great formal beauty.[1] Above all he, like Sunjata or Alexander, is the heroic founder of a state. The cycle opens when, still a child, he flees to his paternal aunt in Karagwe, where his father NDAHIRO Cyamatare has sent him, foreseeing his own death and the destruction of his kingdom. When the time is ripe, Ndori is recalled to the country by a faithful servant of his father. On his return he escapes the clutches of his enemies, the Abanyabyinshi, "those who have many things," and reaches Busigi where he instigates miracles of fecundity that prove his kingship. Then he finds his dynastic drum, Karinga, a feat that in this region announces the birth of a new kingdom. Once king, Ndori surrounds himself with a prestigious army and "this triumpher triumphed in his Rwanda" *("Ruganzu aganza wa Rwanda wé").*[2] By guile and by force he makes numerous conquests and the small kings who occupy central Rwanda fall like "the great trees"[3] under the axe of Ndori, the pioneer. He dies from wounds sustained in an ambush that takes place in the high mountain forests.

Was Ndori a genuine historical figure? Why not after all, as so many other epic heroes. such as Sunjata or Alexander, were? Someone founded the kingdom and RUGANZU Ndori is the name they gave him. In that sense he certainly is a genuine historical person.[4] But as one listens to or reads the series of his numerous supposed conquests one realizes that this Ndori must be more than a single historical person. His name is a holdall, a name to which attaches a series of wars of his successors, a name that personifies the whole founding epoch of the kingdom. Ndori is an "epoch ruler."[5] Thus the name designates both the founder of the kingdom as well as some of his successors.[6]

The appearance of Ndori on the scene in central Rwanda seems to have occurred at a time when other kingdoms, such as those of Nkore, Karagwe, and Ndorwa, were also emerging to the north and the northeast. Although the chronology of these polities still remains uncertain, one estimates today that they emerged around 1700.[7] A more intensive program of archaeological research will be required to date the oldest places associated with kingship in each case. For the moment, the available data indicate that Bweyorere in Nkore and Ryamurari in Ndorwa date to the end of the seventeenth century at the earliest.[8] Today no dates can be proposed at all for the kingdoms to the south and southeast of central Rwanda, to wit, Mubari, Gisaka, and Bugesera, for lack of archaeological research or even reliable dynastic lists. Their chronology before the middle of the eighteenth century derives from references in Rwandan historical narratives, references that are probably mere anachronisms.[9]

One can only speculate about the precise circumstances that triggered the quasi-simultaneous emergence of Nkore, Ndorwa, Rwanda, and Karagwe. It is possible that this simultaneity is a mirage projected by the structure of the oral traditions themselves. Everywhere the emergence of these kingdoms is part and parcel of a foundational epoch that is separated by a chronological gap from a later one when traditions began to be preserved, continuing down until our own time. The duration of this gap may well be quite different in each case and hence the foundations may well have occurred at different dates.[10] But another explanation seems far more likely. These kingdoms could well have emerged at the same time since in Uganda, at least, one encounters just such a state of affairs in a chronology based on archeology.[11] The immediate cause of this phenomenon is thought to have been the foundation of the great kingdom of Bunyoro, an event that would have provoked a sudden break in the older balance of power among the smaller units of western Uganda. The emergence of a single territorial entity that was much larger than any of the older ones had been destroyed the military equilibrium in the region and created a climate of generalized insecurity. To remedy this, and to counterbalance the weight of Bunyoro, the surrounding peoples reacted by also constituting themselves into kingdoms.[12] Some authors have suggested that the deeper cause of the break in the balance of power was a worsening of the climate in Uganda. Such a climate change would have harmed agriculture and favored the expansion of both cattle herding and the development of a large political unit, the kingdom of Bunyoro, whereupon groups of other herders would have swarmed toward the south, leading to the emergence of other kingdoms.[13]

Ndori seems to have appeared from the north, because a dynastic poet calls him "the thunder that rumbled from the land of the Bahinda"[14] and the lands of the Hinda were Nkore and Karagwe. Also, according to certain narratives, he first appeared at Gatsibo, on the border with the region of Ndorwa.[15] Whether or not he first emerged in Gatsibo, one finds him thereafter in Busigi, a small chiefdom in the mountains of the Byumba range, from where he conquered Bumbogo and Buriza.[16] Then he crossed the Nyabarongo to capture the part of central Rwanda located within the great bend in that river that was to become the heart of his kingdom.

Almost nothing is known about his origins. Possibly there were some connections with a royal family from the north since his lineage and then his clan would later be known as *"abanyiginya,"* a word that means "relatives of the king, mainly on his mother's side" in Nkore/Nkiga-Ndorwa.[17] Perhaps his original clan was Sindi.[18] The Nyiginya chose the Zigaba as their own autochton godfathers *(abase)* but they also recognized the Gesera and especially the Singa (the oldest among the autochtons) as such, for several reasons—Ndori apparently already acknowledged some of their lineages as being those of ritualists, he was said to have been recalled to central Rwanda by a Singa (Kavuna), and his queen mother would have been Singa as well.[19]

It is quite important to recognize that Ndori was a Hima. Around 1920 it was still common knowledge that the Nyiginya dynasty was of Hima origin, although at that time one usually included all Hima among the Tutsi.[20] Thus the private name of a king is his "Tutsi name." As a Hima coming from the great grasslands of the north, Ndori probably arrived with the great herds (that likely numbered hundreds of head of cattle) owned by all the leaders of nomadic herders. It was perhaps this profusion of cattle rather than sheer force that was the main cause of his success. For the tales underline that he found a good dozen local allies and that he managed to subdue central Rwanda thanks to their help.[21] Without a doubt, these leaders chose to become Ndori's allies because of his wealth in cattle. For Ndori certainly gave cattle or whole herds of cattle to some of his allies, if perhaps not to all of them. In any case the great herds of the northern Hima had to be divided into small lots of from thirty to fifty head since one could not find tracts in central Rwanda encompassing the hundreds and hundreds of hectares of grasslands needed to maintain the big Hima herds.

To hand over cattle to them amounted to a loan to which certain conditions were attached and Ndori seems to have introduced new conditions that rendered his *ubugabire* contracts different from the existing ones. His unequal contract, called *ubuhake*,[22] was far more permanent and compelling to the client than *ubugabire* was, so compelling, in fact, that to accept a contract of this sort was to submit to the king.[23] The patron *(shebuja)* gives one or more head of cattle in usufruct to the client *(umugaragu)* but maintains the ultimate ownership of these cattle. He assures his client of his protection. In return the client must help his patron whenever needed and becomes his servant or *umuhakwa*. The relation was hereditary and only the patron could dissolve it by requiring not only that the client return the patron's cattle but that he also turn over all his own cattle as well.

The words that relate to the *ubuhake* contract are only found in Rwanda, Nkore, and Havu, but not in Rundi, which goes to show that they are loans from Nkore or Ndorwa (Rukiga). Hence it is likely that they were introduced by Ndori or his companions.[24] The noun *"ubuhake"* derives from *"-hâka,"* meaning "to be with young, to be ready to calve."[25] It is not impossible that at first the word was understood in its literal sense and that the contract involved the offspring of the borrowed cow, but the use of the word *"umuhakwa,"* meaning "calf in its mother's womb," in that sense would have been an anomaly. The term *ubuhake* is obviously a herding metaphor: the *umuhakwa* depends as much on the giver and receives as much protection from him as if he was a calf in the womb of its mother. The word also suggests the image of a being, the patron, who holds others, the clients, inside himself. The relation therefore essentially traded political submission for military protection. Thus the cow as much as the bow and the spear founded the Nyiginya kingdom.

With *ubuhake* Ndori erected the first pillar of his authority over the kingdom. At the outset he probably was the only patron and through

ubuhake he established an unequal and permanent political alliance
between the himself and other leaders, his ritualist allies aside. These
ubuhake relations between the king and the grandees of his kingdom
lasted as long as the realm did. But already in his time or a little later,
similar relations of this type began to be adopted between herders of
unequal power, as the weaker ones sought protectors and the stronger
ones local support.[26] Herders, we said, for the client had to be able to
care for the cattle received. But over time farmers and even Twa came
to be accepted as *abagaragu*[27] (although the only known instance of the
latter was the grant of the Akaganda herd of luxury cattle made by
Mazimpaka to a Twa).[28]

Ndori was confronted by two different political regimes when he
arrived, one north of the Nyabarongo and one to the south. That is
probably the origin of the geographic conception of space in central
Rwanda, which is made explicit in the rituals of kingship by the end of
the eighteenth century.[29] A tale describes the alliance between Ndori
and these regimes as follows "Luck [the fates or gods] have given you
this hill. I confirm that gift."[30] A first group of Ndori's allies lived north
of the Nyabugogo, specifically on the mountains of Jali and Nyamweru
in the angle it formed with the Nyabarongo. There he allied himself
with a lineage of the Singa clan by choosing his queen mother among
them. He also allied himself with the main local ruler of a Kono lineage
and his subordinates by adopting him as one of his major ritualists and
by respecting the latter's own ritual kingship.[31] Thanks to his allies,
Ndori first overcame a king called Byinshi[32] who seems to have ruled
over parts of Bumbogo and Buriza. Later, and still to the north of the
Nyabarongo at Ruganda in Bumbogo, Ndori acquired Karinga, his dynastic drum.[33] Two gripping, commonplace, popular accounts tell of its
discovery in the bush.[34] The keepers of the drum, however, tell us in
a straightforward way that it was made of wood from Buberuka by
Minyaruko, chief of Busigi. He handed it over to the king[35] but without
thereby recognizing him as his overlord. Because in the ideology of the
Great Lakes region a kingdom only exists when it has a dynastic drum,
the message of these tales is that with Karinga a new kingdom was
born, the one we now call Nyiginya. Therefore Ndori did not merely
seize power in a preexisting kingdom, as these very same traditions assert when they claim that he was the son of King Cyamatare, who lost
his life, his dynastic drum, and therefore his kingdom.[36]

Ndori then crossed the Nyabarongo and conquered the lands within
its bend where another kingdom had once existed but had disappeared

long before his arrival.[37] Other allies helped him in this endeavor. Among these some, no doubt the most important ones, also became prominent ritualists, especially a Tsobe group from Rukoma that later was in charge of the annual first-fruit rituals, and perhaps also the Tandura of Marangara.[38] According to some narratives, they lived in Mata in northern Marangara.[39] Having succeeded in occupying central Rwanda, Ndori spent the rest of his life waging wars. During a campaign in Rusenyi he supposedly sustained an eye wound and perished of it at Matyazo in Nyantango. His spirit, we are told, then chose to reside inside the dynastic drum Karinga.[40] After his reign a dark age began, for nearly all recollection of his immediate successors has been lost.

It is not easy to determine the extent of the territory Ndori ruled south of the Nyabarongo because the list of all his allies and the places they lived stems primarily from the single tale known as the message of Kavuna. But that tale is a virtuoso piece, composed to show off all the mnemonic talents at the command of the storyteller. It is therefore not very trustworthy. As to Ndori's capitals, one storyteller lists five of these, all in southern Nduga and northern Busanza, but this seems to have been a case wherein the performer was citing all the famous capitals in the region, irrespective of the king who founded them.[41] Thus many traditions mention Nyamagana in southern Nduga as Ndori's first capital, but Nyamagana was also a celebrated capital in the nineteenth century. Be that as it may, though, the only place that would unquestionably have been a capital of Ndori and his immediate successors was Nyundo in Nduga.[42] All the known traditions locate the center of his kingdom in Nduga[43] and suggest that Ndori incorporated eastern Rukoma, nearly all of Kabagari, all of Nduga, and Mayaga.[44] It was there that his successors were to reside at least until the reign of Ndabarasa. His kingdom was therefore rather small both north and south of the Nyabarongo, covering an area of about forty kilometers from west to east, and sixty-five kilometers from north to south, or perhaps 10 percent of the territory of today's Republic of Rwanda. One could cross it in a single long day from east to west and in two days from north to south. This is the realm Ndori left to his successors.

His son Semugeshi, aka Muyenzi, is said to have taken the dynastic names NSORO, BICUBA, and MUTARA, one after the other.[45] He did not succeed Ndori without challenge. It is obvious that this plethora of names clumsily hides a confusion of ill remembered traditions. Perhaps there was more than one king—for example, a NSORO Semugeshi followed by a Muyenzi BICUBA who on the occasion of a calamity

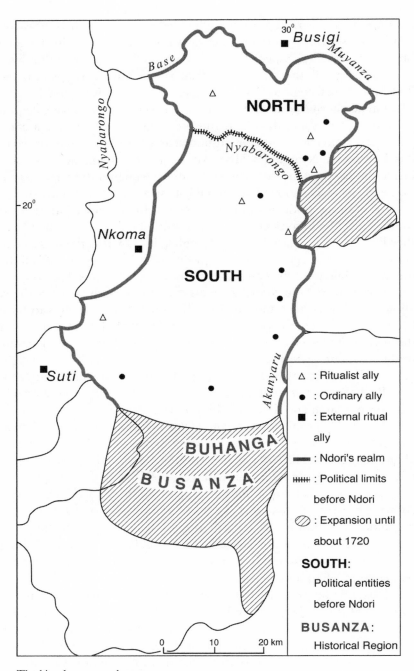

The kingdom around 1700

abandoned that regnal name for MUTARA. Therefore the number of kings involved is unknown; further, it is not known whether these kings all ruled at the same time or in succession.

According to the traditions, KIGERI Nyamuheshera succeeded Semugeshi. Two of his residences, Kamonyi and Shyunga, are mentioned, as is his burial place at Burenga near Sayo where his queen mother Nshenderi is said to have committed suicide.[46] A first blush, this information seems to indicate that Nyamuheshera was king, yet the reasons to doubt this are overwhelming. He is pictured as a great general but the attribution of military campaigns to him is anachronistic and he did not create any new armies.[47] The place names mentioned also refer to locations associated with other, later kings. One can, in addition, doubt the story of Nshenderi's suicide.[48] It is most likely then that this Nyamuheshera is a fictional character and never was king.

This character was probably invented in Rujugira's time when the royal ideology was refashioned in order to complete a dynastic cycle starting with MUTARA and in which a KIGERI was missing. A revealing trace of the mechanism behind a similar rearrangement of ancient remembrances can be found in the commentary about the composition of the dynastic poem *Riratukuye Ishyembe*. Supposedly composed by Rwozi in collaboration with Ndori himself, it was "perfected" by Bagorozi in the reign of CYIRIMA Rujugira for whom he manufactured the verses concerning the reigns from MUTARA Semugeshi to that of CYIRIMA himself.[49] Later on the traditions attributed all the great deeds to the new KIGERI so as to establish precedents for the wars of later kings, especially those of other KIGERI.

Subsequent Military Campaigns: Conquests or Raids?

Nothing is more misleading in the history of the Nyiginya kingdom than the mention of "conquest," for that term usually obscures a very different reality. First, it must be noted that in the Rwandan language there is no distinction between "to defeat" and "to conquer." One speaks of *"gutsinda,"* "to make something fall, to defeat" and even "to kill," and one speaks of *"kuganza,"* "to defeat, to dominate," but also "to win a game of draughts." This verb, from which *"inganji,"* "victory," and *"Ruganzu,"* "the victorious," the regnal name of Ndori, are derived, comes the closest to the notion of conquest, but does not express it either.[50] It follows that the traditions use both words as near synonyms and tell only of "victories," not of "conquests." In fact the narratives do not distinguish among (a) to overcome in a local squabble, for instance, between partisans of different chiefs (b) to succeed in rustling some heads of cattle during a raid (c) to carry out an important raid aimed at the capture of large herds, or finally (d) to assemble thousands of warriors in order to subject a region, that is, to integrate it into the realm.[51] Most historians of the kingdom have automatically concluded that this last sense was intended and have mistakenly understood "to defeat" as "to conquer." In almost every case, however, it was only a matter of raiding, although sufficiently detailed information allowing one to directly evaluate what kind of activity was going on becomes available only after circa 1780.

Given that the information at our disposal for earlier times and even with respect to campaigns attributed to Rwabugiri and Rwogera is still too vague, what to do, then, for example, with the standard pattern of Ndori's tales of conquest? RUGANZU and his warriors attack a small lord, kill him and loot his residence. Is it a raid? Is it an attempt to conquer? What happens after the departure of RUGANZU and his warriors? Data of this sort cannot be used. One must therefore rely on other indicators to document the process of conquest. I have used the following. When a territory had been occupied, an army would have been stationed there for many years, a certain structure, such as a royal residence or an armed camp, would have been erected, and the vanquished leaders would have been removed from command. The whole constitutes a *process*, which takes time. Hence, if after the supposed "conquest" of King X, the same territory must be reconquered by one of his successors, King Y, and this reconquering occurs perhaps several times over, one must consider that the first "conquest" was no conquest at all. Either it was a raid on a lesser or greater scale, or King X never waged war there, but Y did and the court justified his aggression by invoking the invented precedent of X. Moreover, one must always keep in mind that that the technical means available to integrate a region in the realm against the wishes of its inhabitants were quite limited and that a conquest therefore would typically be an enterprise of long duration. All of these considerations suggest that in the absence of other signs, one must understand *"gutsinda"* and *"kuganza"* and related words as referring to mere victories and not conquests. I will take the available indicators related to the interpretation of oral statements into account all the more carefully because the historiographers of the kingdom have for the most part interpreted *"kuganza"* and *"gutsinda"* as meaning "conquest" and tend to reduce the history of all of Rwanda to that of "conquests" by the Nyiginya kings. Unfortunately, such "conquests" are still invoked today as a justification for certain claims.

Nevertheless, "King Ruganzu only became so famous because he was a true warrior"[52] and Ndori certainly waged war outside the borders of the realm that were established after the occupation of Nduga, even though the traditional narratives do not allow one to make a list of them. For a portion of the military operations with which he is credited are likely those of his immediate successors, and there are also campaigns attributed to him that stem from wholly imaginary fairy tales. An examination of the whole lot allows one only to eliminate obvious cases of fictive stories such as his fight with the giant Nyangara[53] and blatant anachronisms such as his adventures in Bugesera.[54] There remain some fifteen campaigns that may have occurred in his lifetime or in that of his immediate successors. To figure out which ones among these were true conquests one can only compare the extent of the realm in the days of Gisanura, who died around 1735, with the territory that was occupied at the outset. The gains were modest. As the maps shows, they include (a) Kigari Mountain and its surroundings,[55] (b) Burwi and Bungwe in the present prefecture of Butare,[56] (c) a small part of eastern Bunyambiriri, and (d) perhaps Marangara.[57] Taking other weak indicators into account, one can attribute the acquisition of Bunyambiriri to Ndori, that of Bungwe and Burwi in the south to his son Muyenzi,[58] and that of Kigari to an unknown monarch.

Other references to conquests by Semugeshi[59] and all references to those of Nyamuheshera,[60] are anachronistic. To cite but one case, let us look at the so-called conquests of MUTARA in the present prefecture of Butare. He is credited with destroying the Ngwe (Abene Ngwe) by capturing their dynastic drum Nyamibande and also with the "conquest" of Busanza, Bufundu, and Bungwe, all in the same prefecture. The first ground for this assertion is the story of Nyagakecuru, located on Mount Huye, which is clearly a fairy tale, attributed by some to MUTARA and by others to Ndori. The second is the presence of the Nyamibande, aka the Rwuma drum, at the court, which does not prove anything by itself as to who captured it, from whom, and when.[61] In addition, although some traditions place MUTARA at Rusatira and relate the capture of a white royal cow in Bufundu by a Ngwe leader they are wrong; these events are obviously taken from another reign, that of Mazimpaka, and from another enemy, the king of Burundi.[62]

A primary goal of all these expeditions was to capture cattle. RUGANZU boasted of being "the man who attacks foreign countries to raid cattle in order to increase his herds."[63] Indeed Ndori is said to have created at least two herds with his loot, one with cattle raided from Bunyabungo,[64] and one with cattle raided from Bugara.[65] But according to many traditions other items were looted as well. A storyteller summarizes: "Finally Rugáanzu's warriors attacked Bugara, killed Nzira with an ax, and took gracious girls with ornaments around their waist; they looted Nzira of just about everything and returned to Rwanda crushed under the weight of the looted objects."[66]Another important goal was to capture "beautiful women" and reduce them to servitude *(abaja)*. Indeed, all valuable objects were taken. Several tales mention, for instance, the looting of goats, dogs, jewels, and metal tools. Moreover, all the houses were burned before the raiders left the place.

These raids were therefore quite destructive. Thus the storyteller complacently narrates how Ndori visited a minor lord who was supervising work on his fields. Ndori proposed to help him and began to hoe, but, coming near him, suddenly killed him with a blow of the hoe, and called forth his companions (his "army") hidden in the vicinity. They killed and destroyed everything on the hill and returned home laden with loot.[67] But for his victims this RUGANZU and his ilk were just highwaymen[68] in search of plunder. Their appearance was the worst of calamities, and to avoid disaster one could only try to flee his neighborhood. Since Ndori and his band were looking primarily for herds, their preferred victims were herders rather than farmers (from whom one could expect to loot no more than one or two head of cattle at a time). Thus, contrary to the overall impression left by the historical tales, it was herders above all who suffered from his depredations. No doubt herders, too, are the ones who attempted to flee in time to escape this scourge that accompanied the emergence of the kingdom. For instance, the herders of Bigogwe recollect that their ancestors arrived at this time, a recollection that is accurate as to the process of cause and effect even if the chronology is exaggerated.[69] The construction of the kingdom was therefore accompanied by some population movement in the form of refugees, among whom many went to the still-empty mountain forests that were less accessible than other lands.

Government: The Ritual Institutions

Two elements were essential to the creation of Ndori's kingdom. First, there was the affirmation of the very idea that it was a kingdom. Ndori was acknowledged as king by his companions from the start and later on by that portion of the population and the leaders of the regions he invaded who rejected the contested sovereignty of Byinshi who ruled north of the Nyabarongo. Ndori's military successes were interpreted as proof of his legitimacy. His legitimacy was later sanctioned by persons who were recognized as genuine ritualists. But they themselves also had to justify their decision to recognize Ndori as king. It is probable that from the very start the rumor circulated in central Rwanda that Ndori was the son of an earlier king.[70] Surely the local ritualists used such a rumor as a justification for their recognition and embroidered it either then or later to form a detailed tradition on the theme of the lost son who returned.

Therefore, ritual institutions became the means by which the very fact that there was a new kingdom was established in the mind of the inhabitants of a region. But in practice a conviction, however strong, is not by itself enough to found a lasting kingdom. It has to be accompanied by the elaboration of concrete coercive institutions that allow a government to find the material means for it to function. We first present the basic ritual institutions and then the instrumental institutions that made the practice of power possible in the realm.

For the population to accept Ndori as king, a more solid legitimacy than that which flowed from his victories was needed. Since he came from a land in which the institution of ritualists was as well known as in central Rwanda,[71] he eagerly sought to acquire the legitimacy it could bestow and to have himself proclaimed king. In order to achieve this, his initial alliances were crucial. We saw that Ndori rallied the support of two groups found in the area, one a Kono lineage in Buriza, the other a Tsobe lineage of Bumbogo, whose leaders he recognized as ritualists. Both of these perhaps had leaders who themselves had been independent kings, or perhaps ritualists for an earlier local king who was not Byinshi. Moreover, Ndori also rallied the support of a third group of important ritualists, the Tege of Kabagari. The Kono and Tsobe each managed a structured organization that included subgroups and corporations of menials who performed the main rituals, and because of this they both were permitted to own unencumbered domains, that is lands free from any interference by the king or his agents.

To establish his authority Ndori also had to be enthroned with a queen mother and he needed a dynastic drum with its following of small drums, as well as a dynastic bull with its herd of cows. This meant that one also had to establish a means of maintaining the service of the drums and of the herd by creating corporations of menials for that purpose.

While the Kono played the main role during the enthronement itself, the Tege were just as essential even then, for they guaranteed the authenticity of Karinga and were in charge of the corporations serving the royal drums.[72] It is not known if Ndori introduced innovations in these rituals that involved drums, herds, and bulls since their use in rituals was probably already widespread in the region, but it seems likely that he introduced at least a few new details.

After the enthronement, the next most important ritual was the annual celebration of first fruits, the *umuganura*, which was preceded by *igicurasi*. Their organization was mainly in the hands of the Tsobe. Although information about the performance of these rituals only stems from the nineteenth century and even though they certainly underwent some elaboration over the years, it is still reasonable to think that their essential features already existed in Ndori's lifetime. These rituals were at the core of the polity because they expressed the unity of the kingdom and the solidarity of its inhabitants in concrete terms by mobilizing not just workers belonging to the corporations of menials, but also providers of the needed paraphernalia who were scattered all over the realm.[73] Moreover, every year these rituals made clear in unmistakable fashion who belonged to the kingdom and who was a foreigner because all the chiefs had to participate and the subjects had to refrain from eating any fruit from the new harvest until the conclusion of the ritual.

Ndori seems to have introduced a new cult, hitherto unknown in central Rwanda, to further legitimize the specific power of the royal dynasty. This is the cult of Gihanga. In the regions to the northwest and the north of central Rwanda, Gihanga, whose name means "creator, founder," was celebrated as the founder of kingship and the first of all kings.[74] Evidently Gihanga never was an historical figure. It would be superfluous to even mention such an obvious fact, were it not that many Rwandans believed, and still believe, that he was one.[75] In those northern regions he was associated with a series of places from Buhanga (same verbal stem as Gihanga) near the Mukungwa River in the Ruhengeri Plain to places in the former province of Mutara. But in the south and east one finds no tales or places associated with this Gihanga. Hence this distribution suggests that the cult was imported from the north to the Rwandan court at a moment when those northern regions enjoyed great prestige, which was the case during Ndori's reign.

The major elements of that cult were the following. First there was the fire of Gihanga, maintained in a shrine for him at the court. It was called "the place where the cattle are milked" and the fire lit there was supposed to be the very fire lit for Gihanga that had never been extinguished since his own days. It served as a proof of apostolic succession: the Nyiginya king truly was the direct and legitimate descendant of the great conqueror Gihanga. This cult was managed by the same Tsobe who were in charge of the *umuganura*. Then a site was discovered at Muganza of Rukoma—as it happens, in the Tsobe domain—that was supposed to be Gihanga's tomb. From time to time the court sent offerings there to beseech his assistance. Lastly a herd was assembled as a memorial to Gihanga that was claimed to consist of the descendants of his personal herd.[76] This was managed by the Heka family of the Zigaba clan, whose leader lived nearby the so-called tomb and was one of the foremost ritualists at court. Let us also mention that the Tege ritualists derived their prestige from their claim to be the descendants of a certain Rubunga, who supposedly revealed the principle of the dynastic drum to Gihanga.[77] Taken all together, the places and the practices of the cult for Gihanga as well as the genealogical data related to it as known circa 1900 certainly resulted from an evolution that only started in Ndori's reign and whose later development thereafter remains unknown. But the first step, the introduction of the shrine for the fire of Gihanga, was taken at Ndori's court.

Among the occasional rituals, those that were designed to control the rainfall were also quite significant, for the effectiveness and the legitimacy of the king were demonstrated to the common folk above all by his power over the rains. One believed that rainfall was controlled by rainmakers who usually were local chiefs in the regions where it rained most and for the longest time, that is, on the highlands bordering central Rwanda and at that time, above all, those of Busigi.[78] So the Nyiginya king found himself depending on these independent leaders, especially the one in Busigi, to perform these rituals. Because of this, the rainmakers were able to maintain the internal autonomy of their kingdoms and keep them free of all interference by the Nyiginya kingdom. Moreover, Minyaruko of Busigi had manufactured the Karinga drum. Then under Semugeshi, Mpande, a diviner who had been Ndori's main confidant, introduced a cult at the court for the rainmaker Kibogo, a person said to be a genuine historical figure.[79] Although no source explicitly states this, a relation of the same sort may well have obtained with regard to a king in Cyingogo notorious for his ability to ward off agricultural calamities and especially to avert devastating clouds of locusts.[80]

Finally, divination was also an essential tool of governance. The king surrounded himself with diviners to scrutinize the world of the spirits, to predict the future, to interpret omens, and then to advise the king.[81] Moreover, the first Nyiginya kings probably used magic for success in war as well as for a long reign, both specialties of the lords of Marangara, which seems to have allowed them to maintain their own autonomy for a very long time.[82] In Ndori's time there were probably far fewer diviners than later on but they were indispensable. According to all the sources, the most illustrious one among them was Mpande wa Rusanga, the main diviner for both Ndori and Semugeshi.

One major cult, Ryangombe's worship, still escaped royal control under Ndori. Only under Semugeshi did the court incorporate it in the corpus of the royal rituals. One story relates how this happened. It tells of a great drought that hit Rwanda and how the diviners claimed that it would only end once the king abandoned his old regnal name NSORO for that of BICUBA ("the milk pot"). The king did so but the drought did not let up. Moreover, the king became bewitched, which caused an infection in one of his eyes. At that juncture, the old Mpande ya Rusanga, who had fallen out of favor, was recalled, whereupon he undid the witchcraft and prescribed that the name of BICUBA should be abandoned in favor of MUTARA, and probably launched the cult for Kibogo.[83] That name probably derives from Gitara, the original home of Ryangombe, and was therefore adopted in his honor. This recalls a second tale according to which the country suffered an epidemic from which it was only delivered by the initiation of the king into the cult of Ryangombe.[84] The basic point of this confused lot of traditions is that from then onward (at least until the reign of Rwaka included), the kings were initiated into this cult.[85] With its integration into the set of royal rituals, the centralization of all the main rituals at court was complete.

Instruments of Government: The Corporations

The ideological institutions were the very foundation of the kingdom. Indeed at the Nyiginya court, to govern meant, above all, to ensure the performance of the appropriate rituals. But to assert itself and to subsist, the realm, and especially the court at its core, also needed institutions to provide supplies necessary for living, such as lodgings and food, and goods to remunerate the loyal partisans of the king, be it by the loan of cattle, the gift of certain luxury clothes, or in other ways. Obtaining these necessities was the task of the corporations. Before Ndori, there were three sorts of these: corporations of menials, corporations for the service of the official herds, and military corporations composed of young men chosen from the families of distinguished herders who were dependents of a local lord. Such corporations were assigned to the service of the king, the court, and the ritualists.

All but one of the corporations of menials were assigned to the ritualists, the exception being a corporation at the service of the court. It was responsible for bringing firewood and water, for keeping the houses and compounds swept and clean, for providing porters, and for supplying other daily services required by a royal house and the pages that it housed. All of that was the responsibility of the king's wives under the direction of the oldest one among them, or of the queen mother when she lived at the court. A good deal of work was carried out by the servants and slaves of these ladies. But still there remained other tasks, from porterage when the court moved, to the routine supply of food and the supply of daily corvée labor to bring water and provide firewood, to the sweeping of the premises, for which there was a team of servants, perhaps already called Abahiza.[86] Was there even then already another corporation in charge of providing the court with hoes, honey, and foodstuffs as needed?[87] And, if so, how was this corporation recruited? Its members came from Buriza, but were all the men of Buriza called upon to serve by turns? Or did only a certain number of them belong to the corporation? From where exactly did they come and who led them? Most of Buriza was in the hands of ritualists, especially Kono, but there also were hills there that were not under their control. Should one imagine that there was a nonritualist chief who was directly subordinate to the king? These are all questions without answers. Let us also observe that certain corporations in charge of cattle were already responsible for the daily supply of milk to the court.

The corporations serving the ritualists had to provide them with all the things and services required for the performance of the rituals. Thus the members of Gakondo[88] grew sorghum and provided the other necessary paraphernalia for *umuganura* to the Tsobe ritualists and ensured the timely transportation of everything to the court. Other corporations were in charge of the drums. They were grouped with the armies because they were constituted in the same way, having seemingly been composed of military corporations retired from active service. In Ndori's days there were the Abanyakaringa Ishyama, which he created himself for Karinga, the Abakaraza for the Cyimumugizi drum,[89] probably the Abariza for the Kono ritualists,[90] and perhaps the Abatsindyingoma who provided the firewood for the Gihanga fire as well as skins and iron-headed arrows.[91]

The members of the corporation of the official herds performed all the necessary usual daily and seasonal tasks for their herds and supplied the court with milk and meat from the slaughter of excess young steers or barren cows. Ndori owned a so-called dynastic herd called Insanga that included the bull Rusanga and supposedly comprised direct descendants of Gihanga's herd. This herd was cared for by the Abanyasanga, led by the foremost ritualist herder, the head of the Heka group of the Zigaba clan, an *umuse* clan of the Nyiginya. Another herd also supposedly stemming from Gihanga was cared for by the Abakaraza corporation and managed by another of the foremost ritualists, the chief of the Tege of Kabagari.[92] Besides these two, four others that served the Kono ritualists and that were all dedicated to the rituals of the monarchy are also mentioned in the oral traditions. Moreover, Semugeshi organized yet another small herd at his court that was at the service of Kibogo, the rainmaker.[93]

Ndori created yet another corporation to keep the Indorero herd, the dynastic herd he raided from Bugara. Its leader, Mpande ya Rusanga, became his favorite, and the king introduced an innovation by attaching this cattle corporation to his own army, the Ibisumizi. Pastures for the herd were assigned at Muyira in Mayaga, and this was the first time that lands were directly given not to an individual, but to an army. In return, the corporation always had to keep two milk cows at the court[94] His successors followed that example and each newly created army was henceforth supplied with corporations to manage their herds, along with pastureland for them, in return for the delivery of a required amount of milk and meat to the court.

This innovation was actually only one facet of the most important of Ndori's innovations: the development of an army. That was a crucial innovation because henceforth this institution, along with the *ubuhake*, came to constitute the very foundation of power in the kingdom. When Ndori arrived, the local leaders already had a system in place whereby their troops of chosen *(intore)* young men also served as a military guard. Ndori transformed this practice. As he needed far more soldiers, as well as more docile soldiers, he began to recruit new companies as the years went by. Outside of the Nyiginya kingdom, this practice was only known in the Nkore and Nyoro kingdoms, so it is possible that Ndori borrowed the idea from the north. The idea of then joining different companies to form a single new entity probably derived from the practice of aggregating a number of small herds into a single large unit, *umutwe* ("head"), an expression that henceforth will also be used to designate an army.[95]

Moreover, Ndori increased the social distance between his warriors and himself by placing his army under the command of a general *(umugaba)*. His first commander was Muvunyi, later replaced by Mpande ya Rusanga, apparently of the same lineage.[96] Ndori created at least four companies in addition to his first *intore,* each with its own particular name, but Ibisumizi, the name of the first one, also became that of the whole army.[97] The captain of the last company to be formed was his successor, Semugeshi. This company became the kernel of a new army that Semugeshi created during his reign, for with Ndori's demise, all the other companies of his army were dissolved.[98] In this fashion, Ndori created, probably unwittingly, a structure of age classes with separate initiations for each class. This aspect of the institution does not seem to have attracted attention for a structure of age classes was never used elsewhere, either in government or in social structures.

The advantages of the new military organization were substantial. In time, Ndori's army became greater than that of his enemies and ended up including from four to six times more well trained warriors than the armies of other chiefs. Moreover, younger and stronger warriors were inducted into it whenever a new company was created. Each new company was instructed by one composed of veterans and learned from their experience so that after a few years the last recruits became the shock troops. Thanks to this organization, Ndori's army surpassed by far the *intore* companies of its adversaries. Even royal security and military discipline benefited from the new organization, since it was no longer possible for a company to wield more than a small parcel of military power. True, every company maintained its internal esprit-de-corps, but the size of the army reduced the effects of any indiscipline. Moreover, that size encouraged the appearance of an esprit-de-corps that expressed itself through its allegiance to the commander-in-chief. And finally, a first step toward a permanent army was taken when Ndori's successor formed his new army from the last company of the preceding one.

The deepest effect of this new military organization was the institutionalization of a glorification of militarism and martial violence that finally permeated the whole of Nyiginya culture as the armies became the foundation of the administrative structure of the realm. For the ties forged by Ndori between the army, on the one hand, and the corporations that provided services to the court, managed the herds, and controlled the pastures, on the other, were to flourish during the eighteenth century so that ultimately all the inhabitants of the realm were incorporated into the military organization. From a cultural point of view the recruitment of *intore* from about ten years of age onward[99] and their indoctrination in the ways of the court was to favor the unification and the development of the Rwandan language as well as the refinement of its artistic expression, which was especially reflected in the practice of different poetic genres that werecultivated there. This indoctrination also favored that exaltation of violence, imposture, and the right of the strongest that became the universal theme of all literary and choreographic artistic forms.[100] To achieve success by whatever means necessary eventually came to justify any and all sorts of behavior, for to succeed is *imana nziza*, that is, "good luck," which justifies all.

The Ibisumizi were Ndori's only army. All of the other armies that were supposedly created by him—to wit, two led by Mpande ya Rusanga before he took over the Ibisumizi, and one that had supposedly been the militia of an immigrant chief of Burundi who married Ndori's daughter—were in fact constituted later.[101]

The Realm

To understand the territorial history of the Nyiginya kingdom one must begin by ridding oneself of preconceived ideas. The realm never was a space with well delineated borders; the court did not first conceive of territorial units and then appoint specialized local administrators such as "governors" or "prefects" to oversee them. Rather, the kingdom was conceived of as a space consisting of a center, its ambulatory capital, and outlying regions that were thought of in two ways. Usually the outer space was rather vaguely divided into natural regions such as "Marangara" or "Cyingogo." The terminology was flexible and certain terms, such as "Nduga" or "Bwanacyambwe," for instance, were applied to a smaller or larger region according to the oppositions implied in the discourse.[102] But when one was talking about political relations one thought in terms of domains pertaining to chiefs, major or small, royal clients, or ritualists, without worrying about the exact extension of these domains. Therefore one spoke of "at X" or "at Y" and one sometimes specified what one meant by that by referring to a natural region. The limits of the country were thought of as the outside limits of the domains that were furthest away. They remained vague and were often theoretical, at least in those places where they did not correspond with the main rivers or lakes such as the Nyabarongo, the Base, the Nyabugogo, the Akanyaru, the Kagera or Lake Kivu.

After his conquest, Ndori became the leader of a set of territories belonging to his allies and of conquered lands, not all of them in one single block. The only centralizing elements at his disposal were the court *(ibwami)* and the residences *(umurwa)*. The court was ambulatory. It shifted from place to place at the king's pleasure on the advice of his diviners. Neither the frequency nor the reasons that prompted the shifts of the courts of Ndori and of his immediate successors are known. Ndori's court was certainly not as populated, or visited as frequently by territorial chiefs, as later courts would be. It included the royal family with its servants, a few diviners, some ritualists, a few essential artisans such as smiths, tanners, potters, hunters, and at least one company of the army. But even if all these people together did not exceed a few hundred, still, the labor necessary for its upkeep must already have put a heavy burden on the surrounding communities. Since it was mainly provisioned by the inhabitants in its neighborhood, the court had to be located in a fertile district where the population density was sufficient to supply its needs. But after a few years, and following the discreet flight of a part of the population scared off by the extent of the corvée labor and tributes demanded, the quantity of local supplies began to be exhausted. Eventually the lack of supplies in the vicinity forced the court to shift to another location. At the same time, these shifts of the court from place to place allowed for the successive exhibition of the power and the splendor of the central government in different parts of the country.

The governmental functions that took place at the court included the usual rituals, the announcement of the king's commands or of those issued by the queen mother, the public meetings in the morning when the king arbitrated or judged, and the evening sessions during which the king and his companions caroused and discussed all sorts of topics. These sessions were the arena in which most political and administrative activity took place. At them, the king found his favorites, his military commanders and other counselors—such as Mpande, for instance—and occasionally one or another of his clients *(abagaragu)*. While amusing itself, this exalted company informed itself, argued about various ways to resolve current problems, or tried to discredit competitors. In this sort of government, administration was not yet institutionalized.

The king personally controlled only a few small districts. When he shifted the capital he sometimes turned over the management of the residence he was leaving to one of his wives or even to a woman servant. In that case, the place became a permanent residence *(umurwa)* managed by a spouse or a servant maid *(umuja)* who was aided by a representative of the king.[103] The king expropriated the lands of the hill on which the residence was located and sometimes even the lands of the surrounding hills. In return, each residence had to supply a large portion of the corvée labor or goods needed by the court. In the nineteenth century (and even perhaps as early as the seventeenth), a distinction was made between residences of wives, which were exempted from having to provide any tribute or corvée labor to the court, and residences of maids, which had to supply them.[104] But not all localities where the court settled necessarily became institutional residences. Most of these places only became *ikigabiro*. After the place was vacated, the trees of the former enclosures were left to grow as commemorative groves and establishing either fields or pastures there was strictly forbidden. Hence the mere mention of a place where the court was located is not enough to determine whether it was a residence or a commemorative spot. So while the names of various places where Ndori is said to have established capitals are known, only one of those has been proven to have been a residence, the one at at Nyundo, and it was a residence only because Semugeshi inherited it. This monarch is thought to have had five or six capitals but seems to have added only one or two residences, both south of the middle Nyabarongo.[105] In fact *imirwa* never became numerous in central Rwanda—in 1895 there were only twenty-one of them in the vast country controlled by Rwabugiri. As to the *ibigabiro*, they acted as visible manifestations of the power of the state in the landscape. In addition to the lands of these districts, Ndori and his successors also seized certain lands as pastures, for example, Murira in Mayaga, and turned over their management to the commander of an army or of a corporation in charge of a herd.[106]

During Ndori's reign a large part of the realm was divided into small chiefdoms headed by allies who were not ritualists but who had still welcomed him into the country. All these chiefs were probably linked to the king by an *ubuhake* contract since such a contract would have reified their submission to and alliance with him. In accordance with the *ubuhake* contract, they would then have sent tribute in food, objects, or cattle to the court according to its needs. The local chiefs *(abatware)* could not be deposed, kept their own *intore*, and governed their lands without any interference by the court. They waged private wars and vendetta without any restriction at all.

The main ritualists also still held territories that were totally free. Some, such as the Remera of the Tege in Kabagari, were apparently of modest dimensions, but those of the Tsobe and the Kono were quite extensive and had their own leaders. The ritualist Kono "king" governed the southern parts of Buriza and Bumbogo and the ritualist Tsobe "king" held lands in Rukoma around Kamonyi as well as a large portion of Bumbogo. Even if the Tsobe lands were less extensive at that time than they would become later on, they still constituted a significant portion of the country north of the Nyabarongo. All these ritualist lands were exempt from royal authority in return for the ritual obligations owed by their chiefs. In addition, a few other hills also became exempt over time because they were graveyards for kings or queen mothers.[107]

One could therefore describe Ndori's kingdom as an amalgam of territories whose leaders stood in a mutually recognized relationship of interdependence with or subordination to the king. But should one, even in this broad definition, include the domains of lords who were the king's ritual allies or not? The most famous among these was Minyaruko of Busigi. He inaugurated Ndori and made Karinga, but he did not recognize Ndori as his king. The same situation apparently obtained in a number of other borderlands such as the Suti region whose rainmaker lords were considered allied ritualists by the Nyiginya court but who thought of themselves as independent.[108] The case of Marangara is slightly different. Its lord, Nkoma Sebibakanyi of Nkondogoro, was an essential ritual ally[109] who thought of himself as independent, yet Ndori stills seems to have established his court at Mata in his lands. It seems reasonable to exclude from the realm all the regions that did not recognize the suzerainty of the king and that contributed neither corvée labor nor tribute. By this measure Busigi, the domain of Suti, and a few small principalities extending from Ndiza to Bweramvura in Kabagari lay outside the realm, but Marangara was part of it, at least as long as Ndori resided there.

Conclusion

Thanks to his valor and his alliances, which were facilitated by the numerous herds with which he came, Ndori succeeded in being recognized as the legitimate king in central Rwanda and created a government there that rested on four institutions, the court-capital, the *umurwa* district, the political *ubuhake* clientele, and a true army. The last two of these remained the innovations that distinguished the Nyiginya kingdom from all its neighbors from that time on. Later on they came to provide an internal cohesion and military power that were quite exceptional within the wider region. But the creation of a kingdom and its acceptance by the population stemmed first and foremost from the fact that Ndori managed to find influential ritualists. After all, the kingdom was only the sum total of the chiefs who recognized the king as their overlord, a recognition that was sealed by the fiction that he was the legitimate successor to a former king.

Yet it would be a mistake to imagine that the first kings ruled as autocrats, although the tales have a tendency to portray the kings as doing precisely that. Certainly the king was the leading actor on the court scene, but he was not the only one. The queen mother enjoyed an independent authority. At the court the foremost ritualists and the diviners-cum-counselors certainly had their say, as did those who had been the king's earliest allies and military commanders such as Muvunyi and Mpande. All these people were stakeholders in this new enterprise that was the kingdom and just as interested in its success as the king was himself. Ndori and his successors were certainly obliged to negotiate with them. Moreover, one suspects that there were already two factions among the courtiers, those who were his first companions from abroad and those who already held high office in the land before his arrival. People in both camps probably competed with each other and the kings undoubtedly exploited such rivalres even while they continued to rely on both factions. In such a political arena, the emergence of favorite counselors (*abatoni*[110]) becomes nearly inevitable if only in an informal way. Thus Mpande ya Rusanga gathered more and more influence during Ndori's reign. He seems to have kept his key position during the first part of Semugeshi's reign but then fled into exile after clashes with the queen mother. Later, however, he was recalled and then remained the king's main ritual counselor until his death. Moreover, according to a single bit of information, Semugeshi also seems to have had an official favorite, Gahenda, an Ega and brother of the queen mother, who was dismissed in favor of Mpande.[111] Despite their tenuous and somewhat speculative character these data have the merit of drawing attention to the importance of the actual practice of power and the inevitable struggles for influence that accompanied it, even during Ndori's reign.

The kingdom survived Ndori and gradually consolidated itself under his epigones. That consolidation was as much due to the great lineages that gravitated around the king as to the efforts of the monarchs themselves, for these lineages were just as much implicated in the construction of the Nyiginya kingdom as was the king himself. Unfortunately, a dearth of sources prevents us from knowing precisely how Ndori's kingdom was transformed into the already much more consolidated one that existed shortly after 1700.

3

Toward the Centralization of Power

Let us pick up the thread of history around 1720 and examine the evolution of the kingdom until the death of Ndabarasa in 1796, which triggered a particularly destructive civil war. Over the course of almost three quarters of a century, the kings and the elite at the court succeeded in creating a centralized kingdom by laying their hands on all the cattle and the land, the essential factors of production, by fashioning effective, multiple, and permanent armies, and by developing the court, which became the pivot of the realm. Thus a system of government was elaborated here that was unique in the whole region of the Great Lakes.

According to the traditions, this period is clearly divided into two parts separated by the rupture that occurred around 1766 when Rujugira seized power. Gisanura,[1] Mazimpaka, and Rwaka ruled before the rupture and Rujugira and Ndabarasa after it. The latter two kings apparently also instituted fundamental reforms. Yet, despite this, the traditions are far more fascinated with the personality of YUHI Mazimpaka than with that of Rujugira or Ndabarasa. They praise his physical beauty,[2] his poetic sensitivity, his visionary talents, his exceptional fertility, which gave him numerous descendants, and his love of cattle, which led him to commit all sorts of follies on behalf of his favorites, especially on behalf of his cow Nyagahoza and his herd of long-horned cattle (Inyambo). This love of cattle also explains why all the subsequent YUHI are supposed to be cattle kings. His beloved capital "Kamonyi in the heavens" was a bucolic and peaceful paradise. In contrast, his martial qualities are not underlined, even in his praise name.[3] But the destiny of this monarch was tragic. This visionary was often drunk,[4] yaws ravaged his beauty, and his sensitivity turned into such paranoia that he ended up exterminating those he loved the most, and turned into a madman.[5] We have here an exceptional personality that could not be stereotyped like that of CYIRIMA Rujugira, the wise reformer, or his son Ndabarasa, the intrepid warrior. The memory of their actions explains why the names of CYIRIMA (and MUTARA) will henceforth open the sequence of regnal names and why KIGERI will henceforth be associated with the picture of a fighting king. But their personalities fade compared to that of Mazimpaka. The two wings of this diptych as presented by the traditions oppose the personality of a king to the great deeds of his two successors. But an historian cannot accept the idea that there was such a complete contrast. Yes, the coup certainly provoked a great rupture that led to the subsequent reform of the royal ideology, and the coup was certainly traumatic since it had a strong impact on all the traditions that speak of earlier times. But the fundamental centralizing reforms had been effected well before the rupture and hence it is better not to subdivide this period.

The Seizure of the Herds and the Land

The curtain rises around 1720 and reveals the following scene: Gisanura is king, but the great chiefs Mpaka in Nduga and Mayaga, Mpumba at Gishubi in Ndiza, Kogota in Rukoma from Kamonyi to Ruhanga, Kazakanyabuseri in Marangara around Kabgayi, and Rugabyi, son of Bwakiya, in the Burembo of Ndiza are all independent. Those are all the chiefs south of the middle Nyabarongo save for Busanza in the far south. But Gisanura succeeds in convincing them to recognize him as overlord, allowing them to remain lords in their lands.[6] We thus learn that practically the whole country south of the Nyabarongo was ruled by five major chiefs, the majority of whom were probably still descendants of Ndori's allies in the region. If one also takes into account the considerable amount of land that was owned by the ritualists in Buriza and northern Bumbogo, it becomes evident that the king still did not control extensive personal domains. Ndori's successors had not managed to extend their authority, and their centralizing power was still as fragile as it had been at the outset.

But starting with Gisanura the kings and their courts attempted to obtain a stronger hold over their subjects and succeeded in this endeavor. It was an enterprise of long duration, which was grounded in part in the strength of the royal armies, but consisted mainly in the seizure of those great herds that constituted the wealth and power of the lords. Remember also that the king could only subject his clients and obtain their services by giving them the usufruct of his cattle. The creation of official herds for other than the service of the ritualists was a central element of the strategy. Not only was an official herd accompanied by pastures and hence by rights over land and not only did such a herd provide milk and meat to the court and thus contribute to its maintenance, but giving usufruct of herds remained the major means at the disposal of the kings to establish their sons, to ally themselves to the great families of the country, to reward their favorites, and to acquire new clients.

From the time of Gisanura onward new herds were created with increasing frequency. Gisanura himself is said to have established two of them, one for the dynastic poet Muguta from a well-to-do family[7] and one called Umuhama for his son Gahindiro. Mazimpaka—Rwaka included?—would have established thirteen of them for herders only and three that were linked to an army, two of which were commanded by his sons. As to the herds for cattle-keepers, he left four of these to his sons (one of whom received two herds), seven to families with whom he wished to ally himself, among whom one notes a herd for a Tsobe lineage, one for the Bena-Gitore, and one to an unknown person. He also kept one herd to himself through the intermediary of a Twa at court: this was the first herd of Inyambo cattle.[8] To evaluate the effects of this attribution of herds one must remember that the beneficiaries only received a right of usufruct, which the sovereign could rescind at any moment. Even if Mazimpaka or Rwaka do not seem to have reappropriated herds from families to whom they had been given, the possibility of this occurrence remained a sword of Damocles always hanging over the head of their clients. Moreover, the king retained ownership over the issue of the herd he gave and at least a subsidiary right allowing him to ask for accounts of all the personal herds of these families whether these grazed with the animals he had given them or not. By contagion, so to speak, these cattle also came to be considered issue of the latter. The herds given to the commanders of armies were even more profitable to the king as the client relationship encompassed not only the commander's own cattle but also all the cattle owned by their soldiers. By these means the king himself claimed an ultimate right over all the cattle raided in war, whatever their nominal attribution as royal cattle, cattle for the army commander, or cattle allotted to his subordinates.

Under Rujugira and Ndabarasa, the creation of official herds accelerated. Rujugira created thirteen official herds for cattle keepers, seven that were distributed over six armies, and one for ritualists. Ndabarasa added another ten for cattle keepers, four for the armies, and one for ritualists. The high point came during the height of the civil war under Sentabyo. In his efforts to attract followers, this king distributed ten herds to cattle keepers and one to an army, all within a span of five years. Thus at the end of a first period extending from circa 1720 to circa 1766, one counts about fifteen herds for nonritualists over about forty-six years, or about one every three years, but between circa 1766 and 1801, the number increases to forty-five herds over thirty-five years, or more than one per year. Under Gahindiro (1801–c. 1847) the number fell to thirty-two herds over about forty-six years and then under the reigns of Rwogera and Rwabugiri to twenty-three over about forty-eight years, or a little less than one every other year.[9] From the reign of Ndabarasa onward the king and the court in fact controlled all the great herds in the country. It is a characteristic of the times that Rukari, Ndabarasa's great favorite, created two herds, which he quickly made safe by having them declared official herds, while keeping control of their management and their main revenues.[10] We are far from the independence of the lords in Gisanura's time.

Where did the cattle come from that constituted the vast majority of these herds given that only two or three of the official herds stemmed from animals raided abroad?[11] A tale concerning one of the two herds of Gisanura informs us. Muguta owned a herd of black cows with white spots that the king coveted. After first refusing, Muguta, who lived at the court, had to give in. "I give you my bovid gift / in order to merit a similar one in return," he is reported to have said, and he did receive another herd called Ingoma.[12] In effect, Muguta had given up his property in return for the usufruct of a herd, underwritten by a patron-client contract, that not only allowed the king to require daily milk production from a milk cow and the handing over at regular intervals of a young steer and a barren cow to be slaughtered for the needs of the court, but also gave him the right to repossess the herd when he wished to do so or to claim other heads of cattle that Muguta or his heirs might have owned under the pretext that these animals were the issue of the Ingoma. Even if the herd remained in the hands of Muguta's descendants the net result was still the loss of their cattle and their complete dependence on the king's goodwill.[13]

The spoliation of the chiefs by the king grew over time in step with the increase in power of the king. Under Mazimpaka a certain Muzigura "of middling wealth" had constituted an exceptional herd of about thirty cows all with the same coat. His neighbor, a courtier, coveted this herd. With the help of a son of the king, he accused Muzigura of the theft of one of his bulls, normally a crime punishable by death. But he graciously accepted to be content with being given the herd. The king confiscated the herd and Muzigura's neighbor obtained its usufruct.[14] By the time of Ndabarasa's reign, an excuse was no longer necessary to seize cattle. The king took all the cattle he pleased, as by then it was accepted that in the last analysis all the cattle belonged to him. In one case, he took the whole herd of a great cattle keeper after having seen a parade of it, although he left its management to the herder.[15] In another case, he ordered his chiefs to come up with a certain number of cows, then added one of his own cows to this, and thus created a new official herd.[16] The occasional practice of creating new herds by requisitioning some animals from each cattle keeper was later institutionalized as a tax called *intore* that was to be collected every three or four years; these animals were then used to set up a new official herd.[17] Given the increase in the number of new herds from Rujugira's time onward, it could be that this practice dates from his reign. But whether it does or not, it is certainly the case that from Rujugira's reign on the king and his court dominated all herders because they were masters of their primary means of production.

What do you think the reaction of independent herders was when they heard the ballad of Muzigura? It must have been evident to them that the king and his court had become the foremost danger to their way of life. Their choices were limited. They could gather their herds, flee the country, and join other herders elsewhere in Kinyaga, Bwishaza, or Bufumbira, and even further away, which some of them certainly did.[18] Or they could draw the conclusion from Muzigura's ballad that it was better to be a courtier with the usufruct of a herd than to lose everything, and that it was better to find a powerful *ubuhake* protector than to stand alone before the covetousness of a more powerful person than oneself. Most herders chose to heed this lesson. No doubt the poet rendered their thoughts when he proclaimed: "Don't suspect me of defecting / for I never despised the king's wealth."[19]

They rallied to the court. Later on the herders, and, above all, those "of middling wealth," would for the most part become particularly faithful and zealous clients, moved by the specter of losing everything. In this way, the king's interests and those of the court also became their own. The result was that well before the end of the nineteenth century the king and his court dominated the bulk of the herders in the country and could count on their support.

Men of rich and outstanding lineages, above all, saw that a clever courtier could make a brilliant career by being awarded usufruct of great official herds or, even better, the command of an army. Such awards were the cradle of many a fortune, especially those of lineages descended from the son of a king, a queen mother, or other royal relatives. The main ritualists also benefited as long as they did not choose

the losing side during struggles for the succession. But others, even simple servants, could sometimes succeed as well. Thus one sees a certain
Nikiwigize, a butcher at the court, form a small herd by managing to get
a few supposedly barren cows sent to be slaughtered pregnant and later
by exchanging his surplus cows for a white-coated heifer issued from
them. When he had obtained a herd in this fashion he presented it to
Ndabarasa who made it official and invested Nikiwigize and his heirs
with its management.[20]

Before 1700 the kings controlled very few lands; most of them stayed
in the hands of the main lords. But the court was ambulatory and inter-
mittently exercised its direct authority over the hills surrounding the
capital. Moreover, after its departure the place it had occupied became
an *ikigabiro* that could not be exploited. The groves that grew there were
visible from far away and signified the king's hold over the surrounding
landscape. Some of these places became residences and others were attached to nearby residences, although we don't know which ones were
which or how many there were of each.[21] Residences were mainly concentrated in Rukoma, which remained the effective heart of the country
during this period, but later on many were founded elsewhere south of
the middle Nyabarongo. Moreover, there were a few residences located
outside the center of the country, in Busanza and Bufundu to the south,
one in Bumbogo to the north, and Kigari in Bwanacyambwe, which became the most famous of all.[22] After Buganza was conquered, one or
two residences were established there, and Ndabarasa founded two in
Ndorwa, but these did not survive him. Finally, two new graveyards,
Kayenzi and Remera (founded by Rujugira), were added to those at
Gaseke and Butangampundu. With the exception of Gaseke, which lay
in Rukoma, they were located in Bumbogo, Busigi, and Buriza.

During the eighteenth century the extent of the direct expansion of
the royal domain through the erection of residences was therefore rather
negligible and was concentrated in Rukoma/Nduga. Royal authority
was far more efficiently established through the acquisition of pastureland, even if this solution offered less direct control over the land since it
was mediated through the client in charge. Each official herd had its pastures. From Gisanura to Ndabarasa one counts forty-nine cattle-keeping
domains, without counting herds for ritualists. Each domain consisted of
a hill or a fraction of a hill and they were naturally concentrated in the
most favorable environments for herding. A map of these would be useful, as it would allow one to follow the progression of the royal expropri-
ations of land, for it is evident that the list of the domains of the official
herds include a number of lands attributed to a herd long after its initial

formation, but unfortunately, no such map can be drawn.[23] Nevertheless, it appears that Mazimpaka concentrated five cattle-keeping domains in Rukoma around his favorite residence at Kamonyi, that Rujugira favored no particular region, and that Ndabarasa founded no fewer
than seven domains in the at-the-time recently conquered Buganza and
three in the adjacent Bwanacyambwe.

Owing to the then prevalent system of land tenure, the seizure of
pastureland was automatically accompanied by that of the hills on
which they were located. Moreover, just as the practice of *ubuhake* involved from the start a right of interference on the part of the patron
over all the herds of his clients, which led, even before the end of the
century, to the patron's claiming the right of ultimate ownership to the
property of all his client's cattle, the very same practice also came to justify the king's claim of ownership over all the land in the realm. Toward
the end of the century, then, the king thus came to own all the cattle and
all the land.

The Armies

This seizure of the means of production by the king was accompanied
and facilitated by the deployment of permanent professional military
forces organized in multiple armies. Ndori had created an army but it
was not hereditary. It was dissolved at his death. That is the meaning of
the tale concerning the collective suicide of the Ibisumizi after Ndori' s
demise.[24] Only the company to which the new king belonged, ideally
the last one that had been formed, survived, and it became the kernel
of a new royal army. At the time of the inauguration of Mazimpaka
around 1735 there was still only a single royal army and every great lord
still had his *intore*. Gisanura's army was called Imitari and young Mazimpaka belonged to it, serving as the captain of its youngest company. He
built his own army, Intaremba, out of that company.[25] As usual, that
army was dissolved upon his death.

Nevertheless, one must date the creation of the first permanent
army to Mazimpaka's reign. It was permanent because conscription in
it became hereditary. The sons of its first warriors were now automatically enrolled in their father's army. At first glance one might think that
this evolution was but a natural reflex in a society where inheriting the
obligations of one's father was the norm and where the leaders of the
ritual corporations succeeded each other from father to son. Yet that is
not so, since no neighboring kingdom had ever owned an army based
on hereditary conscription.[26]

This innovation supposedly evolved as follows. Mukungu, one of Mazimpaka's sons, asked his father to let him have a company of private warriors that was at the time settled at Mukindo near Makwazi in Burwi, then still on the border of the realm. Those warriors were, it was said, descendants of the so-called Nyoro invaders who had fled there after their main army had retreated from central Rwanda north of Burwi. There, their descendants had assumed the positions of their fathers and ancestors within this company so as to defend themselves against the autochthons as well as to be able to raid them. The Indara army is thought to have evolved from this kernel of hereditary warriors and its example inspired the creation of other permanent armies. Be that as it may, Indara is indeed the first case in which one finds an uninterrupted chain of command from father to son, at least until the time of Rwabugiri who handed the command of it over to someone else.[27] The history of the command of an army can be used as an index of the extent of hereditary succession within it, and upon examination one finds that no other army of Mazimpaka knew this type of conscription, but that it became the norm from the reign of Rujugira onward. The practice must be seen as a great innovation for the armies because it not only made them permanent but they also acquired the right to recruit members from a whole set of lineages dispersed all over the country. These people became subjects of the army's commander. He in turn protected them against other chiefs, arbitrated their disputes, and established *ubuhake* relationships with the most distinguished of his own officers. This relationship reinforced the esprit-de-corps within each army and finally created such a strong bond of mutual loyalty between the army and its commander that in some cases the army chose to follow its leader even against the king's wishes.[28]

Before Mazimpaka, the king had only a single army. Mazimpaka organized several of them, however, either on his own initiative or via the initiatives of his sons, such as the one of Nyarwaya Karuretwa who had assembled the kernel of a private army by himself.[29] Imitations of the first supplementary army soon sprang up and armies multiplied more and more rapidly as the century wore on. Mazimpaka created seven of them in a thirty-year-long reign, Rujugira thirteen in far less time, and Ndabarasa ten in ten years.[30]

Moreover, the armies began to develop internal specializations. There appeared a differentiation among warriors, foragers, cattle rustlers, and producers of food. Each army on the warpath usually counted four[31] companies of warriors of about one hundred men each[32] for a total of four hundred combatants, not counting the men who comprised a small headquarters. They were all herders, but the king's own army, his guard, might include a supplemental company consisting of Twa.[33] These companies were assisted by a section of cattle rustlers, whose size remains unknown, primarily recruited from among herders. They had to capture the enemy's herds while the battle raged and drive them to a safe place. Then came the foragers and the servants. Each combatant had an assistant to carry spare spears and arrows. Moreover, the members of this part of the army were in charge of provisioning, lodging, and porterage; in short, of taking care of all the logistic needs of an operating army. Reisdorff estimates that this section included at least twice the total number of combatants and cattle rustlers recruited from among farmers only.[34] According to him, the first systematic differentiation between Tutsi and Hutu evolved in this military context since the combatants and the rustlers were mostly Tutsi and the "servants" were called Hutu in the Rwandan language. The first known Hutu section, Abatabaga, was created under Mazimpaka, as it happens, for the Indara army.[35] All the combatants, rustlers, and foragers together constituted an army. About four fifths of the total number of men comprising the army remained at home. They were the producers who cultivated the army's fields or tended their herds. They also supplied the provisions needed by the armed forces. One special section among these cared for the official herds attached to their army.

Armies existed to wage war. This banal truth must be underlined because the historiography has so much stressed their sociopolitical role as the institution that organized the population in peacetime that the fact that armies are tools of war tends to get overlooked. And from the reign of Rujugira onward the country was almost continually in a state of war.

The operations usually unfolded according to the following pattern.[36] Before any offensive action in enemy lands was undertaken, spies tried to obtain and pass on information concerning the state of its military forces.[37] Once a campaign was determined to be possible, the oracles were consulted.[38] If they were favorable, a general in command *(umugaba)* was appointed and invested with all powers, above all, ritual powers. While the appropriate rituals were conducted at the court,[39] the designated armies prepared themselves for war. The required number of combatants was assembled along with the supplementary troops they needed for their support.[40] Everyone went to the rallying point where each army commander made certain that the warriors were provided with the necessary weapons, bows and arrows, spears, knobkerries, and swords. Once the time came and the last rituals had been celebrated the troops began to march forward. Imagine the passage of fairly compact groups of over one thousand men, plus the train of herds that accompanied them to supply them with milk. All these people were forced to travel across pastures and fields and would end up damaging them on either side of the narrow tracks on which they had to walk, one person after the other. In the rainy season the slippery mud made walking difficult, while in the dry season clouds of dust heralded their arrival from far away. A storyteller describes this phenomenon as follows: "When the captured girls saw dust rising into the sky they said to Nyarwaya: 'Do you believe that this dust is caused by the calves of buffaloes or even elephants?'"[41] All along the way the servants forage relentlessly in the granaries and in the fields. "From time to time the Sultan [Rwabugiri] himself attracted the attention of these [foraging] Hutu to the ripe crops in the fields. During their advance the companies of combatants also took advantage of favorable circumstances to raid communities on whole hills 'just to flaunt their valor.' Only the young have such inspirations. The commanders opposed this sort of abuse and distinguished pages never took part in it."[42]

Once on the battlefield the combatant companies took their places, usually in detachments posted in different places on one or several hills according to the tactics their general had adopted. Then each company designated to participate in the first attack began to engage the enemy by shooting arrows. These shots were accurate up to about four hundred meters. To achieve maximum efficacy, the men arranged themselves in several rows so as to make the fire as continuous as possible. Sometimes the fire was sufficient to sow panic among the enemy and to force its retreat, or, to the contrary, the enemy fire was so effective that the attackers had to retreat. As soon as the enemy's fire lessened, each combatant company charged and began throwing its spears from a distance of about eighty meters. The warriors were supposed to keep themselves assembled in several rows, but all the descriptions leave the impression that they did not in fact maintain this neat order at this stage of combat but rather that each warrior, assisted by his bearer of spare weapons, fought for himself. These archery and spear-throwing engagements are the phases of combat most celebrated in the general descriptions and in heroic poetry.

Often the first shock was not decisive. Then one army retreated and combat resumed later on, either on the same day or during the following days. It even happened that after forces of about the same strength had suffered serious losses a truce was declared and an attempt was made to settle the conflict by a transfer of cattle. Thus in the tale of Nyarwaya Karuretwa cited earlier the Rundi chief declared a truce and proposed leaving all his cattle to the Rwandan assailants.[43] Truces seem to have been declared in the evening after a full day of combat. Once the enemy was sent into flight or reduced in number by the missiles, hand-to-hand combat began. For this, one used mostly swords or knives with the intention of killing and obtaining testicles as trophies to prove the valor of the combatant who secured them. No quarter was given either during the battle or afterward. One mercilessly killed every male enemy one could, adult and child, young and old, uninjured and wounded, healthy and ill.[44]

While the battle was raging, the teams responsible for looting went around the slopes where they were fighting to locate the enemy herds, to rustle them, and bring them back behind the line of combat. As soon as the fighting was over, the combatants burned the houses and standing crops, and, above all, looted. They were especially eager to seize women and young girls for they then belonged to the warrior who had captured them.[45] Even if the king and the army commanders sometimes requisitioned some of these captives they then had to reimburse the warriors who had seized them in heads of cattle. As to the rustled cattle, they were assembled, presented at court, and then divided among the king, the armies, the commander of each army, his main officers, and the most courageous soldiers of the different units. Quite often, though, the way the cattle was distributed provoked bitter disputes.[46]

There are not enough data to estimate the amount of cattle rustled, but in the case of a major war the number could be considerable. Thus Ndabarasa formed an official herd (numbering between thirty and fifty head) with his portion of the loot taken during a single operation in Ndorwa.[47] Considerable numbers of cattle must have been imported into the kingdom during this time, especially under Rujugira and Ndabarasa. For the ordinary combatants, the military campaigns were above all a chance to advance their careers. They hoped for a chance to distinguish themselves either as spies or heroes and thereby to attract the notice of the court, that wellspring of every advancement and all riches. Hence their enthusiasm for war.

For the locals, even in friendly country, the passage of an army was a major plague, comparable to a locust invasion. Such a passage was often followed by local penury, and when the war continued for some time, as happened on the border with Burundi, and if either a drought or a surfeit of rain unfortunately occurred at the same time, penury turned to famine. Large numbers of farmers perished from hunger or fled their lands to seek refuge elsewhere. Many of these refugees without land were then welcomed as land clients *(abagererwa)* in another farming community, but sometimes some among them managed to settle on new lands especially west of the realm's borders.

In peaceful times the army organization constituted the administrative framework of the country, since each army chief must have exercised his authority over about twenty thousand subjects. Therefore, the armies taken together practically encompassed the whole population.[48] The subjects under the authority of the army commander paid taxes to the him and he in return was supposed to protect their soldiers, especially in lawsuits.[49] Indeed, from the end of the reign of Gisanura onward, or during Mazimpaka's at the latest, power in the realm came to be concentrated in the hands of the army commanders, at the expense of the chiefs who had governed the provinces. Their hereditary conscription that occurred across the whole country directly led to its "deterritorialization" and hence to a profound centralization. Army commanders became the foremost chiefs of the realm, eclipsing the few great territorial lords of the sort who had once opposed Gisanura. After Rujugira's coup, the latter actually disappeared altogether. From then onward, only army commanders counted. Thus the creation of armies was an essential step in the unification of the kingdom because their commanders with their dispersed lands were far less menacing to the unity of the realm than the former lords of great provinces forming single territorial blocks had been, for a seceding lord immediately amputated the realm by a whole province. Moreover, by the time of Mazimpaka's reign, army commanders and other great lords had to spend most of their time at the court where it was easy to keep them under observation.[50]

These commanders, often sons or other close kinsfolk of the king, tended to live in the center of the country accompanied by at least one combatant company of their army. Rujugira saw the inherent danger in this practice, which now threatened the court with a loss of control over the core of the realm itself. As soon as the civil war of 1770 was over he began sending clusters of armies to install permanent camps along the borders, mainly those that faced Burundi and Ndorwa. To ensure their food supplies and to ensure border security, each camp was then endowed with a march, that is, a province on the border.[51] To justify this military measure he could invoke the threat posed by these neighboring countries but at the same time he prevented all danger of an unforeseen and sudden coup occurring in the heart of the country. Once more it is said that the Indara army inspired this measure, for even before its official formation it had been concentrated in the south of the country facing Burundi. It was, in fact, one of the first to be assigned a camp and a march in the place where it was already settled. Since Rujugira was so quick in carrying it out, it is certainly possible that the idea of marches itself came from Rwaka.[52]

The creation of marcher camps was a masterstroke. But in establishing them Rujugira again formed territorial blocks since each border army held its own province in addition to the dispersed lands at its disposal elsewhere in the country. Still, this drawback was less serious than it looks at first glance. Indeed, not only were the main armies now camped far from the center at the borders but also their commanders were required to spend most of their time at court and far from their armies. Later on, however, Ndabarasa would prefer to live himself in the middle of his armies in faraway Ndorwa, rather than in the heartland, but this was an exception that was not to recur before Rwabugiri's reign.

At the Hub: Court, King, and Elites

> "O you [the king], center of royalty
> surrounded by a court of great nobles."[53]

Here we have in two lines a definition of what the core of the realm was, the pivot around which all else gravitated from at least the eighteenth century on. For the centralization of power and the building of a true state were the most prominent achievements of the Nyiginya kingdom during this century. *Ubuhake* contracts and armies were the tools used to accomplish the erection of this Nyiginya state but the court was its hub, the workshop in which it was fashioned. Let us then, in so far as the sources allow us to do so, successively examine the development of this court, the kingship that was its reason for existing, and its associated elites

One of the rare anecdotes about Gisanura explains his nickname "the generous." He supposedly organized a distribution of milk three times a day to those who were kept at the court without any supplies, and he was the only king that ever did such a thing.[54] These poor people were obviously Tutsi, since they were milk drinkers, who were there to settle disputes with their chiefs or even with the king. This anecdote draws attention to the importance of the court as an aggregate at this time and to the role of the king as a pole of attraction.

From the outset the court was not just the residence of the king and of the queen mother with their servants, their Twa police, the pages of their guard, their specialized artisans, their ritualists, and their diviners, but it was also the place where the foremost wives of the king resided. The monarch was surrounded by great chiefs and by "people of the customs." The chiefs came with their "household" cattle and attracted in turn the hungry solicitors just mentioned. All throughout the century the number of people who lived at the court seems to have grown endlessly. As the court became wealthier and wealthier through the acquisition of cattle and, above all, of brides to marry off, it attracted ever more chiefs as courtiers and it needed ever more domestic and political personnel. One has the impression that at the outset of Gisanura's reign the lords ruled in their own territories and lived there too. But already under Mazimpaka that was no longer the case. He was the first king to require that the great chiefs spend a good deal of their time at the capital. And also, from that reign onward, the kings had numerous sons, some of whom, at least, were favored by the rulers, and who settled down at court and took root there.

When full data were finally at hand around 1900 one counted among the "people of the customs" dynastic poets and experts in history, musicians for wind instruments, the ritualists of the drums, the ritualists of the Ryangombe cult, the makers of a powder guaranteeing a long life, the exorcists of calamities, the tanners, the magicians, the makers of charms for war, the artisans, the tribute collectors, the cooks and the wine stewards, the fur hunters, the zyther players, those who named the cattle, and the diviners.[55] Even if some specialties in all likelihood did not exist in Mazimpaka's time (such as exorcism) and even if there certainly were far fewer personnel for each specialty around 1750 than in 1900, still this mass of "people of the customs" must already have been imposing. The court was a place of ceaseless coming and going of porters with supplies and tribute, corvée laborers coming to build or to repair structures, chiefs on temporary visits to the king, their patron, and subjects who came to find their chiefs to settle disputes. Although we have little indication of the size of the population of the court, still, it certainly was the greatest aggregate of people in the country, far more imposing than the small establishments of the main chiefs. But its population was mostly floating and varied between some hundreds and a few thousand people.[56]

While reading the descriptions of the first Europeans to travel there, such as Kandt in 1898, one can imagine what the capital must have been. The visitors then were most impressed by the emptiness of the landscape around the court. For several days around it the surroundings were only uninhabited pastures grazed by various herds. One saw many small caravans pass by going toward the court or coming from it, laden with foodstuffs and objects or simply travelers. The heart of the agglomeration was the royal complex of great houses in the shape of beehives, surrounded and subdivided by a medley of circular enclosures. Lugan has established its plan, which was oval in shape, and estimates its dimensions to have been either about 200 meters in length by 80 or 140 meters in diameter.[57]

Around this establishment but at a respectful distance on the surrounding hills were "hundreds "of isolated enclosures without any visible settlement plan. Large, well-built houses of chiefs abutted on small permanent huts of the menials at court and temporary shelters hastily constructed for temporary visitors.[58]

The court reminds one of a city: a large agglomeration with specialized functions, not just a political and spiritual center, but also a manufacturing hub where objects in metal, wood, bark cloth, and plaited stuffs were produced, where one found feathered arrows, game from hunts or from trapping, ceramics, tanned leather, blocks of vegetable salt, and construction teams.[59] It was also an economic center where wealth flowed in the form of cattle that collected and redistributed in the name of the king. But the court was not a city in that it was ambulant. During the eighteenth century it moved at least three times under Gisanura, nine times under Mazimpaka, seven under Rujugira, and five under Ndabarasa.[60] By itself a shifting court was an important means of centralization, since it exercised direct control over a radius of about a day's walk from around the place where it was located and so a change in locality also led to a change in that radius of direct control. Moreover, each locality where the court had resided became a sacred spot. On the other hand, it often returned to the same localities, although never to the exact same spot. The court stayed in certain localities for only a short while and in certain others for a long time, sometimes for many years. In the eighteenth century, the sites of prolonged residence, but not the ephemeral ones, were concentrated on the plateau of central Rwanda, inside the bend of the Nyabarongo, above all, in Rukoma, and especially around Kamonyi. This remained the geographic hub of the realm during half a century or more. From the last part of Rujugira's reign onward, though, capitals were also founded in Bwanacyambwe, while under Ndabarasa nearly all of them were located in Ndorwa and to the east of the Nyabarongo.

The daily round of an ideal court is described in the tale of the war waged by Ntare of Burundi against Mazimpaka in which the storyteller describes the perfection of "the sky of Kamonyi," his capital. This is the image of that eighteenth-century court in the words of both a spy and a woman, according to Kayijuka. The Tutsi woman declares: "The king is at ease in the sky of Kamonyi, he accepts gifts from his clients, he is honored, a guard makes rounds at night, pages are recruited, and they organize parades of Inyambo cattle for him." And the spy adds "the drums are beaten [as is the usual custom]."[61]

In Gisanura's day, the agglomeration that was the royal court had apparently developed to the point that the ancient Gakondo corporation of menials could not longer ensure all the needed services or all the provisions. He is credited with the creation of a new menial corporation, drawn from the people of Cyingogo and called Abangongo, that was in charge of the supply of foodstuffs, milk, and zythers.[62] From Mazimpaka's reign onward, the armies and the corporations that managed the official herds were also responsible for supplying meat to the butcheries, milk, chicks for divination, sorghum to brew beer, skins, and wooden milk churns. It is also striking to note that until Rujugira's reign, the taxes imposed on the armies and on the official herds were all destined to be consumed by the milk-drinking Tutsi of the court and not its menials.[63] Rujugira was the first king to demand supplies of beans, a foodstuff that Tutsi did not eat.[64] From that time onward, the court also began to also provide for the needs of the menials. In the nineteenth century, the diversity of the contributions made by the armies and the supplies of beans for the court's menials would all increase. Moreover, goods demanded from *ubuhake* clients also had to be carried to the royal agglomeration and corvée laborers were certainly sent there for porterage, construction work, and to repair existing buildings, though the traditions do not point this out in their accounts of the court during the eighteenth century because it was such a common occurrence.

The king and the Karinga drum resided at the center of the capital. Together they were the concrete manifestation of the very existence of the kingdom and its unity. For the king was a person of a special kind. Around 1800, after the period we are considering here, a dynastic poet expressed this idea by saying that king was not a person: "Once inaugurated he is separate from the nobility." And the poem ends: "The sovereign is a chosen being, he does not mix with nobles and he accedes to a different rank."[65] The essence of the royal quality is expressed in the saying that "the king, he is God"[66] in which "God" translates as *"imana."* This word refers to the essence of life or of fecundity. This essence manifests itself in all sorts of things, including objects used for a divination of which the result was favorable. Such objects are kept as material proof of *imana nziza,* "a favorable fate." In the abstract *"imana"* now refers to a being who is the creator or God.

The king was the only living and permanent receptacle of that essence.[67] In his activity as a ritualist he consecrated objects or actions and in doing so conferred some *imana* on them. He was then himself neither divine nor sacred, but a priest and at times he became momentarily sacred.[68] Moreover, aside from the authority he exercised as a ritualist, he enjoyed a wholly temporal, supreme authority and lived and acted like the foremost of the political chiefs.[69] At first, his ritual role only imposed a few minor restrictions on his secular behavior. But, following the ideological reform of kingship instituted under Rujugira during the last third of the century, these restrictions increased. The momentarily sacred aspect of the king seems to have become more and more standardized with the passage of time, in step with the growth of his secular power and the centralization of power in general. Like the Mashira of the legends, Mazimpaka was still a visionary who commanded personal creative power as a diviner and an autocrat, but in the last analysis the traditions condemned this power as fatally tragic and destructive.

The king's majesty shone at court. The houses for royal receptions were better made, larger, and decorated with more plaited screens than any other. The king wore the best-made and the most unusual clothes in skin or in bark cloth and he was incomparable when it came to ornaments. Mazimpaka acquired a red bead from the East Coast that became a sensation. A little later glass beads began to make their way into the country and they were so coveted that the word itself to designate such a bead means "coveted thing." Hence one understands the prestige of the nickname "the wealthy one in glass bead collars" bestowed on Ndabarasa.[70] The king owned a special battery of musical instruments and only he had a set of drums that were housed next to Karinga.[71] Moreover, Mazimpaka himself was an exceptional model of physical beauty, a beauty that, like his wealth in dress and houses, no one could equal. Nor was his beauty accessible to everyone's view.[72] Although his successors were not paragons of beauty, nevertheless, the person of the king, his manners, and his language always were the standard of good taste. Finally, the king was surrounded by courtiers and the daily schedule that regulated the life of the whole court was marked by the rhythm of his drum of summons.

Actually, the most coveted thing was not the bead but the cow, and the majesty of the monarch expressed itself particularly in terms of cattle. Under Mazimpaka a new breed of bovids was introduced from Karagwe, long-horned, brown cattle called Inyambo.[73] From the moment of their introduction onward they were considered the most beautiful of all, the true Cadillacs of the bovid world, and from the moment of their introduction they also became a royal monopoly. Mazimpaka created the first herd of Inyambo for himself.[74] Over time its descendants were entrusted to his most favorite chiefs, not as *ubuhake* cattle, but as royal property to be managed for the monarch. The Inyambo were pampered and the requirements for their upkeep were so elaborate that one needed between four and six guardians (hereditary!) for each section of twenty-five cows. Their pastures were designated for their exclusive use for fear of contamination by less noble cattle. But, above all, Inyambo were patiently trained to march in parades and to halt on the great assembly square of the palace in front of the king and his court. Their exhibition was the high point of all the great parades. Breeding Inyambo turned out to be a masterstroke for Mazimpaka: here one sees royal beauty, the unique status of the king and his majestic authority transubstantiated in the world of cattle, capable of impressing everyone who sees them pass by or pasture. Moreover, here is the most concrete expression of the unheard of amount of wealth that the people attributed to the king and the extent of the power of that wealth, since Inyambo required so much land, so many servants, and so much care.

Royal majesty was even expressed by royal whims. Kayijuka tells us that Mazimpaka "loved his cows too much." He kept them nearby, and sent his drums to another hill so as not to frighten his herd. As soon as the grass in the pastures next to his palace was ready to be grazed, he ordered, it is said, honey mead and salt water to be poured over it to pamper his cows, and he often ordered them to be watered at the salt springs or to be provided with salt. His favorite cow was Nyagahoza. She only drank milk and she became proverbial. What whims, but also what power! "Do I have to pay for Nyagahoza?"[75] is an expression that was used as late as the twentieth century to complain about corvée labor that was too heavy. For, in 1938 people were still convinced that all the corvées were the consequence of Hutu from Budaha eating Nyagahoza after her demise. "Ever since then they have had to fill the granaries of the royal palace."[76]

That the king was an autocrat who only acted as it pleased him was, however, a fiction; he actually ruled with an elite that issued, for the most part, from the great families of the country. For them, the court was the place where their fortune was made, as the formula *"Ibwami bagab' abageni,"* meaning "At the court, they give women to marry," puts it.[77] This elite was not wholly homogeneous; it included the queen mother, the ritualists, the lineages of royal blood, the matridynastic lineages, that is, those that were allowed to provide queen mothers, and finally a group of people of more modest means to whom the king had entrusted lucrative or important functions.

The power of the queen mothers was independent of that of the king and in principle equal to his. Among other activities, they supervised the palace maids, whether free or slave, and they gave them away in marriage. They managed the economic activities of the court, established their own militia of pages, constituted a herd of cattle, and distributed a number of their cows in *ubuhake* but probably on a modest scale. Usually they used their power to favor the lineage of their fathers, conduct that could potentially threaten the exercise of royal power. Such a threat to royal power arose in the eighteenth century during Mazimpaka's reign, ultimately leading him to order the extermination of the Kono patrilineage of his mother and possibly inducing him to order her own execution.[78] But the full potential of the power of the queen mothers would only come into play in the next century.

The leaders of the ritualists were practically always on the spot at the court and formed a compact group that exercised great influence over the king through their control of the divinations that preceded every important activity and their control of the rituals of kingship itself. When, under Rujugira and Ndabarasa, military leaders also began to acquire great influence, the ritualists felt threatened and a struggle for power erupted between the two groups.[79] Still, this opposition must not be exaggerated. Thus, despite his status as one of the foremost Tsobe ritualists, Rubona was also entrusted with an army by Rujugira and was killed during a battle with the Rundi.[80] The ritualists were led by three to five of their foremost specialists.[81] They collaborated with each other in performing the royal rituals and supervised all the others. The Tsobe, the Kono, and the Tege were the major ritualist lineages in Ndori's time. With the passage of time, the Tsobe became more and more influential and eventually emerged as the leaders of all the ritualists. Under Gisanura and Mazimpaka, they were the only ones among the great lords to control a single vast block of domains, which included almost all of Bumbogo, and Mazimpaka even created an official herd for one of them.[82] They gained further influence and wealth under Rujugira to whom they had rallied when he staged his coup.[83] During the nineteenth century, happy political choices were to increase their good fortune even further. In contrast, the good luck of the Kono ritualist lineage was intermittent. This lineage was related, as noted earlier, to that of Mazimpaka's queen mother, and once he decimated it, it lost a good deal of its influence. But it regained all the ground it had lost during the reign of Rujugira, who is said to have entrusted the Kono ritualists with the power to designate the matridynastic lineages, that is, the lineages that would henceforth supply the four succeeding queen mothers, and to determine the order of succession.[84]

The word "Nyiginya," in its most restricted sense, designates the sons of the king and their descendants. This category became more important from the time of Mazimpaka onward. He systematically favored certain of his sons in various ways, including by entrusting them with army commands. His successors followed this example.[85] The descendants of Mazimpaka's sons under the succeeding kings still belonged to the high nobility and some among them still managed to exert considerable influence at court. Over time, the sons of Rujugira and Ndabarasa and their issue joined this group and some of them also became army commanders. Yet this whole Nyiginya set did not form a single block at court because bitter rivalries divided the sons and their descendants and these rivalries led them to forge more or less temporary alliances with other elite families.

Then came a group of families that were called matridynastic because they either supplied a queen mother or were entitled to do so. During the eighteenth century, they included Ega, Ha, and Kono lineages. These groups considered themselves to be relatives of one another and hence did not intermarry. Theoretically, a Gesera lineage from Gisaka, which had supplied Ndabarasa's queen mother, was added to the group of matridynastic lineages during Rujugira's reign. But those Gesera never succeeded to gain a prominent position at court. In fact, the Ega dominated the set of matridynastic lineages and had done so at least since the time of Rujugira if not even during earlier periods. Its core lineage wove an impressive matrimonial web with its Nyiginya spouses, and it even obtained a decree from Rujugira that henceforth two out of every four kings would have an Ega queen mother. Yet, not all the famous Ega lineages participated in this good fortune, for the same Rujugira had Makara, "he who hated the kings," executed.[86] It is not known how the Ega lineage allied to the king managed to attain such a preeminent position. Had their forebears once been powerful territorial lords who would have backed Gisanura and Mazimpaka as they did Rujugira after them? Had they instigated or only benefited from the Kono disaster under Mazimpaka? One can speculate but cannot know.

Lastly came "the people of the king." These were individuals who had been assigned to more or less influential positions at court. They were direct clients of the king and he counted on them to counterbalance the influence of the other elites, for they were completely devoted to him if only because their position depended completely on his goodwill. Certain men among these clients occupied a rather modest social position. Among them we encounter, for instance, a dynastic poet under Mazimpaka to whom the king had given cattle and a pasture on the border of Bugesera.[87] Some of them became celebrities. The most illustrious among them is Busyete, who is said to have begun his career as a Twa henchman at court. Having assisted Rujugira at a critical moment he was rewarded with many favors. The king arranged a matrimonial alliance with his family and gave him lands on the northern borders of the realm. The solid foundation with which he was thereby provided allowed his descendants to become one of the most powerful groups in the realm.[88] The first great favorites of the king, men who would manage to gain such ascendancy that they could dictate policy, appeared on the scene a little later. When Rujugira was still ruling, Ndabarasa allied himself to Kamari, but the latter's authority was limited to the armies. Later on, during his own rule, he made Rukari the first great favorite. Still, one must not be surprised that, with the exception of Busyete, very few "people of the king," and none of the great favorites, ever managed to found influential lineages since by definition they were the sworn enemies of all the other elites.

A last set of the "people of the king" was made up of defectors (was Busyete one of these?). These were people of high rank who had left the court of another kingdom to go into exile, often after internal strife, but sometimes simply because they hoped to gain more favor at another court.[89] They were often accompanied by their guard of *intore*. All the kings of the region welcomed them with open arms and used them primarily as officers during wartime.[90] Such cases of defectors seem to have been quite frequent for they are often mentioned. The most famous one is Sendakize, a true *condottiere*, who successively worked for the Gisaka, Burundi, Ndorwa, and Nyiginya courts.[91] The Nyiginya court welcomed defectors mainly from Burundi, Gisaka and Ndorwa,[92] but also lost some of their own to these kingdoms. Thus Rujugira, among others, who is said to have fled to Gisaka with his armed company, married a sister of the king there, and fought for his brother-in-law against Karagwe.[93] On the other hand Rutanda, a mercenary who defected from Gisaka to the Nyiginya court, succeeded in killing Mutaga, the king of Burundi, with a poisoned arrow.[94] The existence of defectors indicates that, as early as the reign of Mazimpaka, the leading elites of different kingdoms thought of themselves as belonging to a single, privileged, and international class and that, to a certain extent, all the courts shared the same elite culture.

The importance of all these elite lineages did not only derive from the posts they were granted by the king and that were accompanied by *ubuhake* contracts with him, but also from matrimonial alliances. These could establish a long-term relationship since marriages between cross cousins were frequent and preferred to others. All the elite lineages, no matter what their origin, married so many partners from other elite lineages and married so frequently that they soon established a single web of kinship. As a result they could think of and express their relationships in the idiom of kinship terminology. Moreover, toward the end of the century, if not earlier, each influential person used his cattle to create his own network of *ubuhake* clients. Unfortunately, no data allow us to trace the development of the network of these relationships during the century. Obviously it was to the advantage of those who managed official or personal herds to use this capital to weave ties of dependence with herders of lesser political weight in order to constitute a following or even a party. But the sources are so deficient that we do not know if any *ubuhake* relationships besides those of the king existed in the early eighteenth century. My feeling is that they did, but that were rare, whereas by the end of the century even clients of the elite had begun in their turn to accept subclients.

The elite was an ally for the monarchy because kingship justified its existence, but with regard to each individual king, it consisted of a collection of potential adversaries who had to be kept under contract. To do so the king could use the following means: give cattle in usufruct,[95] have the queen mother bestow a wife on the person he wanted to rally, maintain his superior authority by arbitrating disputes between members of the elite, divide the set by fanning discord among its members,[96] create a counterelite by privileging either his sons or his sons-in-law or by favoring "people of the king," or lastly intimidate the elite by exemplary punishments and despoilments. The sources do show kings distributing armies mainly to their sons and to "people of the king" but also to others. They have less to say about the other tools of royal power.

Among these the get-togethers at night were exceptionally important because the king and the elite met each other most frequently at these, which were organized by the royal court. All the royal decisions, *amateka*, were made and announced at *ijabiro*, the place where these get-togethers occurred. The get-togethers and the place they occurred were considered to be the very essence of government to the point that the notion of rule itself was rendered as *"guteka ijabiro,"* "to rule in state," or better, "to give orders at the place of get-togethers." Moreover, outside of the royal court, *"ijabiro"* designates the little shrine dedicated to the main ancestral spirit of a family. To attend the nightly royal get-together was therefore equivalent to finding oneself in the presence of the "seat" of the foremost of the spirits.[97] The chiefs who were acknowledged as counselors of the king, the army commanders then at the capital, the military companions of the king, courtiers seeking their fortune there or summoned there by the king, a few invited passers-by, poets and performers of ballads on the zyther formed the company at such a royal get-together. One drank a lot and spent the time listening to musical performances and the recitation of poetry and stories, trading witticisms, and, above all, chatting until late at night. It is there that the kings were informed, there that they heard various accusations and slander, there, too, that they received counsel and settled matters at hand, and it is from there that their orders were sent out. In short, the nightly get-together was the main organ of government.

But it was not the only one. The king and the queen mother also rendered justice during the general audiences that took place at their residences toward the end of the morning. Here is how a storyteller describes one of these:

> After eight days he brought the small drum to the public square and ordered the following announcement to be made "Listen, o people, o people of the king! He who wants to have a word with the king, let him come. He who has cows to offer to the king, let him offer them! He who has a court case: the king calls for the court cases. He who has to lodge a complaint, let him lodge it."[98]

As there existed no codified law, no formal tribunals, no structure for appealing judicial decisions, no separation between civil and criminal law, no distinction between a judicial session and a general audience, the king and the queen mother settled disputes according to their own wishes. When they felt they had been slighted or wronged, they summoned the culprits and sentenced them without further ado. Thus the story, a passage of which was just cited, continues by explaining how the king summoned the Kono to an audience in the same fashion, and how they attended in large numbers believing that they were to be favored as relatives of the queen mother. But once in the main royal enclosure, the little drum called out "seize the traitors" and they were arrested and executed on the spot.[99]

In other court cases the parties were courtiers of the elite since ordinary people had no direct access to these audiences. When it is said that Gisanura became famous for the care he took as a judge, that should not be taken as meaning that he was a learned jurist, nor even that he was impartial. Rather it means that he was well informed and that his decisions were well pondered and reasonable, which amounts to saying that he arbitrated in such a way as not to favor any elite faction at all.[100] The name *"Mazimpaka"* itself means "who ends litigation" and refers to another facet of the system: its expeditious and decisive character. Moreover, Mazimpaka is the first king renowned for his summary executions, which effectively "ended litigation."[101]

It is significant that the only concrete anecdote storytellers add to demonstrate royal justice concerns cruel punishments. It tells us how Gisanura had asked two chiefs to suggest to him exceptional ways to execute criminals and then had them executed in the manner they themselves had imagined.[102] Besides revealing the systematic use of terror as a means of dissuasion the anecdote also tells us that Gisanura or Mazimpaka had achieved enough power to be able to summarily execute important personages.

The Recasting of Royal Ideology during Rujugira's Reign

Before Rujugira no eighteenth-century king meddled with the royal ideology and they were relatively little concerned with the arrangement of the fertility rituals. Gisanura did create the corporation of the Abarembo, drawn from the people of Burembo, their sole task being to supply the necessary charms to avert the devastating plagues caused by swarms of locusts, but that was just one more weapon in the arsenal of charms and rituals.[103] Yet the ideology of kingship was invoked to justify Rujugira's coup d'état against Rwaka and as one thing led to another this justification finally caused a profound reshaping of the ideology in question. Rwaka had definitely been initiated into the cult of Ryangombe, just as the kings who preceded him had been. Rujugira, however, justified his coup by making use of this fact. Rwaka, according to him, was not a legitimate king because he had been initiated and as an initiate had kneeled in front of the person representing Ryangombe. That made him ineligible, since a Nyiginya king never could be the subject of another, even if the other was a mythical hero. Therefore it was decided that from this moment on no king would be initiated himself into this cult but that he would be represented by a "king of the initiates *(mandwa)*."[104] Rujugira designated an inoffensive member of his lineage for this role and had him reside at the court. This solution through delegation allowed the king to maintain control over the cult but also dissociated him from it. Eventually, the "king of the initiates" was endowed with an "army." Under Sentabyo this office passed over to the Yumbu lineage of a clan that stemmed from Ndorwa.[105]

But this minor ideological adjustment was only a start. For unknown reasons, probably linked to the issue of Rujugira's legitimacy, the whole former theory of royal ideology came to be recast. Perhaps the serious illness that afflicted Rujugira at the outset of his reign, which could have been interpreted as a sign of supernatural discontent, had something to do with this reshaping of the ideology.[106] The most concrete expression of this recasting was the elaboration of a cycle for the succession of regnal names that the kings assumed at their accession. From Rujugira's reign on, the number of these names was to be limited, their succession came to be prescribed and invariable, and, in a mystical way, the characteristics of each reign to come were established ahead of time. The ritual "path of the watering" celebrated in principle at the death of every CYIRIMA or MUTARA became the concrete expression of this ideology. Certain authors have attributed this innovation to MUTARA Semugeshi but it actually occurred in Rujugira's time.[107] On the one hand, the regnal names retained as valid after the reform no longer included KAREMERA, Rwaka's regnal name. Moreover, Rujugira happened to be in Bwanacyambwe at the outset of his reign in violation of the strictures of the new ideology.[108] On the other hand, the bulk of the recasting must have occurred before Rujugira's death, since his body was not buried but kept smoke-dried at Gaseke as the "path of the watering" prescribes.[109] Moreover, Rujugira himself named one of his official herds Inturire to commemorate the celebration of this "path."[110] It is he again who installed an army on Mount Rutare and organized a new tomb there for MUTARA Semugeshi to comply with a rule of the new ritual associated with the theory of the cycle of regnal names.[111]

But it so happens that Mount Rutare only came to be incorporated into his realm toward the middle or the end of his reign.

The ideology's starting points were that history repeats itself in cyclical fashion, that the vagaries of each reign are predetermined by the regnal name of each king, and that the regnal names were to succeed one another in a set sequence of four names per cycle. The successive names were CYIRIMA, KIGERI, MIBAMBWE, and YUHI for the first cycle and all odd-numbered cycles that followed, and MUTARA, KIGERI, MIBAMBWE, and YUHI for the second and all even-numbered cycles that followed. The other old regnal names, such as RUGANZU, NDAHIRO, and NSORO, were proscribed for they had proven to be of ill omen in the past. This vision of the regnal names consecrated the triumph of magic ascribed to an utterance as well as that of the idea of predestination.

In this scheme of the world the royal actors played predetermined roles and the reigns of each cycle fell into two sets. The first and last kings of a cycle were strongly bound by their ritual restrictions because they opened and closed the cycle. Any misstep during their reigns could have disastrous consequences for the kingdom and its dynasty. An error in its inauguration could lead to a wholly unfavorable cycle, while a faulty conclusion to the cycle could block the accession to the next cycle and hence interrupt the continuity of the kingdom. The two kings in the middle had fewer ritual obligations since the middle of the cycle was perceived as a protected and rather safe period. The kings of the middle, KIGERI and MIBAMBWE, were held to be warrior kings and so they were expected to be constantly on the road.

The kings of first regnal name (CYIRIMA/MUTARA) were to preside over complex rituals of magical renewal. These "cattle kings" were to stay south of the middle Nyabarongo until the "path of the watering" had been performed. Thereafter, they had to live in the land across the Nyabarongo until their death. The ritual geography of the realm opposed the lands inside the bend of the Nyabarongo to the lands of Bumbogo, Buriza, and Bwanacyambwe. as well as Kigari east of the river. All the YUHI who concluded a cycle always had to live inside the Nyabarongo bend. Their role was to celebrate the path of Gihanga's fire, which would ensure the continuity of the kingdom.[112] But it was the "path of the watering" that tied one cycle to the next. It did so in the following fashion: the smoke-dried corpse of a CYIRIMA was honored and kept at Gaseke until the moment came when the MUTARA who would start the next cycle came to power, which had to be somewhere south of the middle Nyabarongo where he succeeded a YUHI.[113] Once his queen mother had died, this MUTARA was to cross the Nyabarongo and go to the lands beyond. At that moment a complex choreography occurred, which consisted in the simultaneous movement of two large herds belonging to CYIRIMA and MUTARA, the movement of the living MUTARA, and the transference of CYIRIMA's body across the Nyabarongo to Rutare where it would then be buried once MUTARA died. The corpse of this MUTARA was then smoke-dried in its turn and transferred to Gaseke where it would be kept until the reign of the next CYIRIMA. This grandiose conception of the movement from one cycle to the next was, however, never put into practice. Rwogera, the first MUTARA to follow CYIRIMA Rujugira, did not carry out the ritual because his queen mother was still alive and when MUTARA Rudahigwa was inaugurated in 1931 it was decided that CYIRIMA would be buried at Gaseke itself.[114]

One of the consequences of the theory of cycles was that the worship at the court of all royal ancestors before Rujugira was abolished at the time of Ndabarasa because each CYIRIMA was supposed to inaugurate a new order. As a new pair of cycles abrogated any necessity of honoring the preceding kings, once a pair of cycles had been completed, no more commemorative shrines were built for spirits of the kings who had reigned during them and their genealogies were forgotten. Apparently, during the reigns of Ndabarasa and Sentabyo this rejection of the worship of royal ancestors went so far that ancestor worship in general was abandoned throughout the country and not a single initiation into the Ryangombe cult took place.[115] However, formal ancestor worship was abolished at court only to be permitted again under Gahindiro.

Moreover, the theory of cycles dictated that during the celebration of the "path of the watering" the first king of a cycle, CYIRIMA or MUTARA, would compose a secret testament of succession to be entrusted to the foremost ritualists. This testament amounted to a major political action, for its content determined the clan of the two queen mothers who would rule along with the succeeding KIGERI and MIBAMBWE (the queen mothers of kings inaugurating and concluding a cycle were always Ega). The queen mothers of KIGERI and MIBAMBWE had to belong to one of the four *ibibanda* or matridynastic clans, to wit the Ega, Gesera, Ha, or Kono.[116]

Let us first observe the accidental inclusion of the Gesera here. The only Gesera queen mother ever was that of KIGERI Ndabarasa, immediate successor of CYIRIMA Rujugira, and the Gesera are not included in the founding myth that lists the genealogy of the clans who fell from heaven and which are the descendants of "Mututsi." Moreover, given their common origin, Ega, Ha, and Kono did not intermarry.[117] These rules, then, could not have been invented before CYIRIMA Rujugira and thus the designation of the matridynastic clans would date from his reign or succeeding ones. Since the rules of succession profited above all the Ega linage of Makara[118] which did supply six queen mothers after the reign of MIBAMBWE Sentabyo, and since the dictates of this testament were apparently only mentioned in relationship to the coup d'état of Rucunshu in 1896, once again in favor of the Ega, we are rather inclined to believe that the idea of political testaments was a further elaboration of the notion of matridynastic clans and was invented in 1895–1896. In the days of Rujugira or Ndabarasa one was content only to designate the four clans.[119]

The new theory of kingship considerably increased the mystical authority of kingship itself. In contrast, the individual king merely became a person fulfilling a role in a sequence of successive actors. He was reduced to no more than the occupant of the throne.[120] Moreover, the reforms tended to restrict the effective political freedom of the king, even while exalting his ritual role. Part of the elite benefited from this weakening of royal power. The theory was certainly elaborated at first by the great ritualists and the new measures considerably increased their prestige and their influence over the king. But it also strengthened the position of the great matridynastic lineages after Rujugira's coup in which those lineages probably played a decisive role.

The theory of the cycles triggered a profound reshaping of historical awareness at the court. For it implies that as history repeats itself cycle after cycle, there always are historical precedents that parallel each contemporary situation. To know these precedents allows one not only to foresee the immediate future, but, above all, to justify today's actions by citing the precedents that they merely repeat. Historical remembrance and its knowledge thus became the ultimate legitimation. As a result, the importance of historians and dynastic poets, along with that of the ritualists, increased from then on and it is quite possible that the posts of official historian and official poet date to that reign. It is clear that all the official historical traditions were fundamentally reshaped around 1780–90. It is at that time that regularized cycles with the standard regnal names were projected into the past before Rujugira, so as to make historical memories coincide with the theory. Two earlier cycles were built from CYIRIMA Rugwe to YUHI Gahima and from MUTARA Semugeshi to YUHI Mazimpaka using the traditions about earlier kings and were completed by the addition of the "missing" names of YUHI Gahima and KIGERI Nyamuheshera and by eliminating NSORO, KAREMERA, and perhaps BICUBA. From the end of the eighteenth century onward the invention of precedents continued, as did the elaboration or refinement of the ready-to-wear stereotypes of each regnal name.[121] Moreover, the abolition of the worship of distant ancestors certainly led to a regrettable amnesia, since the commemorative shrines and their worship acted as mnemonic means of keeping the memory of these long-gone ancestors alive. In sum, then, the ideological use of the historical awareness of the court affected not only all official oral traditions, whatever their literary genre, but also most popular tales and genealogies. Historians aware of the rules of evidence should never forget that.

The Weight of the State

At the outset of the century, five great territorial lords controlled southern central Rwanda. At its conclusion, none remained. Barring only the domains of the Tsobe ritualists, all great territorial masses had disappeared. During the century, a genuine centralization had occurred, resulting from the institutions of the royal *ubuhake* and the armies, which had become multiple and permanent. This centralization benefited the whole court, the elites as much as the king. The descendants of those great lords of yore were co-opted by a system that promised them more wealth and more influence than they could ever have acquired by themselves. And, finally, let us not forget that the modest dimensions of the country, no part of which was more than a three days' walk at most from central Rukoma, made such a centralization feasible.

The centralization that occurred is all the more remarkable because there was no central administration in the country except for the ritualists.[122] The administrative structure of the realm was formed only by the conscription of the whole population into the armies, on the one hand, and by the chains of patron-client relations whose supreme patron was the king, on the other. But this type of centralization remained limited. We saw, for instance that neither the king nor the court could impose any justice in the case of murder, but had to let vengeance run its course. For that was prescribed by the ancestor cult and therefore obligatory. The court attempted in vain to at least restrict avenging in case of accidental death. The most it managed to force was that no one was allowed to avenge kin executed by order of the king. The exercise of vendettas often gave rise to local conflicts on a small scale, yet no one could extinguish them.[123] Moreover, the court's control over the behavior of its armies was also inadequate. Some armies on the borders, eager for loot, raided on their own initiative.[124] And rivalries between armies more than once threatened to break out into confrontations, although none of those that are remembered date to this period.[125]

Moreover, the cost of centralization was considerable, and that cost became greater and greater over time. For it was grounded in the continual co-optation of influential people who had to be bought mainly by giving them cattle, but also spouses. As the court increased in size, ever more cattle were needed, especially by the great clients of the king to give to their subclients, while more and more maids were required at court to supply spouses to increasing numbers of young courtiers of lesser importance. In theory, cattle increase at a faster rate than people,[126] and hence, more pastures were always required, even though in reality, the rate of increase was too slow to meet requirements. The case of the children of kings illustrates this well. According to certain tales, the sons of Rujugira were discontent because their father had not endowed them and they threatened to seek a better future in another kingdom. To pacify them, armies had to be found for them as well as a good number of official herds.[127] And Rujugira was not exceptional in this regard. Mazimpaka and Ndabarasa also had to endow their numerous sons.[128] Yet the sons of kings were but one category among the elite and one also had to place the sons of the others. Clearly neither the natural increase of cattle nor the periodic levy of cattle could meet this demand. Obviously a frequent influx of cattle accomplished by raiding abroad was also required.

Indeed, the multiplication of the armies from the time of Rujugira onward or a little earlier and the direct testimony of the sources lead one to think that the number of wars waged increased significantly from the previous period. But each increase in military operations also led to an increase in lives lost, especially at the higher levels of society. While the booty captured by an official expedition went in part to the king and in part to those who had taken it, the bulk of it remained in the hands of the army commander and his main officers. One also recalls that beside cattle, the booty also included women who were enslaved and small children who were adopted. Finally, one must not lose sight of the fact that an army in the field was expensive for farmers as it foraged, looted, and plundered the standing crops all along its passage. And if by ill luck a military operation of some duration was accompanied by a natural calamity the situation became dire. Then famine broke out followed by a whole array of aftereffects.

But even wars did not supply the necessary capital with the frequency required. Thus it is no surprise that the volume of taxes and corvée labor increased in parallel with the growth of the capital and the extension of *ubuhake* in the provinces. Periodically the king directly levied dues by exacting a tithe on the occasion of visits to the provinces during which all the cattle were paraded before him. By the middle of the nineteenth century it is thought that the great herders were taxed between 2.5 percent and 3 percent of the total number of cattle in their herds.[129] We think that this levy did not exist at the onset of the eighteenth century and that it only became more and more generalized with the growth of royal power during that century. Moreover, herders without protectors were always liable to arbitrary and total expropriation. Indeed, it was the disgrace of some that allowed the king to find the wherewithal to endow others. As to the farmers, they paid a tithe on the production of their crops in the form of cereals or beer or certain manufactures such as bark cloth, skins, honey, and new and used hoes. The frequency and the amount of that tribute varied according to the needs of the armies to which the farmers belonged as well as those of their patron on the hill, but they paid at least once a year on the occasion of the celebration of *umuganura*.[130]

The situation with regard to corvée labor was more worrying. In this type of economy corvée labor is more important than tribute in maintaining the upper class. The use of the same word, *"ikóro,"* for dues and corvées underlines the preeminence of the latter, for the word derives from *"gukóra,"* "to work." The court and the elites always required many laborers in the form of porters, domestic servants, and construction workers to build or repair buildings. The people required for more or less long periods of time were recruited by their armies or their patrons from among the farmers under their control. But such corvées were far more troublesome than tithes for the patron could levy them at any moment of the year without taking the requirements for tasks on the farm into account. A requisition during the slack season merely caused some irritation, while a levy at reaping time or when the gardens near the marshes were tilled, endangered the harvests. Moreover, these corvées always fell to the socially weakest people as local leaders and *inzu* heads decided who would go in answer to the call of their patrons. They always designated the same people, preferably those who rented land from the family heads who held an *isambu*.

Unfortunately, the sources contain no information at all that would allow us to better estimate the burden the kingdom imposed on the bulk of the population. There are simply no data on the amount of goods demanded, the frequency of such levies, or the duration of corvée labor. Still it is evident that centralization exacted a heavy toll on the kingdom. Moreover, it required not just the levy of an ever-increasing number of dues but also an increase in the number of wars. In return, the only benefits that the exploited classes, whether herders or farmers, could hope to derive from all of this was the protection of their patrons against the rapacity of others of their ilk and that of the king against both the raids conducted by neighboring kingdoms and the ravages of natural calamities.

4

Government in the Eighteenth Century

Having offered a general presentation of the progress of centralization in the Nyiginya kingdom during the eighteenth century, we now come to a discussion of government in action in which we will focus on the doings of the historical actors. These actors formed a community at court that included the leaders of the elites as well as the kings. It is important to emphasize the role of the leaders of the elites, for the personal role of the kings has been quite exaggerated in the historiography, depicting the situation as if it all depended only on the whims of the kings. In fact, political action seems rather to have been the result of the partly contradictory goals pursued by a variety of actors. The data allow us to examine two different facets of this activity: the internal struggle for power and the attempts made to extend that power over new lands, either directly by the use of force or indirectly by diplomatic means.

Government from Gisanura to Rwaka

As the source material stemming from the court portrays political history as a succession of autocratic actions by the sovereigns who were accountable to no one, such a history is therefore mainly determined by the character of each individual king in succession and its natural unit is the individual reign. A few, vague remembrances about Gisanura the Just are followed by the lurid portrait of a demented Mazimpaka. Better not even to mention his son Rwaka. Rujugira towers over all others in this century as a result of his ritual and military reforms, his wars and his conquests, and even his long life, but his personality comes across as that of a rather dim administrator. Then comes a martial Ndabarasa, long in the shadow of his father whose footsteps he followed without introducing any further innovations. But this official history obscures the play of politics and the struggle among individuals, families, and elite groups for the ear of the king, as well as the attempts of the king to obtain support and obedience by manipulating the rivalries among persons and among groups. Yet, nevertheless, the existence of such struggles and rivalries have left fairly many traces in the memories of the past.

Such rivalries were particularly pronounced during the succession crises. On the occasion of each succession, even the most straightforward one, the kingdom entered in a state of crisis. Nearly always, several candidates were eligible and the political elites had to choose whom to back and to evaluate what advantage they could derive from doing so. If the lineages of the queen mothers and the groups allied to a candidate by marriage, or again by a direct *ubuhake* contract, backed their son, husband, or patron, the other important families, especially those of the ritualists or the descendants of earlier monarchs, found themselves faced by a sometimes difficult choice on which hung their future. Support at the right time for a winning candidate could yield a fortune, while a miscalculation could lead to disgrace and sometimes to persecution or exile. Thus a time of succession always provoked a high fever at court and in the country. Even following the succession crisis and its aftermath, the struggle for influence among the leaders of the great families did not completely abate. Everyone tried to exercise as much personal power as possible in the name of the king and to ruin their enemies. The internal political history of the country is the tale of these unceasing rivalries among the great leaders as well as between them and the king.

After an unknown period of time since Ndori's reign, the curtain rises on the dramatic scene of the refusal by the lords living south of the Nyabarongo to recognize Gisanura as the new king, a scene that underscores the point that the king did not rule alone.[1] We think that this occurred during a struggle for the succession. In explaining that they all ended up recognizing him but that every single one of them remained in control of his own territory, the tradition, in effect, documents, even though camouflaging it, a whole struggle for power. Gisanura was certainly supported by the Ha lineage of the queen mother-to-be and by those of his wives among whom one counts a Kono lineage that was probably related to the lineage of the Kono *abiru* kings. He was certainly backed by his Imitari company and probably also by the foremost *abiru* north of the Nyabarongo and in Rukoma. His coalition must have been stronger than that of his five opponents for he became king. But not that much stronger since the five lords retained power over their lands, which is tantamount to saying that he accepted them as his clients.[2]

Gisanura died young and suddenly from an infected wound. Mazimpaka did not succeed without difficulty as the fact that he first had to take refuge in Gatsibo and then in Ndorwa suggests.[3] Once he had seized power, he exterminated almost all of the sons of his brother and rival Nyagasheja in Ndara because they remained opposed to his succession.[4] Once king, he was himself several times the target of attempts to overthrow him. First there were the murders of both his half-brothers at the instigation of the Kono relatives of his own queen mother. The king then decreed the massacre of all the Kono in spite of the intercession of the queen mother who then supposedly committed suicide, whereupon the persecution of the Kono ended.[5] Some time later Mazimpaka found out that, at the instigation of the king of Bugesera, two of his Cyaba wives had bewitched him with a charm to enrage him. He had them executed and forbade anyone in the royal lineage to henceforth marry any Cyaba.[6] Then followed a reign of terror during which he is said to have killed even his son Musigwa by mistake.[7] Faced with this royal paranoia, all the important personalities, including Rujugira, fled from the court.

But all of these assertions are found in the official traditions approved by Rujugira's court. These traditions reflect the propaganda that was used to justify the latter's coup d'état. The point of this set of anecdotes is to stress that Mazimpaka was a mad tyrant and that his reign was very short. And yet this is the same Mazimpaka who obliged the great chiefs by allowing them to live at his court and who is celebrated as the progenitor of over a hundred sons.[8] He saw most of his sons reach adulthood and he placed three of them at the head of six new armies, which certainly is not the kind of political move that one would expect a paranoiac to make. All this leads one to think that his acts of repression were reactions to perceived threats emanating from the factions of his mother, his wives, and some great chiefs.

According to the official version, the ritualists finally inaugurated his son Rwaka as coruler and in this fashion deprived Mazimpaka of effective rule.[9] Rwaka is said to have succeeded without open opposition after Mazimpaka's accidental demise and was approved by the ritualists who bestowed the regnal name KAREMERA on him. As one storyteller has it, he was successful because "the forces of his maternal lineage were stronger [than those of Rujugira]."[10] But his queen mother stemmed from a Nyiginya lineage close to that of the royal lineage and that hurt the powerful Ha, Kono, and perhaps Ega lineages that until then had provided the queen mothers. Rwaka is said to have ruled for sixteen years, twelve as a coruler and four by himself after Mazimpaka's death. His rule was ended either by his death or by a debilitating attack of yaws whereupon a coup d'état took place.[11]

Mazimpaka had systematically favored his sons by entrusting them with major military offices. But the failure of this political strategy became glaringly evident when his sons split into opposing factions, which occurred long before his death. According to the official view, Rujugira had to flee to Gisaka where he was well received.[12] He was even given a daughter of the ruling Gesera lineage as a wife, who engendered his son Ndabarasa. Meanwhile his mother was condemned to death but, Busyete, the executioner in charge of carrying out this order, hid her in Bumbogo in the lands of the Tsogo ritualists. It is thought that Busyete was a Twa, no doubt because he was given the job of executioner and around 1900 the court's royal executioner always was a Twa.[13] A version that was even more favorable to Rujugira claimed that he was the designated heir, unjustly ousted by Rwaka who was only a make-believe king. Rwaka was given the regnal name KAREMERA because a certain KAREMERA who had emigrated from Gisaka with a strong following had wanted to carve out a small kingdom for himself in Rwanda and Rwaka had been ordered to drive him back.[14] The most unfavorable versions to Rujugira, however, only mention the coming of Rujugira from Gisaka after Rwaka's death without specifying his parentage.[15] These versions also note that in Gisaka Rujugira received a wife who engendered Ndabarasa, and add that he participated in the invasion of Gisaka by Karagwe.[16]

After Mazimpaka's death and Rwaka's inauguration, Rujugira supposedly returned to the realm to Gitovu in Mayaga. Four years later, Busyete is said to have informed Rujugira of Rwaka's death and to have led Ndabarasa, Rujugira's son, to Kabjyonjia, the eldest son of Rwaka. The latter was an ally of his uncle Nyarwaya Karuretwa, a son of Mazimpaka, who was renowned as a formidable warrior. Nyarwaya gave the royal drum to Ndabarasa. According to the most likely scenario, which is supported in part by the next tradition, the young Ndabarasa came to an understanding with Nsigaye, a son or a nephew of Mazimpaka,[17] and commander of the Intaremba army that had been Mazimpaka's guard and that was perhaps still stationed at court.[18] Thereupon Ndabarasa encouraged his by-now aged father to invade Rwanda and to claim the throne. Meanwhile, the conspirators received the backing of some influential lineages that were either in disgrace at the court (the Kono) or that had lost much of their influence, especially by the installation of a Nyiginya queen mother (the Ega and Ha). And then Busyete joined as well. I think that he was neither Twa, nor ritualist, but a chief from Gisaka who was in command of a small detachment composed of his pages and reinforced for the occasion by troops provided by the king of Gisaka who was the brother or the father's brother of the future queen mother and who stood everything to gain from Rujugira winning the succession struggle in the Nyiginya realm. Whatever the case was, the Gesera were later rewarded by officially by being designated one of the matridynastic lineages *(ibibanda)*. The foremost ritualists (Tsobe, Kono, and Tege) at the court itself sided with this faction, no doubt because it seemed to them to be the strongest, and so Rujugira was inaugurated with an adoptive queen mother, probably stemming from a Kono lineage.

Their main opponents were Rwaka's oldest son, Bicura, and his ally, Nama, Mazimpaka's son, who commanded the Imitari army. Bicura was only able to procure feeble support and soon fled to Burundi. Later on he was to fight at the side of Mutaga of Burundi against Rujugira. Nama, chief of Bugamba, a portion of Cyingogo, used the Imitari army to make a bid for the throne, but he was defeated by Nsigaye at Hogwe on the Rukoma border and his army was integrated into that of the Intaremba of Nsigaye.[19] Following this battle, Busyete then brought the genuine queen mother back to the court, which was equivalent to saying that Rujugira was rejecting his maternal aunt Turira and choosing an Ega woman as queen mother instead,[20] certainly for political reasons, even though we will leave aside here what they were. This was an unheard of action in the annals of a kingdom where the queen mother was the equal of the king. Busyete's support in this matter was crucial. Whether that was so because the authority of his testimony concerning the identity of the woman designated as the new queen mother was decisive, or simply because he had military force at hand at the right moment does not matter much. The effect was a loss of influence on the part of Turira's lineage and a victory for the Ega of Kirongoro. That lineage soon exploited its political advantage. Gihana, one of the two favorite sons of Rujugira, married an Ega,[21] as did Ndabarasa. The three following queen mothers would all be Ega as well.

Rujugira's seizure of power was a coup d'état and not just an ordinary succession struggle. This conclusion is based on the fact that all the detailed traditions that underline his legitimacy were manufactured later on at court and that one of them even denied that Rwaka had ever been king. And what an accumulation of arguments as to why Rwaka could not be king there were: he was king of the *imandwa,* he was a make-belief king called KAREMERA for magical reasons, his queen mother was a Nyiginya.[22] But he actually had been king! All this, added to the affable description of Mazimpaka's furious madness, reinforces the impression that of the two it was Rujugira who was the usurper. Given this, it becomes clear why Rujugira refashioned the whole kingship ideology, ordered the armies to the borders and away from court, and limited the royal matrimonial alliances, and it explains why his court was so anxious to appropriate predynastic kings as supposed ancestors of his dynasty and thereby deny that Ndori had been an invader. By such means Rujugira wished to wipe out even the remembrance of his usurpation while at the same time correcting the structural weaknesses of the kingdom that had allowed him to seize power. Certainly these reforms resulted from other causes as well and many were effected by other rulers, but Rujugira's successful usurpation certainly seems to have wonderfully made everyone forget that he was an usurper.

Government under Rujugira and Ndabarasa

Following the coup d'état, the king and his advisers took measures to prevent a similar coup from occurring in the future. One such measure was relocating most of the armies far from the court. In addition, long before his death Rujugira proclaimed his son Ndabarasa to be his successor, perhaps in imitation of Mazimpaka who had designated Rwaka as his successor while he was still alive. But the crucial decision was to restrict the number of lineages that could be matridynastic lineages *(ibibanda)*. For on the occasion of every succession, all the lineages of the mothers of the challengers with all their clients and allies each rallied behind their candidate and made trouble to the point that the nineteenth-century ritual, foreseeing the possibility of contested succession, includes entreaties for the matridynastic lineages to stay out of it and threatens them if they don't: "We tell you: 'crush the competition / of the Nyiginya and that of the *Ibibanda.*'"[23]

But the dictate that henceforth associated certain lineages with the king also weakened the absolute character of kingship. To cope with this, the ritualists, probably as much as the king, thought that the moment had come to strongly underscore everything that made a king different from other chiefs, however illustrious or wealthy. They refashioned the royal ideology by the elaboration of the theory of cycles for the regnal names and backed the reformulation up with explicit new rituals. This project was ongoing in Rujugira's reign and was perhaps still being completed during Ndabarasa's reign. But neither the elaboration of the matridynastic lineages nor the exaltation of the monarch's ritual role were enough to avert catastrophe when the rivalries among the many sons of Ndabarasa, "the Nyiginya" of the ritual, plunged the country into a disastrous and prolonged civil war.

Rujugira had to concede a lot to his allies. The designated matri-dynasties were the Ega, Kongo, Ha, and Gesera, the last one being included because Ndabarasa's mother was Gesera. From that moment onward those lineages constituted an aristocracy superior to all the other great families. Among them the Ega were to become first among equals. For they were granted the privilege of supplying queen mothers for all future CYIRIMA and YUHI kings, which guaranteed that two out of four would be Ega.[24] From this moment onward it also appears that Ega, Kono, and Ha ceased to intermarry so as to signal their supposed common ascendancy. They also seem at this point to have begun to identify themselves as children of Mututsi "who had fallen from heaven" exactly like the supposed forebear of the Nyiginya and in contrast to all others.[25] Still, it is not clear how the Ega had managed to achieve the position of strength at the time of Rujugira's take-over that permitted them both to provide a new queen mother and be granted concessions beyond those granted to the other matridynastic lineages. One can only observe that the coup d'état turned this Ega lineage into a formidable political power, a force almost comparable to that of the kings. Some time later, though, and as the result of unknown intrigues, one of their number, Bukuba, attempted to murder Rujugira. The attempt failed and Bukuba fled to Ndorwa along with his father Makara Rwangabami ("he who hates kings"), a close relative of queen mother Kirongoro. Yet Makara was to be the forebear of the Ega lineage that would dominate the monarchy after 1796. But soon after the assassination attempt Rujugira tracked them down and had them killed by his armies operating in Ndorwa.[26]

Then Rujugira had to reward Busyete. He gave him a Nyiginya daughter as a wife and married a daughter of Busyete himself. He also endowed him with extensive domains in the northern boundary regions, especially those that adjoin Ndorwa in Bumbogo, Buriza, and Rukiga. Moreover, the king granted an army to Busyete's son, Semakamba.[27] Among the ritualists, Rujugira rewarded the Tsobe by raising an army for their leader Rubona and by granting what were then regions on the border in Bunyambiriri and Bufundu to his sons when Rubona was killed during a war with the Rundi.[28] Lastly, Nsigaye was permitted to add the Imitari and Bisiga armies of Nama to his own[29] and also was allowed to take control of Nama's herds, including the Mikara.

He was so influential during the whole of Rujugira's reign that he fell into disfavor as soon as Ndabarasa succeeded.[30]

On the other hand, Rujugira persecuted all his vanquished opponents, especially the great families that had sided with Bicura and Nama, even though the traditions only mention the case of a family of drummers.[31] Many in these families probably fled to Burundi, Gisaka, or Ndorwa. But the descendants of Rwaka apparently established themselves in Budaha where they were left to their own devices.[32] Rujugira's reign also saw the onset of a fairly considerable migration of herders toward the lands located west of Bunyambiriri and north of Bumbogo, especially in Bwishaza, and toward Bugoyi as well as toward the tiny kingdoms along the lower Mukungwa, and Kibari.[33] But contrary to Nahimana, I don't think that these migrations were planned by the court as a preliminary to the conquest of these regions. Rather we have here refugees either fleeing the victor of the coup d'état or the operational theatres of war in Burundi, Gisaka, and Ndorwa, as well as herders attempting to avoid the veiled seizures of their herds in the guise of *ubuhake* contracts, and finally some adventurers in search of wealth.

The details of the main struggles for influence at the court of Rujugira remain unknown.[34] It is only accidentally that one learns that Bukuba wanted to assassinate him. But a few poems reveal growing tension between ritualists and army commanders on the point of their respective importance. This quarrel would have begun at the time of the first wars with Burundi (around 1772) and it was decided in favor of the military. Its first manifestation in the sources comes in the form of a poem about a dispute between a military man who was also a dynastic poet and a smith at the court who had not delivered a spear on order. The smith argued against his adversary that in times of war the manufacture of knives for divination is more important than that of weapons. Then the discussion was transformed into an oratory joist about the respective merits of the bulk of the warriors and of the *abatabazi*, those heroes who willingly sacrifice their lives in order to win a war.[35] This controversy is above all important as a sign of the growing militarism in court circles at the time. Still, one should not exaggerate the extent of the conflict, for at the same time the power of the ritualists was also increasing considerably. Nevertheless, this opposition between ritualists and armies surfaced again in the reign of Ndabarasa who sided with the military.

Like Mazimpaka before him, Rujugira promoted the careers of some of his sons and that of the husband of his favorite daughter. But the traditions give the impression that he hesitated some time before doing so. And despite his considerable needs he still found the means to offer three official herds to favorite courtiers.[36] Among them only the career of Kamari (yet another Ega but from Ndorwa) was truly remarkable. The king trusted him to the extent that he made him Ndabarasa's right-hand man and endowed him with three armies as against Ndabarasa's two. One might think that Kamari was assigned this position to counterbalance Ndabarasa's military clout, yet he was clearly appreciated by the latter, even during his own reign. At a certain moment during that reign, Kamari had become so powerful that a deserter from Gisaka accompanied by his armed guard went to him in order to obtain Ndabarasa's hospitality rather than straight to the king. Subsequently, this guard then became the kernel of yet another new army under Kamari's command.[37]

When Rujugira died at the advanced age of about sixty-five his succession was not contested, such a rare occurrence that the sons of Rujugira have been celebrated as "Abatangana," "those who agree with each other." Actually, the transition was peaceful in part because Ndabarasa had already been invested as coruler before Rujugira's death just as Rwaka had been in Mazimpaka's lifetime, although it seems likely that the memory of the coup d'état also inspired this gesture. At the same moment, Ndabarasa, who was already an older man, designated Sentabyo, "the lanky one," as crown prince.[38] Perhaps the succession was simply not contested because Ndabarasa was then at the head of the by far most powerful set of armies in the land and obviously supported by Kamari as well. Moreover, both of the two favorite sons of Rujugira, the army commanders Gihana and Sharangabo, had already predeceased him, which left the field to Ndabarasa. And, finally, one also recalls that he had been very active right from the onset of Rujugira' s reign.

Ndabarasa succeeded as a mature adult and a seasoned warrior, but without much experience at the court.[39] As his mother, Rwesero, of the royal lineage of Gisaka, had died earlier on, he was inaugurated with "a close cousin" as an adoptive queen mother. She was probably also a Gesera, which, given the hostilities between Gisaka and the Nyiginya kingdom, would not have brought her any backing at court. His weak position at court certainly played a role in the king's decision to settle in the military camps in Ndorwa far away from the center of the country. The courtiers, and, above all, the ritualists among them, did not follow him there and the king was therefore freed from their interference. The ritualists kept exhorting him to return to the heart of the country but in vain, so that finally even their messenger to the king chose to stay with

Ndabarasa. In the end, though, Ndabarasa resolved this problem by sending his young son Sentabyo, the coruler, back to the court while he remained himself in Ndorwa.[40] But at the same time the king did not neglect the elite at his court. He gave them a little more than a third of all new official herds created during his reign.[41] Even if Kamari was Ndabarasa's indispensable military assistant during nearly the whole reign he did not acquire a political influence commensurate with this position. It was Rukari of Muhabura who became the great favorite of the king. The latter was so partial to him that Rukari ended up commanding two official herds and two active armies, one of which was taken from Kamari.[42] Indeed, it is probable that Rukari was Ndabarasa's lover; many of the favorites would be lovers of the king in succeeding reigns, for homosexuality was admitted at court and quite common in military circles. But that does not necessarily imply a major political role. The real innovation was the recognition of an official favorite and what distinguished the favorite was that he eclipsed all the other advisers to become the right arm of the king as happened under Ndabarasa. In the nineteenth century the point would be reached where a favorite was *de facto* to take over the government in the name of the king. To be efficient the great favorite had, as Rukari did, to amass more and more wealth to attract ever more numerous clients.

Wealthy and powerful in the king's shadow, Rukari was the main inspiration behind and the executor of royal policy, and the real leader of the faction at court devoted to the person of the king. The speed with which he obtained this position was certainly eased by the absence of the other factions of courtiers who had remained at the capitals in the center of the country.

Ndabarasa was a prudent man. Like his predecessors he favored his sons[43] but less exclusively than they did. His policy of appointments to military commands was far more nuanced. Thus, in addition to Kamari and Rukari, he appointed his son Semugaza to head his own army and another one of his sons, Kimanuka, the older brother of Sentabyo, was endowed with three other armies.[44] And when he needed to replace one of Rujugira's sons who had commanded another important army he picked Nyarwaya, the grandson of the same Nsigaye who had fallen into disgrace at the outset of his reign, for the job. With these maneuvers, he probably hoped to avoid a war of succession. And hence, when he suddenly died in 1796 following surgery to alleviate venereal disease, one might have expected a peaceful transition.[45] That did not happen. His unforeseen demise hastened the succession and provoked a long civil war among his sons. The traditions have labeled them collectively "Ibigina," "the color of a flood of blood," in contrast to Rujugira's sons, the "Abatangana," those "who give themselves to each other." This war signaled the failure of both the policy of associating the princes to the exercise of power by assigning them to the command of an army and the policy of attempting to preserve power by keeping them away from the court. Indeed, once the war was over, the monarchs had lost their political autonomy and found themselves firmly under the thumb of their court.

Foreign Relations under Gisanura and Mazimpaka

At the dawn of the eighteenth century the Nyiginya kingdom was located in between two very different sets of polities. To the west and northwest were very small political entities governed either by dynasties or by lineages of farmers. From the northeast to the south, however, the realm was surrounded by a series of new kingdoms all headed by an elite class of herders who all belonged to the same set. This state of affairs can only be understood in reference to the ecology of the region. The hypsometric line of nineteen hundred meters was wrapped around the kingdom from the southwest to the northeast. This was the limit of a major ecotone for it nearly coincided with the isohyetal line of twelve hundred millimeters of rainfall and with the limit of forested vegetation. This ecotone separated two contrasting regions with respect to relief, vegetation, axes of communication, and commercial trade. One is particularly struck by the existence in the nineteenth century, and probably much earlier, of a network of trade around Lake Kivu that communicated with central Rwanda by a series of markets all located in the ecotone between an altitude of nineteen hundred to two thousand meters. There was no such a market system in the east.[46] Information of all sorts regularly spread all along this commercial network, which probably also channeled a few small population movements. Since these mechanisms were absent in the east, where trade was only carried out by hawkers who do not seem to have followed well-defined commercial routes, one understands that the way of life of the settlers in the high country to the west or to the north of this line was fairly different from that of the inhabitants of in central Rwanda.

The exchange of information on the markets of the Kivu network probably to some extent fostered the spread of a characteristic and homogeneous political style, practiced all around Lake Kivu as well as in the region of the volcanoes to the north, a style that was clearly different from the one practiced further east.[47] Located to the south and the east of the ecotone, the Nyiginya kingdom was part of a political region composed of kingdoms, most of which had taken shape almost simultaneously during the seventeenth century. They were all led by a ruling class of Tutsi or Hima herders and their courts maintained fairly frequent contacts with each other. No doubt such contacts among courts account for the spread of a few exotic prestige items such as a few glass beads, cowries, and conus shells from the Indian Ocean, as well as rare objects in copper or in copper thread.[48]

At the dawn of the eighteenth century the kingdoms surrounding central Rwanda in a half-circle from the northeast to the southwest that maintained direct contact with the Nyiginya state were Ndorwa or Mpororo,[49] Mubari, Karagwe, Gisaka, Bugesera, and, a little later, Burundi.[50] These kingdoms can be divided into three groups based on their physical features. Ndorwa, Burundi, and central Rwanda were backed by the high mountains and enjoyed more, more regular, and better distributed rains than the kingdoms further east with a climate that was more favorable to herding. In this group, Ndorwa and Burundi (around 1730) were larger than Rwanda, but Ndorwa's population was probably smaller than that of Burundi or the Nyiginya realm. A second group included Gisaka and Karagwe, both located within well-defined natural spaces that included ranges of hills in their center, which herders found useful during the dry season. But the amount of rainfall was smaller and the rains were less regular. Karagwe was somewhat bigger but less populated than the Nyiginya kingdom, whereas Gisaka was comparable to it both in size and in population. The third group included the weakest kingdoms: Mubari and Bugesera. The first occupied the unhealthy and sparsely inhabited depression of the Akagera, while the second included rather barren and sparsely inhabited savannas south of the bend of the Akanyaru and the lower Nyabarongo, but also more fertile land between this depression and the Ruvubu river.

Most of the time hostile relations prevailed among all these kingdoms. They usually fought each other in order to rustle cattle, but sometimes also to increase their territory. They welcomed fugitives from the neighboring kingdoms and sometimes gave shelter to foreign princes or kings from these kingdoms, especially during succession struggles. Sometimes two kingdoms allied themselves against a third one. But one does not find any systematic pattern of alliance among the kingdoms, not even on the order of my neighbor is my enemy and my neighbor's-neighbor

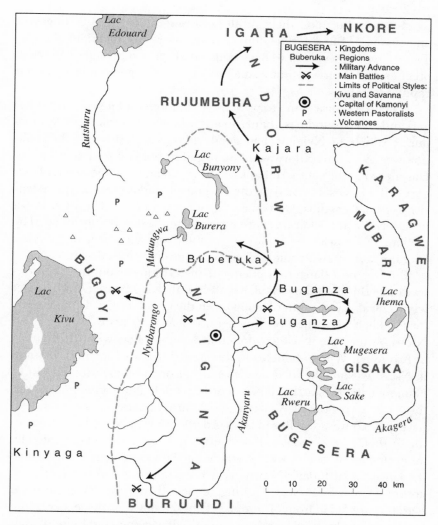

Political styles and military campaigns in the eighteenth century

is my friend. Thus, during the first third of the eighteenth century, Ndorwa successively attacked central Rwanda and Gisaka but also allied itself to Gisaka in an attempt to seize lands in central Rwanda. At another moment, it invaded Karagwe. Sometimes Mubari waged war with both Karagwe and Gisaka, and sometimes it was allied to Karagwe. Karagwe and Gisaka were bitter enemies but the relations between Gisaka and Bugesera seem to have been unremarkable.[51] As we shall see, Burundi, then in full expansion, invaded both Bugesera and Rwanda. But interkingdom relations were not invariably hostile. The ruling houses seem to have concluded some marriages with each other and from time to time a small traffic in exotic goods joined various capitals together.

When Gisanura came to power the kingdom had just acquired Kigari and its surroundings, thanks to a war between Gisaka and Ndorwa during which the Nyiginya had sided with Gisaka. Although the coalition was victorious Ndorwa still managed to hold on to the enclave of Gasura along the southern bank of the Nyabugogo to the north of Kigari.[52] But in Gisanura's time the Nyiginya kingdom was on the defensive, especially against Gisaka, east of Kigari, and also against Ndorwa in eastern Buriza. After trading a series of insults supposedly initiated by the king of Gisaka, war apparently erupted and a Tsobe leader died as liberator, a story that could well camouflage a Nyiginya defeat.[53]

But the most dangerous enemy of the Nyiginya from the 1730s onward was Burundi, then in full expansion. Its King Ntare made contact with central Rwanda after having taken the greatest part of Ngwe territory.[54] Then he turned on Bugesera, defeated its army, and pursued Nsoro Nyabarega, its king, who finally sought refuge with Mazimpaka at Kamonyi. Whereupon Ntare threatened to invade central Rwanda if Nsoro was not handed over to him. Nsoro was then forced out of Kamonyi, the capital, but he was not extradited. Ntare then moved into the Nyiginya regions of Buhanga and Ndara. Mazimpaka seems then to have gone to Rusatira (Busanza) in order to prevent Ntare from advancing further. Negotiations followed and a nonaggression pact, sealed by an exchange of blood, was concluded at Utwicara-bami, "the seat of the kings," near today's Nyaruteja. Here a tale ought to be mentioned according to which Ntare, having requested that the Nyiginya royal herd be paraded in front of him, was knocked down by the leader of the herders when he tried to seize cattle. Whatever the credibility of that story, it is evident that Ntare invaded the southern parts of the Nyiginya kingdom with a great army consisting of several formations. Mazimpaka was too weak to immediately counter this invasion militarily and Ntare settled at Kami in the middle of Bufundu from where he is said to have organized a raid to Kinyaga. But he fell ill and died on his way southward. The Rundi army evacuated the lands it had occupied and Mazimpaka claimed victory—but only by magic. Actually, the whole war had demonstrated the great military weakness of the Nyiginya state.[55]

The experience of such military weakness certainly played a major role in the formation of multiple, permanent armies based on hereditary recruiting from the time of Mazimpaka onward. Perhaps the external situation was not the main reason for the creation of this new type of army, but it certainly favored its rapid development. Once deployed, these armies proved their efficiency by redressing the military imbalance. The following incidents give a concrete idea of the situation at the time of the formation of the armies. In the later years of his reign, Nyarwaya Karuretwa, one of Mazimpaka's sons, constituted the Ababanda company of pages by himself and went to rustle a herd in Ndorwa with them. He was successful, which incited him to try again by attacking a chief Rusengo in Burundi. His father was opposed to the endeavor because he wanted to raise a whole army before proceeding with the attack. But Nyarwaya disobeyed and raided Rusengo. He first captured cattle and women but then Rusengo counterattacked, inflicted heavy losses on the Ababanda warriors, and apparently succeeded in reclaiming a good part of the booty. After these events Nyarwaya apparently fell into disgrace for some time, but later Mazimpaka finally pardoned him and even transformed the Ababanda into a true army.[56] This stands in sharp contrast with the situation a few years later when Gakombe, another of the king's sons, went to war in Ndorwa and settled nearly unopposed in the region of Gabiro at the head of one of the new Nyiginya armies.[57]

Around the middle of the century precious and exotic goods such as copper, glass beads, and perhaps fragments of conus shells *(ibirezi)*, as well as cowries, which had all been extremely rare until that time, began to arrive along with two wholly new products: brass and a large red cotton wrapper that was kept in Mazimpaka's treasury. These things came from Bushubi and Buzinza and it is probably on the first occasion of their arrival that the court learned about the existence of those two kingdoms. It is not known, however, what was given in return for these objects.[58] On that occasion Mazimpaka must also have learned about the existence of the Indian Ocean and the ships that traded there. The information he received was sensational and is at the origin of a famous vision attributed to him. He saw a big ship in heaven whose oars made a crashing noise (cannon?). He wanted to attract the beings in the ship and shot two arrows toward them to which gifts had been attached, one with honey, the other with a banana.[59] To the historian this tidbit reminds one that from that time onward a more or less intensive trade in exotic goods began between the Nyiginya court and the principalities southwest of Lake Nyanza (Victoria).

But the external history of the Nyiginya kingdom was not restricted to its relationships with the kingdoms in the savannas to its east. Its relationships with the high lands to the west and the north were no less important, even if the sources stand mute on this topic. With the exception of the great forests inhabited only by foragers, most of these regions were organized, or were being organized at the time, into small kingdoms of farmers, although in Kigezi and Murera there remained domains governed by the leaders of large lineages.[60] The two main axes of communication, which structured the whole region, were the road between Kabagari and Bwishaza along the shores of lake Kivu through the Rugabano pass, and another road that, starting in central Rwanda, crossed a mountain pass in Ndiza, and then followed the Mukungwa upstream to the lava plain around the volcanoes and regions beyond. These roads were frequented by hawkers who, no doubt, already carried salt from Lake Edward, hoes from Bugoyi, and perhaps raffia bracelets (*amatega*) from north Kivu. Quite probably the court already had a good idea of the political geography of the lands lying along the western road to Bwishaza, perhaps even as far as Kinyaga and Bukunzi, and of Bugoyi to the north. The existence of Lake Edward, the source of salt that was highly appreciated in central Rwanda, was probably also known, as were the lands of the northern territories as far as Kigezi, the region of the volcanoes, and the lands north of Lake Kivu.

At the outset of Gisanura's reign, the valley of the upper Nyabarongo still constituted the western boundary of the kingdom. But this frontier was attracting more and more families of herders who settled in the piedmont to the west of the river, notably in Cyingogo and in Budaha, and especially in Bunyambiriri, where they went the furthest west they could by ascending the river valleys that form the western headwaters of the Nyabarongo. The court claimed authority over the herders and farmers in the lowlands but further away the local political entities maintained a independence. Gisanura succeeded in rallying a woman magician who ruled over Burembo between the Ndiza chain and Rukoma province and she later on helped him to establish his authority in the Nyabarongo valley beyond the Ndiza mountain range.[61] He is also said to have set up a corporation of menials drawn from inhabitants of the Nyabarongo valley in Cyingogo.[62] Mazimpaka established the pastures of an official herd in the same valley, but in Nyantango, and he got farmers in Budaha to supply foodstuffs for the court.[63] And when Rujugira effected his coup d'état, Nama's army occupied the Bugamba district in the piedmont of southern Cyingogo.[64] By the beginning of Rujugira's reign, then, the realm's border had advanced westward but only by a few blocks of hills. Beyond this border zone several petty kings of the region were already trying, no doubt, to establish relations with the court in order to enhance their prestige, as they were wont to do later on. But this process of expansion has left no known traces before the reigns of Rujugira and Ndabarasa.

The most important repercussion of the Nyiginya military activities at the time was that it caused an emigration by herders and others from the east toward the regions to the west and northwest of the realm or intensified one that had already been in progress. The following story should be dated to this time or perhaps even earlier. A certain Kagongo left Ndorwa to immigrate to Suti of Bunyambiriri. His son Rwenga, a professional hunter, then left Bunyambiriri with his friend Kanyoni to settle in Bugoyi. Three generations later their descendant Macumu succeeded in establishing a kingdom in Bugoyi, helped in part by his marriage to a girl from the Abeshaza group that had just emigrated from the east and established a small principality on the Mpembe Peninsula in the region, later called "Bwishaza" after them. Macumu was coeval with Rujugira, which would date the arrival of the Abeshaza in Bunyambiriri to this period. The emigration of the Kagongo group from Ndorwa to Bunyambiriri would then date to long before Gisanura's reign.[65] This tale is certainly suspect. The creation of a political entity by a hunter is a classic cliché in the lands surrounding Lake Kivu. The chronology before Macumu is suspect precisely because it is a tale of origins and one can certainly not accept the three generations in Bugoyi as gospel truth. The arrival of the Abeshaza, however, certainly occurred earlier than Gisanura's reign.[66] And finally neither Kagongo, nor the first Abeshaza, are actually described as herders.

Be that as it may, some individual lineages of herders did leave the border regions of the upper Nyabarongo far behind at this time, crossing the great forest to settle in Bwishaza and then pushing from there southward into Kinyaga and northward into Bugoyi. The size of such a migrating lineage varied between fifteen people with about twenty head of cattle or so to a hundred people with nearly a thousand cattle.[67] No doubt such a large group was strong enough to maintain its autonomy in remote, sparsely inhabited parts of these regions where they settled in the cracks between the small local principalities.

Foreign Relations under Rujugira and Ndabarasa

A genuine territorial expansion of the Nyiginya realm, supported by the new armies, was begun under Rujugira. His and Ndabarasa's reigns were characterized by almost continuous military campaigns in the area of the eastern kingdoms. Kagame presents this development as the result of a calculated strategy. Rujugira would have been aware of a joint conspiracy hatched by the kingdoms of Ndorwa, Gisaka, and Burundi to attack him and would have elaborated a precise plan to face that conspiracy.[68] Yet no evidence supports this scenario and it is far more plausible to view these campaigns as successive developments, each of which had been inspired by the circumstances at the time. It is therefore important to attempt to place the events in their chronological order.

Not long after Rujugira's ascent to power, Mutaga was installed as king in Burundi and immediately launched a campaign against the Nyiginya king. Accompanied by a company of deserters from the Nyiginya kingdom that had taken refuge with Bicura in Burundi, he appeared with his army at Nkanda in today's prefecture of Butare. This invasion was connected with Rujugira's coup. It was also the opening move in a long war that, more than any other, would leave an indelible imprint on the official memory of the court. At first, the surprise element gave the advantage to the Rundi. But they were stopped by a Nyiginya army led by Gihana, one of Rujugira's sons. A second campaign ended in a Nyiginya defeat and the death of Gihana. This event had major repercussions at court where Gihana was declared to be *umatabazi* or "liberator," a word that refers to a person of high rank who lets himself be killed by the enemy in sacrifice in order to secure final victory. I believe that the concept of liberator was invented by the ritualists at court on this occasion to mitigate the shock of the defeat and to console the king.[69] The court then sent another army, which also suffered a severe defeat and whose commander was also killed as a "liberator." The troops that Rujugira raised for a fourth campaign included among others a group of deserters from Gisaka. This formation had just arrived in the kingdom and knew the secret of poisoning arrows. The struggle began again and several persons of high rank perished on both sides until a poisoned arrow killed Mutaga.[70] The Rundi left Bufundu, which was then incorporated along with a part of neighboring Bunyambiriri in the Nyiginya realm under the Tsobe commanders of the Abadahemuka army.[71]

Considering the number of campaigns and the truce at Utwicarabami, the war lasted about four or even five years and the fighting always took place in the same region. No wonder that a general famine broke out there during the hostilities and that it lasted for several years.[72] Faced by this disaster and having become embroiled in a new crisis of succession for the throne, the Rundi abandoned the field and left all the land east of the uppermost Akanyaru to the Nyiginya. Thereupon, Rujugira seems to have decided to put the whole border region under military rule. He divided it among several armies and installed them in defensive camps to ward off future invasions.[73]

Once the struggle with Burundi was over, Rujugira seems to have decided to attack Gisaka, either to rustle cattle in Buganza, which was the most important herding region in Rwanda outside of Nduga, or perhaps even in order to conquer the province. The official version of the court—that the king of Gisaka provoked Rujugira—seems to be a justification after the fact. Why would Gisaka have attacked him when the much stronger Burundi had just lost a war to him? Rujugira raised several armies commanded by his sons Sharangabo and Ndabarasa, whereupon they attacked Gisaka as well as the Gasura enclave. They won a decisive battle at Gasabo, and Sharangabo's army then advanced eastward, south of Lake Muhazi. But he died and so under the command of his son, the army completed the occupation of all of Buganza and set up a military camp in Munyaga on its border.[74] Meanwhile Ndabarasa, assisted by Kamari, seized the Gasura enclave from Ndorwa and occupied the Rutare Mountain massif after the battle of Gasabo. Not much later Sendakize, a defector from Gisaka on the Ndorwa side, went over to Ndabarasa and murdered the commander of the Ndorwa armies.[75] The Ndorwan forces disbanded, thereby allowing access to Buganza north of Lake Muhazi. One of Ndabarasa's armies invaded it, defeated the local Gisakan forces, and then clashed with those from Mubari. In spite of all this, it still managed to reunite with Sharangabo's army east of the lake. At this point the leading herding families of Buganza fled their province and left the place to the Nyiginya elites.[76] This was a total victory. Later, during Ndabarasa's rule, the former army of Sharangabo, claiming provocation in the form of a raid against them, invaded the heart of Gisaka and destroyed its army when the king was away in Ndorwa. But having received an appeal from the Gisakan ruler who was his mother's brother, Ndabarasa ordered an immediate halt to this unauthorized invasion and his order was carried out, albeit grudgingly.[77]

After Ndabarasa's victory over Ndorwa, his armies camped north of the Rutare Mountain massif at Muhura. There they were informed that

Ndorwa's ruler, Gahaya, had died and that a civil war for his succession had just broken out among his sons, which prompted Kamari to occupy Mutara. Soon afterward Rujugira also died and Ndabarasa succeeded. That did not stop him from continuing to direct the Ndorwa campaign in person. He now conceived the extraordinary notion to enter the lists as a pretender to the throne of Ndorwa on the grounds that he was the legitimate successor designated by Gahaya himself, and waged war on the other pretenders in the richest districts of the country, those that lay between fifteen hundred and nineteen hundred meters' altitude, abutting the highlands. He ravaged Kajara, Igara, and Rujumbura, not far from Lake Edward, where he captured thousands of cattle, and finally Nkore further east.[78] He thus spent most of his reign in Ndorwa. According to certain storytellers, this worried the court in central Rwanda to the point that Ndabarasa had to quell two successive revolts, although the relevant dynastic poems merely testify that the discontent at court was orchestrated by the ritualists and only consisted in exhortations to return home.[79]

Mubari was also drawn into this great war. Even in Rujugira's lifetime, there was at least one clash between Mubari forces and one of Kamari's Nyiginya armies, since one of Rujugira's nephews was slain there as a "liberator."[80] During his operations in Ndorwa, Ndabarasa also attacked Mubari, which was then under Karagwe's protection. Its king fled to Karagwe but was handed over to Ndabarasa at his request. Ndabarasa killed him, took his dynastic drum, and seized his queen mother Nyirabiyoro, whose prophecies are still famous.[81] But Ndabarasa's whole lifework collapsed at his death. Mubari was returned to Karagwe's protection and the local princes in Ndorwa recovered their independence. The Nyiginya lost practically all the conquered lands including even Mutara with its sparse and nomadic inhabitants.

The most remarkable effect of the wars under Rujugira and Ndabarasa was not their failure to incorporate Ndorwa, Mubari, or the western lands, but to the contrary the success of their integration of Bwanamukari, north of the Akanyaru, and of Buganza. The conquest of the first of these two provinces is not so surprising for that territory had been claimed by the kingdom since the dark age after Ndori and earlier on Mazimpaka had succeeded in incorporating one territory, that of Nyakare. Even so, it ought to be observed that Rujugira had to permanently station troops there and put the whole region under a special military regime. But in the case of Buganza there is no doubt that the whole territory was rapidly integrated without any difficulty. Given that such conquests were typically very difficult to achieve, the ease with which Buganza was incorporated does constitute an anomaly that must be discussed.

Let us recall that Buganza was a land of Cocaigne with plenty of excellent pastures, a country worthy of integration, and the one from which the great herders who were linked to the royal house of Gisaka had fled during the conquest of their country. Their settlement in turn allowed the settlement of many emigrant herders and even farmers from central Rwanda, and probably, first among them, the families of officers. Other emigrants certainly arrived from ravaged war zones in Ndorwa and Gisaka. They all availed themselves of the protection of the great conquering chiefs. Most of these were descendants of Sharangabo who maintained governance of almost the whole of Buganza until Gahindiro's reign.[82] One should also recall that there was a permanent military presence here, just as there was in the south. A strong army was camped at Munyaga facing Gisaka, a second one at Gakuta in northern Buganza, facing Mubari, and a third one on Mount Rutare, although after Ndabarasa's demise the one in Gakuta and the one on Mount Rutare were abandoned.

An extraordinary operation of ideological integration also occurred here. Buganza was declared to be the cradle of the kingdom, finally recuperated by its legitimate kings to the great relief of its liberated inhabitants. Had not the decisive battle of Gasabo taken place on the very hill where the kingdom had been born? The ritualists and historians at Rujugira's court did all they could to justify his conquest and to attract the goodwill of the remaining inhabitants by borrowing their local history to turn it into that of the dynasty. South of Lake Muhazi other battlefields besides Gasabo were also recognized as places tied to the destinies of the first kings RUGANZU Bwimba and CYIRIMA Rugwe. These kings were wholly fabricated from characters in popular fairy tales, tales well known throughout the country as well as in Buganza. Moreover, the Rutare Mountain massif, which already enjoyed the reputation of being a sacred place where former kings were buried,[83] was annexed by the dynasty. Rujugira settled a military detachment that had metamorphosed into a ritual army (and that also was a disguised occupation force) around tombs that, according to the court, were those of MUTARA Semugeshi. Rutare was also integrated into the rituals concerning the CYIRIMA and MUTARA kings.[84] Places for the supposed tombs of the KIGERI and MIBAMBWE kings were also identified and honored.

KIGERI Ndabarasa was buried at Rutare in 1796, and with this symbolic gesture of appropriation all of Buganza was integrated into the realm. Hence the integration was rapid and total. Before 1800, a royal capital had already been founded there and official herds, including two of Sharangabo's and no less than seven during the short reign of Ndabarasa, were installed in pastures there. Even the ordinary pastures of the ritual royal herds themselves and those of the Inyambo cattle were located there from the Ndabarasa's reign onward.[85] And finally, already before Ndabarasa's death, all the new masters of the great, landed domains had become *ubuhake* clients of the king or of Sharangabo's descendants.

Our description of the military operations during the lifetime of Rujugira and Ndabarasa should not be taken as implying that there was a central headquarters at court that planned the campaigns, season by season, and that these plans were then blindly adhered to by all the armies. The saying "Rwanda attacks, she is not attacked"[86] attributed to Rujugira may have been uttered by him but it is a boast. It does not imply a thorough centralization of military operations. Leaving aside the campaign against Burundi, which was defensive, the initiative to attack remained with the army commanders, and we saw that in the case of Gisaka under Ndabarasa a major operation was undertaken by an army for its own benefit. Furthermore, the kings, whether on their own initiative or that of their sons or great chiefs, raised armies and named their commanders and main officers, but once those armies were in the field, they acted mainly to their own advantage in order to acquire glory, loot, domains, and, if possible, more than other armies did. It is from this angle that one must view the numerous cases of deserters usually accompanied by military contingents. These deserters were important lords, often emigrants who had left their countries during a succession struggle, as well as genuine *condottieri* who, like Sendakize, moved around a lot, serving one country and then another. But the result of a the ambitions of these various groups was a certain disorder, especially in times of war and especially along the borders. Even if at the time rivalries among different armies had not yet led to out-and-out confrontation, that danger was not remote, for such clashes did occur during the civil war and later in the nineteenth century.[87]

Rujugira's and Ndabarasa's wars also had repercussions in the lands in the west beyond the line of nineteen hundred meters' altitude. One of the consequences of the great famine of the 1770s and of the military operations in Gisaka and Ndorwa was the migration westward of such a large number of Tutsi refugees toward the shores of Lake Kivu that it became almost a cliché among the inhabitants from Kinyaga to Bugoyi who knew that their forebears had emigrated from the east to say that one came from Ndorwa or Gisaka.[88] The immigrants joined other herders already settled on good pastures along the valleys or near the shores of lake Kivu. Thus the Abazimya group in the region of Kibuye was established in Rujugira's time.[89] Nahimana, as well as some other Hutu historians, maintain that this migration was planned by Rujugira as a means of introducing a fifth column in these regions in preparation for their eventual conquest.[90] This is absolutely false. At the time, the Nyiginya kingdom did not possess authority sufficient to order its subjects to live in such and such a place, especially outside the realm. Moreover, the court probably did not have enough detailed geographic knowledge to devise such a plan. One might even wonder whether this massive immigration of herders under Rujugira was not a mirage created by the nature of the sources, for we reach here the outer limit of the genealogical memory in most families. Herder mobility is natural at any time and certain groups of herders labeled "Tutsi" were already living in the western lands, long before Rujugira's time, such as, for example, the herders of Bigogwe. Further, in neighboring Bugoyi the first "Tutsi" families allegedly arrived during Mazimpaka's reign.[91] Nevertheless, the bulk of the known family traditions suggests that the immigration of herding families to the west increased considerably during the reigns of Rujugira and Ndabarasa.

In addition, adventurers also went there. Thus Busyete and his folks (where and how had he raised an army?) crossed the border in Bumbogo on their own initiative and carried out an operation in the valley of the lower Mukungwa[92] where they eventually settled, creating pasturelands there. There is no indication at all that this operation was instigated by Rujugira. At best, the court merely registered the results. In the same vein, another Tutsi adventurer, Rusimbi, invaded Bukonya and established a small domain there. Rujugira merely endorsed his activities retroactively and probably at the behest of Rusimbi himself.[93] And finally the descendants of the famous deserter, Sendakize, himself a grandson of a king of Gisaka, are said to have finally settled in Kigezi.[94]

Yet all armed incursions were not the work of adventurers; there was at least one important official operation. Not long after having seized power, Rujugira allegedly sent an army to the northwest but soon had to recall it to cope with the Rundi invasion. A long time later the court sent another army against Bugoyi, the main principality in the northwest.

This expedition ended when a battle in the forests of the mountains halted the progression of Nyiginya forces. Negotiations followed and Macumu, king of Bugoyi bought peace by accepting a proposition for a political alliance. The Nyiginya court asked him to send a few of his diviners to court, for their talent was judged to be superior to those that were available there. The more or less regular remittance of tribute to the court, to be disguised as gifts, in the form of honey mead, shell beads, and used hoes, among other things, was also promised. In return "friendly" Bugoyi was to spared during later raids. Macumu agreed because he thought that his diviners would defend his interests at the court. But this arrangement actually was the start of a gradually increasing Nyiginya hold over the small Bugoyi kingdom and finally led to its incorporation into the realm about a century later.[95] According to other sources, however, it was the invasion of Bugoyi by people who spoke a foreign language and came from Congo that pushed Macumu to request an alliance from Rujugira. But clearly we have a chronological confusion here between the much older settlement of Bugoyi by Macumu's forebears and events dating to his reign.[96]

But the foreign relations of the Nyiginya kingdom with those lands to the west and the north were not necessarily hostile. Ordinary or ritual marriages linked the kings to other courts; this was mainly accomplished by dispatching girls from renowned families to be married at court. That is what one deduces from the family reminiscences of Kayijuka. In Ndabarasa's time, the daughter of an illustrious Singa-Renge family of the Gishari region arrived at court as a spouse for the spirit of Gihanga and this lady's companion married an ancestor of Kayijuka.[97] Such ties were accompanied with moral support by the Nyiginya for the leaders of these small northern and northwestern kingdoms. Thus a story of far away Butembo relates how during the nineteenth century the prestige implied in the offer of a Nyiginya girl to the local king served as a tool to win over the local princes.[98]

Conclusion

At the dawn of the eighteenth century, the Nyiginya kingdom was still a fragile entity, a coalition more than a kingdom and not very different from the polities that surrounded it. By the end of the century, it had been transformed into a unified, centralized, and aggressive entity. In Gisanura's days, great lords could still rule over compact territories and could still threaten to secede. Secessions of this sort did actually fragment the neighboring kingdoms of Ndorwa and Gisaka. But as Rujugira's coup d'état had revealed, power was vested in those who commanded armies and no longer in those who controlled territorial domains, and this is the way it was to be thereafter in the kingdom. Henceforth only succession, not secession, struggles would take place. Centralization was achieved by the direct *ubuhake* relationships of the king and by the territorial dispersion of the recruits and of the lands given to the armies. Not a typical centralized government this one, for it did not require an administration and rule rested on royal ties of the patron-client relationship that the king could revoke at any time.

Moreover, from Gisanura's time on or maybe even earlier, an ambulant court became the focal point of the unification of the realm, the hub toward which tributes and corvée labor flowed, the place where the majesty and the justice of the ruler and his mother were displayed, the magnet that attracted all the ritual and secular elites of the realm, for, henceforth, to make a career one had to be a courtier. The second characteristic of the kingdom was its utter militarization. When Ndabarasa died, the court had a military machine at its disposal that included about thirty armies with about twelve thousand combatants, and it could make the kingdom's power felt far away. These armies ensured security for the realm and its ruling class, and it is in that context that the saying "Rwanda attacks, she is not attacked" must be understood. At the same time, though, the armies effected an ever growing rift between a well endowed elite class with its warriors and the bulk of their subjects. For these armies continually pillaged the inhabitants of the theaters of war and prevented them from farming to the point that they caused at least one great famine in Rujugira's time. Moreover, they seem to have provoked the emigration of herding and farming populations that fled as far out of reach as they could, seeking shelter from all manner of exactions as well as from the arbitrary seizure of cattle and pastureland alike.

With such armies, who would not be tempted by territorial expansion? The court was as much if not more interested in expansion than the king. For each conquest offered an opportunity for the main lineages at court to acquire more land, more cattle, and more power. Private initiatives such as those of Rusimbi in Bukonya or Busyete's people in the same region must be understood from that perspective. Hence one observes that the relative decline over time of the king's personal power in comparison to that of the elites did not affect the pursuit of expansion. The decades of expansion following Rujugira's coup d'état occurred in a context in which the unconditional supremacy of the king over the

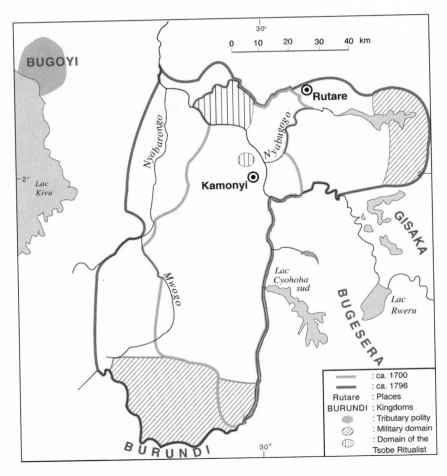

The realm in 1796

elites began to be contested, despite the recasting of the royal ideology and the affiliated rituals that were supposed to strengthen his authority. Similarly, the long civil war that followed Ndabarasa's death would not prevent the kingdom from acquiring Bugesera. Conquests were less crucial for the welfare of kings. Certainly they gained by them but they gained less than the great lineages of their court. And one king at least, Ndabarasa, was less interested in the expansion of his country than in his personal advantage. Did he not end up claiming to be the heir of the Ndorwa kingdom rather than claiming its incorporation into central Rwanda? If he had lived longer, would one have seen central Rwanda incorporated into Ndorwa rather than the reverse?

The territorial gains of the realm in the west during the eighteenth century consisted first in the incorporation of Burembo, then of all of Ndiza and the piedmont west of the upper Nyabarongo in Cyingogo, Budaha, and part of the Nyantango Piedmont (excluding Mount Nzaratsi). Further south, Bufundu and Bunyambiriri, which until then had been a forest uninhabited by sedentary populations, were integrated and royal authority was consolidated in Bwanamukari. Northward, there were small gains of pastureland in Kibari and in Bukonya immediately to the north of the middle Nyabarongo. The most significant conquest, though, was that of Buganza to the east. Finally, beyond the Congo-Nile divide, the threat of raids led Bugoyi to recognize a theoretical Nyiginya suzerainty and the first Nyiginya tentacles reached the eastern shores of Lake Kivu and even some lands to the north and northwest of that lake. But still more important than such territorial gains was the brute fact that its armies had transformed the kingdom into a great regional power. Its most dangerous enemies had been contained, Ndorwa had collapsed, Gisaka was pushed back to within its natural stronghold, Bugesera was no longer of any importance, and Burundi had been forced back even though it remained the kingdom's equal in force. By the end of the eighteenth century, the policies and activities of the Nyiginya kingdom affected a vast region that included all of the territory within the present Republic of Rwanda as well as Kigezi and the lands beyond the volcanoes to the northwest.

5

Social Transformations in the Nineteenth Century

A new political dynamic appeared in the kingdom after the civil war of 1796–1801. It grew in importance during the whole nineteenth century and ended up transforming the overall structure of society.[1] The essential steps of this process were the following. The civil war destroyed the personal power of the king to the advantage of the great families at court whose aspirations will henceforth dictate the internal policy of the kingdom until at least 1875. Meanwhile, as a result of continual population growth, this group constantly increased in size, which drove each of its component families to find new profitable posts for its adult sons. Yet the number of such posts remained quite limited in relation to the growing number of candidates and hence new positions had to be created by means of further territorial expansion, by multiplying positions within the realm, by dividing domains while increasing exploitation of the subjects to make up for smaller size, or by managing to oust rival families so as to seize their posts and their goods. The elite acted on all these options at the same time and, in consequence, the internal rivalries at the court grew, becoming evermore bitter. This competition fueled an expansion of the realm, which ultimately resulted in the incorporation of nearly all the regions that form the present Republic of Rwanda and even some beyond. But it also provoked greater and greater internal violence and fueled a process of social transformation that affected all the inhabitants of the kingdom and gave birth to the stratified social categories, known today by the labels "Hutu" and "Tutsi." As everyone knows, this fatal division was henceforth to dominate the whole subsequent history of Rwanda.

This chapter is dedicated to describing this process of social transformation, which underlay all of the internal and external politics of the kingdom during this period. Because it unfolds during the whole century, we follow it here to about 1900. In the next chapter, we go on to analyze the internal and external politics of the kingdom, starting with the civil war (1796–1801), which ushers in this age and the subsequent reigns of Gahindiro and Rwogera (1801–c. 67). The last chapter deals with Rwabugiri's reign and the events following it that led to the inauguration of Musinga in early 1897.

The Transformations of Society

All the indirect indices (new clearing of land, dynamics of land tenure, reforms under Gahindiro) lead one to think that the population within the kingdom, and elsewhere in Rwanda, grew considerably during the eighteenth century and continued to do so in the next century, in spite of famines, which become more numerous from about 1850 onward. The foremost agricultural calamity occurred at the end of the eighteenth century and broke out when a great drought, which had hit Rukoma and Nduga especially hard, further aggravated the destructive effects of the civil war. There is no trace concerning human epidemics before 1801 when smallpox is mentioned for the second time. On that occasion, all crossings of the Nyabarongo and Akanyaru were closed in order to attempt to check the spread of the scourge, which recalls the practice of quarantining victims of yaws, a practice already attested to in the days of Mazimpaka.[2] The first epizootic epidemics of which memory has been preserved date to the reigns of Mazimpaka and Ndabarasa.[3] All in all, however, it appears that such disasters were neither numerous nor extensive enough to prevent a natural increase in the population. This trend continued during the nineteenth century despite the droughts and famines that became far more numerous from around 1850 onward.[4] No doubt the causes of natural population growth in the eighteenth century already were many and complex, but the most basic one was the wish of everybody, ordinary people as well as elites, to have many descendants, whether that be because of the desire "to reproduce oneself in children" or simply because the more members a lineage had, the more secure it felt in relation to others. Indeed, the dynastic poem *Ukwibyara*, composed for the inauguration of Rwogera around 1845, became so famous in good part because of the feelings expressed in its first two verses and its conclusion:

> To be reproduced in one's children, gladdens parents
> O you, who acclaim the joy
>
> .   .   .   .
>
> May you always have the fecundity

> That perpetuates the succession to this kingship!
> This dynasty has been reassured by the good omens of the oracles
> That you will engender without interruption for the reign
> And that your sons will be successful.[5]

In this pronatalist context, one of the elements responsible for the increase in population seems to have been an increase in the quantity and the quality of cultivated foodstuffs—the American bean *igishyimbo (Phaseolus)* This was introduced around the middle of the eighteenth century, and it was an especially important addition, since its yield was higher than the older *Vigna* and they preserved well.[6] The cultivation of tobacco was apparently adopted in various parts of the country around the same time and its leaves quickly became a highly appreciated product for exchange, especially in return for food.[7] Meanwhile, the population continued to increase during the nineteenth century, attaining important densities in the northwest and the center well before the century ended.[8] The continuing adoption of new farming practices, then, would be an expression of the pressure that resulted from an increase in population. Around or just after 1800, farmers also began to plant sweet potatoes (*Ipomoea batatas* L.) called *ikijumba*.[9] Then, in Rwabugiri's day, followed the first cultivation of marshland, which increasingly helped to remedy the shortage of food that occurred during the farming season.[10] At an unknown date, but well before the end of the century, farmers also began to practice irrigation here and there, notably along the upper and middle Nyabarongo in Budaha and Ndiza, as well as north of Lake Muhazi.[11] The beginnings of the earthworks found around 1900 in the whole northwest of present-day Rwanda also probably date to the nineteenth century.[12] The pea that came from Buberuka was, however, only introduced to central Rwanda during Rwabugiri's reign. But as its cultivation is the agricultural mainstay in lands of over two thousand meters' altitude, it had certainly been planted for many centuries in high mountain country, for instance, in Bushiru.[13]

Not only was the yield of these *Phaseolus* beans far higher than that of *Vigna*, but because beans were already a main crop before *Phaseolus* was introduced, its farming characteristics were well known and, in any case, beans were already the most basic staple food of farmers. The introduction of *Phaseolus* did not therefore raise any major technical or cultural problems. Sweet potatoes seem to have ousted taro and water yams. At first they were mainly cultivated in marshy soils on the lowest slopes of the hill during the dry season, but from there the practice of planting them into the main fields as well spread rapidly, for the sweet potato matures faster and has a higher yield than taro or yams and its cultivation is easier. In addition to the quantitative increase in foodstuffs all year round, an increase in fecundity was probably also fostered by the new diet that was richer in vegetable proteins. Thus, despite infant mortality, which remained quite high and does not seem to have been affected by the new crops, the population increased in part as a result of the introduction of new plants.[14]

Another element that contributed to the rapid growth of the population was immigration. This was probably most spectacular in Bugoyi where it is well documented and where it seems to have begun around the second half of the eighteenth century or later. Most emigrants came from the northwest and their arrival was accompanied by an accelerated rate of clearing at the forest's edge on the Congo-Nile divide, which ended up giving Bugoyi a population density just as high as that of Bushiru or Murera to its east.[15] The accelerated rate of clearing in the nineteenth century also affected the edge of the forests facing central Rwanda, especially Bushiru and western Budaha, as well as the region from Bufundu to the middle Akanyaru. In the present prefecture of Butare, a hill such as Nyaruhengeri in the middle of western Mvejuru was apparently only cleared during Gahindiro's reign.[16] This migration toward the edge of the great forest may well have been caused in part by droughts in the savannas of the central plateau since the regions located to the north of the great Nyabarongo bend and west of the Congo-Nile divide were almost always spared and became refuge havens (as they did, for instance, during the great drought of 1797 to 1802). But the molestations endured by farmers of the central plateau also gave rise to a nearly continuous trickle of emigrants. For one thing, being close to the court meant being burdened with a lot of extra corvée labor. Moreover, as the number of cattle herds continually increased in these regions that were near the hub of the kingdom, more pastures were needed and they were obtained by seizing the lands occupied by farmers. Given these conditions, many chose to emigrate. Emigrants from Marangara, Kabagari, Rukoma, and Nduga first cleared the highlands of Ndiza and then later pushed west of the upper Nyabarongo, settling in areas from Bushiru to Bunyambiriri, while emigrants from Nduga, Mayaga, and Busanza moved to Bufundu and Buyenzi.[17]

The effects of this increase in the density of population were many. It immediately affected land tenure by reinforcing the power of local chiefs. In the longer run, it led to a new type of land tenure and to a new territorial organization. The borders of the *ingobyi* domains became

more and more carefully demarcated while the local chief began inter-
fering more and more in the internal affairs of each small *inzu* lineage
by approving of and guaranteeing the borders of the plots called *umunani*, or "eight," within each *ingobyi* that were given as bequests to sons
on the occasion of their marriage. Moreover, as time went by, these plots
became smaller and smaller.[18] Although no evidence is available that
would allow for dating the introduction of *umunani*, it seems likely that
they began around 1800, or perhaps somewhat earlier. Later, during the
nineteenth century, and especially toward the end of it, farmers without
lands or with insufficient land began to appear. These were genuine
proletarian day laborers *(umucancuro)*, forced to hire themselves out to
whomever would pay them in foodstuffs. The oldest instance, that of a
rich Hutu in Bufundu to whom the child Rwabugiri had been entrusted
who hired day laborers to till his fields, can be dated to around 1865 or a
little earlier.[19] Some were forced to offer their services for hire in order
to feed themselves during food shortages. But later on, many of them
would be forced to work in this manner because their lands were too
small to pay the dues required by *uburetwa*. Among them, a distinction
was made between those who had hoes and those who didn't.[20] Before
1900, these farmers were mainly young men who waited for the death of
their fathers and uncles in order to inherit their tracts of land, but soon
afterward, day laborers began appearing without any hope of an inheritance or of access to a plot of land big enough to feed them.

In the eighteenth, and especially in the nineteenth, century the
volume of corvée work required and the amount of dues in foodstuffs or
in manufactured goods levied per family *(inzu)* probably rose in direct
relationship to population pressure on arable land. The lack of lands
strengthened the position of the chief who owned it with respect to newcomers and gave him a means to exert pressure on the farmers already
settled on the land. These effects were most pronounced in the middle
of the kingdom, far from the edges of the forest. During the nineteenth
century, the political domains there were increasingly broken up, to the
point that, around 1900, all of Buriza and Marangara had been reduced
to an array of tiny domains, none of which could ensure the subsistence
required by any lineage with political pretensions.[21]

This crumbling of the land-tenure base resulted from population
growth among herders and, above all, among aristocrats, for the number of new lineages that managed to gain a place at court increased
without letup from Rujugira's reign onward. Their rivalries became increasingly bitter, and they used all the resources available to them to

ameliorate their social position, in particular by attempting to ratify as many *ubuhake* ties with as many clients as possible. Finally, the raising of new armies, which reached its zenith around 1800, went hand-in-hand with a demand for more services and goods from the farmers under their command. From about 1840 onward, this pressure on land led to the emergence of substantial innovations in matters of land tenure and territory, which then further multiplied the amount of corvée labor and dues required from the farming population.

The pressure of the population and the cattle on the lands in the heart of the county was certainly in large part responsible for the invention of a reserved herding domain, that is, one not accessible to all herders.[22] This invention probably dates to the end of Gahindiro's reign, that is, to the 1840s.[23] The traditions recall it by the use of a concrete image. One day Rugaju "asks for the grass growing on the paths in the whole country" and received it.[24] A reserved herding domain consisted in a hill or subhill rich in pastures that was detached from the province to which it belonged. The king entrusted it to a herder who became his direct client and only had obligations to him. Hitherto, all herders had had access to all pastures that had not been set aside for Inyambo cattle. But as the land available for grazing shrank, it became more and more difficult, especially for herders with a lot of cattle, to find tracts that were large enough for a herd. Thus they came up with the idea of reserved pastures. For, as Schumacher's interlocutors put it, "cattle is the most precious thing in existence. It surpasses all other goods, even command posts, the aim of which, in any case, is [to have the means] to enrich oneself in cattle."[25]

The invention of the reserved domain seems to have been inspired in part by the practice of giving pastures to armies for use by their official herds. It also seems to have derived in part from the status of the domains wholly dependent on the king that had been created to sustain royal residences. In Rwogera's time, this innovation flourished in the heartlands[26] but the practice became common only in Rwabugiri's time (c. 1867–95), at which point it spread beyond the central plateau. At the end of his reign, the central plateau had been so broken up by the creation of new reserved domains that all territorial authority beyond that granted to those who managed these tiny reserved domains had practically vanished.[27]

The creation of reserved domains whose beneficiary was accountable only to the king or to the person who had endowed him favored the most powerful herders at the expense of a very large number of other herders who were just as Tutsi as their peers. These herders were now condemned to a precarious existence. As the pastures of the new type of domain were reserved only for the cattle of the beneficiary and his clients, other herders who had used these tracts "since always" were now refused access to them. Either they had to become clients of the beneficiary or they had somehow to graze their cattle on the public pastures that were continually shrinking as a result of the creation of new reserved domains. In the latter scenario, their herds also shrunk rapidly, for the size of a herd is limited by the size of the pastures where it can graze. And as soon the number of cattle in a herd falls below ten head or so, it becomes too small for the needs of the herder, who is then driven into poverty. So, because the amount of land available to them for grazing their cattle became too limited, the great majority of those among them who had failed to be accepted as clients by one or another of the beneficiaries of reserved domains ended up getting rid of some or even of all of their cattle.

The beneficiary was no longer subject to any territorial authority whatsoever and paid his dues directly to the king. Moreover, he was perfectly entitled to give a portion of his lands as a reserved domain to someone else, and he could, of course, accept new clients, regardless of whether they were herders or farmers. In addition, the army commanders who ruled over military domains began to imitate the king and also handed off reserved domains within the territories of their command.

A decade or so after the creation of the first reserved domains, another innovation followed. This was the nomination at the level of the territorial provinces of "chiefs of the long grass," the *abanyankenke*, whose task was to manage all the remaining pastureland in the province, with the exception of pastures used for the official herds, and to command the herders who used them. It is likely that the emergence of this new institution was prompted by the scarcity of public pastures that developed after the distribution of reserved domains. At this time, then, leaving *ubukonde* domains aside, the following types of tenured domains existed: the domains of royal residences, the free domains of the ritualists and the royal cemeteries, the reserved domains, the military domains, a few provinces that did not have a "chief of the long grass," and the provinces that did. In the latter, the herders became subjects of the chief of the long grass so that the former provincial chief now ruled only over the farmers. This new reality resulted in a new title, and henceforth these chiefs were no longer called "chief of the province," *umutware w'intara*, but "chief of the land," *umunyabutaka*.[28]

The result was the fashioning of multiple local authorities. Both the chiefs of the long grass and of the land gathered dues, the first in cattle, the second in foodstuffs, manufactures, and, above all, corvée labor.[29] As might be expected, friction between the chiefs of the land and the chiefs of the long grass occurred from the very outset, especially in relation to the question of which tracts of land were to be used as pastures and which as arable land.[30] Moreover, army commanders had exclusive rights to the dues and services of the members of their army wherever they resided, while *ubuhake* patrons had rights to the services of their clients and were entitled to receive gifts from them. Finally, cases are known in which great chiefs of the provinces and army commanders appointed their own chiefs of the land and of the long grass. Over time, these practices led to more and more inextricable situations. We must recall, however, that these innovations, which first appeared in the 1840s, only spread rather slowly. By Rwogera's death in around 1867, the existence of reserved domains were still rare. Further, few appointments of chiefs of the long grass had been made as of yet and the title "chief of the land" was practically unknown.

Modern authors have attempted to account for the coexistence of multiple local authorities by appealing to legal and administrative rules and have elaborated complex schemes that do not always agree with each other. One becomes lost and the complexity is such that one cannot but become lost. In fact, given the multiplicity of chiefs, one cannot account for how they coexisted without appealing to the fact that they were political actors who held some measure of power at the local level. According to the equilibrium of local forces at any given moment, the leaders on the local scene would invoke one or another argument to seize all the goods and services they possibly could to the detriment of their competing peers as well as of the leaders of the smaller or larger lineages that they hoped to exploit. On their side, the "subjects" sought shelter by invoking arguments demonstrating that they stood in a relation of dependence with someone other than the person who at that moment was clamoring for what was due to him. The titles certainly existed, but I think that the functions, obligations, and prerogatives that were claimed to have been associated with them were dreamt up by those who held the titles.

The process unleashed by the invention of the restricted domains in fact generated a chaos that allowed the elites to multiply pretexts for exploiting their inferiors, whether herders or farmers. The result was the general pauperization of the bulk of the inhabitants of the country affecting herders just as much as farmers. But the process had not yet reached its conclusion. In this transformation, the great losers as far as revenue was concerned seem to have been the provincial chiefs. They had no other option left them than to increase the dues and corvées that they could extract from their taxpayers. Around 1870 or shortly thereafter, one individual, believed to be Seruteganya, invented a new system of exploitation called *uburetwa*.[31] At that time, the word was used to designate the obligations of tenants to their masters on *ubukonde* land.[32] By analogy, the chief of the land who considered himself to be master of the arable land now began to impose such obligations on all the farming families established in his jurisdiction by the pretence that they were all his tenants. In addition to the dues, which included a significant portion of the family's crops, these obligations mainly consisted in the delivery of services. From now on two out of every four days of the Rwandan week had to be set aside for services to the chief. The loss of about half of their available time was a very heavy burden for most taxpayers.[33] Moreover, as one thing led to another, certain chiefs of the land began exploiting the farmers mercilessly, a situation that Classe described in 1916 as follows: "The chief, especially the chief's wife, takes what he wants; the *nyamunyu* (cooking bananas), yams, etc., that are ripe and the *muhutu* does as he is asked so as not to lose his field."[34]

Hutu and Tutsi

The imposition of *uburetwa* on farmers and not on herders was the straw that broke the camel's back. Very soon it provoked a rift that was to divide society from top to bottom into two hierarchized and opposed social categories, henceforth labeled "Tutsi" and "Hutu." The history of these terms is complex. We have seen that at first "Tutsi" was an ethnonym by which a *fraction* of Rwanda's herders designated itself. Later, and already before Ndori, its meaning had been widened to designate the political elite within that fraction and that is the meaning that became the most common one after the Nyiginya kingdom was founded. The word "Hutu" was a demeaning term that alluded to rural boorishness or loutish behavior used by the elite. Even before Mazimpaka's time, masters at court called their servants, even those who belonged to the Tutsi ethnic group, "Hutu."[35] The first group to be collectively called "Hutu" probably was the Gakondo corporation because it was a corporation of menials. Somewhat later, at the time of Rujugira, the term also came to be applied to a collectivity in the case of the inhabitants of

Budaha. They were Hutu because they were servants in charge of supplying provisions and services to the court.[36] Moreover, "Hutu" was also applied without any discrimination to all foreigners, that is, those people who did not live within the realm.[37] In early times, then, the word does not seem to have been applied systematically to all those who lived by farming.

Within the framework of the internal development of the armies, hence, under Rujugira's rule at the latest, the words "Tutsi" and "Hutu" came to be applied to new categories of people. In this environment any combatant was a Tutsi and the term stood in opposition to *mutware*, "chief," as well as to "Hutu," meaning "noncombatant."[38] Since the political elites were Tutsi, and as the first company was always recruited from among the pages, this equivalence between warrior and Tutsi makes sense. As to "Hutu," that term was applied to the noncombatants in the army because they were in service.[39] It is in this context that the first direct and *institutionalized* opposition between Tutsi and Hutu arose. As most noncombatants happened to stem from lineages of farmers, the elite eventually began to call all farmers "Hutu" and to oppose this word to "Tutsi," now applied to all herders, whether they were of Tutsi origin or not.

As the political and cultural influence of the capital grew, as the kingdom was enlarged, and as the armies multiplied, these distinctions between Hutu and Tutsi gradually spread all across the country and beyond. Among other developments, the meaning of "Hutu" as "foreigner" expanded to the point that all the farmers living north or west of central Rwanda were called by it, including their leaders, as long as the latter were not important herders. Thus an absolute equivalence was effected between "Hutu" and "farmer."[40] On the other hand, the realms of the peoples northeast, east, and south of central Rwanda who were ruled by herding dynasties and in which cattle held a major role were considered to be similar to the Nyiginya kingdom and were thought of as containing both Tutsi and Hutu.

This situation remained unchanged until the mid-nineteenth century when the distinction between chief of the long grass and chief the land again *institutionalized* a division between Tutsi herders and Hutu farmers. A while later, the emergence of *uburetwa* aggravated that division and poisoned it. For only Hutu owed *uburetwa* because of their tenure of arable land,[41] and only Hutu were obliged to perform the menial work required by the chief of the land in contrast to the less humiliating obligations of his Tutsi clients. *Uburetwa* seems to have provoked a new awareness across the whole society that resulted in the emergence of the two hierarchized social categories.[42] From this point on, "Hutu" and "Tutsi" would no longer designate a relative category with respect to class or dependency or occupation but became an absolute one. The tale about Shongoka of the Abareka during Rwogera's rule (c. 1845–c. 65) underscores this. She let the evening fire at their meeting place die out because all her servants were Tutsi and to tend the fire was Hutu work. Thus contrary to the olden days, a Tutsi servant was no longer a Hutu.[43]

The absolute division between Hutu and Tutsi institutionalized by the daily practice of *uburetwa* rapidly displaced the older social class consciousness, in spite of the fact that this consciousness itself resulted from a political phenomenon rather than from a pure notion of class. Until then class consciousness had elaborated a very fine social scale in which families were deemed to be more or less "good or bad" according to their occupations and their relative well-being but it also made a rough distinction between the elite *(imfura)* and the bulk of the people, or between wealthy and poor people.[44]

From the 1870s onward, the awareness of the division between Tutsi herders and Hutu farmers thus spread all over Rwanda following the spread of the practice of naming chiefs of the long grass and then of that of *uburetwa* with the rancor it caused. Rebellion began to ferment among the exploited. After 1885, several spontaneous revolts broke out led by farmers driven to distraction by too much oppression.[45] They were all easily crushed. Tensions between Tutsi and Hutu also appeared in the south of the country during the fighting in Bwanamukari before 1890 and again in 1897–99, where the lineages of the high aristocracy opposed themselves to the "new men" of Rwabugiri, whom they decried as Hutu. In both cases the aristocrats sought revenge for what they chose to interpret as an insult to "Tutsi."[46]

Following the succession crisis ushered in by the coup at Rucunshu in December 1896 the exploited populations exploded with resentment. In the east of the country the millenary aspirations that had already revealed themselves during Rwabugiri's reign were now expressed almost openly. In Gisaka, the whole local population, farmers and herders alike, were waiting for the coming of a royal savior who would deliver them from the Nyiginya, and they welcomed the first Europeans who crossed the country as if they were such kings.[47] Meanwhile, to the northwest the Ndorwans joined the cult of Nyabingi, a woman who was believed to be the daughter of the last independent king of Ndorwa/Mpororo before the Nyiginya conquest. Supposedly she was still alive and would return one day to recover her kingdom. When Muhumuza, one of Rwabugiri's spouses, fled there in 1897 with her young son, one of the pretenders to the throne, she was hailed for a few years as Nyabingi returned on earth.[48] Since all the local populations in Ndorwa and Gisaka, participated in these movements regardless of whether they were herders or farmers, with the single exception of the chiefs and new herders who had come from central Rwanda, these movements were not entirely anti-Tutsi. Rather, they were liberation movements directed against the Nyiginya kingdom that were colored by anti-Tutsi animosities.[49]

But before these events took place an insurrection specifically aimed against Tutsi, an ominous portent of the future, had already broken out in the south of the country either in 1892 or around 1895. Here follows the only known detailed report:

> At the time of Rutarindwa, the brother of Musinga, the mentally ill Nyirashirembere, nicknamed Nyirafugi, was the wife of a certain Nyabubare of the mountainous province called Budaha to the west of the Nyabarongo. Having succeeded in freeing herself from her bonds she began to travel all over the forest regions until she succeeded in developing a special activity at Fugi, south of Rwanda. Hence her name Nyirafugi, "mistress of Fugi." She called herself "Imana" ("God, blessed by God") like the Baheko of Nyabingi, and without more ado they brought offerings to her. From then on she was called Rutenderi ("bull of the herd of the lakes") and she said: "I want to increase your herds." They brought pots of beer and filled a hole-watering trough with them. She let a head of cattle be conducted to the trough and as its image was reflected on the surface [of the liquid] she exclaimed "Look." A man who until then had engendered only sons wanted girls and that was given to him. Whereupon the Hutu said: *"Umwami n'uwishe"* ("A true king is one who kills, who orders executions"). And they added "Free us from the Tutsi." The latter were attacked, many of them were killed and two chiefs were impaled. Whereupon the Tutsi arrived and attacked Nyirafugi, but she managed to flee to Burundi. Later on she was sent back to Rwanda and Rutarindwa had her executed.[50]

Here, then, we have a magician who promised to fulfill the dearest wishes of the inhabitants, such as getting cattle and girls for them. Therefore it was not she but the local Hutu inhabitants who asked to be freed of the Tutsi. It was the Hutu who rose in large numbers and who treated her as a savior *mwami*.

This rebellion was soon followed by an armed anti-Tutsi movement that broke out in the northwest in 1897 and engulfed countries from Bugoyi to Kanage in Buberuka, including Rwankeri, Bushiru, Cyingogo, Buhoma, Murera, Bukonya, and Bugarura. Led in most of the small districts by the many former local kings who lived there, the insurgents did not succeed in forming a front united enough to withstand the counterattacks by the armies of the court. In 1899, after two years of combat, these armies managed to repress the insurrection, but at the price of having to surrender the power to directly interfere in the governance of the small kingdoms that had been tributaries under Rwogera's rule. Moreover, a substantial part of the population, especially in Murera and in Buberuka-Ndorwa, was not subdued and participated in a set of insurrections against Musinga, fostered in part by Muhumuza, aka Nyabingi, in the name of the restoration of a legitimate king.[51] One might object that this was an independence movement rather than an anti-Tutsi one, but the fact that people were willing to pay dues to the court but did not want any Tutsi residents in their midst is evidence against this argument. Moreover, in light of the Nyirafugi episode, it would be difficult to claim that there was no anti-Tutsi rancor in Fugi either.

The 1897 insurrection is particularly significant because it proves without any ambiguity not only that the population at this time was conscious of a great divide between Tutsi and Hutu, but also that the antagonism between these two social categories had already broken into the open.[52] One can therefore summarily reject the views of those who attribute the distinction between Tutsi and Hutu as well as the engendering of their mutual hostility to each other to the first Europeans. The Europeans merely adopted a practice they found on the spot and the terminology they used to express it derived from the speech of the local elites.

Their first error was to attribute the Tutsi/Hutu opposition to feelings of racial hatred, as Captain Bethe did in 1898 when he spoke of "Rassenhaß," which reveals his opinions about race more than it reflects any reality on the ground.[53] Indeed, it became commonplace for Europeans to equate Tutsi with Hamite and to apply the racist theories that Speke's book had introduced in the Great Lakes region to Rwanda. From there it was only a small step to imagine that Hutu was a special racial designation accepted by all those who were so designated. Yet, at that time, the farmers in the country absolutely did not think of themselves as members of a single ethnic group, and they all rejected the insulting epithet that was bestowed on them. They distinguished themselves as the "people" of Bugoyi, Kinyaga, Nduga, Rukiga (Kiga or

Cyiga), or even Rundi (in the southern center[54]), not as "Hutu." An awareness of their common quality was to arise only as the result of their common experience as Hutu subjects of the same colony and by its registration in all manner of census and identity papers of an awareness that then was openly appropriated and further refined during the political struggles of the 1950s.

6

The Triumph of the Great Families
and Its Consequences

In this chapter we examine the political history of the kingdom from the death of Ndabarasa to that of Rwogera in 1867. The internal affairs of those seventy years were characterized by the political weakness of the kings in countering the activities of the elite and by the internecine rivalries of the great families at court. In foreign affairs, the most important consequence of these activities and rivalries was an extension of the kingdom through the more or less effective incorporation of nearly all of western Rwanda as far as the shores of Lake Kivu as well as Bugesera and Gisaka to the east of country. For it is around 1867, and not in Rwabugiri's time, that the kingdom first achieved the borders that it was to retain after this eventful reign.

Civil War and the Supremacy of the Elites

The death of Ndabarasa in 1796 triggered a catastrophe: a succession war. Several of his most powerful sons were bent on seizing power despite the fact that he had designated Sentabyo as his successor. More than ten of the main lineages of the country played an active role in this struggle. Sentabyo was assisted by his brother Kimanuka[1] and three armies, Vuningoma of Nyarwaya, a grandson of Mazimpaka with two armies,[2] his mother Nyiratamba who belonged to the foremost Ega lineage, and a set of lineages led by chief Nkebya.[3] He was recognized by the Tsobe ritualists and installed as the rightful successor. Another set of Ndabarasa's sons, including Ruzamba with one army, and Rukari, Ndabarasa's favorite, with two armies,[4] refused to recognize him and backed the claims of Gatarabuhura and his mother. A third minor faction backed Gasenyi.[5] Finally, a fourth faction, which had rallied around Semugaza and his army, ended up remaining neutral, no doubt because Semugaza was hemmed in by Kimanuka and Vuningoma's five armies.

This faction simply waited. It did not recognize Sentabyo, but did not back Gatarabuhura either. Sentabyo succeeded fairly quickly in getting rid of Rukari, despite his armies, and Gatarabuhura fled to Gisaka. But Sentabyo was not strong enough to attack the factions of Semugaza and Gatarabuhura at the same time. During his reign he only succeeded in raising two new armies himself while his ritualists raised three.[6] The situation remained stalemated during his whole reign. The crisis was severe and left echoes in dynastic poetry, especially in the poem *Umwami si umuntu*, "The King is Not a Person," according to which the king is not a Tutsi like any other, but a special being chosen to be king by a supernatural power that no one could resist. And to declare:

> The king is a person before being called to the throne
> But once named,
> He separates himself even from the aristocrats and puts himself aside
> The sovereign cannot not have a rival: He is unique.[7]

As to the message of the poem *Ko bavuga iridakuka abami*, its very title "The Word of the Kings Cannot Be Repealed" already says it.[8]

The crisis was not resolved when smallpox suddenly cut down Kimanuka and young Sentabyo in 1801. The latter left no known descendants. No wonder that this demise immediately provoked a coup d'état. Nkebya, a chief whose forebears are unknown, and Barinyonza, Ndabarasa's son by a mother from the illustrious Ega lineage descended from Makara,[9] produced Nyiratunga, an Ega woman already famous in the country as the widow of that Gihana, son of Rujugira, who had died as a liberator in Burundi. She had just given birth to a son called Gahindiro and they pretended that the child had been engendered by Sentabyo. They immediately enthroned the baby with the support of a Tsobe ritualist, probably the same one who had installed Sentabyo as king. At the same time, though, Gatarabuhura, backed by his numerous warriors and by Semugaza's army, was triumphantly greeted by the population east of the Nyabarongo and entered Nduga.[10] After a failed attempt to murder the baby,[11] battle was waged near Butare (Kigoma), the residence of the court of Nyiratunga. For a long time the matter of who would be the next king remained undecided until finally Semugaza suddenly changed allegiances and rallied to the side of Gahindiro's faction, which carried it to victory.[12] This was a decisive battle (1802?), and not long thereafter Gatarabuhura was betrayed by one of his party, captured, and executed.[13]

The civil war demonstrated the failure of the political regime. Its deep cause was the excessive proliferation of the elite lineages at court. One estimates that ten sons of Mazimpaka founded important lineages, seven of Rujugira, and another seven of Ndabarasa. To these twenty-four Nyiginya lineages must be added at least three important Ega ones, as well as a few others among the matridynastic lineages linked to the Nyiginya by marriage, for a total of about thirty lineages of the first rank, excluding the five or six lineages of the foremost ritualists. As to positions, besides those of the ritualists, the foremost ones were army commands. In 1796, there were about twenty-eight active armies, but only twenty-one commands because some chiefs commanded several armies at once.[14] Let us also recall here that the combatant troops were closely tied to their army commanders by *ubuhake* ties and were faithful to them. That means that there were only enough command posts for roughly one third of the sons of the lineages of the first rank.[15] It is therefore not surprising that these lineages found themselves divided after Ndabarasa's death and that civil war broke out among the elite families who each wanted access to the benefits of power. Nor is it surprising that some left this political arena to seek fortune elsewhere. The immigration of Rwanteri and his army to Kinyaga is but one example of this. The famine of circa 1797–circa 1802 that accompanied the civil war in central Rwanda further favored such an exit solution.

The conflict was a collective triumph for the elites and a disaster for the kings because it transformed the balance of power at court. By 1802, power already lay in the hands of an oligarchy that included about twenty great families and it stayed there during the two following reigns. Despite the fact that it was rent by intestine dissensions, this elite none-theless ruled. Gahindiro did succeed in raising a rival power, that of his favorite, but in vain, for it was his favorite, not him, who ruled. Rwogera was so embroiled by the elites that one might say that the king belonged to one of two rival factions rather than that he had created his own.

Meanwhile, though, the elites at court continued to multiply and the struggle among lineages of the first order became more and more ferocious as the years passed by. This rivalry manifested itself mostly in the form of lineages informing against each other at court, although rival lineages did also fight each other from time to time in order to eliminate the leader of their opponents. Under such conditions no lineage felt se-cure. To cope with potential threats to their power, each of their leaders tried to attract as many clients as possible to strengthen their position at court, while the same climate of insecurity pushed herders of less illustrious lineages to seek protectors. In consequence, we believe that from the end of the eighteenth century onward, and in the heartland of the country, the practice of forming *ubuhake* ties rapidly spread downward through the social layers to the point where, certainly before 1867, all the owners of sizeable herds and even some prosperous farmers were affiliated with a protector. But this protective shield had its obverse side: disgrace or the spectacular destruction of a patron also redounded on his main clients of lesser rank. Still, until the personal rule of Rwabugiri, this kind of disaster was rare. Yet from that moment onward catastrophes became so frequent that men of inferior rank became less and less inclined to accept illustrious men as patrons and the number of new *ubuhake* contracts plummeted.[16]

One can better grasp the strengths, the weaknesses, and the relative permanence of lineages of the first rank by following their family histories. So let us give two well documented examples from two of the most important elite groups at court, the Nyiginya and the Ega. The first traces the history of a Nyiginya lineage founded by a son of Mazimpaka and the second that of the descendents of Byavu, an Ega. One would also have liked to have at least one detailed family history of a great ritualist lineage at one's disposal, preferably a Tsobe one, but no such detailed histories have been recovered.

Gakombe, one of Mazimpaka's sons, was a warrior who held lands on the border with Ndorwa and who grew rich by rustling herds of cattle, among which were the Imikara.[17] He married one of the women he had captured and had two sons by her, after which he died, supposedly of smallpox.[18] His son Nsigaye gained fame as a champion of Rujugira, and, seized both of Nama's armies to add to his own. However, he fell into disgrace under Ndabarasa who only left him with his Imikara herd, his "household" cattle, and a few enclaves where he had built enclosures. He married Nyiramuhanda, a foreign woman from Gishari who had joined the court in connection with the cult for Gihanga. This Nyiramuhanda succeeded in gaining Sentabyo's favor, whereupon he left her the Abangancuro corporation of menials[19] with domains in Bufundu and Kabagari. After Gahindiro, who was a baby at the time, became king, she played a crucial role in the ongoing succession crisis, for, according to the official history, she saved him from certain death in her capacity as the decisive witness on behalf of the queen mother, attesting to the fact that the baby was indeed Gahindiro, son of Sentabyo. She had been able to serve as such a witness only because she had been initiated as ritualist, it being absolutely necessary to be a ritualist in order to be an effective witness. Her initiation did not constitute a precedent for installing women as ritualists—she is the only woman to have ever been initiated—but it did set another precedent, that of admitting a member of a lineage of high rank to the ritual sphere. Soon thereafter her example was used as an excuse to install some other political leaders as ritualists as well.

In addition, she was granted the Impundu herd and a few hills. Her son Nyarwaya inherited all her goods, including her position as ritualist. This man distinguished himself as an outstanding warrior during Gahindiro's rule, gained several herds in consequence, and was appointed as commander to the important Nyaruguru army. Moreover, he became one of Gahindiro's lovers[20] and his most respected ritualist. He owned residences and domains in Rukoma, Marangara, Mayaga, Nduga, Nyanza, Busanza, and no less than six of these in Nyaruguru. During his lifetime, his son had the good fortune to save Rwogera's life when an attempt was made to murder him and so, in reward, he gained several more herds as well as the management of an Inyambo herd in Buganza. But the fortunes of two among his brothers, who had at first been as lucky as he, went bad when Nyiramongi, the queen mother at the time, had them blinded because they belonged to the political faction that was opposed to her. King Rwogera was furious and forced her to give them herds in compensation. But their active political careers were over.

Nyarwaya died almost at the same time that Rwogera did.[21] Nyantaba succeeded him and it is under his aegis that the family reached its apogee during the rule of Rwabugiri's queen mother, Murorunkwere. Nyantaba was then the main ritualist. He had enthroned Rwabugiri, he oversaw the whole of recently conquered Gisaka, and he commanded the personal army of the young king. But before 1877, and shortly after the king came of age, he lost command of the Nyaruguru army. He regained it some time later before being deprived of it for a second time and was then executed in the early- to mid-1880s. His sons also perished on this occasion, except for young Kayijuka who was entrusted to Queen Kanjogera.[22] When she became queen mother in 1896, Kayijuka succeeded in recovering the Nyaruguru army once again but fell from favor soon after 1900 because he had chosen the side of Ruhinankiko who was ousted from the court by Kabare's faction. Following an accusation at court according to which he had betrayed secrets to the Europeans, the queen mother had him blinded in 1906.

The history of the family shows that it had much luck. Three times in a row it chose the correct pretender and harvested the rewards for this. But Nyantaba had hitched his wagon to Murorunkwere's star, whose lineage of origin, that of the Kono, was not powerful. Moreover, Nsigaye's descendants did not succeed in concluding advantageous political alliances with other lineages of the first rank, which spelled its ruin in the long run. This history also shows us the scissions that occurred from generation to generation within the elite lineages and the crucial importance for the good fortune of a family of being recognized at court and of constantly seeking occasions to curry favor. Birth, even an illustrious birth, was not enough. Thus, one of Kayijuka's cousins, descendant from another of Nsigaye's sons, had become so poor by the later 1890s that he had to marry a Hutu woman and hence was on the way "to becoming Hutu." Another closer cousin, a descendant of Nyantaba's brother, had then become "a lesser chief." The example illustrates the proliferation of the great elites well enough, but also the fact that most of their members could not acquire a position of high rank and rapidly faded into obscurity. It is this dynamic that underlies the frequency and the rancor of the struggles for influence at court.

The second family we follow here is that of Byavu's descendants.[23] Byavu, an Ega, was a son of Buhura, grandson of Sesonga, and a nephew on his father's side of Nyiratamba, queen mother of Sentabyo.[24] He married one of Ndabarasa's daughters and was given the new Imvejuru army with its official herd on that occasion.[25] His wife bore him five sons, all of who were appointed to important posts. He fared well at Sentabyo's and Gahindiro's court. Nyiratunga, the queen mother of Gahindiro, was one of his relatives, although she belonged to the lineage founded by Sesonga's brother. In Gahindiro's time, he commanded his army, three official herds, and the provinces of Bwishya, Bufumbira, and Bugoyi to the north, Kinyaga to the southwest, plus a portion of Buganza and all of Bugesera to the east.

His son and successor, Nyarwaya, married Shongoka, a daughter of Gahindiro. She bore him three sons who all managed to be appointed to important posts during the reign of Rwogera. For Nyiramongi, the latter's queen mother, was also a relative, albeit from a new collateral branch descended from Gaga.[26] This Nyarwaya became Nyiramongi's favorite and he gave her a sensational gift: after a great famine he succeeded in filling two granaries for her, one with beans, the other with sorghum.[27] In return he received the governments of Busanza in southern central Rwanda, Gisigari and Jomba north of the volcanoes, and

Buriza to the northeast, in addition to the lands of his father. But this Nyarwaya was aggressive by nature and was always involved in intrigues at court. At one point he provoked a violent quarrel with Nkusi, Rwogera's favorite half-brother. After Nyarwaya had made a bet with Nkusi, the queen mother gave him the command of a second army, even though this army had previously been set aside for another of Rwogera's half-brothers. Finally, the king was driven to distraction and personally killed Nyarwaya. His brother Rugereka, who led the family during the minority of Nyarwaya's son, was designated to succeed him.[28] Hence the name Abagereka by which the family is known. Despite the manner of Nyarwaya's demise, his son Rubabazangabo still succeeded in marrying one of Rwogera's daughters and a sister of Rwabugiri, and the family continued to prosper.[29]

When Rwabugiri succeeded, the Abagereka became so powerful that the government of Murorunkwere, the queen mother, attacked them by accusing them of having killed Rwogera in order to avenge Nyarwaya's death. They fought a battle at Rwesero (Nyanza), which the Abagereka lost, upon which all of them, including their allies by marriage and their main clients, were exterminated. About two hundred people died in this vendetta, excluding the soldiers of the Imvejuru who had died during the battle itself.[30] Rubirima, the grandfather of the biographer Mazina, and his six children, however, escaped, although they lost all their possessions. Long after these dramatic events, Biyenzi, Mazina's father, who was a renowned warrior, finally managed to gain the esteem of Rwabugiri who returned the command of the Imvejuru, the government of Busanza, and two official herds to him. Biyenzi then married, among others, a Nyiginya woman from a lineage descended from Ndabarasa. But around 1893–94, he and his family once again lost the goodwill of Rwabugiri after he was bested in a struggle for influence by the faction of the main Nyiginya sons of the king. Biyenzi and his folks had to flee to Burundi and lost their lives there about a year later. But the baby Mazina, born in 1892, and abandoned on the wayside during Biyenzi's flight was saved and taken in by a daughter of Mwezi, the king of Burundi. Shortly before Rwabugiri's death (1895), Mwezi sent him back to Rwanda and Queen Kanjogera took him under her wing. Mazina was then educated by his Nyiginya "aunts," who were descendants of Ndabarasa, and made a career as a diviner in charge of the cult for Musinga and Kanjogera's ancestors.

The most striking points in this tale are the following: the prosperity of the lineage stemmed mostly from marriages its members made with members of the royal family; all the "Ega" at court, although kin, split into different lineages nearly once every generation; and thirdly, and contrary to the norm, this lineage managed to find posts of the highest rank for all of Byavu's eight sons and those of Nyarwaya, his son, which amounted to about one third of the existing posts. It was this last success that rendered the Abagereka so powerful but also so envied and hated by the other elite lineages that in the end it was this very accumulation of posts that caused their final fall. Moreover, one observes the resilience of the ties between a commander and his army, revealed in this case first at the battle fought at Rwesero, and then confirmed by the restoration of the family at the head of "its" army. Lastly, one also takes note of the attitude of the court in Burundi, which obviously recognized the great families of Rwanda as equals to its own. Mazina was ultimately saved by this web of multiple alliances that had linked his family to the royal line.

A detailed family history of one of the foremost ritualists, and especially of the ruling Tsobe family, would show another foundation for the acquisition of power. The Tsobe ritual position was permanent and protected the whole family, but not always its leaders, from the ill-fated consequences of struggles at court. Besides, the support of the Tsobe ritualist was absolutely indispensable to guaranteeing the legitimacy of each king. Well protected in an unassailable position, certain leaders began to interfere in secular affairs. Already under Rujugira, a Tsobe chief owned an army and his descendants kept its command. Moreover, the Tsobe of this and related lineages began step-by-step to enlarge their Bumbogo domain both by internal expropriation and by the gradual annexation of hills on their northern and eastern borders.[31] They managed their affairs so well that by 1900 they had become the third great political "family," surpassed only by the Ega and Nyiginya lineages. But not all the ritualists at court were so fortunate. The Tege of Kabagari held their own, but did not succeed in extending their influence beyond the ritual sphere. On the other hand, the Kono seem almost always to have been losing influence despite the fact that, in addition to their holding the office of a great ritualist, another one of their lineages had produced some queen mothers. In the end their loss of influence seems even to have restricted their ritual role.[32]

Struggles for Power at Gahindiro's and Rwogera's Courts

After the civil war, a coalition consisting of Nyiratunga, the queen mother, her brother Rugagi, chief Nkebya, and Barinyonza's lineage took control. After the battle of Butare near Kigoma in 1801–02, different leaders of Gatarabuhura's party were killed or shoved aside and the partisans of the queen mother were rewarded.[33] But the major sequel of this battle was a struggle for influence between the factions of Nkebya and Barinyonza, on the on hand, and Semugaza's, on the other, with the queen mother tending to favor the latter. After a few months, the conflict ended when Semugaza, along with the best combatants of his army, left the court. He defeated all the armies that pursued him and carved out a small autonomous principality in Ndorwa for himself. Meanwhile, though, at the court the queen mother's faction had been bested by Nkebya's.[34]

But the queen mother's government took steps to increase royal prestige. The worship of the royal ancestors, which had been abandoned during Ndabarasa' rule, was restored and a codification of the royal rituals was undertaken whereby the ritualists had to learn by heart the liturgies or instructions for performing them. All that, however, did not prevent the aristocratic lineages from attempting to reinforce their position within the ideological institutions at court. The queen mother's faction instituted a new practice whereby their male maternal ancestors would be included in the list of dynastic succession, which reinforced the weight of the matridynastic families and especially that of an Ega queen mother.[35] The direct irruption of the high-ranking lineages into the ritual affairs of the kingdom was far more significant, however. When an epidemic broke out in the country the courtiers suddenly became aware that they were on the point of losing the whole ritual relating to Gihanga's fire, precisely the one that was to supposed to halt epidemics.[36] To prevent any possibility of the rituals being forgotten, the government of the queen mother then decided to multiply tenfold the posts of ritualists in charge of the memorization of all the ritual paths of kingship. The reader will recall the precedent set in 1801 by the initiation of Nyiramuhanda, which now was invoked as a justification for naming many members of the most aristocratic lineages to these positions. The epidemic was perhaps no more than an excuse to do this, for these measures created a whole set of new posts for some of the sons of these prolific lineages. Moreover, this measure broke down the Chinese Wall that had hitherto protected the set of ritualists from all direct interference by the secular elites, to the detriment of the autonomous political position of the ritualists. From then on, some powerful lineages were even to take a leading role in the process of designating successors, and they took advantage of it, as we have seen in the case of Nyarwaya of Mbyayingabo.

During his youth Gahindiro became friendly with Rugaju, a child of his age from a modest herding lineage who had attracted attention by his skill as an animal trainer on the occasion of the presentation of an Inyambo herd.[37] Rugaju acquired great influence over the king and when the queen mother handed over the government to Gahindiro around 1820, Rugaju became his main favorite and foremost adviser. One might think that the king made a clever calculation in choosing Rugaju, perhaps hoping thereby to establish an independent power base, but I doubt it. Not only was this a childhood friendship, but there was no limit to the favors the king granted to Rugaju. He received the command of the three armies that Gahindiro raised for himself and also was given the first of the two armies that the queen mother had created for her brother. The second one went to Munana, her son by Gihana.[38] Rugaju accumulated herds,[39] and rapidly obtained important territorial commands, especially on the northern borders of the realm. The storytellers recall that his ascendancy was so complete that he ended up by ruling the country almost like an autocrat: "All those who received something, it was Rugaju who gave it to them. All those who lost their possessions, it was Rugaju who took them,"[40] or again, "whomsoever wanted to be the king's servant began by being Rugaju's. . . . He ordered the king's men about and made himself master of all of Rwanda."[41] His star attracted clients, which further strengthened his position, and this then attracted others, empowering him even further, until the king himself was no longer able to oppose him. If the intention had been to use Rugaju as an instrument of the personal policy or the king, it had failed. To the contrary, Gahindiro was well on his way to becoming Rugaju's man.

Yet there were disagreements between them, particularly when Gahindiro killed Rugaju's brother, but they always made up.[42] Because the aristocratic lineages at court were divided as a result of their mutual rivalries, they did not succeed in countering Rugaju's ascent. Some rallied to his side, and others were opposed to him, but in a disorganized fashion. Nevertheless, at the outset of Gahindiro's personal rule, probably in the early 1820s, Ruyenzi, son of Semugaza, returned from exile with his army and competed with Rugaju for royal favor. But Rugaju managed to have him sent to the border of Burundi where he perished during a Rundi attack.[43] After this Rugaju was not effectively challenged for many years. New rivals, which he could not entirely get rid of, appeared only toward the end of the reign, although his own position remained as strong as ever. The important Abashakamba army, which he commanded, hated him. Around or after 1840 a mutiny broke out and the soldiers chose Nkusi, a king's son, as commander. The king and Rugaju had no choice but to accept the situation. Not long thereafter Marara, grandson of Gihana, who had inherited the command of the fifth army, challenged Rugaju during a campaign in Ndorwa and won his challenge. Although he had to be rewarded in cattle, he did not succeed in lessening Rugaju's influence.[44]

It was during the last years of Gahindiro's reign that Rugaju introduced the institution of the reserved herding domain, which was soon followed in the first years of the next reign by the creation of chiefs of the long grass. Rugaju was prompted to invent the reserved domain because of the ever growing number of members in the principal lineages at court who needed positions and it was favored by the steady increase in the number of herds owned by the most powerful courtiers. These new institutions provided posts for some of them, Rugaju's clients in the first place. At the same time, these institutions reinforced the hold of the court over the rural populations and allowed for their more efficient exploitation as well, which was especially of benefit to the aristocratic lineages. It has been held that either Rugaju or the king came up with the idea of putting two competing chiefs in place to rule over the same territory as a way of strengthening central power by instituting a mutual check between the chiefs commanding in the same region. That certainly was one of the results, although the main aim simply seems to have been to multiply the number of posts that could be granted. Hence the foremost enactors of this policy on the ground were the great lineages who sought to place their sons.

Rwogera was still a young child when Gahindiro died around 1845. Nevertheless he and his queen mother succeeded without any known contest.[45] This is remarkable and Rugaju was no doubt responsible for the smooth transition. In any case, he still remained all-powerful for a few more years.[46] At first the queen mother Nyiramongi, abetted by her brother Rwakagara, contented herself by persecuting some people who had thwarted her in her youth. She also resented Rugaju, supposedly for the same reason, but in fact probably because in effect he still ruled the country.[47] Some years passed before his enemies, led by Marara and backed by the queen mother, felt themselves strong enough to accuse him, seize him, and have him executed together with his whole family.[48] Whereupon the queen mother redistributed his vast possessions and those of his clients to her partisans and in the first place to Marara.

The queen mother ruled by herself as a regent helped by Rwakagara, head of her lineage, and by their Ega relative, Nyarwaya of Byavu, who commanded the Abakemba army. When Rwogera came of age in the early 1850s, a royal party appeared that mainly included Nyiginya chiefs. Nkusi, Gahindiro's son, and his Abashakamba army led this party and Nyarwaya of Mbyayingabo with his Nyaruguru army was one of its main backers. But Nyiramongi did not give in. The two factions, which were about equally strong, continued to compete during the whole reign and several favorites fell victim to the rivalry. Thus Rwogera, on the one hand, exiled Marara and killed Nyarwaya of Byavu, Nkusi's rival, while Nyiramongi, on the other, had one of Nyarwaya of Mbyayingabo's sons killed and later supposedly had him murdered as well. Toward the end of the reign she gradually began to favor Nkoronko, Rwogera's younger brother, thereby hoping to recover an equilibrium that was becoming precarious. For while her personal ascendancy over the king had often ensured the success of her faction, he was beginning to question her mastery more and more.[49]

Rwogera reinforced royal authority by establishing an important cult for the spirit of Mazimpaka at Ijuru of Kamonyi, where he placed two armies, one corporation of menials, and an official herd, all of which were dedicated to the performance of rituals.[50] This grandiose gesture must be understood in the framework of the political situation at the time. The lineages issued from Mazimpaka were the flower of the Nyiginya elite at court, constituted the most compact group of the kings' backers, and were probably the inspiration for this move. Not only did this gesture reestablish the importance of their common ancestor, but it also underlined the unique mystical quality of the king, their leader, an attribute that elevated him above all others, including his mother. No Ega could ever match the king in this respect.

The changing fortunes in the struggle for power are reflected in the creation of new armies. The first of four new armies was given by the queen mother to Rwabika, a half-brother of Rwogera, who remained outside the political arena. The second went to young Nkoronko. After Rugaju's execution, his army was taken over by Rwakagara. The king gave the first of the next of two armies to his young son Nyamwesa, installing a Kono commander as trustee, and the second to another son. Meanwhile, those armies of the preceding reign that were still important remained in the hands of the commanders who had held them during Gahindiro's rule. Moreover, two corporations of menials were created, one of which fell in Nkoronko's hands.[51] Shortly before Rwogera's death, the military forces of Gisaka, consisting of three armies, were integrated into the kingdom. One fell under Nkoronko's absolute control. The other two were given to Nyamwesa and to one of Rwabika's sons, respectively, but their former Gisakan leaders remained in place as second-in-command and these formations continued to obey their former masters much more than the new ones.[52]

As could be expected, the long struggle between the factions that followed Rugaju's autocratic rule was accompanied by increasing turmoil in the country, particularly by "revolts."[53] The only uprising about which something is known is the execution of the "king of the Imandwa" of the Abayumbu family whose chief commanded the Impara herd that was dedicated to the worship of Ryangombe.[54] This case draws attention to the turmoil caused by groups of initiates *(mandwa)* roving through the country on official missions.[55] The process whereby reserved domains and positions of chief of the long grass and chiefs of the land were established was similarly chaotic and took place in an atmosphere of rivalry among the king, the queen mother, and even the main chiefs. From time to time, rivalries among chiefs even burst into open combat.[56] As to the armies, not only did they maintain their tendency to mutiny, as in the case of the Intanganzwa who boycotted the king himself until their chief Marara had been reappointed,[57] but they also engaged in battle with another, as the several clashes that occurred between the armies of Nkusi and Nyarwaya of Byavu during a campaign in Bushi attest to.[58] Private raiding on the borders increased and it was one of these private expeditions that triggered the disaster of Nyaruhoni during the war in Gisaka.[59] Finally, one may also wonder what the role was of all this political turmoil in the alleged occurrence of frequent famines during Rwogera's rule.[60] What is certain is that every famine provoked local dislocations and that a severe famine, such as Gikoko, which occurred during the 1850s, triggered the temporary or definitive displacement of the affected populations, which complicated the political situation even further.

Although these struggles for power fueled the rivalry among the great families even more, collectively the court elite became considerably wealthier during this reign and reinforced its power not only with regard to the king and the queen mother but also throughout the country, particularly by the extension of *ubuhake* contracts, which seem to have reached their apogee at the time owing to the fact that the general climate of insecurity that accompanied these factional struggles favored their extension. For the first time, families near the bottom of the social pyramid, be they small herders or even well-off farmers, sought local protectors at any price and those protectors in turn tried to place themselves under the protection of more powerful chiefs.

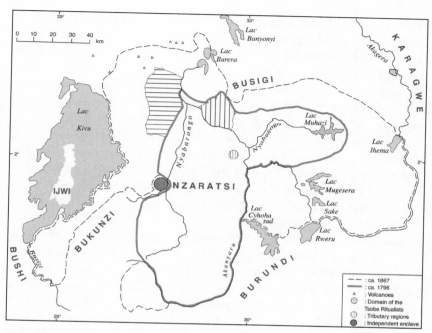

The realm in 1867

Stricken with tuberculosis, Rwogera died rather young in about 1867, around the same time as Nkusi and Nyarwaya of Mbyayingabo. The queen mother was then murdered by her own lineage head and brother, Rwakagara.[61] Even before a succession struggle could develop between Nyamwesa and Sebizoni, better known as Rwabugiri, the fore-most ritualists came out in favor of the latter, albeit against Nkoronko's wishes. The latter then abandoned Nyamwesa "for his mother belonged to a very weak family"[62] and even the two deputy commanders of Nyamwesa's armies had no more urgent goal than to recommend them-selves to the new queen mother. Thus the party of the Nyiginya lineages came into the ascendancy without any struggle, to the detriment of the faction of Nkoronko and the Ega.

Expansion of the Kingdom Eastward and International Trade

After this discussion of the internal politics of the kingdom and their effects on its core, we can now turn to an examination of its external relations. Indeed, this very period that saw the triumph of the elites at court was also remarkable for the extraordinary expansion that occurred in the realm's territory. By 1867, it had more than doubled and had approximately reached the borders it still had in 1900. But just as during the eighteenth century, the dynamics of this expansion were so different on each side of the great ecological and cultural divide between east and west that each side must be examined separately.

Court tradition and its interpreter, Kagame, attribute the expansion eastward to a series of well-planned and always victorious wars: The slogan *"Nunguyurwanda,"* "I broaden Rwanda,"[63] seems to support this view. And yet it would be an error to accept it. Given the political conditions at court, it is much more likely that this expansion was not always organized by it and that it never was perfectly planned. Moreover, the kingdom did suffer some resounding defeats, especially against Burundi, and even against Gisaka. Let us observe, first of all, that the traditions did not keep track of all the wars, let alone all the reciprocal raids along the borders. The war with Karagwe under Gahindiro is only the most evident example of this.[64] Far from being planned by the court, a good many military operations stemmed from the private initiatives of individuals or from armies acting on their own accord. One can even doubt whether a sustained royal will to conquer foreign lands existed because at that time the kings resided only in central Rwanda. And, lastly, the internal struggles between elites at court were sometimes directly related to foreign campaigns.[65] Thus, in reality, the expansion of the kingdom occurred in spurts and resulted as much from the temporary weakness of adversaries like Bugesera or Gisaka than from a concerted plan at court. One may object that the ritual paths numbers eleven to fourteen unquestionably show the court's aggressiveness.[66] But the paths numbers thirteen and fourteen deal mainly with defensive maneuvers and the initial lines of path number eleven are:

> When a foreign country is revolting
> and a rebel has been enthroned there
> In his honor the drums beat in salute.[67]

These lines refer to the installation of a foreign king and a defensive maneuver in response to it even though the ritual foresees a military expedition and foresees, thanks to this ritual, that "this country, one defeats it."[68] Aggressiveness, yes, but initiative of the court—not necessarily. And the slogan of the royal hammers must also be understood as referring to the need to undertake defensive military action.

The very first conquest of the period illustrates the role of serendip-
ity and of private initiative in the process. When a great drought struck
the kingdom and central Burundi in Sentabyo's day, Bugesera was
apparently spared. Whereupon Ntare of Burundi's army, no doubt in
search of food and pastures, invaded the heart of the country, which lay
in its southern part, crushed its enemy, and purely and simply annexed
the part it occupied. At the same time, a group of Rwandan herders
crossed the Akanyaru on its own initiative and invaded northern Bugesera with the hope of seizing the land for its herds to graze on. Bugesera's
army did not have the strength anymore to repel them, and so, at that
point the court decided to intervene and formally annex the country. A
relatively widespread variant of this tale underlines the role of pure
chance even more. A madman had gone to buy foodstuffs in Bugesera
and returned to court complaining about how little he had obtained. As
no one paid any attention to him, our madman took it upon himself to
beat the alarm drum in an effort to call up the commoners to invade Bugesera, a move that the court immediately countermanded. But hunger
listens to no reason and the volunteers invaded Bugesera.[69] The incorporation of the northern portion of this kingdom, a very sparsely settled
land, was concluded very quickly once the drum and the dynastic herd
had been captured. Long after these events, the ousted king tried to return to his country but he was arrested and executed.[70] And as a memorial to the glory of Sentabyo, Bugesera's dynastic herd was installed
at Remera, the graveyard where his predecessors with the name of
MIBAMBWE had also been buried.[71]

The other great success of the Nyiginya kingdom during this period
was the destruction of Gisaka. One remembers that Gatarabuhura and
other rivals to Sentabyo's throne had taken refuge in Gisaka and that reciprocal raiding skirmishes were frequent on that border. The king had
planned a large-scale attack, but then he died and civil war flared up as
before. When peace returned, Nyiratunga instigated at least one expedition against Gisaka. After that the situation remained unchanged, despite the fact that Gisaka became highly unstable in Gahindiro's time.[72]
By the beginning of Rwogera's reign, the country had split into three
practically independent principalities, which prompted the court to
invade the one called Gihunya with a force composed of eight armies,
probably with the aim of conducting an extensive raid there. This expedition was such a success that it was followed by others, official and private ventures alike, among which one at least proved to be disastrous for
the attackers. Finally, toward the very end of the reign, probably around

1865, the prince of Gihunya was overcome, thanks to a deserter from his country who had betrayed him. He was then executed, which led to a general capitulation and the occupation of his whole country. But the dynastic drum was not captured and Gisaka was not yet formally annexed. It was left to Rwabugiri to complete this conquest. Still, the Gisakans were loath to accept their incorporation into Rwanda and several insurrections resulted, the last of which broke out in 1901.[73] Nevertheless, Gisaka had been conquered and from this point forward the Nyiginya kingdom bordered on the confines of Bushubi and the main commercial road to the Indian Ocean.

Both of these successes stand in contrast to the unfolding of relations with Ndorwa and Burundi. Paradoxically, the first one was too weak and the second too strong to be easily conquered. We saw that when Ndabarasa's died, his troops evacuated Ndorwa, abandoning the country to several pretenders who sowed division there. At the beginning of Gahindiro's reign, Semugaza had gone into exile with his army and carved out a principality for himself there, but shortly after Gahindiro came of age, this principality vanished along with Semugaza himself. Thereafter Ndorwa was of little concern to the court until the waning days of the reign when a Hima leader there assumed the regnal name of Murari, managed to rally a great number of Hima chiefs, and began to raid cattle in Rwanda. The court reacted and sent several rival armies to Ndorwa, one group under Rugaju's command and another under Marara's. The latter issued a challenge to Rugaju, claiming that he would defeat Murari before Rugaju would even arrive there. Marara did defeat Murari and appropriated a rather extensive domain there but was unable to subdue all the lands of old Ndorwa. A further expedition under Rwogera was no more than a great raid, and a second one had to be cancelled because of the monarch's death.[74]

Once again, as in past times, Burundi remained the most dangerous and the strongest enemy of the Nyiginya kingdom during the whole nineteenth century. After Mutaga's death, the border of the Akanyaru, well protected by military camps, remained fairly peaceful despite the occasional raid by one side or the other until Gahindiro came to age and Rugaju was in his ascendancy. At that point, the Rundi warriors had slowly begun gaining advantage and so Rugaju sent Ruyenzi and his troops there, but they were annihilated. Whereupon a period of mutual harassment followed that increasingly weakened the Nyiginya forces until the moment when the Nyaruguru army led by Nyarwaya of Mbyayingabo succeeded in redressing the situation.[75] Much later, toward the end of Gahindiro's reign and to strengthen his prestige at court, Rugaju mobilized a great army and invaded Burundi. It was a total disaster and a second expedition raised to avenge the first underwent the same fate. This probably inspired the king of Burundi to launch a huge expedition across the Akanyaru at the accession of Rwogera. But a counterattack by the Nyiginya garrisons along the border was effective and the expedition turned into a catastrophe for the Rundi. It became quite evident that neither Burundi nor the Nyiginya kingdom had the strength to invade each other's realm. Hence, the regime of border clashes resumed.[76] But meanwhile, and later as well, Nyarwaya and his successors gradually succeeded by dint of lavish gifts in convincing one local chief after the other in Buyenzi to switch allegiance from Burundi to the Nyiginya.[77] Thus this whole province was "conquered" and incorporated shortly after the end of Rwogera's reign.

Yet perhaps the most significant development of the times was not the Nyiginya's military expansion eastward, but a commercial expansion stemming from the coast of the Indian Ocean. Before 1800, at least a certain amount of luxury goods such as beads, conus shells, and brass rings from the coast were being imported, at least to judge by the contents of Rujugira's tomb.[78] From about 1800 onward, imports rose in line with the increase in the long-distance trade of the peoples in Nyamwezi. During Gahindiro's personal rule, the first coastal merchants established a commercial center at Tabora (1830–40) and the first cotton textiles are said to have been imported into Rwanda at that time. In 1844, around the beginning of Rwogera's reign, the first Arab trader arrived in Buganda and, in 1855, Rumanyika rose to power in Karagwe with the decisive help of Arabs who intervened on his behalf in a succession struggle there.[79] Still in the 1850s a whole Arab or Swahili caravan even reached Rwogera's court. But a great drought struck the country at the time and the king's diviners accused the caravan of having caused it. As a result, foreigners from far away were henceforth barred access to the country, although their products still continued to flow into the country, thanks to hawkers.[80] Two of Rwogera's capitals became famous for the profusion of their decoration in glass beads, and on great occasions the cream of society began to drape itself in cotton togas.[81] The hawkers probably quickly found their way to the easternmost markets of the Lake Kivu system, such as those in Buberuka, Nduga, and Marangara, and no doubt sold some of their products there as well.

The decision to close the country to foreign caravans was to be of unsurpassed importance for the subsequent history of the kingdom as the contrast with Buganda's destiny shows.[82] Despite this decision, though, the effects of trade led to a gradual intensification of elephant hunting, especially in the northwestern forests, a further intensification of the practice of capturing young women and children during raids and military campaigns for sale as slaves, and an increase in the prestige of king and elites alike.

However much the court attempted to prevent the kingdom from participating directly in the east African trade, it was still the case that as early as the second third of the century a new geographic pole of great interest had arisen to the southeast of the realm. This pole was ambiguous in value; on the one hand, its wealth made it attractive, but, on the other, the menace posed by the military strength of the caravans and perhaps in part the exoticism of these coastal merchants made it at the same time repulsive. The traditions do not speak of the lands to the southeast, but certainly there was a lot of talk about them at the court of Gahindiro and Rwogera. One may also surmise that the decision to close the country was as much influenced by the spectacle of Karagwe in 1855 as by the divination blaming a caravan for a drought. Might one even suppose that the traditions concerning the prophecies of Mazimpaka about the coming of foreigners date from this time and that the arrival of merchants from the east coast at the borders of Gisaka was one of the motives for the renewal of Mazimpaka's cult at Kamonyi?

A Spontaneous Expansion toward Lake Kivu and the Land of the Volcanoes?

The political expansion of the kingdom from central Rwanda west- and northward had barely begun before 1796. But from the onset of this period and while civil war was raging, an official interest appeared first in Kinyaga and only later in Bwishaza, even though that region was closer to the Rugabano road. Still, the kingdom was to expand mainly from footholds in Bugoyi and Kinyaga.

After Rujugira's expedition to Bugoyi the local king, Macumu, allied himself with the court and began to send gifts ("tribute" in the eyes of the court) as well as messengers in order to avoid further raids and to prevent his local opponents from allying themselves with the Nyiginya. This state of affairs persisted unchanged for almost half a century. But after around 1820, Rugaju, whose main domain was Ndiza, had himself appointed as nominal chief of Bugoyi. He accepted the customary gifts,[83] but never went there and did not appoint any representative there. After his demise in circa 1847, the post fell to Nkusi, who appointed one of his sons to collect the tribute owed by the local king and the new dues that were directly imposed on the local Tutsi, who may well have conceded to pay them in order to strengthen their autonomy with regard to the local Gwabiro dynasty. But even Nkusi's sons never resided in the country. Only by the end of Rwogera's rule was an attempt to control Bugoyi made more directly by sending chief Buki to live alongside the local king. They were jointly responsible for handing over tribute and both controlled detachments of well known armies. The result was an unending series of clashes between their warriors and a situation that rapidly degenerated into chaos. Bugoyi was only to be fully integrated into the realm under Rwabugiri's personal rule, well after 1875.[84]

In the land of the volcanoes beyond Bugoyi, the first Nyiginya incursions also date from Gahindiro's time and followed the same pattern as in Bugoyi. Rugaju managed to be recognized as chief by the herders of Bigogwe, in Murera, and of Bukamba, but without appointing any delegate from central Rwanda and without the payment of any dues. Delegates and dues arrived only after military operations in Rwogera's time.[85] In neighboring Bufumbira, the first Nyiginya incursions also seem to date from Gahindiro. Later on, several attempts to send delegates from the court and impose dues on the country failed before Rwabugiri succeeded.[86] On the other hand, in Bwisha and Jomba, where there also was an ancient population of herders, Gahindiro is said to have appointed three local delegates who did succeed in ruling the southern part of the region that bordered on Bugoyi.[87]

An adventure much further to the northwest of Lake Kivu apparently occurred during Gahindiro's rule. According to the official local version, a Nyiginya army was dispatched to the kingdom of Karinda. Its commander exchanged blood, a common procedure in the region, with Karinda and paid him a tithe in cattle. He is said to even have proposed a dynastic marriage with a daughter of Gahindiro to him. But when Karinda visited the Nyiginya camp he was suddenly overpowered and killed. His testicles were then sent to the court to decorate the dynastic drum. It looks though as if, once more, we have a private raid here that was recast as official business later on after the testicles had been sent. In any case, from then on this faraway region was to be completely uninvolved until Rwabugiri's campaigns there.[88]

A group of herders known as the Abazimya, which the Nyiginya court considered to be an army, had settled in Bwishaza a very long time ago. Rugagu, an indigent brother of the Ega queen mother of Gahindiro, plagued by famine, had sought refuge in Budaha at the entrance to the road from Nduga to Kivu. Later, in 1801, he used the good fortune of his sister to claim the command of this so-called Abazimya army. This was granted and he went to Bwishaza, probably accompanied by a guard. There he succeeded in being acknowledged by the herders. But he probably never sent any dues at all to the court, and no one even remembers that he had any obligation to do so.[89] Indeed, it is not known when the first dues from Bwishaza arrived at court or when the rulers of the local farmers began to acknowledge this chief from central Rwanda. The silence on this subject suggests that it was not earlier than Rwogera's reign, and perhaps even as late as in the first years of Murorunkwere's rule.[90]

According to the court's view, Kinyaga was occupied in accordance with Sentabyo's wishes who had sent two chiefs there with new armies.[91] But things were not what they seemed. The two chiefs in question were ritualists, but ritualists were usually excluded from military appointments. Rwanteri, an Ega, led the followers of Ryangombe at court and Rukoro, a Kobwa, and one of the foremost ritualists, was responsible for the service of Karinga itself. The first one recruited an army from within his congregation, while the second one recruited part of his people from the ancient corporation of the dynastic drum and the rest from among followers of other ritualists. These were totally unheard of ways to raise an army before this time. Moreover, all this occurred during a civil war when the king needed all the available troops in the center of the kingdom to fight his enemies. On top of that, the great famine of circa 1797–circa 1802 was raging. I think that both chiefs withheld their support from Sentabyo during the civil war. But once the court recognized him they feared his vengeance and mobilized their partisans. When the famine struck, the favorable conditions in Kinyaga, a country renowned for its lack of droughts, attracted them. Informed of a chance to carve a landed domain out for themselves there—for at that moment Kinyaga was in political turmoil—they decided to join the pastoralists who had been immigrating there since Ndabarasa's reign or even earlier. The new armies were the first organized military formations ever seen in these parts and easily defeated a certain Bijeri of unknown origins who was in the process of occupying a domain in this region. Western Kinyaga went to Rwanteri and Rukoro and they divided it between themselves. Later on either Sentabyo's court or that of Nyiratunga was prompt to capitalize on this situation. She recognized the command of both chiefs but in return they were to send her dues for the hills that they had been occupying. The success of these two chiefs and their armed followers then attracted further lineages related to the Ega and Kobwa pioneers. But Rwanteri did not stay long in the region, since he was in Mutara after the victory of Gahindiro's party and was executed there with his whole family, probably as a partisan of Gatarabuhura. Only one of his sons survived and succeeded him as head of the Impara army.[92]

It is in this overall context that the circumstances under which the first Rwandan herders arrived in the Itombwe Mountains overlooking Uvira must be understood. Their first leader, who is now believed to have been a Tutsi, is said to have immigrated there with his kith and kin around the beginning of the nineteenth century. Was he fleeing the famine and the war in central Rwanda, or did he actually only come from central Kinyaga, fleeing there to escape from Rwanteri or Rukoro? No one knows.[93]

Kinyaga was next door to the Shi kingdoms and principalities across the Ruzizi and the Rwandan court soon took advantage of this. Unfortunately, a detailed and critical study of Shi traditions for the period has still not been made so that the assertions of the Nyiginya court cannot be matched to those coming from the country itself.[94] According to the available data, the first contacts between the court and this region supposedly occurred during Gahindiro's reign when the Ngweshe court supposedly sent a delegation to announce the installation of a new king. Later, still during Ngweshe's reign, Gahindiro's court supposedly sent three or four military expeditions to raid Bunyabungo, one of which, at least, ended in defeat. Moreover, Makombe, a pretender to the throne of Bushi proper (kingdom of Kabare) is thought to have taken refuge at the Nyiginya court before he seized power at home. Later, the rivalry between the favorite army commanders of, respectively, Rwogera and Nyiramongi triggered a raid by their competing armies against the same Makombe. Until these data are confirmed or refuted, it is wise to retain only from all of this that Nyiginya raids were conducted in this region well before the better known campaigns of Rwabugiri.

The case of Ijwi illustrates why considerable caution is required. According to the Nyiginya court traditions, the first king of Ijwi, Mwendanga, was helped in his struggle to found the kingdom by relatives who had settled in Bwishaza during Gahindiro's reign.[95] Later on, and after Rugagi's settlement in Bwishaza, the two countries entered into diplomatic relations with a mutual exchange of gifts. Indeed, at the very moment of Rwogera's death in 1867, a delegation from Kabego, Ijwi's king, arrived at the capital with just such gifts but it was turned back. However, local Ijwi historians have never heard of any of these assertions and David Newbury, the historian of the island, is convinced that these so-called events never occurred.[96]

The dynamics of the expansion of the kingdom northward, especially east of the Mukungwa, is partly different in nature. Here it started at the border and went from hill to hill. The initiative came from various local chiefs of the Syete, Tsobe, and Shambo aristocratic lineages who vied with each other. This rivalry began as early as Rujugira's reign with the arrival of Busyete on the Mukungwa, but progress was very slow until Rwogera's time and he only gave an official stamp of approval to the local commands the Tutsi chiefs had instituted for themselves.[97] But these private initiatives worried the small local kings, especially those of Bushiru, Buhoma, Rwanteri, and Bukonya, who chose to become tributaries of the Nyiginya, but not to allow any authority from central Rwanda to settle on their lands, just as they refused to grant even the least autonomy to groups of herders who wanted to settle among them.[98]

Hence most of the expansion, especially westward, was but the institutionalization of a preceding spontaneous colonization. The court never had a grand strategic plan by which herder settlers were first introduced into a region and then later followed by the arrival of an army. To the contrary, because of its spontaneous character, this expansion was very irregular. One of the consequences of this state of affairs was that, even at the time of Rwogera's death in 1867, there subsisted a host of enclaves in which local kings or lineages did not recognize any Nyiginya rule at all, not even a nominal one. Among the largest enclaves were the small kingdoms of Bukunzi, Busozo, Bushiru, Rwankeri, part of Cyingogo, and Nyantango, the Abarashi lineages of Muhabura,[99] and the smiths and other inhabitants in Buberuka and on a few adjacent hills in Ndorwa. With regard to most of these territories the court was content to accept dues or gifts, gathered by the local authorities and transmitted from time to time to the court in central Rwanda. Finally, as ancient ritual allies greatly needed by the Nyiginya kingdom, Busigi, and Kibari also remained as autonomous as they had been up to then.[100]

Conclusion

The severe crisis of 1796–1802 consecrated the political supremacy of the aristocracy at court to the detriment of the personal power of the king. Its continued growth, in numbers as well as in the size of their herds, as well as the strong pressure this growth placed on the land, led to internal rivalries that grew ever more ferocious over time, and because the kings were weak, they could not halt them. Everyone attempted to obtain the most power, the most cattle, and the most land possible, and necessarily did so to the detriment of the others, since there were not many additions to the twenty-odd positions of the first order during the whole period. One must see the creation of the reserved domain, actually tiny provinces, as well as the multiplication of territorial positions in this light. The growing impoverishment of all other subjects, herders as well as farmers, was a direct consequence of the attempt of the aristocracy to acquire ever more positions, cattle, and land. Some lost their pastures, and others were crushed by new corvée labor. Yes, the aristocracy ruled but in a climate of general insecurity, a climate in which they all attempted to ratify their position by further extensions of *ubuhake* contracts and by the use of sheer force. But such actions only made the insecurity worse. In the end, the frantic search for resources and positions of authority produced a total rent of the whole social fabric into the two hierarchical social categories of Hutu and Tutsi.

In this climate, the king, unable to arbitrate among the factions or to play on their rivalries to ensure his own personal power, was reduced to allying himself to one of the factions among the elite. The results were, first, that Rugaju totally dominated Gahindiro and later that Nyiramongi and Rwogera completely stalemated each other. And so it came to be that the only firm and unified government during this period was that of Rugaju (c. 1820–c. 1848).

In foreign affairs, the expansion of the population, the famines, and the political uncertainties at the court favored westward emigration. At the same time, the aristocracy's need for cattle, domains, and prestige fostered great raiding expeditions and resulted in the acquisition of new territories to exploit. The result was the more or less accidental incorporation of, among others, Bugesera, Kinyaga, and, in the end, also Gisaka. Thus, thanks to the chaotic cupidity of its elites, the realm more than doubled in size and had, by 1867, acquired the borders it would still have in 1900.

7

Nightmares

The Age of Rwabugiri (1867–1897)

The overwhelming impression one is left with after a study of the age of Rwabugiri and his successors is that of the unrelenting rise of a tide of terror that starts at court and engulfs the whole country, finally erupting into a social crisis that has now lasted for well over a century. We witness here the tragic paradox of increasing centralization (for the court comes to control what happens elsewhere more and more), which sows anarchy as it unfolds.

Yet it is not this theme that has struck historians. In the classical historiography and for some other historians as well, King Rwabugiri was such a great man that his reign put its stamp on an epoch.[1] Supposedly he wrung the reins of power from the elites whom he subdued by means of terror and he established a dictatorial power that, all things considered, turned out to be beneficial. The violence that accompanied his reign was merely unfortunate but a necessary by-product of the process of building a large centralized state: "One does not make an omelet without breaking eggs." For he centralized the country while launching a set of wars that considerably enlarged it. All the changes that had occurred since the previous period owed to his personality. Authoritarian, impetuous, vigorous, and pitiless, he had an unclouded political vision and was a military genius.

But one can reject this interpretation. Rwabugiri was not an extraordinary personage and his reign did not constitute an age apart. One can underline the continuities with the preceding period, not only during the regency, which no one denies, but also beyond this, arguing that while the major directions of a new social and political evolution emerge during his reign and the use of violence with its whole train of consequences starts to become especially prominent, nevertheless, there were precedents for both. The trend did not change, and would not in fact change until after the Belgian conquest of 1916.[2] Despite the fact that he appointed newcomers to important posts, Rwabugiri did not succeed in breaking the hold of the ancient elites, so that, barely a year after his demise, one group among them was able to seize power. In this view, increasing centralization was a by-product of the struggles among the factions at court; the kingdom's wars, for instance, were even more strongly characterized by the vicissitudes of these internal struggles than they had been up to then. As to the king's personality, it needs to be emphasized that he was thoughtless, that he did not succeed in fashioning a clear long-term policy, and that his impetuousness only manifested itself in the unthinking way he reacted to the demands of the moment. Moreover, his authoritarian and irascible character went hand-in-hand with limitless distrust and a lack of personal discipline that made him but prey for the factions at court. As to his military talents, they were rather modest.

Which of these two versions should one choose? As one has seen, we have treated the passage of time between 1867 and 1897 as a separate period, despite evident continuities. This is a period of transition, no doubt, but one during which the dynamics of power are no longer what they were hitherto, and that the alliance of the Germans with, in particular, the court of queen mother Kanjogera, would transform again. To allow for a more nuanced understanding of both the period and Rwabugiri, we will briefly describe the main events that characterized the internal and external policies of the kingdom at the time. But we refuse to be drawn into a set of speculations concerning the king's personality because to us this is a question of secondary importance. It is more important to follow the rise of the tide of violence and its effects, which typifies the period and that will continue to affect the next one.[3]

Political Crises and Wars from 1867 to 1889

Internal politics and externals wars are so intertwined during this period that we will treat them together, and it is the internal politics, rather than the external wars, that are the driving force shaping the kingdom at the time. The dynamics are characterized by a succession of major upsets in the balance of power at the court with an apparent periodicity of about seven to nine years.[4] Each of these cycles was followed by a wave of executions and persecutions as well as a realignment of the various factions. The great turning points were the destruction of the Abagereka around 1869–70, the murder of the queen mother in about 1877, shortly after

Rwabugiri's coming of age, the death of the favorite Nyirimigabo in 1885 or 1886, the proclamation of Rutarindwa as coruler in December 1889, and, finally, the coup d'état at Rucunshu that placed Musinga on the throne in January 1897.[5] In this section, we follow these upheavals and their consequences, except for the last phase of 1889–97, which coincides exactly with the period when the realm's isolation began to crumble, a trend that finally led to the loss of independence.

The enthronement of young Sebizoni,[6] soon to be called Rwabugiri, in preference to Nyamwesa, came as a surprise. While it did not immediately provoke an armed struggle for the succession, that was merely delayed. The choice was a victory for the royal faction of Rwogera over that of Nyiramongi, the queen mother. The victorious faction included several important princely Nyiginya lineages, and it succeeded in rallying Nkoronko, who abandoned the party of his mother Nyiramongi and reconciled himself to Murorunkwere, his divorced wife and the new queen mother. Actually, Rwabugiri was Nkoronko's son rather Rwogera's.[7] Even more important to the royal party was the fact that Rwakagara, the actual leader of the party of his sister Nyiramongi, rallied to its support. He now killed her himself. Thus he separated himself from the other Ega lineage of Nyiramongi's party, that of the Abagereka of Rugereka, who was the son of Byavu and brother of the Nyarwaya whom Rwogera had killed himself. After the demise of Nyarwaya, Rugereka became head of the family and continued to enjoy Nyiramongi's favors and to be her political mainstay. The choice of Sebizoni left him isolated, but he was still too powerful to be sidelined, for he was in command of the imposing Imvejuru army, which had been led by his ancestors since Ndabarasa's time, and he was backed by many influential clients spread over the whole country as well as at court. Moreover, a great drought and a major famine, Cyabaherera, is said to have struck the country at this moment.[8] But every drought always raised doubts about the efficacy of the king. It did so in this case question the legitimacy of the ruler himself since he was both newly installed and a child to boot.

For at least a year, the Abagereka possessed enough power to continue to attempt to discredit the new queen mother. But finally she became strong enough to organize an attack on them led by Nkoronko and Rwampembwe, a son of Nkusi. After a battle near Nyanza between their respective armies, Rugereka was vanquished and killed. All the members of his family and his best-known adherents, more than two hundred aristocrats in all, were also tracked down and killed. It was a hecatomb never to be forgotten.[9]

The considerable possessions of the Abagereka were given to Rutezi, a brother of the queen mother, who thereby was able to begin to strengthen the political weight of his Kono lineage to the detriment of the Ega. But, far from restoring calm, the extermination of the Abagereka by a governmental coalition that was, however, as yet not powerful enough to dominate the political arena, created a temporary vacuum. Acute rivalry erupted among the major chiefs accompanied by a confused free-for-all among lesser chiefs looking for new protectors. Following the massacre, Murorunkwere immediately decreed a campaign against Ndorwa, but the hostility among the armies participating in it threatened to turn it into a civil war and the troops had to be recalled. Whereupon the queen mother sent them to fight Ijwi, making the highly unusual decision to accompany them herself. She entrusted her brother Nzirumbanje with this expedition and everyone camped on Nyamirunde facing Ijwi Island. Apart from a short-lived mutiny by the Abakemba army,[10] the chiefs and their troops became less turbulent. Soon after this campaign, she managed to coax the former pretender Nyamwesa and his brother back from Burundi by promising not to harass them. But as soon as they were back she had them blinded, thereby rendering them unfit to rule. After this clarification of the political situation, calm returned among the chiefs and for the next few years the queen mother's regime did not encounter any serious opposition. Ostensibly, the government and the court were less divided than they had been before. Around 1873, Murorunkwere even succeeded in marrying three daughters of her brother Nzirumbanje to the king all at once, this despite the fact that two of these daughters were already married and had children, whom Rwabugiri now adopted as part of his triple marriage. Among these children, Rutarindwa and Muhigirwa were later to play important roles. These marriages seemed to guarantee that the queen mother of the next reign would come from Murorunkwere's Kono lineage.[11]

Meanwhile, military activity on foreign soil remained limited. There were only two campaigns spread over eleven years and they merely consisted in completing the unfinished business of the previous reign. The preparation for a great raid in Ndorwa with the aim of capturing enough cattle there to reconstitute the herds of ravaged Gisaka had been interrupted by Rwogera's death. Shortly after the question of the succession had been settled, this operation, labeled "the war of Mirama," was undertaken again and ended successfully. A second expedition against Ndorwa, called "the war of Humure," took place immediately after the

Abagereka massacre but, as we saw, had to be aborted.[12] Soon after this, Murorunkwere, as we noted, called up all the chiefs for a campaign against Ijwi, encamping with the troops at Nyamirunde.[13] After a fairly long wait, the troops managed to land on the island with the help of Nsibura, a Havu chief of the west coast of Lake Kivu. But because they were unable to seize Kabego, the king of Ijwi, and hence the "insult" to them remained unpunished, they captured Nsibura and executed him instead, which allowed them to proclaim a great triumph on their return to central Rwanda. Six or seven years followed without any remarkable military activity in foreign parts. But around 1871, an Arab caravan that took the risk of entering the country is said to have been totally destroyed.[14] Was that the one led by Omar Marvati who was detained for three years at the court according to a note dated January 20, 1878?[15] Whatever the case, the lack of direct access to the coastal caravans did not prevent but rather animated indirect commercial activity on the markets of Karagwe, Buganda, and even Bunyoro, where colored mats from Rwanda were in great demand even before 1878.[16]

As time went by the situation worsened. Whether from political calculation or because of a sentimental attachment, Murorunkwere let herself be influenced more and more by one of her favorites, Seruteganya, who was also her lover. He was a Tsobe, just like the leading ritualists of the realm, and probably Tutsi as well, but stemmed from an unremarkable lineage. He was in charge of the tanneries at court when he became a protégé of Rwogera who gave him two herds that had hitherto belonged to a deceased member of his maternal family. During Murorunkwere's rule, he received command of the Cyingogo province and of some domains in Ndiza and Bumbogo, as well as another herd, but he did not succeed in being entrusted with an army command.[17] Nevertheless, Seruteganya became so powerful at the court of the queen mother that he began to eclipse even Nkoronko, which prompted the latter to withdraw his support from the queen mother and ally himself more closely to the young king when he came of age (around 1875). He is thought to have started the rumor that the queen mother was pregnant by Seruteganya, which, if true, would have constituted an unheard-of crime against kingship. At the time, Seruteganya had become so powerful that even Nzirumbanje and his daughters abandoned Nzirumbanje's sister, the aunt of his daughters, to choose the king's side, thus dividing the small Kono lineage issued from Mitari, Murorunkwere's and Nzirumbanje's father. For his part, the leading Tsobe ritualist was convinced that the accusation was true. He took sides against his

Tsobe colleague and proclaimed that the scandal had to end. Finally, Nkoronko and his faction caused such an uproar that the king supposedly ordered the elimination of Seruteganya, but also the safe return of his mother to his residence.[18] Nkoronko, Rwampembwe, and an Ega, son of Rwakagara, were ordered to execute this mission. They did so, and Murorunkwere was killed during the ensuing fight. News of this event provoked great fear in the country. For had the king not killed his own mother?

When he came of age and took command, the king surrounded himself by four influential advisers, two of whom had led the royal party right from the outset of the reign and two of whom he had chosen himself. Foremost among the first was Nyantaba, the descendant of Mazimpaka who commanded the Ingangurarugo, the king's personal army and the best equipped of all, as well as his own army Nyaruguru. Moreover, he was the ritualist who had enthroned the king. The other one was Nyirimigabo, son of Marara, descendant of Gihana and Nyiratunga who was in charge of the Intanganzwa army, which had also played a prominent role at the time of Rwabugiri's accession. At the time of Murorunkwere's death, he was the most heeded of all the king's advisers.[19] The advisers that Rwabugiri had chosen himself were Bisangwa[20] and Mugugu, both from unremarkable families, who owed their standing to the king. Never once during the whole reign, which saw so many fall out of favor, were these two compromised. They kept the king's trust until the end and were the executors of his will. As soon as the powerful party of Nkoronko and his allies abandoned Murorunkwere for Rwabugiri, Nyirimigabo attempted to ruin it, for in Rwogera's day his father Marara had belonged to the royal faction and suffered a good deal at the hands of Nkoronko's and Nyiramongi's faction. He used the death of Murorunkwere to destroy Nkoronko.

For the murder of the queen mother profoundly affected her son. After hesitating for a few months, he fell ill and concluded that this illness could have stemmed from the fact that he had not avenged his mother, for he rejected all personal responsibility in the matter. He charged Mugabwambere, a Tsobe and the commander of the queen mother's own army, to enquire into the matter.[21] He concluded that she had not been pregnant and that her accusers were responsible for her demise. Thereupon a plan of revenge was initiated. It was to last about five years, in part because it was interrupted by a great raiding expedition in Bumpaka. But in large part it took so long mainly because of the eminence of the accused. These included the Tsobe Karamira, the first in rank of the ritualists, as well as Rwampembwe and Nkoronko whose faction was too powerful to be attacked without more ado. With the king's backing, Nyirimigabo ordered the pursuit and the massacre of all the members of this faction one after the other, beginning with its weakest links, the groups affiliated with the Kono and the Tsobe. First, the king married the beautiful Kanjogera, an Ega daughter of Rwakagara, and promoted her brothers Kabare and Ruhinankiko,[22] while the three queens and their father were eliminated. Thus the leading Ega lineage triumphed over the leading Kono lineage, taking its revenge for its defeat at the time of Rwabugiri's accession. After this, he exiled Karamira, whose post was given to Mugabwambere, and several years later he had him killed.

In the case of Rwampembwe and Nkoronko, both army commanders, more caution was required. At the time, both armies were in the field in Ndorwa under Rwampembwe's command. Soon after this campaign, Nyirimigabo found a way to weaken Nkoronko's army, the most formidable one in the kingdom. Little by little he succeeded in luring away its senior officers by giving them the chance to become direct clients of the king. Then he managed to launch a great military campaign against Burundi to mask the fall of both chiefs. Nkoronko's and Rwampembwe's armies were among the mobilized armies and the murder of Nkoronko was to occur in Burundi during a battle with the enemy. But Nkoronko was informed and his army kept its distance from the others during this campaign, known as "the war of Rito." Hence a border raid took place that ended more or less in defeat.[23] Rwampembwe was blamed for this failure and executed, which in turn provoked a series of suicides among women of the highest rank.[24] Meanwhile, the failure of the campaign led to the beginning of a set of long diplomatic negotiations with Burundi that resulted in a nonaggression pact concluded in 1888 or 1889.

The emotions stirred by the events surrounding Rwampembwe's death are said to have inspired Rwabugiri to leave court immediately himself on an expedition to Buhunde with only a single army, albeit it a formidable one, the Uruyange, which had just returned from the borders of Burundi.[25] The king's own participation was an extraordinary event, for, since Ndabarasa, no monarch had accompanied his troops in the field. The excuse given for this operation was that it was necessary because a Hunde chief had rustled Rwandan cattle in Kamuronsi. Following this, and supposedly out of curiosity, the king and his army then penetrated into the forests of Butembo, where there was no cattle to be had.[26] I believe that the goal was rather to raid for ivory, as the traffic in ivory under royal direction was then developing in the Bushubi and Bujinja markets.[27]

On his return to Rwanda the king lingered in Bwishaza. He founded a residence there at Rubengera, the outlet of the well traveled road by the Rugabano pass. After Sakara, which had been founded in 1875–76, this was the second of a set of residences destined to integrate the whole periphery of central Rwanda by the erection of a territorial organization under the direct control of the king. Meanwhile, though, his absence from central Rwanda allowed him to order the execution of his own father, Nkoronko. In 1882, the latter was brought to the border of Burundi where he was killed, supposedly as a liberator of Rwanda.[28] But even after the elimination of Nkoronko's party, Nyirimigabo was not satisfied. He aimed to destroy Nyantaba, the only other person at court who was as powerful as he was. It is not known exactly how he managed to convince the king that Nyantaba was a traitor, but about two years later he finally succeeded in having him arrested and executed.[29] Moreover, he took advantage of the confusion and had a son of Nyantaba murdered on his own initiative.

This wave of persecutions of a sizeable segment of the old aristocratic families and their clients favored the Ega to the detriment of the Kono and ended with the disappearance of the flower of the Nyiginya aristocracy, barring only Nyirimigabo himself. Rwampembwe was replaced by a creature of the king, a person from an undistinguished family, while Nkoronko's army went to a person of lesser social rank.[30] Royal authority benefited, but by eliminating all his Nyiginya rivals, Nyirimigabo benefited even more. He was the only surviving scion of an illustrious family and a favorite at court from the earliest days where his influence now became predominant until his accidental (or not?) death on the battlefield in 1885.

But the king's vengeance was only one of the court's preoccupations. The consolidation of Gisaka and the raiding expeditions in foreign lands claimed its attention as well. When the queen mother was murdered, Rwabugiri was in Buganza and much concerned with Gisaka. Chief Kabaka had succeeded in obtaining its dynastic drum so that the country could be ritually annexed. Rwabugiri founded a royal residence there at Sakara, the first of a new type that he was to establish systematically in all the regions outside of central Rwanda conquered by the realm. These residences were more extensive than earlier ones; they directly ruled over a large region rather than just a hill or two. Even though they were headed by a spouse or a royal maidservant, they also were entrusted to an army commander of the first rank. At Sakara that commander was Kabaka.

Two wars in Ndorwa, both provoked by local chiefs, followed the foundation of Sakara. The leaders of the first expedition, known as "the war of the waters" were still Rwampembwe, Nkoronko, and Nyantaba, but this raid was not a great success, which incited a chief in Ndorwa to proclaim himself king in this ancient realm shortly after their return to Rwanda.[31] In response, Rwabugiri organized a huge expedition from which the three former military leaders were barred.[32] The expedition took place in 1879–80 and expanded northward in the direction of Lake Edward as far as Bumpaka. It captured a huge booty in cattle, most of which the king confiscated, allowing him to establish ten new chiefs as the heads of new official herds.[33] The expeditions to Burundi and to Butembo already mentioned followed this one.

When the king ordered the execution of Nkoronko, he was on the point of invading Ijwi Island yet again. He had succeeded in winning over Nkundiye, one of Kabego's sons who had risen against him. Kabego was killed and Nkundiye installed as his successor. But Ijwi was integrated into the realm and the king built two residences there, each with its own governor. These two were, however, rapidly ousted by Nkundiye. Then Rwabugiri moved to Murera and Bufumbira where he stayed for about two years and where he built several residences. He was there still when the expedition known as "the war of Gikore" broke out south of Lake Bunyoni in Kigezi. Nyirimigabo had provoked this war to seize lands that were under the nominal control of the Abashakamba army. But the autochthons held their ground against the royal troops and the expedition was a failure. Nyantaba was executed during this operation and Nyirimigabo found himself at the pinnacle of his power.

Following this "war of Gikore," the king decided to personally launch a raid in Bushi, which immediately turned into a general war against Kabare, the main kingdom there. The Nyiginya armies were destroyed. It took more than a year to recover from this disaster and to prepare a second expedition," the war of Kanywiriri," to avenge this defeat. Bushi was invaded by a powerful force composed of eight armies, but they underwent more defeats than victories and the expedition was aborted. For the court, this was a disaster because many highly influential chiefs perished there. Nyirimigabo was killed during the first battle at Kanywiriri itself.[34] His death instantly created a huge void at court and immediately provoked a new struggle of influence among the royal favorites of lesser rank. For with him, the last of the great Nyiginya princes had disappeared.[35] With the exception of Kanjogera's brothers, the king' main advisers were now only his "new men" who owed everything to him.

The void created by Nyirimigabo's death was filled momentarily by Ntizimira and Nzigiye, two Tutsi linked to illustrious families, but of unremarkable collateral lineages, whom the king had singled out and protected.[36] Right after the defeat at Kanywiriri, Ntizimira appeared to be the foremost favorite at court, which immediately led to a rebellion in Ijwi. For Nkundiye detested Ntizimira, and so he refused to accept his new position at court and seems to have felt that the defeat at Kanywiriri allowed him to declare his independence. But as soon as Rwabugiri learned of this, he launched an expedition to repress him. Despite some initial difficulties, he managed to invade the island and to kill Nkundiye.[37] This time Rwabugiri left a strong garrison there and thereafter his chiefs maintained effective control.

Meanwhile, Ntizimira and Nzigiye vied with each other at court. Not long after the Ijwi affair, the king had the fiancée of Nzigiye's son marry one of Ntizimira's sons, an insult that Nzigiye attributed to Ntizimira's machinations. He therefore accused his adversary in public during the daily evening meeting at the royal palace of having plotted Nyirimigabo's death on the battlefield. The accusation was all the more credible in that the court itself had concocted a similar plot to rid itself of Nkoronko. Rwabugiri, who wanted to avenge the death of his great favorite, believed him and ordered the assassination of Ntizimira and his sons. Nzigiye also used the occasion to arrange for the massacre of many renowned officers of the Ingangurarugo army who had been friends (and clients?) of Ntizimira.[38] He was rewarded by numerous possessions confiscated from his enemies and above all by the ransom of those whom he pardoned.[39] Following this wave of terror, he became the foremost favorite, but a year or two later in 1889 he was eclipsed by the rise to power of Rutarindwa and Kanjogera.[40]

Isolation Breached and the Hatching of a Coup d'État

It is not known why Rwabugiri took the fateful decision to designate Rutarindwa as his successor and to install him as coruler in December 1889. Later, contemporaries at court who became partisans of Musinga declared that a series of disasters, including a famine, a epizootic epidemic among cattle, smallpox, and an epidemic of jiggers pushed the king to appoint puppet kings. Their role was to combat the catastrophe specified at their accession and hence to relieve the real king of any responsibility. Rutarindwa was supposedly made king to combat the jiggers and in 1894 Muhigirwa was installed to fight the bovid plague.[41] But all these disasters, with the exception of the onset of a great drought, only struck after Rutarindwa's accession. Did the king make this decision because he felt himself to be gravely ill? That does not seem likely, given that he only fell ill during the following year. Was he harassed by the ritualists on the occasion of the first appearance of gray hairs, or again, did he need to sacrifice his life to put an end to the calamities as Schumacher's collaborators would have it?[42] Did a foreboding about the threat that the European posed play a role? A popular tale seems to tie this event to the arrival of the Europeans (though this is yet another anachronism), an arrival that had supposedly been predicted by Nyantaba at the time of his execution.[43]

The most likely reason is that Rwabugiri was forced to act. Apparently, he had soothed his favorite wives and their families for years by promising each one that one of their sons would be chosen.[44] Did such promises raise hopes and exasperate the tensions among these families, especially between Kanjogera's Ega lineage and the Kono lineage of his adopted sons, to the point that there was no way out anymore? What was the advice of his personal and trusted friends of long standing, Bisangwa and Mugugu? And what did different ritualists suggest? We don't know. All we do know is that he came up with a compromise, choosing Rutarindwa, his adopted son, to be his successor, but giving him Kanjogera as an adoptive queen mother. He is even said to have promised to Muhigirwa that he would become king a few years later! But the compromise was too artificial to last and some seem to have foreseen as much at the time.[45]

Rutarindwa's accession coincided with the collapse of the policy of keeping the borders of the country closed. Intercontinental trade on the borders of the country had grown during throughout Rwabugiri's reign, coming mainly from the east, but also from the Rusizi valley.[46] Although the court had no knowledge at all of the 1885 act of the Berlin Conference partitioning Africa, it was conscious of the increasing frequency of European travelers to the east of the country. The passage of Stanley and Emin Pasha in July 1889 was the last prelude to the scramble for colonies. On his return in November 1890, Emin Pasha founded the permanent post of Bukoba and with this colonial conquest began.[47]

Meanwhile, though, the court had come to believe that the Europeans were invincible.[48] How, then, could it prevent their arrival? Faced with this predicament, Rwabugiri had pursued the policy of keeping the borders closed to caravans from the east coast after the departure of Omar Marvati. But Rwandan hawkers and Sumbwa merchants from Nyamwezi continued to participate in intercontinental commerce.[49] These hawkers appeared on the markets of Nduga and Marangara, which were part of the Lake Kivu commercial network, and even at Save in the south, which facilitated the spread of their products all over the country.[50] The most important part of this commerce consisted in official consignments of ivory, female slaves, and children to the markets of Bushubi and Bujinja. Rwabugiri had been involved in this trade since his accession, obtaining luxury goods, textiles and some guns from it, and had established a warehouse to store these products. The expedition of Butembo in 1882 was probably in part a raid for ivory and his decision to settle part of his personal guard at Minove, west of Lake Kivu, in around 1888 might also be explained by his desire to collect ivory and slaves.[51] Kabaka, chief of Gisaka, was his commercial agent in dealings with Bushubi. He is thought to have advised the king to considerably reduce the volume of this commercial traffic so as not to attract the attention and the greed of the Europeans. But his advice was not heeded.[52]

In any case the effectiveness of this policy of participation from afar collapsed when, despite the closure of the borders, a number of diseases carried by the traders spread into the country.[53] The country was recovering from a drought that had struck from 1889 to 1891,[54] when rinderpest appeared, which was immediately followed by an outbreak of foot-and-mouth disease. That was introduced in 1892 by infected cows that had been raided in Ndorwa and presented by a chief to the court, then in Kinyaga, a gesture he payed for with his life.[55] The rinderpest destroyed about 90 percent of all affected cattle[56] and very few herds could be led to safety before they were struck.[57] Foot-and-mouth disease killed others. These epizootic diseases led to the dissolution of many *ubuhake* contracts because of the death of the cattle involved. As soon as the rinderpest passed, the king began to reconstitute his herds by taking a large number of the surviving cattle in all the herds.[58] He then redistributed them anew among the great chiefs and by reconstituting his *ubuhake* ties thus reaffirmed his power. Hence most of the surviving cattle fell into the hands of the most powerful chiefs while the small herders were ruined.[59] Many of them did not recover and became Hutu farmers.

The next year a murderous smallpox epidemic that started in Burundi broke out as well, in addition to an epidemic of jiggers, which incapacitated Rutarindwa himself.[60] The smallpox plagued the country during several years. In 1895 it was smallpox still that provoked Rwabugiri's withdrawal from Nkore.[61] And finally, after 1893, several invasions by locusts ruined the harvests.[62]

The foreigners followed. Rwabugiri is believed to have defeated Rumaliza, a famous trafficker in slaves and ivory, first in 1887 or 1888 and later on the banks of the Kivu River in December 1891.[63] But Oscar Baumann crossed the south of the country in September 1892 without let or hindrance. He was followed in May–June 1894 by von Götzen who crossed the kingdom diagonally from Gisaka to Bugoyi and visited Rwabugiri at Kageyo. In August of the same year, Lieutenant Wilhelm Langheld traveled in Ndorwa and north of Buganza. This was the first official colonial circuit, for he was head of the Bukoba residence.

The wars of Bushubi, which broke out in 1890 on the occasion of a struggle for the succession in that country, must be placed within this overall context. One of the pretenders, Nsoro, called on the Nyiginya for help and Rwabugiri sent elements of five different armies to reinstate him. But his adversary did not give up and a second Nyiginya expedition under the leadership of Kabaka, the military commander of Gisaka, occupied the country for several months. This force was eventually recalled because an epidemic broke out in Bushubi.[64] The expedition then brought the new king of Bushubi and his family back with them before executing them without further ado. Soon thereafter Rwabugiri fell seriously ill[65] and this disease was attributed to the vengeance of Nsoro's spirit. Whereupon the king had Kabaka executed to satisfy this vengeance.[66] Meanwhile, Bushubi had collapsed and Kasasura, king of western Bujinja, henceforth attracted trade to his country. Rwabugiri then appointed Mugugu, his long time favorite, to the command of Gihunya and entrusted him with overseeing the official trade between the court and Bujinja.[67]

Meanwhile, Rwabugiri himself had visions of conquest in Bushi. A young child had just been enthroned there under his mother's regency and at the same time famine had struck. The king saw this as an extraordinarily good occasion to invade the region. He raised a very large army, composed of elite companies provided by the most renowned military commanders, and he invaded Bushi. After a murderous campaign, he succeeded in occupying most of the country but failed to capture either the king or the queen mother. They had fled with their dynastic drum to the piedmont of the Rusizi valley.[68] The local king there refused to surrender them, which triggered a second campaign. This time around the queen mother was captured and executed, but the young king escaped. Thereupon Rwabugiri left his guard encamped there and returned to the center of the country. Some time later however, in the spring of 1894, these soldiers began to feel so threatened that a general mutiny broke out in their ranks. They deserted in large numbers and returned home. As there were far too many to all be executed, the king contented himself by depriving their families of their possessions, which were then granted to others.[69]

Thus once again Bushi eluded him. The king at once organized a new expedition and by the end of July 1894 had gathered troops at ku-Mira. But just when he was about to join them there himself, he learned that Ntare, the king of Nkore, had launched a great raid on official herds in the part of Ndorwa that was under Nyiginya control. Rwabugiri turned around and went to war against Nkore in September or October. He reached Ntare's capital, went beyond it, and defeated the Nkore several times, even those detachments that were armed with guns. But by late February or early March 1895, smallpox broke out in his army and he had to abandon his campaign.[70] Moreover, he knew that an English officer as well as the German resident of Bukoba were both preparing to go to war against him if he did not withdraw. Shortly after his return to central Rwanda he learned that Ntare had died.[71] He then returned to his plan for the conquest of Bushi, but fell ill on the way and died in September 1895 on the boat that was bringing him back to Kinyaga.[72] His death triggered the immediate loss of Bushi, Ijwi Island, and other territories. As a storyteller puts it: "All the foreign countries that Rwabugiri had defeated reconstituted themselves, all of them! No foreigner remained within the country. They all reconstituted themselves right away."[73]

At court, the ritualists recognized and installed Rutarindwa as king with Kanjogera as his queen mother.[74] His accession launched an unspoken struggle between the Ega and the royalists. Both parties had military forces but those of Bisangwa, Mugugu, and especially the Nyaruguru army of Muhigirwa combined were far stronger than those of the opposition. Despite this advantage, and disregarding Muhigirwa's advice, Rutarindwa did not attack his enemies. But Kanjogera succeeded in having Mugugu—with whom she had earlier clashed over revenues from Gisaka—murdered. The situation was thus already quite tense when it was then learned that a Belgian officer had established a post at Shangi.[75] After a long debate about the invincibility of Europeans, the brothers of Kanjogera managed to convince the court to send an army

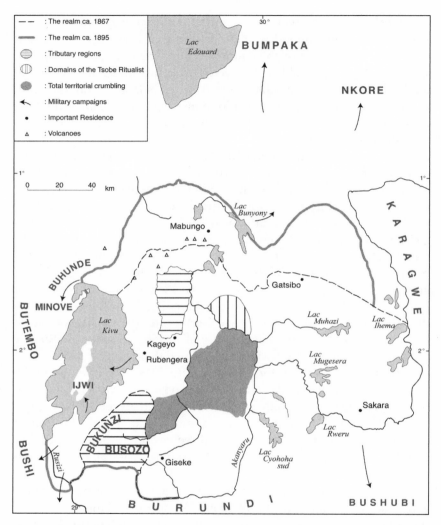

The Rwanda of Rwabugiri

there led by Bisangwa and Muhigirwa. The post was attacked by four elite companies, about six hundred warriors in all, who were decimated in minutes by regular volleys of gunfire. Bisangwa returned to attack again but was killed on the spot. As to Muhigirwa, he withdrew with his army and headed back home to Nyaruguru. After the demise of Bisangwa, several partisans of the king were murdered on the orders of Kanjogera or condemned to death by her. Finally, a direct confrontation

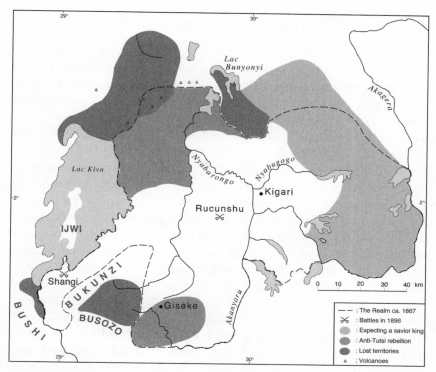

The realm in 1897

between the king and the Ega lineage of Kanjogera erupted by accident at Rucunshu in December 1896. After bitter fighting, which cost the lives of hundreds of warriors, the king and his party perished. It was mainly an Ega triumph, but also a Tsobe success.

In February 1897, Kanjogera had Musinga, her son, who was then about thirteen or fourteen years old, enthroned. But this assumption of power was immediately contested and continued to be so for many years to come. It is likely that without German backing, Musinga would not have been able to remain on the throne. But by the end of March 1897, only a few months after his accession, von Ramsay, a German officer, appeared at court and proposed an alliance between the king and the colonial authorities that Kanjogera immediately accepted. Thus began the colonial era. During the following twenty years, however, the German authorities did not interfere with the internal affairs of the realm and thus the customary intrigues and violence continued as before.[76]

The Nightmare of Violence Used as a Political Tool

What stands out from the overview of the political history of the realm at this time that we have just sketched is the growing role of violence during the period, not just in the practice of government, but also more generally in society as a whole. Rugamba observes that "in this society one is respected in as far as one has power"[77] during this period. This is so true that the slogan of it might well be "Might makes Law."[78] Yet in the eyes of the bulk of the population the legitimacy of the Nyiginya government did not rest on sheer might. It had always been based on the mystical quality of the king as expressed and periodically reaffirmed by the appropriate rituals. It was the ritual face of royalty that guaranteed order and prosperity. In this perspective, physical coercion was only an accessory. But the experience of rule had taught the courtiers especially that the manipulation of physical force was the true key to success. For did a man's prestige not rest in the first place on his exploits in war? The personal panegyrics celebrated violence and wallowed in detailed descriptions of the wounds, the mutilations, and the tortures inflicted on one's enemy. This use of brute force, or the threat of its use, had become the ultimate tool guaranteeing subjection long before Rwabugiri came on the scene. But what is novel from the very start of Murorunkwere's rule is the blaze of violence attested to by the number of massacres[79] and the frequency with which her government resorted to force. Rwabugiri's reign is punctuated by successive waves of persecution and executions from which no one was immune. Terror ruled.

Why this blaze of violence? It was not the result of a ubiquitous anarchy; to the contrary, it was engendered by the very regime that was ruling. One cannot attribute it to Rwabugiri's character either, even though is said to have been sanguinary. For the blaze began before he came of age and was to continue until the installation of the Belgian colonial regime, long after his demise. Yes, one can reply that the political regime of the kingdom had always been based on a certain degree of violence and that this period was no different from ones preceding it. Yet it is evident that resorting to violence became much more common during this age than at any time before. One must look for the cause of the more frequent use of violence in the changes that affected the composition of the elites and their mutual interrelations, especially after the king came of age.

The new elements were a very active king and a new elite surrounding him whose members were men of modest origins, men such as

Bisangwa and Mugugu, or men such as Ntizimira, Nzigiye, and even Kabaka, who, although of more aristocratic families, belonged to undistinguished lineages. These men were faithful because they owed everything to the king. But these upstarts were confronted by a government that remained in the hands of the old elite, by now a true aristocracy, precisely in opposition to these "new men" of the king. Yet, at the same time, this exalted nobility continued to devour itself as the number of its members grew, and as some groups, such as Rugereka's, succeeded in concentrating great wealth and great power in their hands.[80] The massacre of the Abagereka was a consequence of their success. But this event did not stop anyone; every ambitious aristocrat still continued to try to concentrate as much power and wealth as possible in his own hands. As these struggles unfolded, the presence of a king or a queen mother remained essential, however, if only as a platform for action. For the hostilities mainly consisted in accusations being brought to the king in the hope that he would order the destruction of one's enemy, whereupon the accuser would be granted the enjoyment of the possessions of the fallen in his name. Thus Rwabugiri was a pivot in the functioning of this regime. Yet he could not do himself without help of the aristocracy, as he discovered after Nyirimigabo's death when most of the high nobility had been swept from the scene. It appeared as if he finally had obtained personal despotic powers based on the support of a mass of common people.[81] But, paradoxically, it was then that he realized that if he did not want to see the kingship disappear he could not dispense with the aristocracy, for its participation was essential to ensuring the royal succession. It is then that he fashioned the disastrous compromise between Kono and Ega.

In the last analysis, then, the blaze of violence owed to the growing number of adversaries facing each other. In the end, this overgrowth of the aristocracy generated a sort of anarchy in which everyone threatened every one else and in which an active king was always ready to give credence to any accusation and to order its immediate resolution. The nearly permanent recourse to violence finally engendered so much tension and created such a climate of insecurity among the common people as well as among the elites that it succeeded in dissolving the cohesion of even the most basic social groups. Everyone reacted by resorting to violence him- or herself, hoping thereby to rid oneself of one's enemies and to build up wealth so as to obtain more power.

We begin this section with an exploration of the institutionalized role of violence in the government of the realm, examining the armies, wars, and spoliations of the court. Then we discuss the struggle to acquire possessions in the context of centralization, the accelerated exploitation of the population in general, and the local disorders that resulted from this. Finally, we come to the consequences: a significant degree of social disaggregation and an increase in the number of popular revolts, inspired or not by a millenarian utopia.

Ever since the end of the eighteenth century, wars had been one of the main instruments of power of the Nyiginya kingdom. They were essential in the first place as a means of importing new wealth into the country to endow the elites and the kings. Most of this wealth assumed the form of cattle, but women and children who could be sold into slavery. Ivory for exchange in foreign trade also became more and more important over time. Under Rwabugiri, most foreign expeditions were raids whose purpose was to acquire cattle.[82] Gisaka was totally devastated both by its conquest and by the later raids by Rwabugiri, raids that then apparently triggered the first expedition into Ndorwa with the aim of restocking Gisaka with new herds. At the same time, the restocking of the herds also allowed the introduction of a new Rwandan order there based on *ubuhake* contracts.[83] With his part of the booty from these raids, the king could set up new official herds and use them to promote his authority. But soon the king was no longer satisfied with his portion of the booty from such expeditions. After the second campaign against Ndorwa, he decreed that from that point forward the king would divide the booty himself, thereby enabling him to take the largest portion of it.[84] We know the source of eleven out of fifteen new official herds whose constitution is attributed to Rwabugiri. Almost two thirds of these new herds (seven) stemmed from booty, of which five came from the single campaign in Bumpaka, and about a third (four) derived from the spoliation of chiefs.[85] Rwabugiri gave his first three herds to his favorites, but used almost every one of the next eight herds to supply the services and the food necessary to keeping up the new kind of residences he had instituted. These herds were essential to the endowment of these new residences and benefited both the women who managed them and the leaders he appointed as governors of them. Thus Kanjogera acquired a lot of revenue as the manager of two residences, while the foundation of Bisangwa's power was his military control of the provinces that were ruled from Rubengera.[86]

Actually, wars benefited the great noble families at least as much as they did the king. If Gisaka had been emptied of its herds before 1867, where had these cattle gone? If the king gained five herds in Bumpaka, how many went to his commanders? If the king truly needed bovid booty to establish residences and to obtain faithful men, such men were for the most part not newcomers at all but old aristocrats. Lastly, the unceasing competition among members of the elite meant that each leader needed ever more cattle to attract ever more clients so as to surpass and eventually destroy his rivals. This is the reason why war was at least as welcome to the aristocrats at court as to the king, despite the losses they sustained, for many among them remained on the battle-fields from one war to the next.[87]

Were wars waged in a systematic fashion in order to conquer foreign lands? The answer to this question is not clear. The will to conquer and to incorporate is incontrovertible with respect to the small independent enclaves in the kingdom, such as those to the northwest. The king founded residences by force of arms and sometimes established reserved domains staffed by military units to gather tribute. This was also the case for the small territories north of the volcanoes and in Kigezi. But in the most celebrated instances, those of Ijwi and Bushi, annexation and effective conquest seem to have been an accidental outcome of a set of raids. The first campaigns were a set of more or less unfortunate raids, followed by reprisals ordered by a Rwabugiri who was insulted by his initial lack of success. The king then committed a larger number of forces to the expedition and made the objective the capture or assassination of the enemy's king to punish him for his insolence. After great victories, as on Ijwi, the territories were then occupied, residences founded, and reserved domains granted. Finally, the will to formally annex a country was reflected in the search for the local dynastic drums. Their capture put the final seal on the annexation process.[88]

Whether inspired by greed or by policy, wars were far more frequent during Rwabugiri's personal rule than before. There were thirteen campaigns over less than twenty years, which amounts to saying that the country was at war two years out of every three. And that doesn't even include the border raids by local chiefs such as that Munigankiko, who brought rinderpest into the country, which, although collective memory is silent on the matter, one suspects were certainly as numerous as the official operations. Given the frequency of wars and their economic significance for the country, it is not surprising to learn that eight new armies were raised during Rwabugiri's own rule.[89] But on closer examination one observes that they were not important armies. Among them only the royal guard, the Ingangurarugo, became a first-class army with seven main companies. Further, and this is wholly unexpected, far from increasing the total strength of all of his military forces, Rwabugiri actually dismantled most of the existing great armies to the point that at the end of his reign only Muhigirwa's Nyaruguru and Kabare's Uruyange armies were still at full strength.[90] For the armies were too loyal to their commanders, as Imvejuru was to Rugereka and Inzirabwoba to Nkoronko, or they were mutinous as the Abakemba army had been during the first campaign against Ijwi when it rose up with the aim of choosing its own chief. The court undermined the power of such great armies in three main ways: by separating them from their official herds, which deprived their commanders of the means to establish patronage and hence diminished their prestige,[91] by luring away some officers to make them direct clients of the king as happened in the case of Nkoronko's army, and by detaching whole combatant units to create a new army with them. Thus Bisangwa's new army was but a detached portion of Abakemba.[92] These measures allowed the court to regain some control over the armies, although the mutiny of ku-Mira toward the end of the reign revealed the limits of its power.

Moreover, the role of the armies changed over time. Eventually, a whole army was no longer mobilized for a great campaign. Instead, an expeditionary force was constituted out of a number of combatants companies from within several armies.[93] This approach diminished the independence of each army and its revenue from booty.[94] Moreover, nearly all the armies were territorialized and tied to a specific locality, residence, or marcher camp[95] and the previously nonterritorial character of the army was only maintained for a portion of its recruits. The dangers of such a territorialization soon became evident in Bugoyi, especially when several armies began to quarrel and even to fight for control over some bits of land.[96]

War was but one manifestation of the politics of violence. Judiciary violence directed against one's rivals was another one. Its mechanism consisted of accusations launched at court. One praises Bisangwa "because he did not accuse others, seeking to have them killed in order to obtain their possessions or to be well-spoken of. . . . Thus he intervened for those who had been denounced to Rwabugiri and whom he wanted to kill. They were denounced by the members of their own families and they corrected themselves."[97]

Such accusations or denunciations made during the evening meetings were the main tool of the courtiers for eliminating their adversaries, whether for the purpose of obtaining their wealth or out of sheer hatred. It was a terrible weapon in part because of the king's character.

Rwabugiri, who was touchy, impulsive, irascible, very suspicious by nature, and thought himself to be crafty, was easily convinced of treason. Quite frequently he immediately condemned the accused and his whole family to death, sparing a child to provide for their ancestor worship. In the proceedings, even the condemned's clients lost their possessions and sometimes their lives. The accusation was above all a political tool and it is through denunciations that this credulous or Machiavellian king ratified the shifts in power that occurred during his reign. Thus one first saw Nyirimigabo direct wholesale massacres against his Nyiginya rivals for years by accusing them of complicity in the murder of the queen mother. Then, new men succeeded in bringing down great pillars of the regime. Nzigiye, for example, ruined Nyantaba, even though the latter had been the most devoted and important of Rwabugiri's partisans at his accession, and, at a more regional level, Ntizimira succeeded in destroying a great many notables in Bwishaza and Kinyaga.[98]

After Nyirimigabo's death, Nzigiye cried foul and managed to get rid of his rival Ntizimira, a set of bothersome officers of the guard, and even members of Nyirimigabo's family, despite the fact that he represented himself as Nyirimigabo's avenger. By 1885, the old Nyiginya guard was gone except for two or three chiefs who were ill-considered at court, but, and this is an ironic reversal, who survived thanks to the protection of one of the king's "new men."[99] The struggle then continued among rivals of the king's men, as well as among all of them and the old *ibibanda* families at court, especially Kanjogera's.[100] And, in the end, indeed, as early as 1896, she supplanted them all.

The king and the denouncers, the former rivals of the now deceased, then grew rich on the spoils. For spoliations of the great herders produced a lot of cattle. One third of Rwabugiri's new official herds stemmed from judicial spoliations. Thus one royal son was endowed with several thousand head of cattle all at once when the commander of the Abakemba army fell out of favor and was executed.[101] It is then not surprising, then, that sometimes the only motive for a denunciation was lust for the goods of the accused.[102]

At a less exalted level, denunciation, disgrace, execution were everyday events. Thus denunciations to Rwabugiri literally transformed a struggle between big men into a fight to the death. The whole reign is characterized by a series of cascading disgraces accompanied by many executions. A first effect of this pattern of disgrace followed by execution was that almost everywhere one saw a rapid turnover of chiefs at the head of almost all important institutions, be they armies, residences, official herds, reserved domain, posts of chiefs of the land or of the long grass. Even some of the foremost ritualists were executed. The numerous replacements of key posts in the realm have often been interpreted as having resulted from a royal will to centralize the realm, but it is more likely that it was but one effect of the internecine struggle that devoured the courtiers and that Rwabugiri's condemnations owed more to his credulity than to his supposedly Machiavellian cunning. Apparently, the king did not even seek to increase his own personal power by replacing aristocrats with his creatures, for even a cursory check of the known replacements of the leaders of armies and official herds shows that he did not.[103] Yes, many scions of illustrious lineages were ousted, but many other children, sometimes from the same lineages, were also appointed and sometimes to the same position. One discerns no trace at all here of a planned royal policy, but merely the fatality of violence without bounds. The king seems to have been more the toy than the master of this autodestructive elite of courtiers.

The result of all these struggles were the great waves of massacres, from the extermination of the Abagereka (c. 1868–169) to those that followed upon Murorunkwere's murder (1877–82), Nyirimigabo's death (1885–87/88), and the coup at Rucunshu (1896–1898). Exterminations on a smaller scale (that is involving "only" from ten to twenty people) did occur, however, throughout the reign and after. The last one dates from 1912 or 1913.[104]

But each execution triggered consequences that could last for a generation. For each condemnation fanned the flames of new hatreds and new vengeances to be satiated. Despite the attempts to exterminate all the male members of a family, a survivor often remained, even, for instance, among Rugereka's descendants.[105] Moreover, sometimes the king felt obliged to return important posts to the descendants of the chief he had persecuted. He was sickly and when he fell ill he sometimes attributed his illness to the vengeance wreaked by someone who had been executed. To return a post to the family of the deceased was a way to redress that situation.[106] But it did not settle much. For the family naturally attempted to avenge those who had made accusations against it. Actually, vengeance was a duty imposed by the worship of the ancestors. Hence when family members succeeded in capturing the culprit or a member of his family, it was proper to torture them in front of the shrine that commemorated their ancestor. The more cruel the torture inflicted, the better the deceased was avenged. There were cases that lasted for several days and were exceptionally cruel.[107]

In addition, each act of vengeance might lead to one of countervengeance. Thus the waves of executions had a cumulative effect. As the reign progressed, more and more accounts remained to be settled and the elite, in particular, tore itself apart more and more. But not just the elite. A local tale about a certain Sebihubi narrates a case of vengeance at the local level between relatives of the same lineage.[108] As to the aristocracy, it was destroyed to a large extent by these massacres and the cycle of vengeance and countervengeance that followed in their wake. Thus another one of the effects of the violence was an (unintentional) alleviation of the pressure caused by the constant growth in the size of the upper nobility. Although precise numbers are lacking, it is clear that the massacres, even more than the losses during combat, decimated the ranks of the nobility.[109] Yet the sizeable loss of human life also contributed to the concentration of power, especially at the level of the great chiefs.

While judiciary violence justified the spoliations practiced at the court, simple spoliation was the rule on the hills, especially in the center of the kingdom and in Kinyaga. Favorites who were clients of the king or even of great chiefs were granted reserved domains without regard to the rights of the current occupants. Moreover, there were at least as many men of low extraction as members of illustrious families among the favorites of the king who were thus endowed. A person parachuted into a region, took pastures and arable land, and no one could be sure of exactly what he had obtained. Naturally, the old masters tried to resist these incursions.[110] Similarly, new leaders parachuted in as chiefs of the long grass or of the land abused their power and extorted all sorts of arbitrary tributes and corvée labor from their subjects. Appointments of this sort, especially endowments with reserved domains, almost invariably triggered a series of quarrels that erupted from time to time into violent fights on the hills, pitting the newcomers against the previous officeholders who lived there. At this local level, the nobles then jointly opposed the upstarts. Sooner or later they attacked the despised newcomers and tried to kill them or drive them out. For them, these new men were Hutu, even if they were of Tutsi or Hima descent, because they did not issue from an illustrious family. The slightest insult toward a member of the nobility then provoked a private armed response.[111] Finally, and in spite of Rwabugiri's support for some of his local representatives, the old elite managed so well that in the end not one family of Rwabugiri's new men managed to keep a sizeable fortune. In addition, especially along the borders, other local disturbances were caused by private expeditions into foreign lands for the purpose of raiding cattle and even by armed confrontations between units of different armies that were garrisoned there.[112] Overall, one cannot but conclude that the use of violent, armed force and an appeal to the right of the strongest were endemic at the local level and that the king and his representatives merely let it happen.

This overall context allows one to better appreciate the effort toward centralization undertaken by Rwabugiri. Its first and most significant element was the creation of a new sort of residence. At the time of Muro-runkwere's assassination the king was at Sakara, in Gisaka, waging war. He founded his first residence of the new type there. It received jurisdiction not just over a few hills, as had been the case with residences before founded before it, but over all three provinces of Gisaka. He endowed it with official herds, with a chief of the long grass, and with an army led by a commander who held supreme authority in parallel to one of the king's wives or maidservants. Sakara was entrusted to Kabaka, but the king left the provincial chiefs in place as his subordinates. The latter, a Gisakan nobleman and an army commander of the Gisakan army called Abarasa, succeeded in finding Gisaka's dynastic drum and its handing over sealed the formal incorporation of the country into the Nyiginya kingdom. But for the aristocratic courtiers Kabaka remained a new-comer and Rwabugiri's creature. He had obviously been chosen because other chiefs were not successful in quelling the continual local insurrections. Further, he and his army were easily accepted because they were natives of Gisaka.

Thereafter Rwabugiri established other residences of this sort, especially on the western and northern periphery of the realm. The most famous one was Rubengera. Its territory stretched from Bwishaza to beyond Bugoyi northwards and it was commanded by Bisangwa, the commander of the royal guard Inganguraruog. On the other hand Rwabugiri did not alter the organization or the extent of the existing residences at all in the center of the realm. When he died the kingdom counted twenty-one official residences, two thirds of which though were still of the old classic type and included only a very small domain. This is why a map showing residences as if they were the capitals of a homogeneous royal administration is wholly misleading.[113] In fact a certain centralization obtained only west of the Nile-Congo divide (and even so without Bukunzi and Busozo), in Mutara, and in Gisaka, But to what extent did this centralization result from a clear political vision of Rwabugiri, to what extent was it but a practical solution to subjugate regions that were difficult to overcome, and to what extent was it merely an outcome of the search of the courtiers to find new positions for their noble sons? To my mind the last two motives predominated by far. For I don't see evidence for a true will to centralize, in the sense of a systematic will to implant direct royal authority by means of a homogeneous bureaucracy composed of men who were particularly indebted to the king.

Similarly, the endowment of reserved domains and the assignment of chiefs of the land and the long grass did not manifest a will to centralize or even a desire to introduce the king's men everywhere. These appointments seem to have been but an effect of the rise and ebb of political struggles at court. The frequent removal of chiefs from office resulted from the same dynamics, since the great majority of new appointments ended up in the hands of the same nobility that had held them earlier on.[114] Even the breakup of the great armies seems to have been motivated in part by the need to find new positions for courtiers and in part by the wish to curtail the might of the great military commanders rather than by a desire to establish a centralized and homogeneous royal army.[115] Still, all these developments did strengthen the centralizing power of the court and the king.

In this context, one must also mention the king's ceaseless travels. He was nearly always on the road in the country, which, once again, has been interpreted as reflecting a deliberate will on his part to impose his authority directly without any intermediaries. But, in practice, his traveling constituted a provocation and a source of irritation and oppression because of the constant looting that accompanied it. Here is a case that struck the imagination. Rwabugiri arrived in the domain of a well-to-do lady; she saw how the Twa of his guard were pillaging and destroying the crops and so complained to him. But he merely replied that this was a case of normal foraging and refused to intervene. So, when she got back home, she tipped over her many beehives and her furious bees chased the Twa away. Apparently, the king appreciated this gesture and did not punish her for having "rebelled."[116] But in other cases, clashes of this sort provoked serious insurrections, such as those at Save around 1890. Thus the frequent passage of the king exacerbated local conflicts rather than eliminated them, which certainly did not help to centralize the realm.

One might also credit a centralizing effect to the epizootic epidemics since one of their effects was that the king ended up seizing all the remaining cattle and redistributing them to the chiefs, as happened, for instance, between 1892 and 1895, although such confiscation did engender some bitter resistance, as, for example, in Cyingogo in 1894. It is significant, however, that the king used these opportunities to restore the status quo rather than to reinforce the power of his new men and to eliminate the aristocrats, although, actually, he probably could not have done this without provoking a generalized uprising of the nobility.

The growing turmoil and insecurity during the reign were so significant that in the end they destabilized the solidarity of even the most cohesive social groups and led to a certain amount of social disaggregation. One sees this in the evolution of the number of *ubuhake* contracts. The frequency of the downfall of even the most powerful patrons was such that many people of lesser social rank no longer sought protectors among the most powerful for fear that the disgrace of their patron would also drag them down. Moreover, clients lost even the protection they looked for when they concluded such contracts, whether it be with army commanders or other patrons. For, in practice, the commander or other patron intervened only on behalf of his favorites and even then only to the degree that by so doing the existing balance of power would remain favorable to him.[117] Thus even at the level of the hill, arbitrary behavior, based on the threat of power, was eroding the regulatory function of the institution, replacing it with pure and simple coercion. Consequently, people of modest rank no longer looked for patrons. The number of *ubuhake* contracts seems to have dropped considerably and the people were well aware of it, since a prophetic tale foretelling "the end of *ubuhake*" apparently refers to this period and not to colonial times.[118] The new clients were mostly people whom a powerful man could force into contracts. In this perspective the epizootic epidemics of 1890–91 had at least the merit of freeing some clients, for the death of all their cattle also brought their liberation.

A similar phenomenon occurred at the level of kinship groups, especially in the most exalted circles and among those most directly involved in power struggles. Rwabugiri set the example. Not only did he kill his father and his mother, but toward the end of his life he openly lived in incest with his daughter Berabose.[119] The most powerful lineages broke up. Thus one sees a Kono brother, Nzirumbanje, actively collaborate in the downfall of his sister Murorunkwere, just as his daughters also actively strove to have their aunt killed.[120] A Tsobe ritualist of the highest rank condemned not only his distant kinsman Seruteganya, but also one of his closest relatives, Mugabwambere, and was the cause of his elimination.[121] Among the Ega, one recalls Rwakagara personally killing his sister Nyiramongi after Rwogera's death. Later, his daughter Kanjogera was accused of having killed or provoked the death of her own brother

Giharamagara during the Butembo expedition.[122] Shortly after the coup at Rucunshu, Kabare and Ruhinankiko, Kanjogera's brothers, clashed, and she finally renounced both of them. One may certainly call this a rise of individualism, but, if so, then it was individualism in a climate of "every man for himself."

One might observe that all these cases concern only people at the very pinnacle of the social pyramid and hence those who were the most exposed to the risks of politics. But the beginnings of disaggregation are also apparent at much less exalted levels. Thus in Bwanamukari, a certain Sebihubi denounced at court a rival who belonged to a collateral branch of his lineage. The man was the father-in-law of a survivor of the Abagereka who was still being tracked down. The man was put to death. But later on the injured branch of the family managed to secure Sebihubi's condemnation, and he was therefore to be executed with his whole family. He lost his spouses and his grandchildren and in his panic he was about to kill one of his older grandchildren who was holding him up in his flight, but one of his cousins who was fleeing with him saved the child.[123] The case is fascinating because it not only shows a rift in ties of kinship, but also solidarity operating within the kin group. One understands why Sebihubi's close cousins would remain devoted to him since all his paternal relatives seem to have been slated for extermination. The loyalty of the father-in-law to his son-in-law even when the man was being tracked down is perhaps more surprising than the loyalty of a paternal uncle to a grandchild.

This case gives us reason to reject any generalizations. All ties were not weakened, in part because collective responsibility unified people doomed to the same fate, and in part because individualism had progressed to the point where everyone cherished some relatives over others. Moreover, this disaggregation did not affect to any degree at all the requirement that the group show solidarity in pursuing revenge. Thus Rwabugiri was forced by his illness to avenge his mother and, after another illness, the followers of Ryangombe seem to have obliged him to make some appointments in restitution to descendants of lineages that had been exterminated. Indeed, certain offspring of lineages condemned to death were spared in order to carry out the worship of their dead. All in all, then, people still accepted that there was a religious foundation to the duty to demonstrate solidarity among relatives, despite a certain degree of disaggregation.[124]

Finally, one might also understand the scission of society into the Tutsi and Hutu social categories as a case of disaggregation between a ruling class and its subjects, at the level of the whole society. Given the Tutsi vengeance against the "Hutu" Nkiramacumu (c. 1889),[125] the anti-Tutsi uprising instigated by Nyirafugi, and the killing of Mbanzabugabo (1897–98?), which all occurred in the same region, it is hard to pretend that the rift had not by then occurred.[126] But to interpret this cleavage only as an effect of a general social disaggregation is disingenuous. For, one should bear in mind that this rift did not directly grow out of personal insecurity or from violence in general but from the *institutionalization* of a humiliating differentiation made between Tutsi and Hutu in the exploitation of the population both within the armies and especially within the corvée labor imposed on farmers but not on herders. The struggles at court, the multiplication of local authorities, the increase in local turmoil, and the court's increasing interference in local arenas went hand-in-hand with the ever-increasing exploitation of the population that we discussed in chapter 5. The apogee was the introduction of *uburetwa*. An anecdote about the rout of a Hutu unit assaulted by the Nkore army at the end of 1894 or in early 1895 alludes to *uburetwa*. A counterattack of the Ingangurarugo (all Tutsi) redressed the situation. But a resentful Rwabugiri supposedly decreed that the Hutu could farm for themselves by night, since by day they would have to work for the courageous Tutsi![127] Can one conceive of a more unbearable oppression? This exaction was invented between 1870 and 1876 in Cyingogo and spread first into Kinyaga during the 1880s before being adopted in central Rwanda during the 1890s, at the very moment when the great natural disasters broke out in the country.[128] At this point, the least straw would suffice to break the camel's back.

It was the bulk of the population that suffered most from the politics of violence during this whole age. And, in first place, through the devastation caused by the armies. Remember the theaters of war where men were killed, where women and small girls were captured, where houses, and sometimes the crops as well, were burned.[129] The local population could only flee more or less far away, for a more or less limited period of time. Farm production suffered and local food shortages appeared. Let us also not wholly forget the depredations caused by military might, sometimes used to gather tribute, as Rwabugiri did at Kageyo in 1894.[130] His work there was visible from the other side of the upper Nyabarongo:

> A mountain range rose before us like a gigantic wall and on the slopes one saw blazing fires and thick clouds of smoke issuing from

burning villages everywhere. Schirangawe declared in a triumphant tone of voice that that was his father gathering the dues of the inhabitants and punishing them for their recalcitrance.[131]

Just as important was the devastation caused by an army on the march, even in friendly country. The foragers, and sometimes even the combatant companies themselves, pillaged[132] the harvests that were in the field or stocked in the granaries and requisitioned cattle for slaughter, not to mention what they stole along the way. The inhabitants of one or more hills frequently had to provide food for hundreds or even thousands of people (since the armies included many women and servants). The devastation of an army on the march was comparable to an invasion by locusts and in the heart of the country such plundering occurred two years out of every three! Moreover, the king and his escorts were perpetually traveling from one residence to another and their passages were also accompanied by a host of requisitions and stealthy thefts.

On several occasions during the last decade of the reign, such military passages proved to be too much to bear. The sources at court recall specific clashes in three parts of the country but add "insurrections had to be continually quelled."[133] How many others have been forgotten? The Save case is the best known and is probably typical. According to a disdainful aristocrat for whom "a few Tutsi are enough to drive a whole army of Hutu away"[134] the turmoil had been caused by the theft of a single goat by the royal Twa guard. A more detailed account explains that when the royal army passed by Save at a time when famine raged elsewhere, but not in Save, the Twa guard began not only to pillage but also to seize women, raping them and stealing their bracelets with the intention of reselling them to buy food. Whereupon the whole population, which was considerable, rose up and attacked the royal retinue. The army intervened in strength and repressed the revolt. Rwabugiri wanted to exterminate the population of the whole district, but less irascible minds pointed out to him that this was one of the rare places where one could reliably obtain food as it was not subject to famine. Thus it was the famine that provoked the looting and the famine again that saved the rebels.[135]

The calamities of the 1890s and a foreboding that the end of the reign was coming since a coruler had been appointed inspired millenarian hopes among these excessively oppressed farmers. Nearly everywhere in the eastern parts of the country a liberation from all ills was expected, thanks to the coming of a new king, a truly legitimate and beneficent ruler who would do away with all calamities and warrant prosperity. In Ndorwa, the cult of Nyabingi, a mysterious queen in these parts, explains the reception Langheld received there, and in Gisaka the hope of seeing a return of a native king explains that of von Götzen there.[136] But in the heart of the country, the peasant's utopia now included their liberation from their Tutsi oppressors. That was the hope that Nyirafugi incarnated for them. During the years 1879–99 a sizeable portion of the inhabitants elsewhere also rose up, particularly in Bugoyi and Jomba, sometimes with the aim of restoring the ancient small monarchies of the region and always with the goal of "chas[ing] the Tutsi away."[137] Thus the polarization between Tutsi and Hutu was already at the forefront of people's consciousness before Rwabugiri's death. And it was to remain there.

A Balance Sheet

Faced by the relentless, mounting tide of this centralized anarchy, these internecine struggles that were affecting the whole country, the question whether Rwabugiri was a great man or not really becomes secondary. Butare, for example, thinks that he attempted to establish an absolute monarchy and that he introduced territorial centralization accompanied by frequent reshuffles of all the secular and ritual positions, especially with regard to the command of the armies, which he tried to transform into a single national army. On this account, he also took control of all the sources of revenue, whether from booty or from internal dues, but in the end all his personal power and all his efforts to reinforce the personnel of his own house to counterbalance that of Rwakagara did not succeed in preventing the rise to power of that Ega family.[138]

But is this seemingly plausible interpretation really likely? It seems doubtful. First, the conquest of new territories ended in failure. With the exception of Bufumbira, Jomba, and Bwisha, the lands conquered by the king were lost as soon as a few months after his death. So were a good many of the northwestern enclaves, and almost as quickly. Let us then insist on the nature of this much-vaunted centralization. It did not consist in the creation or the extension of a homogeneous network of royal administrators, in the imposition of a network of uniform territorial subdivisions, or in a territorial homogenization with regard to tributes or corvées.[139] Certainly Rwabugiri acquired personal power beyond that of his predecessors, but it mostly derived from the internecine struggles among the aristocrats. And, in the end, Rucunshu proved that the king had failed to subdue them. One must therefore conclude that Rwanda as a fully centralized state is a colonial creation. Rwabugiri's much-vaunted centralization amounted, in the last analysis, to an increase in the power of the court as a whole and in the export of its bloody rivalries all across the country. It was a centralization that sowed terror and reaped social disaster.

The personal role of Rwabugiri was more limited and passive than has been believed. But he did put his stamp on the age. He tried to rely on new men for support and he may have come up with the idea of the new residences, but he does not seem to have pursued a grand political goal. He was first and foremost a warrior, inclined to resolving all difficulties by applying brute force. When Shongoka of the Abagereka cursed him before her suicide, her "curse" was "no longer to have any favorite; from then on he began to kill everyone who became his favorite. There were always victims because of the slandering by the Ingangurarugo whose profession it was."[140]

Indeed his habit of immediately and impetuously following up on denunciations turned him into the perfect instrument for courtiers who wanted to settle accounts, and resulted, in the end, in the terrorizing of the country, but also in its transformation. So rather than "Rwabugiri: A great man," it is "Rwabugiri: a king accursed."

In Conclusion

History and the Present

$\mathbf{A}$s we reach the end of this study, the reader will remember that the main objective of it was to present a starting point for thinking about Rwanda's past in the light of the present. Let us hope it has achieved that goal. To enter into a series of reflections about and detailed recommendations for the future does not fall within the province of an historian and hence I refrain from doing so. But it is pertinent and proper for an historian to offer some advice as to the way in which to approach the question of the relations between past and present since historians are capable of evaluating continuities and ruptures between a more remote and a more recent past, or even between a past and a present. I will first offer a commentary on the subject of the value of different concrete propositions about the past and follow that with a discussion of the various approaches used to draw "lessons" from history. But before I do so it will help to briefly recall the main features of this history.

The Nyiginya kingdom was but one among several that arose during the seventeenth century. It is not older than that. It emerged from a coalition between a newcomer and small local lords and was based on a notion of kingship that was then already well established in the region, according to which ritual power was exercised by a set of specialists who were distinct from those who held secular power. Only the king was the connecting link between the two spheres, for he expressed the very notion of the social unity that formed the state and he was considered to be the person responsible for the public weal, since he was believed to be the spiritual author of the well-being of all the inhabitants. After it was established, the kingdom became very different from its neighbors when nonterritorialized, multiple, and permanent armies were put in place. True, Ndori had introduced the *ubuhake* contract that via the patron-client relationship linked each of the great chiefs directly to the king, but ties of this sort were common in the region, whereas no other realm knew a military organization similar to the one the Nyiginya developed during the eighteenth century. The combination of multiple, permanent armies based on an hereditary recruitment from lineages living all over the country and linked to the management of lands and herds, also spread all over the country, led to an effective centralization. This structural innovation will henceforth shape the destiny of the kingdom and truly distinguish it from all others. For, even though it suffered from the same weaknesses as the others, especially succession crises and the untrammeled growth of turbulent elite lineages, the military structures functioned in such a way as to make the effects of these phenomena different from what obtained elsewhere. The crises did not lead to territorial secessions and the centralized nature of the realm ensured that the growth of the aristocracy led to more violent and more constant struggles among their lineages than elsewhere, for their leaders were forever facing each other at the court where everything was decided.

The main theme of the internal history of the kingdom from the end of the eighteenth century onward is the hold over power sustained by the high nobility at court. The creation of a court culture with its customs, its way of thinking, its language, and its aesthetics was their work, as was the expansion of the realm beyond the central plateau. But unlike the king, the courtiers were not responsible, not even in theory, for the well-being of all the inhabitants of the country. The public weal was not their concern and their internal struggles did not take it into account at all. In the nineteenth century, these struggles led to the triumph of the law of the strongest and its train of troubles, insecurity, and clamor for revenge. These unending conflicts necessarily led to growing disturbances that, from the second half of the century onward, unsettled the country more and more. At the same time, the high nobility increasingly exploited the bulk of its subjects, and its scorn for them manifested itself more and more in their humiliating treatment of the populace. The combination of the humiliation suffered and the heavier and heavier exploitation finally provoked a rift that tore the whole society apart, so that, by 1890, it teetered on the brink of total anomy. Far from constituting an apotheosis of a great united nation encompassing almost two million people, the kingdom of Rwabugiri and his successors offered the spectacle of nearly two million people standing on the verge of an abyss.

In order to understand the relationship between the past before 1900 and the present, it is necessary to brush aside a whole set of false propositions or assertions found even in the most recent literature. They are false because they wholly contradict the known data.[1] Here is the list of the main ones. (a) There never were successive immigrations of Twa foragers, Hutu farmers, and Tutsi herders since these social categories were only slowly developed as a means of labeling persons who were in the country. The settlement history of Rwanda is actually very ancient and quite complex. (b) No one fell from heaven and there never was a real person called "the Creator" (Gihanga) who founded an immense kingdom. (c) The Nyiginya kingdom is more recent than has been imagined hitherto: it only dates from the middle or the end of the seventeenth century. It is therefore not the oldest of all the kingdoms of the Great Lakes region, but appeared at the same time as most others. Rwandan culture is not heir to an atavistic talent for organization or centralization. (d) Neither the first king nor his immediate successors conquered all of present-day Rwanda and the history of the Nyiginya kingdom is not synonymous with that of Rwanda. As has been seen, the history of the territorial additions to the Nduga of Ndori is quite complex and unfolded especially after 1770. (e) The king was neither an all-powerful autocrat nor necessarily benevolent. (f) The kingdom was not a State endowed with an impersonal, homogeneous, and centralized administration, and in which all change—internal change as well as that involving the expansion of the realm's borders—was the result of careful planning by the king assisted by his advisers. (g). The linguistic and cultural unity of the country today did not exist in the seventeenth century and Rwanda is not a "natural" nation. It is the product of the expansion of the culture of the Nyiginya court that began in the eighteenth but occurred mainly during the nineteenth and early twentieth centuries. Rwanda really became a nation in the twentieth century. It is an error to imagine that all the forebears of the present-day speakers of the Rwandan language must have spoken it in the past and in the same way as now, and therefore that the language was always as unified and standardized as it now is. (h) Formerly, neither abundance nor order flourished in the country and it is false to think that everyone was happy with their station in life and all lived in peace under the shepherd's staff of wise kings. False not only because it runs counter to the evidence but also because it is biased, for it only reflects the point of view of a well-off courtier (and, in any event, the perpetual struggles among the big men at court rendered such moments of harmony practically nonexistent). (i) Clans are not unchanging entities nor did each of them immigrate by itself. They were in fact alliances concluded on the spot between lineages and these alliances varied over time. (j) The clearing of forests did not just begin under Ndabarasa's rule, but was as old as the practice of agriculture itself in the region, although it did intensify during the nineteenth century. Local traditions tell how, when Ndori arrived, Minyaruki of Busigi had just finished clearing his mountain of forest. (k) *Ubuhake* was not born in Rwabugiri's age but appeared as early as Ndori's rule. Moreover, the meaning and the frequency of this sort of contract have considerably varied over time.

The reasons for the elaboration of such erroneous propositions are evident. First, there is the projection of a nostalgic utopia into the past, a past that contrasts with a painful present (propositions e, f, h). But the error of retroactively projecting the present into the past is far more frequently committed. It has been greatly facilitated by the practice of the famous ethnographic present, which consists in painting a static picture of "traditional culture" in which nothing ever changes. Those who commit this sort of error do not realize that institutions, customs, values, and practices have changed over time (propositions a, d, g, i, j, k). Then there are chronological errors that are committed either by lengthening or, in reaction to that tendency, compressing processes (propositions c and d, on the one hand, and j and k, on the other). Finally statement i relates to cosmological speculation, not to a recollection of the past.

Once obviously false propositions such as those that have been cited are put aside, one can address the nature of the relationship that obtains between the present of this year and the past before 1900. It is not a direct relationship, since a whole century has lapsed and it was a century during which demography, technology, economic, political and social structures, education, information, and ideological modes of thought all profoundly changed. Nevertheless, one easily recognizes that present-day society is a descendant of that of 1900, if only in the language it uses and in its historical memory. The relationship between an older past and the present is thus indirect and the continuities and differences are not merely superficial. Moreover, one must always remember that the present does not flow from the past as if it was the only possible future that could have emerged from that past. Hypothetical questions speculating what would have happened "if" show this very well. "If the Germans had not supported the court . . . ," "if there had not been a great depression . . . ," "if Rudahigwa had not died in 1959 . . . ," and so on. If the present flowed from the past according to an inexorable fate, then one could predict the future by interpreting the precedents of the past, as the diviners at court used to do. But past and present are linked by other fetters than the inevitable.

The active tie between past and present is the collective memory (written, oral, collective, familial, and so on), a memory that is, moreover, exploited by propagandists on all sides. This collective memory influences present-day perceptions and sometimes guides today's behavior, according to the principle that what happened once can happen again. But, between 1900 and 2000, most memories about the past were put aside and forgotten. Who wants to know whether Rujugira was bald, or whether Marara had a beer belly? The small number of recollections—in the shape of traditions—that have survived have done so because those traditions carry a meaning that is related to themes of present-day interest. Moreover, they have been strongly colored and often skewed by the impact of events subsequent to the date to which they refer. Often, even speculations without any substance at all have been added to them. Collective memory consists in this set of recollections and speculations, a memory that praises and blames, a memory that continually acts on the present and that is given expression in books, media, and also, as before, in the spoken word.

Given this circumstance, it is useful to propose an overall view of the past rooted in the great bulk of traditions that have been gathered since 1900. This is exactly what this book, written by a professional historian who is not implicated in the affairs of present-day Rwanda, does. By placing specific concrete present-day recollections within the context of the whole body of the traditions, one obtains perspective and often succeeds in casting doubt on weaving together the warp of the remembrance of an event or a situation pertaining to the past and the woof of an event or situation in the present. Moreover, such a work helps to draw attention to the relevant data that have been overlooked. Who really remembers that it was the small herders rather than the farmers who were the foremost target of the rapacity of the powerful during a good part of the history of the kingdom? But a book such as this one is only a first step. It is up to Rwandan historians to elaborate as impartial an history as possible on the basis of data that are uncontested and acceptable to all, a history that could then serve as a common foundation for everyone in thinking about the future.

Always keeping the nature of the links between the present and the pre-1900 past in mind, one can then evaluate different reflections about the past in a spirit of positive skepticism. Thus one can rightly be suspicious of so-called lessons of the past when the lessons alluded to are based on a direct parallel between some characteristic of an undefined past and one in the present situation. For such lessons are always ambiguous. Thus one may deplore the principle of collective vengeance because it produces endless hostility, but one could also recommend it because it is at the same time the cement of the vaunted solidarity of kin groups. One can deplore the education of the *intore* companies in old Rwanda because it inculcated militarism and an absolute scorn for all outsiders, but one can also praise the esprit de corps, the loyalty, and the sensitivity to the performing arts that were also products of that education. Moreover, the ambiguous character of a bridge hastily constructed between a single element of the past and the present becomes glaring once one starts to thinks about the difference between the present of yore and the present of today and no doubt between the present of today and the present of tomorrow. In this sort of comparison the meaning of the past constantly changes according to a changing present! Yesterday, the *intore* were but parasites; today they probably are the paradigm of a sophisticated system of education.

Among this class of so-called lessons, one will particularly distrust those of the following type that attribute a national or collective character to people: "Such a family of Twa executioners was renowned for their cruelty, hence their descendants must be equally cruel," or even worse, "one Twa was reputedly cruel, hence all Twa were cruel and today all Twa must also be cruel." It only takes a little reflection to see that nothing holds together in this type of false syllogistic reasoning that presupposes either the operation of an inflexible genetic law unknown to science or an ongoing, relentless, and intensive indoctrination of subsequent generations by their forebears, and this all in a century of great changes, which is equally unthinkable.

How then should one start to think about the past? By conceiving it as a laboratory of human experience from which conclusions can be drawn. It is perfectly acceptable, for instance to assert the proposition that any rule that is based on the right of the strongest leads to perpetual instability. One saw this during the nineteenth century: a rise in the number of executions triggered by the arbitrary denunciations of interested adversaries, combined with the application of the principle of collective responsibility, produced a general atmosphere of insecurity in which violent reactions inspired by fear were not uncommon. Moreover, each execution was the starting point of an infernal chain of vengeance and countervengeance that, in the context of the rule of collective responsibility prevailing at the time, caused even more insecurity. The tensions and turmoil generated by this state of affairs were such that the internal cohesion of all social groups began to be eroded by it. The proposition that rule based on the law of might results in permanent instability is as true in the present as it was in the past because, with the exception of the technology of coercion, the general conditions that undergirded such a process in the past have persisted. One can therefore refer to such a proposition in making recommendations about the management of the society of today. Let us observe in passing that it is an awareness of such a process that explains why one deplores Sebasoni's romantic admiration for a society where law does not obtain, "where action and behavior are dictated by personal ties, rather than by laws, where the execution of one's duty depends on affection to a person rather than compliance with cold laws."[2] He may be well-intentioned, but he is in fact promoting the most untrammeled arbitrariness in the conduct of social relations.

Finally, a particularly fruitful point of departure for plumbing this ancient past for what it has to offer the society of today and tomorrow seems to me to be the following. Many Rwandan readers will have been surprised to learn how preponderant the high nobility of the country has been in its governance. They will have been especially surprised by the magnitude of the effects produced by the dynamics of its internecine struggles both with regard to the territorial expansion of the country and its internal development. They will also have observed the tendency of the rulers to resist any delegation of power, both by excluding whole social groups from participation in the government and by eliminating their immediate competitors. Rwandans know that Kanjogera almost succeeded in concentrating all power in her own hands, but have long forgotten that Rugaju had succeeded in this endeavor well before her time. Finally, most readers will also have been surprised to learn to what extent anomy, caused by dynamics from which the public was wholly excluded, had corroded the whole country.

All that is something to think about. Despite the great changes that occurred during the last century, the overall social and cultural conditions in the country today are not so different as to render the experience of the eighteenth and nineteenth centuries invalid. This experience allows one to ask questions. Which group today should take over the role of the aristocracy of yore? How can one counteract the nefarious tendency whereby power is concentrated in the hands of a smaller and smaller group, a tendency which seems to be inherent in a comparable situation? How can one prevent processes of exclusion that allow such a concentration of power in so few hands? How to prevent possible anomy? How to mitigate the alienation of the bulk of the population that such a concentration of power can engender? In other words, how to mobilize the population? Only the visible and tangible pursuit of a public good, recognized as such by all, could achieve this and only such a pursuit can legitimate a political regime. Indeed, didn't some populations spontaneously mobilize themselves at the end of the nineteenth century in the hope of finding a new king who, once again, would be the guarantor of the public weal?

The Nyiginya kingdom was not the only one in the world where power tended to be concentrated in a few hands and where the bulk of its citizens were alienated. Indeed, practically all the centralized polities of large-scale societies today fit this description. And in different parts of the world subsequent experience has suggested remedies, even while leaving the management of public affairs in the hands of very few persons in proportion to the large number of people they administer. Today's Rwandan thinkers might therefore draw on foreign experiences and theories in order to elaborate a system of government that would avoid an excessive concentration of power and the alienation of the people, since there was a time when those foreign experiences were also those of Rwanda, first in the eighteenth and nineteenth centuries, and then in the last one. Starting from this set of questions and experiences, further thought about the meaning of this past history for the present may yield fruitful initiatives for a new construction of the country.

APPENDIXES

NOTES

WORKS CITED

INDEX

APPENDIX I

Chronology

Chronology is an essential foundation for history and any change in the calculation of a chronology can have quite substantial effects. That is the reason why here we focus once again on the chronology of the Nyiginya kingdom even though the topic has already been the object of much research, including some of my own.[1] For none of the earlier attempts has proven to be satisfactory. Moreover, the new chronology at which we arrive here entails major consequences. Among others, let us observe, for instance, that the kingdom was probably founded around 1650, almost six centuries after the 1091 date proposed by Kagame.[2] Further, the new date is not earlier than most of the dates proffered for the emergence of other kingdoms in the immediate vicinity as well as elsewhere in the Great Lakes region.[3] The sources only become credible and more numerous from the middle of the eighteenth century onward, as is also the case elsewhere in the region. A great territorial expansion only starts here circa 1780 (Buganza) and not centuries before. Rugaju's rule stretched over more than twenty-five years and not over a few years as some had thought. Such examples show that the adoption of a new chronology brings us to a new understanding of the history it relates to, and that justifies the presence of this appendix.

The Foundations

Until now all authors have established a chronology for Rwanda before 1895 on the basis of the official dynastic list of kings, by accepting the claim that the monarchs nearly always succeeded from father to son, and using an average number for the length of a dynastic generation.[4] Moreover, authors have used references to eclipses of the sun and comets to attempt to make such calculations more precise. This procedure does not resolve the following problems. First one has to determine who really founded the kingdom, if all the kings who appear on the dynastic list are historical personages or not, and if the succession did indeed pass from father to son. Secondly, one needs to take into account the fact that an average of generation length is an *average*. It can only be valid for a number of generations, not just for one or two. Moreover, this average number does not take male longevity into account. Most adult men died before or around forty years old.[5] As far as the kings are concerned, one observes that no less than eight of those about whom data are extant suddenly died or died at a fairly young age, to wit: two died in an accident, one was killed in war, and five died of illness (5). Among the two remaining kings one was reputed for his longevity. On the other hand, three kings were enthroned as children, and a fourth one when he was just about a young man. Moreover, readers should realize that a researcher always chooses an eclipse or comet by looking for it within a window of time previously determined by a calculation based on an average generational length.

The first step is to determine the list of kings. One observes that the kingdom begins with RUGANZU Ndori and not with RUGANZU Bwimba as has hitherto been believed. In the next appendix, we will see that the list of the so-called predynastic kings is not credible. Moreover, one of the later kings on the usual list, KIGERI Nyamuheshera, seems to be fictional as well.[6] He was probably added later on to construct a complete cycle of dynastic names. But that means that there is a gap in the dynastic list that prevents us from dating the preceding kings. Among these, MUTARA Semugeshi, aka BICUBA, aka NSORO Muyenzi,[7] may well refer to two or even three different kings, either in succession or as coevals. One can only observe, then, that RUGANZU Ndori's reign was followed by a dark age during which the number of kings who reigned cannot be determined. An absolute chronology can only be reconstructed from Gisanura onward. It is true that two kings, KAREMERA Rwaka and MIBAMBWE Rutarindwa, have been deleted from the official list, but nonetheless they were remembered and even the length of their reigns was not forgotten. Finally, one observes that Rujugira is supposed to be a half-brother of Rwaka and Rutarindwa the half-brother of Musinga who was to succeed him.

The second step consists in obtaining a date in absolute chronology for the annular eclipse of the sun that occurred a few days after the inauguration of MIBAMBWE Sentabyo.[8] To find this date, one makes a rough calculation of generations by counting three of them or a little less within a century, thereby locating a window of time within which this eclipse could fall. As this king is said to only have ruled for about five years[9] it is better to calculate the date of his death and then subtract the duration of his rule in order to determine when he was enthroned. After his death, three generations passed until Rwabugiri's death in 1895. By counting a century at most backward from Rwabugiri's death, one obtains 1795 for Sentabyo's demise and 1790 for his accession. If one counts thirty years as a generational average, then king died in 1805 and acceded in 1800. And one does find that there were two annular eclipses that occurred during this ten-year window, one in 1792 and one in 1796.[10] But the first was practically invisible, achieving a magnitude of only 0.74 percent, while the one of 1 October 1796 that occurred shortly after dawn attained a 0.93 percent magnitude. In good weather, that is an observable magnitude.[11] We therefore assume that MIBAMBWE Sentabyo was inaugurated at the end of September 1796 and died in 1801, which then leaves ninety-four years for the three succeeding generations, hence probably a little over thirty years per reign.

One could, however, reject the tradition that an eclipse occurred during his reign by observing that the only other eclipse remembered is that which occurred at the accession in December 1889 of that other MIBAMBWE, Rutarindwa.[12] Perhaps the coincidence is too striking to be credible. But, even so, Sentabyo would have been inaugurated between 1790 and 1800. Indeed, this dating is reinforced by the case of Muhunde who was born during his reign and became famous for his advanced age. He died around 1900, when he was over 100 years old, but probably not a very improbable 105.[13] 1795 is the earliest possible date for this birth. Given the proximity of all these dates, one can in fact accept that Sentabyo was installed as king in 1795, and that there really was a coincidence of eclipses that occurred around the time of the inaugurations of the two MIBAMBWE. Therefore, four generations elapsed in ninety-nine years (from 1796 to 1895). As a first approximation, one may well postulate the same figure for the four generations from MIBAMBWE Gisanura to MIBAMBWE Sentabyo, in which case Gisanura would have been inaugurated in 1697 and the average length of a dynastic generation for each king on the list would be twenty-four years and nine months.

But let us calculate a more realistic chronology for the period of the four kings between 1796 and 1895, on the one hand, and for the four kings before 1795, on the other. We will do this reign by reign and take into account all sorts of relevant data, from the length of a given king's reign, to the length of his life,[14] to his age at his accession or at his death, to overlaps between several reigns, and the longevity of certain subjects. However, we do not accept any alleged synchronisms established between the Nyiginya and other dynasties before the nineteenth century because such synchronisms are learned, recent, and speculative elaborations.[15]

Dating Rwabugiri's Reign

Let us start by examining the reigns between 1867 and 1895. Rwabugiri died between his meeting with von Götzen on 30 May 1894 and the attack by a Congolese detachment, which occurred during his successor's reign in August 1896. In this case, detailed recorded reminiscences referring to a succession of events allow one to date his death to September 1895.[16] An examination of his skeleton suggests that he died before he reached the age of forty.[17] He was therefore born around 1855 at the earliest, and as he became king at the age of between seven and twelve years old,[18] his reign had to have begun between 1862 and 1867,[19] probably closer to the latter date. Some others indications, including the age of the queen mother at her death, lead me to accept 1867. The 1853 date proposed by Kagame must certainly be rejected.[20] The more plausible date of 1858, proposed by Delmas, must also be rejected in favor of 1867.[21] The 1870 date proposed by Van Overschelde is probably a bit too late.[22]

The chronological sequence of events during Rwabugiri's reign after December 1889, which was the date of the inauguration of Rutarindwa, is attested to by many sources from Rwanda and its vicinity.[23] But any earlier dating remains quite hazy. A good example of the difficulty is Kagame's proposed 1861 date for the murder of the queen mother, which is a few years before that of Nkoronko, the chief held responsible for it. Accepting a date of accession of 1867, the death of the queen mother should have occurred around 1877 at the latest. For she was killed because it was believed that she was pregnant. Being about twenty years old when she married, she would have been a little more than thirty when Rwabugiri was installed, since he was about ten years old or a little older at that time, and, ten years later, at over forty she would be near the outer limit of a possible pregnancy.[24] But in 1876 Stanley speaks of "the powerful Empress," so it seems very likely that she was still alive then.[25]

The next event that can be linked to a date recorded in writing is the war of Bumpaka. On 7 January 1880, CMS missionary Pearson, then at the capital of Buganda, Rubaga, informed his colleague Wright that large numbers of Ganda warriors had left for Rwanda, "to the northwest of Karagwe," and on 5 March he reported that the Ganda raiders in Rwanda, "southwest of Karagwe," had been utterly routed and that the remnant of the army was on its way back, "despoiled, rather than bringing back cattle and slaves." The diary of the Catholic mission reports what seems to be the same expedition.[26] The Rwandan traditions do not mention any Ganda at all, probably because they confused them with Nkore. Hence there is no neat, direct, and obvious correspondence between the written data and the oral traditions. On the other hand, it is not likely that this encounter was so insignificant that it was wholly forgotten, for the White Fathers mention a very large number of cattle. So the question is, to which of the Ndorwa or the Nkore expeditions could these written texts correspond?[27] It cannot be the last Nkore campaign in 1895, which is also dated by contemporary documents. The 1880 letters and diary must relate to one of the two earlier campaigns in "Ndorwa." The earliest, the "campaign of the waters," was obviously fought in or near Mutara and movement was greatly hampered by heavy rainfall that made it difficult to cross the rivers. Given such conditions, it is not likely there was anything to attract the Bugandan army to join the fray. Hence the "campaign of the waters" was probably not the one of 1880. The expedition to Bumpaka is a much more likely candidate. It overran the whole of Nkore, and raided even further, as far as Bumpaka, which is not very far from Buganda, and it captured an immense booty in cattle. Such a booty and its close proximity to Buganda could certainly have tempted a Ganda army.[28] All in all, then, the 1880 campaign seems to correspond to the latter part of the Bumpaka expedition and we can date the latter to 1879–80.

One other event can now be dated by reference to the Bumpaka expedition, namely the Rwakabyaza comet. The comet was seen a year after the execution of Rwampembwe and the suicide of Kabyaza at the time of return of the Butembo expedition, and, therefore, at the time when Nkoronko was executed. All of these events follow well after the Bumpaka campaign. Kagame identified it with the comet of Coggia seen in 1874,[29] but other comets were also visible in 1880 and 1882. It is now obvious that the Rwakabyaza comet is the one of 1882 and that Rwampembwe and Kabyaza probably died in 1881.[30]

The only other date that can be directly derived from written records is that of Musinga's birth. The careful assessment by Kandt, a physician, dates it to around 1882–83.[31] Since this occurred during the Gikore expedition, one can also reckon forward from the comet in 1882 to obtain 1883 at the earliest. Finally, one can estimate the date of Rwabugiri's first marriage from the date of his death. Young men were married from about the age of eighteen onward, which would date Rwabugiri's first marriages to 1873 if he was forty in 1895, but it could have been a little later if he died at a younger age or was married a little later.

The internal chronology of the reign can then be deduced from the succession of events during the reign.[32] An absolute chronology can be derived from this succession of events by a dead reckoning to and from the dates of 1877, 1882, 1883, and 1889 that we have already obtained. The margin of error of the dates given is probably on the order of one or two years and certainly less than five.

THE REIGNS OF RWABUGIRI AND RUTARINDWA

1867: Inauguration of Rwabugiri. Murorunkwere and Nkoronko rule.

1868: Mirama expedition.

1870: Humure expedition. First expedition against Ijwi. Nyamwesa blinded.

1873: First marriage of the king.

1875: The king comes of age.

Late 1876 or 1877: Murder of Murorunkwere. Nyirimigabo in the ascendant.

1878–79: Expedition of the waters.

1879–80: Bumpaka expedition.

1881: Rito affair. Execution of Rwampembwe. Kabyaza's Suicide.

1882: Butembo expedition. Comet. Execution of Nkoronko.

1882–83: Second expedition against Ijwi.

1883–84: Birth of Musinga. Gikore expedition.

Late 1884: Buntubuzindu expedition.

1885: Kanywiriri expedition. Death of Nyirimigabo.

1886–87: Expedition against Nkundiye. Ntizimira and Nzigiye in the ascendant.

1887: Fall of Ntizimira.
1888: Fall of Nyiringango and Ndungutse.
December 1889: Inauguration of Rutarindwa as coruler.
1890: Expedition to Bushubi.
1890–91: Cattle plagues. ku-Kidogoro expedition.
1891–92: ku-Rusozi expedition. Defeat of Rumaliza.
1892: Smallpox epidemic. Jiggers.
1893–94: ku-Mira affair.
1894: von Götzen's passage. Aborted expedition to Bushi.
1894–95: Nkore expedition.
September 1895: Death of Rwabugiri. Rutarindwa rules.
December 1896: Coup d'état at Rucunshu and death of Rutarindwa.
February 1897: Inauguration of Musinga.
March 1897: Arrival of von Ramsay.

From 1796 to the Death of Rwogera

Having established a date for Rwabugiri's accession we now go back and use 1796 as a starting point for establishing a chronology for the reigns between then and 1867. Sentabyo is said to have been quite young on his accession and to have only ruled for five years, although according to another source he died in his fourth year.[33] His death and Gahindiro's accession occurred in 1801. According to all the data, Gahindiro was then a very small baby, born in 1800 or 1801. He therefore came of age around 1820. But no Rwandan tradition enables one to date his death and hence the accession of Rwogera, who died himself in 1867 when Rwabugiri was inaugurated. But Gahindiro's death is mentioned in a tradition from Karagwe. He seems to have died during the last part of the reign of their king Ndagara. According to information given to Grant, this Ndagara died around 1854 (1853–55).[34] His succession was disputed and Rumanyika, his successor, only seized power with the help of the Ganda troops of Ssuuna II aided by a group of traders from the east coast.[35] As Ssuuna did not die immediately after this event and as his demise dates to October or November 1856, the circa 1854 date gains in credibility.[36] Which leads us to postulate a date circa 1850 or before that for Gahindiro's death.

The sources from the Nyiginya kingdom do not agree as to Gahindiro's longevity. For Kagame, he died aged, between sixty-five and seventy-five, but according to Schumacher, he was sixty and as far as Mugina is concerned, he died young.[37] One can obtain an idea of the length of his reign by looking at the career of Nyiramuhanda. She came from Gishari as a young girl under Ndabarasa, married Mbyayingabo, and had two sons. Since girls were married between the ages of eighteen and twenty (let us say nineteen) she was therefore about twenty-two when Ndabarasa died in 1796 and twenty-seven when Sentabyo died in 1801. She became old at court and died under Rwogera, from whom she still received some gifts.[38] Supposing that she achieved the respectable age of seventy-five, a generous figure for an "ordinary" case given the conditions for longevity at the time, then the total of Gahindiro's reign with a portion of that of Rwogera added on would have been about forty-eight years. Moreover, considering the latter's youth at his accession, the benefit given to Nyiramuhanda under his reign probably stemmed from Nkoronko with whom one of her sons was allied. Therefore, she would have received this benefit after Rugaju's fall, that is two or more years after Rwogera's accession. By subtracting two years from the total of forty-eight, then, we surmise that Gahindiro's reign would have lasted for forty-six years at most and that he would have died in 1847. But as this figure derives from attributing the longest reign to Gahindiro it is possible to attribute to him, it is probably somewhat forced. A death circa 1845 would be more realistic. This result does not contradict Kagame's chronology, which is quite vague for this reign, and for lack of any better evidence we accept it.[39]

It then follows that Rwogera reigned between 1845 and 1867. He was inaugurated as a young child of about ten[40] (and so therefore was born around 1835) and supposedly died from TB at age thirty-two, yet after a long reign of twenty-two years. And indeed Mugina and Bourgeois's informant noted that he died when still quite young, but the Kagame's and Schumacher's collaborators claimed he was at least fifty years old.[41] The calculated length of reign seems plausible. When he died his mother was beginning to see her first gray hairs.[42] She was therefore about fifty and would have been about thirty when she became queen mother.[43] The available evidence about the sequence of the main events that occurred during their reigns is not sufficient to propose a detailed internal chronology for either the reign of Gahindiro or that of Rwogera. But one observes that the campaign in Gisaka was still ongoing when Rwogera died.[44] The dates given in this table have, I believe, a margin of error that does not exceed five years.

From Sentabyo to Rwogera

1796–1801: Civil war.

1796: Accession of Sentabyo.

1798–1802: Rukungungu famine.

1799: Conquest of Bugesera.

1801: Accession of Gahindiro. Nyiratunga rules.

1820: Gahindiro comes of age. Rugaju rules.

1843: War with Karagwe.

1844: Famine.

1845: Accession of Rwogera. Nyiramongi rules.

1847: Fall of Rugaju.

1855: Power is divided between Rwogera and Nyiramongi.

1860–67: Expeditions in Gisaka; the country is subdued.

1867: Death of Rwogera. Execution of Nyiramongi.

Before 1796

The following data are available as a starting point for further calculations: the age of Rujugira when he died, the death of Ndabarasa in 1796, the fact that Nyiratunga, widow of Gihana who was Rujugira's son, is also the supposed mother of Gahindiro, and the fact that Nsigaye and Ndabarasa were adults and quite active during the coup d'état that made Rujugira king.

A first computation starts from the unknown length of Ndabarasa's reign. In the total absence of data, we assume that he ruled well over five years, for otherwise the traditions would have remarked on it, since they noted that Rwaka lasted only four years and Sentabyo five. Let us say for the sake of argument that he ruled seven years at least. In that case, Rujugira would have died in 1789 at the latest. An examination of his skeleton suggests that Rujugira was sixty-five years old at most when he died, but probably much less.[45] On the other hand, given that all the traditions insist on his longevity, we will attribute a life-span of sixty years to him.[46] He would then have been born in 1729 at the latest.

A second computation starts from the fact that Nyiratunga conceived Gahindiro in 1800. Given the usual age at menopause she would then have been forty-five years old at the most, at least if she did have a baby. But even if it were only ascribed to her she still could not have been over fifty, for otherwise that claim would have been unbelievable.[47] Since she was Gihana's widow and he died shortly after the conclusion of their marriage but after she had already borne him a son, so she must have been at least twenty years old at his death. This puts Gihana's death between twenty-five or thirty years before 1800, hence in 1770–75. Gihana' death occurred in the first years of Rujugira's reign, since the war with Burundi occurred shortly after the coup d'état that brought him to power. By estimating the duration between the coup and the war at one to five years one arrives at a window of time between 1765 (1770 minus five) and 1774 (1775 minus one) within which the coup could have occurred.

On can more or less determine Rujugira's age when the coup occurred since his son Ndabarasa was then already a married man. In the hypothesis, which I am inclined to endorse, that he was a usurper from Gisaka, he would have been at least forty years of age. Since he died in 1789 at the latest, the coup happened by 1769 or earlier and Gihana's death falls between 1770 and 1774. If he really was Mazimpaka's son, Rujugira fled the country at the accession of Rwaka when he was at least thirty-eight years old, as his son Ndabarasa was nineteen years old at the most, given that he was not married yet and a spouse was found for him in Gisaka during their exile there, which lasted four years. Even if he was a usurper, he must have been about the same age, since the adult Ndabarasa was the main instigator of the coup. Thus at the time of the coup d'état Rujugira was slightly over forty, let us say about forty-three. Given his age when he died and 1789 as the last possible date for that, we now come to 1772 at the latest date for the coup d'état and reach 1773–77 for Gihana' death.

No matter what hypothesis one chooses, all the data suggest that Rujugira was fairly old at the time of his coup d'état and that agrees well with the tenor of the tales about it. All in all we *estimate* that the following dates are the most likely: death of Rujugira in 1786,[48] which means that Ndabarasa ruled for ten years, death of Gihana in 1773, the coup d'état in 1770 when Rujugira was about forty-three, and his birth in 1726. Rujugira would then have ruled for about eighteen years. Ndabarasa came to power at about age thirty-five and died at around age forty-five. The fairly short duration of his reign is plausible when one remembers that he performed almost all of his great deeds when his father was still alive.

Rwaka's length of rule poses no problem if one accepts the data proposed by Kayijuka and Kagame. Rwaka would have ruled alone for four years before the coup and for twelve as Mazimpaka's coruler.[49] He therefore ruled from 1766 to 1770 and was a coruler from 1754 onward. At that time he had to have been at least twenty years old and was therefore born before or in 1734.

Mazimpaka, who died in 1766, lived long enough to engender a hundred sons before he died "at the age of an adult man" and he ruled long enough to found eleven capitals.[50] He was fairly old when he died, because four years later Nsigaye, one of his adult grandsons, commanded the rebels during the coup d'état of 1770.[51] Mazimpaka must have been born at least sixty years before this date, that is, he must have been born at least by 1710. If so, this king was forty-four years old or a little older in 1754 when Rwaka was put in control and at least fifty-six when he died accidentally in 1766.[52] These dates are the oldest one for which one can estimate a margin of error of about five years.

For the period of Mazimpaka's reign before 1754, there is only one bit of useable information. It relates to the war for the succession after Gisanura's death at forty-five years old or older.[53] At that time, Nyagasheja, Mazimpaka's brother and rival, was in his twenties and perhaps over thirty for he had several children, but they were still too young to fight.[54] On the other hand, Gisanura was at least twenty years old when Mazimpaka was born in 1710. He was therefore born by or before 1690, a date for which one has to allow a fairly great margin of error (ten years at least) because it is derived from 1710, which itself includes an appreciable margin of error. By combining both data, we can estimate that Gisanura's death and Mazimpaka's accession occurred at the latest in 1735, a date that includes the same large margin of error as the 1690 one. That would give a reign of thirty-one years to Mazimpaka and one of unknown length to Gisanura.

The date of Gisanura's accession remains to be calculated. In the absence of any data can one rely at least on statistical computations derived from dynastic generational averages? Not really, for we are dealing here with a single generation and statistical averages can only be applied to a fairly large number of generations; moreover, they yield only a general likelihood in any case. All one can do is use the lengths of the dynastic generations already obtained between 1735 and 1895 to estimate Gisanura's. These are twenty-eight, twenty-two, forty-four, five, ten, twenty, and thirty-one years. The longest is Gahindiro (forty-four years) and the shortest Sentabyo (five years) As the average, 22.85, may be too much influenced by the two extremes, the median of 22 is more likely. But it makes even more sense to figure between twenty to thirty-one years for the duration of a reign since a majority, four out of seven, fall into this window and the two extremes are separated from these by ten and thirteen years respectively. Although we refuse to propose any concrete dates, we can conclude nevertheless that the whole of Gisanura's reign probably fell in the eighteenth century.[55]

The hiatus between Gisanura and Ndori is of unknown duration for no private genealogy allows one to bridge it. On the one hand, the Kono genealogy posits a span of only two generations between the queen mother of the predynastic king Mukobanya and Mazimpaka, and the Ega genealogy posits three generations between those of Ndori and Mazimpaka but these genealogies have been falsified before one reaches a notional Mazimpaka/Gisanura generation. In the Tege genealogy, on the other hand, the list of names given to Delmas by Sezibera are different from those the same Sezibera gave to Kagame for the forebears of Nyabirungu, a ritualist who would have corresponded to the generation of Gisanura (or Mazimpaka's?). Finally, there is the genealogy of the Ganzu. For Delmas, their founder Nzuki, supposedly Ndori's grandson, belongs to Gisanura's generation, which implies that the kingdom was founded two generations earlier. But in his version, Kagame inserts a certain Mutabazi, just after Nzuki, and his genealogy is in harmony with the royal one.[56] All in all, then, we are forced to admit that the known private genealogies are not any more credible before Gisanura than the royal one. Hence any estimation of a precise date for the foundation of the kingdom is dubious. One must therefore remain vague. The kingdom was certainly founded before 1700. Probably any kingdom based on an alliance of chiefs around a king, such as this one was based on between Ndori and Gisanura, would not last for long. Hence the Nyiginya kingdom was probably founded around the middle of the seventeenth century.[57]

From Ndori to Ndabarasa

Seventeenth century (c. 1650?): Ndori founds the kingdom.

After 1700: Gisanura's accession.

1735 (rough estimate): Mazimpaka's accession.

1754: Rwaka, coruler and regent.

1766: Rwaka, sole ruler.

1770: Coup d'état. Rujugira's accession.

1772: War with Burundi begins.

1773: Gihana's death. Famine.

1775: Mutaga's death.

1786: Ndabarasa's succession.

1796: Ndabarasa's death. Civil war.

APPENDIX 2

Predynastic Fairy Tales: Central Rwanda before Ndori

Although RUGANZU Ndori was the real founder of the Nyiginya kingdom, almost all historiographers[1] start the known history of the kingdom much earlier with another RUGANZU, whose personal name was Bwimba.[2] He lived on the hill of Gasabo and ruled over several adjacent hills, as well over the historic province of Buganza, south of Lake Muhazi. And even Bwimba was not the first king, but of his predecessors only the names are known, a chain of names linked to the mythical fall from heaven of Kigwa, the ur-ancestor of the royal dynasty, and, later on, to the first mythical ruler Gihanga, "the Creator," who is said to have ruled over all the known lands of the Great Lakes. But Bwimba is the first king whose deeds are related "when the curtain finally opens"[3] on history. From that moment onward, a set of traditions seems to report the emergence of this embryonic kingdom of Gasabo and its growth through the acquisition of lands, first to the north of the Nyabugogo, and later in Rukoma and Nduga.[4]

Yet an analysis of the literary coherence of this set of traditions reveals that it is really a disparate body created by stitching various odds and ends together with bits of various tales of origins.[5] First comes a set of beautiful romantic tales about RUGANZU Bwimba and CYIRIMA Rugwe, which also includes the later story of MIBAMBWE Mutabazi's marriage to a princess of Buha and the war for succession that followed that event. Smith realized[6] that these stories are in fact fairy tales, or perhaps disguised myths. Everything pertaining to them is fictitious down to the very names of the protagonists, except for MIBAMBWE Sekarongoro whose names are identical to, and borrowed from, those of Gisanura.[7] Second is a set of traditions that tells stories about campaigns of conquest conducted more or less together by KIGERI Mukobanya and his son, or, according to some, by his younger brother, MIBAMBWE Mutabazi, a set of traditions that concludes with the depredations and the final defeat at Ishinjaniro of a group of foreign invaders called "Nyoro." As far as we can tell, there are no convincing parallels between these traditions and known tales of fiction. Mukobanya could actually have been a real person and the polity the traditions claim he created in Buriza, Bumbogo, and Rukoma may well have existed. A third set of traditions constitutes the cycle of the last king of

217

Nduga, Mashira, or "the End." It consists in divinations and prophecies that display the magic powers of kings.[8] These stories are part and parcel of a genre of tales of fiction, related to riddles, for which parallels can be found elsewhere. The whole cycle is fictitious, even the part that portrays Sekarongoro Mutabazi as the tenacious adversary and later victor over Mashira.[9] For a character called Sekarongoro Mutabazi does appear in all three sets of traditions and serves to unify.

Then follow some bits about a certain YUHI Gahima, an imaginary king. The data supplied for this king are derived either from the preceding cycle (Nzaratsi) or based on anachronisms (the conquests). Then comes the tragedy of NDAHIRO[10] Cyamatare, which belongs to the cycle of Ndori, for Cyamatare lost his realm and his life after having sent his son Ndori to Karagwe where he was kept safe. Once again, this king is a figment of the imagination, but his story could have been conceivably inspired by the fate of some lord in Nduga, who was overcome and killed in the mountains to the west of the upper Nyabarongo.

The intelligentsia at court molded this disparate batch of fictions and reminiscences into a single whole by imposing a chronological sequence on them that turned their protagonists into a series of kings succeeding each other from father to son. The fabrications consisted not just in tying the cycles of tales together, but also in providing them with a concrete context of places (capitals, battles, cemeteries) and kinship with dynastic names, queen mothers, and even the latter's clans. This process may well have begun in Ndori's lifetime or shortly thereafter, when the ritualists came up with the idea of making him a scion of a legendary Cyamatare, thus turning him into not only the legitimate successor to the whole of Nduga but also to all the lands in the north that had been ravished by Byinshi the usurper.[11] Because the scenery of the Mashira cycle is set in Nduga, it was probably annexed to the rest of the cycles shortly after Ndori's conquest. But the whole, including the dynastic names, acquired its definitive shape only after the conquest of Buganza by Rujugira.[12] Actually Nkurikiyimfura concludes from an analysis of the dynastic genealogy that its final version was only established after the reign of Ndabarasa and would therefore date more or less from 1796.[13]

When the Nyiginya conquered Buganza, many of its earlier habitants fled and were slowly replaced by the newcomers.[14] They were therefore no longer in a position to dispute the assertions made by the courtiers. It is worth recalling that the systematic cycle of dynastic names was elaborated under Rujugira. The first cycle from CYIRIMA Rugwe to YUHI Gahima (a total invention needed to complete the cycle) was created at that time or shortly thereafter. And in order to forge a parallel with the genuine founder of the dynasty, the traditions put RUGANZU Bwimba before these names. Besides Gahima and Sekarongoro, the names of the other heroes were perhaps already then considered to be genuine historical figures, either at court (Cyamatare) or in Buganza itself. Finally, the fact that the decisive victory in this campaign occurred at Gasabo explains why this place was henceforth considered to be the cradle of the embryonic kingdom that supposedly existed in Buganza. The accession in 1796 of MIBAMBWE Sentabyo at Nkunzuzu explains why this place was thought to be the domain of the first MIBAMBWE Sekarongoro Mutabazi. Further, it looks as if the content of the forged traditions came from some favorite local stories—fairy tales no doubt—about the earlier history of Buganza, which were annexed by the intelligentsia of the court. Let us also note that the tradition about the Nyoro was known to Rujugira since he created a company called Ababito after the name of the ruling clan in Bunyoro. Ababito became an army under Ndabarasa, while another army called Abanyoro was also raised under his rule.[15] The popularity of these names at the court in those days suggests that there may have been something novel about them, but what exactly? The substance of this tradition was certainly well known because two places in Rukoma are directly associated with it, but the attribution of the name "Nyoro" to the foreign invaders may have been novel at the time.

It is not feasible here to scrutinize all these narrative traditions in detail to present all the details relating to the period from Bwimba to Cyamatare, or to explain from where each little element derives. Let us be content with discussing the few elements that might have some historical foundation in the period before Ndori. They are mostly limited to parts of those traditions that relate the exploits of Mukobanya and of persons who were later fused into a single Sekarongoro personage. The mention of small-scale conflicts between chiefs mainly located north of the lower Nyabugogo and in adjacent eastern Rukoma may have some historical basis. The world represented by these tales is one in which leaders held ritual powers and had a modest personal following of warriors. They did not just rustle cattle but quarreled over effective control of hill after hill within a small territory. Some forged temporary alliances with neighbors against third parties. A more stable form of alliance resulted from the more powerful lord delegating the ritual powers to his weaker associate. Thus emerged the first ritualist kings and their territories, especially the Kono king of Nyamweru. Over time one group gained the upper hand over the others and Mukobanya succeeded in lording it over Buriza, Bumbogo, and even eastern Rukoma, in part by allying himself to the Tsobe and in part by conquest (including the defeat of Murinda).

Thereupon appeared a powerful army of invaders called Nyoro today.[16] Since a set of traditions in Nkore as well as in Buhaya also mentions a Nyoro invasion it is possible that there was a single invasion of the whole region. But it is just as likely that the historiologists at the court of Rwanda borrowed the name from their neighbors to designate the invader of central Rwanda whose misdeeds were similar to those ascribed to the Nyoro by their neighbors. It is possible that the story according to which one of the detachments of these invaders was annihilated at Ishinjaniro, presumably by Mukobanya, has a real historical foundation.[17] This would then be a case of a local reminiscence being imported to the court by an important ritualist who lived near the place where the battle of Umuganzacyaro was fought.

Finally, one may accept that at least two personages, conflated today under the single anachronistic label MIBAMBWE Sekarongoro Mutabazi, were chiefs in Rukoma and fought rulers in Nduga.[18] After a set of clashes, the first of these was forced to the *statu quo ante bellum*. Later, one of his successors succeeded in killing the king of Nduga. But contrary to what has traditionally been claimed, he failed to take the country, for Nduga ended up being fragmented into a large number of small independent domains.[19] In Ndori's time, only one entity that claimed to be a kingdom remained, namely, Byinshi's territory. The names of the predecessors of this king in ascending order are Bamara and Juru, both brothers of Byinshi.[20] But Bamara is also the name of the last of the celebrated Cwezi half-gods, the one who descends into hell,[21] while Juru means "the sky" or "heavens". These names refer to a variant of the Ryangombe cult. Contrary to the declarations of the traditionalists, therefore, there is no tie of kinship between Byinshi and Cyamatare and Byinshi was not just a usurper of the so-called kingdom of Cyamatare.

In the end, one can no longer doubt: Ndori was the founder of a new kingdom and not just a successor to or a usurper of an older one. Before him, there was a leader of a small territory in Buriza and Bumbogo who claimed to be king, but his legitimacy was contested by the ritual Tsobe and Kono kings. For there were kings, but no kingdoms. Certain leaders had people call them *umwami* and claimed to possess supernatural and ritual powers enabling them to ensure the prosperity of their lands, their cattle and their subjects. But their realms comprised only a couple of hills. The greatest polity in all of central Rwanda before Ndori was probably Nduga, but even that had been ephemeral and had vanished by the time he arrived. Around central Rwanda, kingdoms of the size of Karagwe, Gisaka, Bugesera, and Burundi all emerged at about the same time as the Nyiginya realm did. So within central Rwanda Ndori's work succeeded in creating something novel, something never seen before: a kingdom that was completely different from the miniature chiefdoms that had preceded it, even if it did incorporate older elements such as the magical ideology of kingship or the participation of a ruling class.

NOTES

Introduction

1. C. Wrigley, *Kingship and State*, 1. He also notes that all of the four main kingdoms of this region were quite different from each other.

2. The quantity of oral sources of information about this kingdom is extraordinary, even compared to Bunyoro or Buganda. These sources comprise over 300 historical tales and 175 different dynastic poems, among others, as well as the only considerable body of ritual texts known in Africa.

3. See articles in *History in Africa* from 1974 onward and a fairly recent overview by J. Vansina, *Oral Tradition as History*.

4. The last of these is B. Lugan, *Histoire du Rwanda*. J. P. Chrétien, *L'Afrique des Grands Lacs,* is more recent, but Chrétien writes from a wholly different perspective from the others and is less under the influence of Kagame's vision.

5. A. Kagame, *Un abrégé de l'ethno-histoire du Rwanda* and *Un abrégé de l'histoire du Rwanda,* henceforth cited as *Abrégé* 1 and *Abrégé* 2.

6. Notably F. Nahimana, *Le Rwanda*.

7. Wrigley, *Kingship and State*, 41.

8. Elsewhere in the region such an organization was totally unknown.

9. Besides oral data we have also used some auxiliary archeological, biological, and linguistic sources.

10. For a general overview, see J. Vansina, *L'Évolution du royaume rwanda à 1900* with the bibliographical supplement of the 2000 edition. See also his "Historical Tales (Ibiteekerezo) and the History of Rwanda" and "Useful Anachronisms."

11. A critical edition of this liturgy is contained in M. d'Hertefelt and A. Coupez, *La Royauté sacrée de l'ancien Rwanda*. Further comment by Vansina can be found in "Useful Anachronisms."

12. Editions of these poems can be found in Kagame, *La Poésie dynastique au Rwanda* and "Étude critique d'un vieux poème historique du Rwanda" as well as in A. Coupez and Th. Kamanzi, *Littérature de cour au Rwanda* and "Poèmes dynastiques rwanda." C. Rugamba provides critical analysis in *La Poésie face à l'histoire.*

13. An edition of this list of succession is contained in A. Kagame, *Inganji Karinga*, 1:93–97, and in his *Notion de génération appliquée à la généalogie dynastique et à*

l'histoire du Rwanda, 15–17. See also Nkurikiyimfura, "La révision d'une chronologie," 151–54.

14. Rugamba, *Poésie*, 328, n.80, deplores that a poem cannot be directly interpreted, commenting that "the piece would have been a first rate source of historical information, if the names it contains could have been identified."

15. One can object that esoteric information was separate from this reservoir. But this secret knowledge related only to the liturgy of the rituals and did not include any historical information.

16. The passages in a poem that evoke kings before the one in honor of whom the poem was composed are easily interpolated at any later time and must be considered suspect.

17. The oldest publication is P. Loupias, "Tradition et légende des Batutsi sur la création du monde et leur établissement au Rwanda," gathered at the latest in 1907, the same year that J. Czekanowski conducted the research published in *Forschungen im Nil-Kongo Zwischengebiet*. The latter was the first author who tried and failed to gather traditions at the court.

18. R. de Briey, "Musinga." De Briey probably obtained this list at Nyanza, either directly from court historians through an interpreter or from a White Father.

19. Pagès, "Au Ruanda sur les bords du lac Kivu," 377. These articles were followed up by a work that included further data: *Un Royaume Hamite au centre de l'Afrique*. He obtained the list of kings around 1920 ("Au Ruanda. À la cour du Mwami," 476).

20. Schumacher arrived in Rwanda in 1907. From 1928 onward he was a full-time researcher. He left Rwanda in 1936, obtained a doctorate at the university of Vienna in 1938, finished his synthesis in 1943, and returned to Rwanda from 1950 to 1954. He was very competent in the Rwandan language. See P. Schebesta, "In Memoriam Peter Schumacher." He differs from other authors in that he carefully cites his sources and gives some details about the discussions with his collaborators that yielded those sources. Delmas arrived in 1905 and spent his life in Rwanda as a practicing missionary until 1950. Abbé Alexis Kagame (1912–81), the most renowned Rwandan scholar and the one who has exerted the most influence, was born in a family of ritualists *(abiru)* educated by the White Fathers. He began his research into the history of Rwanda in 1936. See "Alexis Kagame: l'homme et son oeuvre," P. Smith, "Entretien avec l'abbé Alexis Kagame," and C. Vidal, *Sociologie des passions*, 45–61.

21. Most of his manuscript dates from 1938 and the text was completed in 1943. The synthesis was published on microfilm in 1958. P. Schumacher, *Ruanda*.

22. Kagame, *Inganji Karinga*. A second edition was published in 1959.

23. Schumacher underlines the independence of his information from the data given in Pagès, 122. G. Van Overschelde, *Bij de reuzen en dwergen van Ruanda*, while he cites Pagès (61 n.1), was strongly influenced by Schumacher (6).

24. Kagame, *Notion*, 15, and Schumacher, *Ruanda*, 122 (indirectly through Mazina, who obtained it from Rwanyange in 1928).

25. Kagame, *Abrégé* 2, 20, and Delmas, *Généalogies*, 6 n.1, 13, 40, 152. Apparently Schumacher did not consult him.

26. Schumacher, *Ruanda*, 121, 425; Delmas, *Généalogies*, 6 n.1, 13, 14 n.1, 33, 40, 106, 152, 177–78; Kagame, *Notion*, 100 n.1; Van Overschelde, *Bij de reuzen*, 70. Kayijuka was also one of the main informants of the anthropologist J. Maquet.

27. Kagame, *Notion*, 100 n.1; *Abrégé* 1, photograph 6; *Abrégé* 2, 39 (he worked with Kagame in 1936); *Introduction*, 280 (he worked with Van Overschelde before 1936); Schumacher, *Ruanda*, 121 (the collaboration began around 1928), 749; Delmas, *Généalogies*, 1 n.6, 33, 106, 161 (deceased in 1946), 166, 185; Van Overschelde, *Bij de reuzen*, 59, 70 (an octogenarian by the time of his death in 1946).

28. Let us also mention Ruzigaminturo, a relative of Kayijuka, consulted by Schumacher and Kagame, as well as Karera, who worked with Kagame and Delmas (Kagame, *Notion*, 95 n.1, 100 n.1; id., *Introduction*, 280, id., *Abrégé* 1, photograph 3).

29. Pagès, "Au Ruanda," 392, 568–69.

30. An argument often resorted to by Kagame. But once the text of the liturgy of the royal rituals became available it was found that it did not contain any *intekerezo* that had been transmitted as "explanations."

31. Schumacher, *Ruanda*, 137–43, 145; see also Van Overschelde, *Bij de Reuzen*, 70, about one point concerning the first king of Burundi raised during this encounter.

32. Kagame, *Notion*, 98 n.1. He corresponded with Baranyanka about these topics in 1949 and 1957.

33. With the exception of most of the oldest among them, kings are called by two names: a regnal or dynastic name, which is an element in the royal ideology, and a personal name. In this book the regnal names are rendered in capital letters. However, we will avoid citing them except when providing the list of dynastic succession and when discussing the royal ideology.

34. See appendix 1 for a discussion of this list.

35. Vansina, "Historical Tales."

36. Those myths were the first traditions to be reported that showed their importance for the ideology. See Loupias "Tradition," Czekanowski, *Forschungen*, 286–87, and E. Johanssen, *Ruanda*, 72–73, whose discussion of these myths is rudimentary. They have been the object of passionate debate since at least 1930 (Schumacher, *Ruanda*, 145–58, e.g., 151) and reflect the history of the political struggle since the 1950s (d'Hertefelt, "Mythes et idéologies dans le Rwanda ancien et contemporain"). Today they, among others, are still invoked to justify the territorial claims of today's Rwanda (Gihanga!) and also to legitimize the present government. But because they are speculations, these myths have no direct historical foundation at all and hence find no place in this work.

37. A similar situation occurs in Buganda where the data become detailed and credible from the mid-eighteenth century onward. See Wrigley, *Kingship and State.*

38. I prefer Schumacher, *Ruanda,* because his five collaborators are well known.

39. A. Kagame, *Les Milices du Rwanda précolonial* and *L'Histoire des armées-bovines dans l'ancien Rwanda.*

40. For the armies, see L. Nkongori, "Les Bashakamba" and the *Ibitéekerezo* texts recorded on tape, Gahindiro file, nos. 1, 17, 22, 27, and texts recorded by hand, Gahindiro file, no. 12 (Abakemba). Hereafter this collection will be cited by the title of a file, accompanied by T (tape recorded) and/or H (recorded by hand). For family reminiscences and the link between them and the Nyaruguru army, see Kayijuka, "Lebensgeschichte des Grossfürsten Kayijuka und seiner Ahnen seit Sultan Yuhi Mazimpaka, König von Ruanda."

41. Vidal, *Sociologie des passions,* 58–59.

42. Kagame, *Abrégé* 1, 121.

Chapter 1. Central Rwanda on the Eve of the Emergence of the Kingdom

1. For the application of this technique, see D. Schoenbrun, *A Green Place, a Good Place,* 37–55, 265–69, and his *The Historical Reconstruction of Great Lakes Bantu Cultural Vocabulary.*

2. See maps 1 to 3 for the location of the old historical regions cited in this book.

3. See C. Prioul and P. Sirven, *Atlas du Rwanda,* plates 2 to 11, for the position of central Rwanda in relation to the other natural regions of the Republic of Rwanda today.

4. D. de Lame, "Instants retrouvés," comments that "the anthropologist who respects the rhythms of the hill is integrated into that universe but remains a stranger on the next hill."

5. In altitudes over two thousand meters one can no longer farm beans or bananas and these are replaced by cowpeas. See E. Everaerts, *Monographie agricole du Ruanda-Urundi,* 61, 64; Prioul and Sirven, *Atlas,* plate 19.

6. Prioul and Sirven, *Atlas,* plate 6.

7. R. Heremans, A. Bart, and F. Bart, "Agriculture et paysages rwandais à travers les sources missionnaires," 9–10, note that the soil are too sandy and that there is a lack of rain.

8. The sorghum cultivated for the first fruit ritual was grown in Bumbogo.

9. To a large extent map 4 follows E. Roche, "Apports de la palynologie à la connaissance du Quaternaire supérieur au Rwanda," 63, which traces the vegetation of Rwanda from around the onset of our era. This map more closely reflects the realities of the seventeenth and eighteenth centuries than

more recent vegetation maps, particularly in regard to the rain and the piedmont forests.

10. J. Hiernaux and E. Maquet, *Cultures préhistoriques de l'âge des métaux au Ruanda-Urundi et au Kivu (Congo belge)*, 6–31, 68–83; J. Nenquin, *Contributions to the Study of the Prehistoric Cultures of Rwanda and Burundi*, 272–87; F. Van Noten, *Histoire archéologique du Rwanda*, 33–49, and appendices; C. Desmedt, "Poteries anciennes décorées à la roulette dans la région des Grands Lacs." But the sites with X/Y ceramics cover the whole period from the fourteenth century onward to about 1900. They can therefore give a spurious impression of the population density, since not all of them date to the seventeenth century. But even the sites where archaic hoes and hammers, which probably are earlier than the seventeenth century, have been found are also well distributed over the whole region.

11. Ikiremera is the ancient name designating Burundi according to F. M. Rodegem, *Dictionnaire rundi-français*, 347.

12. Nenquin, *Contributions*, 18–70, 295; Van Noten, *Histoire*, 1–8. A site in the region (Nyarunazi in Burundi) probably dates from the older Acheulian period, the oldest known industry associated with *Homo sapiens sapiens*.

13. Urewe ceramics are part of the east African Chifumbazi complex. See D. W. Phillipson, *African Archaeology*, 187–91. The oldest sites in Rwanda with Urewe ceramics date at least to c. 500 BCE according to B. Clist, "A Critical Reappraisal of the Chronological Framework of the Early Urewe Iron Age Industry," 43, 48–55. Even at that time all the inhabitants were not necessarily recent immigrants.

14. M. C. Van Grunderbeek, "The Iron Age in Rwanda and Burundi," 27. See also Van Noten, *Histoire*, 32, who notes that the teeth of cattle found at Remera are probably of the Inkuku variety and date from the first centuries CE.

15. See Van Noten, *Histoire*, 66, for a specific date of 700 rather than "about the eighth century" in Desmedt, "Poteries," 175.

16. Only ten sites are known in Rwanda and Burundi. See Desmedt, "Poteries," 178; Hiernaux and Maquet, *Cultures*, 68–74; Nenquin, *Contributions*, 283–87.

17. Desmedt, "Poteries," 183. She looks at the distribution and the chronology of this ceramic in the whole Great Lakes region and ends up attributing it to herders who stemmed from the east of Lake Victoria and had turned around the southern end of the lake.

18. The sites are Cyinkomane and Akameru "of the ninth or tenth centuries." See Van Noten, *Histoire*, 34–35, 62, and A. Gautier, "Les restes osseux des sites d'Akameru et de Cyinkomane (Ruhengeri, Rwanda)," 104–20.

19. Nenquin, *Contributions*, 281–82; Desmedt, "Poteries," 181, 182–83; Schumacher, *Ruanda*, 120–21; illustrated in G. R. Célis, "La métallurgie traditionelle au Burundi, au Rwanda et au Buha," 31–32. R. Bourgeois, *Banyarwanda et Barundi*, photo 1; Van Overschelde, *Bij de reuzen*, 51. Desmedt counts nine W sites (Muramba, Karama, Muginga, Ruli, Kabuye, Gishubi, Bweya, Kansi, Kinkanga) but there are others such as at Gisagara near Butare.

20. Desmedt, "Poetries," 185–92.

21. For Muyaga, see Nenquin, *Contributions*, 272–75. I have also consulted my personal notes of the dig.

22. Desmedt, "Poteries," 188, notes such a discovery at Dahwe, Muyaga. F. Van Noten, *Les Tombes du roi Cyirima Rujugira et de la reine-mère Nyirayuhi Kanjogera*, 23–41, describes a host of metal (iron, copper), bone, shell, ceramic, and stone objects as well as glass beads found in Rujugira's tomb, but the chronology is unsatisfactory since the burial occurred in 1931.

23. This person was called Muyenzi, a personal name of MUTARA Semugeshi. Contra Desmedt, "Poteries," 182. See also Kagame *Abrégé* 1, 109, and *Ibiteekerezo*, Semugeshi file, T, nos. 1.1, 3.1, 7.1; H, nos. 2.1, 4.1, 7.1.

24. On the other hand, neither the spearpoint nor the axe underwent any changes. Let us remember that the more efficient and lighter new hoe facilitated farm work in general but especially benefited women's work.

25. Célis "La métallurgie," 39–46. The distribution of the three existing types of furnaces correlates relatively well with the territory of various kingdoms. Moreover, this distribution suggests a relative chronology for their spread that would only have begun well after the onset of the later Iron Age, for one of the earliest W sites is associated with still another type of furnace.

26. Van Noten, *Histoire*, 64, asks himself the question.

27. At the dawn of the colonial period in 1907, Czekanowski, *Forschungen im Nil-Kongo-Zwischengebiet*, 109–14 (table with numbers, 114), is probably the first to give us an estimate of the distribution of the population in Rwanda and of its density in various regions. Heremans, Bart, and Bart, "Agriculture," 12, summarize the impressions the missionaries had of Rwanda as "a mosaic of islands already settled by many and intensely cultivated" alternating with zones with little settlement.

28. Bwanamukari is a region that stretches to the south and east of the modern town of Butare.

29. Van Grunderbeek and H. Doutrelepont, "Étude de charbons de bois provenant de sites métallurgiques de l'âge du fer ancien au Rwanda et au Burundi," 2 (maps 1 and 2, formations 1–3). Despite the fact that the maps represent the state of affairs around the year 1 CE they give a better idea of the extent of the forests in the seventeenth century than modern maps do for clearing has increased considerably since the end of the eighteenth century. See Reisdorff, *Enquêtes foncières au Rwanda*, 17, 19 (Bumbogo and Ndiza), 50 (Butare region); P. Schumacher, *Expedition zu den zentralafrikanischen Kivu-Pygmäen: Die Physische und soziale Umwelt der Kivu Pygmäen*, 14, and id., *Ruanda*, 110, 250–51; Nahimana, *Le Rwanda*, 127, 131.

30. At least that part of northern Bugesera that is presently in Rwanda. All the sources maintain as much and N. Leleup (personal communication) confirms it for the last five hundred years on the basis of entomological data.

31. Archeological sites succeed one another on the banks of the Mukungwa

and a dense cluster of population lived there around 1900. See Czekanowski, *Forschungen,* 111–13.

32. Ibid., 109, 114, and von Ramsay, "Über seine Expeditionen nach Ruanda und dem Rikwa-See," 310. But R. Kandt, "Bericht der Forschungreisenden Dr Richard Kandt aus Ruanda," 118, reports very high emigration from there caused by drought and looting by Rwandans. This case (and the one in Bugoyi mentioned later in this chapter) shows that one cannot just project the population distributions reported around 1900 three centuries back.

33. P. Schumacher, *Physische,* 17, 20 (Bugoyi). D. Newbury, *Kings and Clans,* 44–45, insists on the "individual" (of families?) character of this mobility.

34. The definitive and massive emigration of a local elite is reported only during the conquest of Buganza c. 1780, and perhaps also in southern Ndorwa around the same time. See Reisdorff, *Enquêtes,* 142.

35. The determined resistance of the hunters of the Rugezi marshes as well as those in neighboring Kigezi (Uganda) is only the best-known example of this behavior. See Schumacher, *Expedition zu den zentralafrikanischen Kivu-Pygmäen: Die Kivu-Pygmäen,* 47, 51–53, 61, 67, 77–78, 80–81, 84–86, 88–89; id., *Physische,* 94–95, 97–99, 149–53.

36. For supposed clan migrations, see A. Nyagahene, *Histoire et peuplement.*

37. Czekanowski, *Forschungen,* 118–21; Schumacher, *Physische,* 59–61 (Bugoyi); Prioul and Sirven, *Atlas,* plate 19 (commentary by J -F. Gottanègre); R. Botte, "Rwanda and Burundi, 1889–1930," 55–57 (especially 57 for epidemic yaws). Rwogera died of TB. But had the disease been around earlier in time? Smallpox is reported well before the coup of c. 1770 (Kayijuka, "Lebensgeschichte," 138) and especially mentioned ever since the epidemic of 1801 that killed Sentabyo. This epidemic spread from the east and must be linked to the extension of the Indian Ocean trade. But was the disease in these cases really smallpox?

38. Schumacher, *Ruanda,* 332, and his *Physische,* 60, where he points out that around 1930 there still was a 50 percent mortality rate overall and that it was highest among Tutsi; Czekanowski, *Forschungen,* 115–18; Prioul and Sirven, *Atlas,* plate 18, for the demography of the recent past.

39. Eyewitness account of Kandt, "Bericht über meine Reisen und gesammte Thätigkeit in Deutsch Ost-Afrika," 254. Kandt was unaware that the famine resulted in part from the various military operations of Musinga's troops in the province. As we shall see, Rwandans have recalled extraordinary famines since about 1775. The citation reminds one also that the first victims were always also the least prosperous (slaves in this case).

40. One sees mention of epizootic diseases in the reigns of Mazimpaka and Ndabarasa (*Ibiteekerezo,* Rujugira file, T, no. 15.1 and 5, and id., file *Ndabarasa* H, no. 11). The great epizootic epidemics of 1891–92 (Botte,"Rwanda," 72–73) destroyed most of the herds. Before this date neither the frequency nor the severity of epizootic diseases are known. See D. Adamantidis, *Monographie pastorale*

du Ruanda-Urundi, for a discussion of the reproduction of cattle (39–40) and veterinary practices (50–53) at the time. The cattle that died consisted mainly of young steers and sterile cows and hence did not affect rates of reproduction.

41. J. Sutton, "Archaeological Sites of East Africa," 49–56, 59, 69–70; P. Robertshaw and D. Taylor, "Climate Change and the Rise of Political Complexity in Western Uganda," 14, 17, 18, 19; A. Reid and P. Robertshaw, "A New Look at Ankole Capital Sites," 86; T. Tshihiluka, "Ryamurari, capitale de l'ancien royaume du Ndorwa," 150–51. Yet, although the contrast among sites is striking, our argument from lack of evidence found at them always remains vulnerable in principle.

42. Schumacher, *Physische* and *Kivu-Pygmäen*, for a general overview of such groups in the northwest of the present Republic of Rwanda.

43. d'Hertefelt and Coupez, *La Royauté sacrée de l'ancien Rwanda*, 443 (*"-úmwé,"* meaning "hoe of the unity of the country"). This hoe is used in path seven (renewal of the dynastic fire) and path seventeen (enthronement). The hoe as symbol must be very old for it does not mesh well with the usual symbolic language used in those rituals in which dynastic unity is expressed by the drum and the dynastic bull.

44. The placement of the houses is evident from the archeological sites. General descriptions can be found in Heremans, Bart, and Bart, "Agriculture," 6–10. According to their sources (23–24), the bottom lands would absolutely not have been cultivated at that time.

45. The description is backed by the existence of a sizeable, old agricultural terminology like that documented in Schoenbrun, *Historical Reconstruction*. See Everaerts, *Monographie*, 61–70, for an introduction to the description of their agricultural practices. See Chrétien, *L'Afrique des Grands Lacs*, 46–50, for a description of such practices in the wider region.

46. We only cite two terms of the relevant comparative vocabulary having to do with tools: "hoe" and "sickle." Schoenbrun, *Historical Reconstruction*, no. 76 (*"-suka,"* "hoe"). *"Isuka"* is "hoe" in Rwanda, Rundi, Ha, Sukuma, Vinza, Konzo, Nande, and Kwaya. *"Umuhoro"* is "sickle" in Rwanda, Rundi, Ha, and Kiga/Nkore. The two words are older than the common ancestral language for Rwanda, Rundi, and Ha. The sickle was first used as a bush knife and later as a pruning tool for banana trees.

47. See d'Hertefelt, "Le Rwanda" 25–29; Czekanowski, *Forschungen*, 137–39; Schumacher, *Ruanda*, 924–44, for the whole associated vocabulary; ibid., 870–74, for the cattle-breeding calendar, and id., *Physische*, 22–25, for the agricultural calendar.

48. These are both found on archeological sites. Terminology: *"amasaka"* is "sorghum" in Rwanda, Rundi Ha; *"uburo"* is "finger millet" according to Schoenbrun, *Historical Reconstruction*, no. 68, to which Rwanda, Rundi, and Ha must be added.

49. Schoenbrun, *Historical Reconstruction*, no. 56. This probably is the legume

found at Ruli (Hiernaux and Maquet, *Cultures,* 14). These are sometimes erroneously called cowpeas.

50. *"Iteke"* in Rwanda, Rundi, and Ha.

51. *"Igikoro"* in Rwanda, Rundi, and Ha. This is *Dioscorea alata* L.

52. Schoenbrun, *Historical Reconstruction,* no. 66, "Yam sp.," and no. 73 (*Dioscorea minutiflora* Engl.).

53. *"Umwungu"* is "gourd" in Rwanda, Rundi, and Ha; *"igisura"* is "gourd" in Rwanda; *"umusora"* is "gourd" in Ha. *"Igisora"* in Rundi is probably *Urtica massaica* Milder.

54. Schoenbrun, *Historical Reconstruction,* no. 38 (*"*-caabo,"* "calabash"). It is found as such in Ha, but in Rundi it has the meaning "churn made of a calabash" and in Rwanda it can mean any churn. See Schumacher, *Ruanda,* 153.

55. *Urunumbu* or *uruhombo,* but this name also refers to *Vernonia hochstetteri.* In Rundi *"inumbu"* refers to a salsify bush and *"umuhumbo"* to *Vernonia karaguensis* Oliv. and Hiern.

56. Type AAA. See G. A. Rossel, *Taxonomic-Linguistic Study of Plantain in Africa,* 206–7, 210, 219. The banana would have been imported from the north and its introduction is often linked to that of the so-called Nyoro invasion. Schumacher, *Ruanda,* 153, 936, argues they were imported from Bunyoro and Kagame, *Abrégé* 1, 79, claims their introduction was linked to a Nyoro invasion. But for F. Géraud, "The Settlement of the Bakiga," 32, 34, the banana was introduced from Rwanda into Mpororo during the reign of Mazimpaka and into Kigezi also from Rwanda. These attributions are only valid for AAA and not for the AAB cultivars around Lake Kivu. If they are correct, the introduction dates from the seventeenth century. Botte, "Rwanda," 70 n.75, claims that the famine of 1894–97 led to a considerable expansion of the banana groves, which is hard to credit considering the profusion of large banana groves noted by all travelers from 1897 onward. Moreover, famine conditions obtained in fact from c. 1898 to 1901 in Bugoyi and in Gisaka.

57. See Delmas, *Généalogies,* 3, for its meaning and use. In Burundi the three-pronged fork *(isando)* symbolized an alliance between two lineages and was part of the dowry (Rodegem, *Dictionnaire,* 394).

58. Schumacher, *Ruanda,* 940–42.

59. See A. Gautier, "Les restes osseux," 114, for an account of archeological traces of goats, sheep and chicken. As for cattle, Adamantidis, *Monographie,* 30, speaks of one to four cows per family of farmers. Forty percent of the bovine cattle in Rwanda was kept by Hutu as compared to 49.5 percent by Tutsi in 1955. These numbers are, of course, not valid for central Rwanda in the seventeenth century, but suggest that farmers may well have kept a substantial quantity of cattle.

60. Everaerts, *Monographie,* 95–96.

61. Nahimana, *Le Ruanda,* 34–37, 40.

62. *"Ubushyo"* is "herd" also in Rundi, Ha, Nkore/Kiga, Nande, and Shi.

For the old cattle-breeding vocabulary, also consult Schoenbrun, *Historical Reconstruction*, nos. 52, 63, 65, 78. See Adamantidis, *Monographie*, 22–25, for an instructive comparison between Rwanda and Rundi terms; see Schumacher, *Ruanda*, 858, for herd size.

63. Schumacher, *Ruanda*, 825–923, is the best account of the herding economy and its vocabulary. But see also Adamantidis, *Monographie*, 16–53. In the forests, the herd attained about seventy head, which shows that the extent of available pasturage was more important than the amount of available labor. An ordinary herd must have a single tract of pasture of 60 to 100 hectares, since each head requires 1.70 hectare of pastureland per year (Adamantidis, *Monographie*, 69; J-N. Nkurikiyimfura, *Le Gros bétail et la société rwandaise évolution historique*, 288, tells us that by local decree no. 7 1954 it was proposed to allow at least 1 hectare of pastureland per head and at most 1.5 hectare). This number is roughly twice the surface required to feed a monogamous family, which amounts to less than one hectare.

64. Schoenbrun, *Historical Reconstruction*, no. 45. The herd there was called *engana*, a word derived from one meaning "one hundred." See also J. Roscoe, *The Banyankole*, 93, as well as R. Burton, *The Lake Regions of Central Africa*, 2:181, who describes herds in Karagwe around 1858.

65. For the salty wells, see Nkurikiyimfura, *Gros Bétail*, 141–53, and Schumacher, *Kivu-Pygmäen*, 21–22. For transhumance, see Heremans, Bart, and Bart, "Agriculture," 16.

66. See both Schumacher, *Ruanda*, 870–79, 881–84, and L. Classe, *L'Organisation politique du Rwanda au début de l'occupation belge (1916)*, 9, for an account on transhumance and the need for herds returning from the mountains to be reacclimatized during their descent into central Rwanda.

67. Schumacher, *Ruanda*, 880–81.

68. Later on a herd of cattle of the Inyambo breed will require twelve herders for thirty to forty head, that is one person for every three head of cattle. Schumacher, *Ruanda*, 885; Adamantidis, *Monographie*, 42–44.

69. Among cattle-breeding nomads these teams were permanent during the whole year. As herders in Central Rwanda became more sedentary their role was less prominent but did not disappear. See Classe, *Organisation politique*, 10, who notes incidences of looting committed by herders in the forest.

70. Schoenbrun, *Historical Reconstruction*, no. 194 *("umuja")*.

71. *Ibitéekerezo*, Gahindiro file, T, no. 15. The matter was serious enough for the hero to transgress a royal decree.

72. Schumacher, *Ruanda*, 876–79. This reconstruction of the division of labor by gender is in part based on the fact that it was universal in the region of the Great Lakes.

73. See H. Cochet, "Burundi: quelques questions sur l'origine et la différentiation d'un système agraire" 15–62, for manuring in Burundi.

74. Classe, *Organisation politique*, 5, 7–8. This text of 1916 finds Kandt's

affirmation that every head of cattle needed four hectares of pasture to be exaggerated. But Classe attributes the low population density of Marangara in part to "the Tutsi [who] prevent[ed] larger fields in order to have more pastureland."

75. See Schumacher, *Ruanda*, 487–97, for the theory, and his *Physische*, 102–3, for the reality. To deny that one eats any solid vegetable food (which was associated with the farming status of farmer) amounts to asserting herding status.

76. Schumacher, *Physische*, 72. "Famine is not our concern: it kills only those who have no cattle."

77. Looting fields was par for the course during military operations. Thus the first known great famines around 1770 and from c. 1798 to c. 1802 were mainly caused by a state of war, as was also true in the case of the famines at the end of the nineteenth century and the one from 1916 to 1918. But this was not always so—it was not so, for instance, in the case of the Gikoko famine of Rwogera's time. On the other hand, a famine easily led itself to hostilities: "Rwanda was struck by famine, but Bugesera was rich" and later in the tale "invade Bugesera! These then are famished people. Those who were in the fields, those who were at court, those who were in their households . . . instantly arrived with their spears and their bows" (*Ibiteekerezo*, Sentabyo file, T, no. 2).

78. Everaerts, *Monographie*, 69–70. See also Lugan, *Histoire du Rwanda*, 323–28, and id., "Famines et disettes au Rwanda," 151–74, for the impact of recent famines and an estimate of the number of victims. Unfortunately, the sources do not relate the behavior adopted by the different components (e.g., sexes) of the population during such disasters.

79. R. Kandt, "Gewerbe in Ruanda," and Schumacher, *Ruanda*, 960–61. Célis, "La métallurgie," finds three different regions of iron smelting, only one of which was in central Rwanda. The smiths of Buberuka were the greatest purveyors of hoes for northern central Rwanda also according to Lugan, *Histoire du Rwanda*, 187.

80. Schumacher, *Ruanda*, 696–98, 957a–59 (see 959 for his discussion of the standard of value); id., *Physische*, 30–31; Kandt, "Gewerbe in Ruanda," 361; Czekanowski, *Forschungen*, 160–61. Does the fact that packets of new hoes were found on the late Iron Age sites of Muginga and Kansi suggest that hoes were already being used as standards of value at that time? See Nenquin, *Contributions*, 281.

81. For markets and trade, see Czekanowski, *Forschungen*, 161–65; D. Newbury, "Lake Kivu Regional Trade in the Nineteenth Century," 6–30; see also id., "'Bunyabungo': The Western Rwandan Frontier, c. 1750–1850," 181–83, where he argues that this trade is thought to be very old. See also Lugan, *Histoire du Rwanda*, 162–89; Schumacher, *Ruanda*, 957–59, and id., *Physische*, 29–33.

82. Glass beads, cowries, and copper objects have been found at Ntusi, Bigo, Munsa, and Kibiro, dating from well before 1500 according to Sutton,

"Archaeological Sites," 49, as well as Robertshaw and Taylor, "Environmental Change," 15, 16.

83. For kin groups in general, see d'Hertefelt, "Le Rwanda," 41–48. For *inzu*, see Schoenbrun, *Historical Reconstruction*, nos. 121–22. For kinship terms, see ibid., nos. 95, 99, 120, 128, 136, 141. The fact that the word *inzu* implies a common residence for the married sons but not for the daughters suggests that it was a purely patrilineal group. The whole terminology of kinship is quite old, but that only demonstrates the antiquity of the structures, nothing more. There certainly must have been changes over time in, for example, their size, their precise functions, and the detailed mutual behavior of their members about which we remain ignorant. This gap in our knowledge must be taken into account when twentieth-century ethnographic data are used.

84. *"Guhora,"* "to avenge." See Schoenbrun, *Historical Reconstruction*, no. 302.

85. Thus Binama refused to rally his army, which was then fighting against the Rundi, despite an explicit order of the king, before he had exacted retribution from the murderer of his older brother. The king (Semugeshi) congratulated him on that decision! See *Ibitéekerezo*, Mazimpaka file, T, no. 4.

86. *Ibitéekerezo*, Gahindiro file, T, no. 3.2.

87. Despite the difference between *"umuryango,"* "lineage," and *"umuryângo,"* "entrance to the house, portal of a compound," the first derived from the second and both words are attested to with both meanings in many languages in east Africa. See Schoenbrun, *Historical Reconstruction*, nos. 101, 106, and 135, for the obsolete term.

88. Czekanowski, *Forschungen*, 237–38; Schumacher, *Ruanda*, 727–34. Mazina, "Nachtrag zur Lebensbeschreibung des Kayijuka," 162–63, describes a case of a particularly macabre case of killing by torture lasting for four or five days in front of the shine of the murdered ancestor, so that she could witness the avenging.

89. Schumacher, *Ruanda*, 437. The genealogical depth of the whole, then, did not dictate a scission, which makes sense considering the hazards of demography.

90. For this social position in action the bundle of P. Smith, *Le Récit populaire au Rwanda*, is an eye-opener.

91. See Smith, *Récit*, 326–33, for the charming tale of a girl who chooses her own husband, and 62–63, 180–85, for the theme of the warrior-girl.

92. The most famous among the rather many woman prophets were Nyirabiyoro during the reign of Ndabarasa and Muhumuza, aka Nyabingi, in Ndorwa after Rwabugiri's death. For the role of women in possession and healing cults, see I. Berger, *Religion and Resistance*, 22–25. An historical vignette tells how the fleeing mother of Rujugira subsisted by making herself out to be the priestess of a new cult she had invented (*Ibitéekerezo*, Rujugira file, H, no. 16).

93. Schoenbrun, *Historical Reconstruction*, no. 267. Slave women were never sold. After a term of service, they were given in marriage by their wealthy owners, often without payment of any dowry at all.

94. Ibid., no. 201, *"ubukire,"* "wealth, fortune, blessing"; id., no. 209, *"ubukungu,"* "wealth, wealth in stocks of food and in small stock, wealth in fields and in cattle." *"Ubutunzi,"* "wealth in commercial goods, trade" (from *"-tunda,"* "to trade, to take away").

95. For a description of what wealth was and how a Hutu could acquire it, see *Ibiteekerezo,* Gahindiro file, T, no. 5. In this tale Mirenge became wealthy by his mastery over the agricultural calendar. He sold his agricultural surplus for old hoes and for a few head of cattle and ended up being made a direct client of the king *(ubuhake).*

96. Especially between herders who themselves owned no animals at all and owners of cattle. No numbers are available to measure the differential in the seventeenth century between a poor herder and a rich one, but it was certainly lower than c. 1900 when the wealthiest owned more than twenty thousand head of cattle according to Schumacher, *Ruanda,* 602.

97. The words *"ubugabire"* (literally "distribution for X") and *"shebuja"* (literally "father of the servitude") were also known in Burundi, Buha, and Ijwi (Newbury, *Kings and Clans,* 149, 299–300). The concept and its two terms are certainly quite old but the modalities of this type of contract were always quite flexible. It must be stressed that such contracts did not allow for a perpetual exploitation of the client, or for exploitation without bounds.

98. The term is found in Rwanda, Rundi, and Ha with the same meaning. It is therefore old.

99. Thus Kagame, *La Poésie dynastique du Rwanda,* 189, no. 123, *"Ubwaami bugira ubwoko"* ("Kingship belongs to a lineage"); Coupez and Kamanzi, *Récits,* 24, discussing branches of a clan, Nyagahene, *Histoire et peuplement,* 204–5, and Chrétien, *Afrique,* 62, 329 n.18, all claim that *"ubwoko"* only came to designate the three social groups after 1950, "following colonial corrosion." Given the overall meaning of the word one may doubt this. In 1925, E. Hurel, *Dictionnaire Runyarwanda* already defined *"-oko" ("ubw-," "ama-")* as "race, family, species" and uses "race" with regard to the Hutu category (327).

100. For the clans, see M. d'Hertefelt, *Les Clans du Rwanda ancien,* Nyagahene, *Histoire et peuplement,* and D. Newbury's critique "The Clans of Rwanda."

101. d'Hertefelt, *Les Clans,* 5–6, 43; Nyagahene, *Histoire et peuplement,* 259–64; A. Kagame, *Les Organisations socio-familiales de l'ancien Rwanda,* 209–13; Schumacher, *Ruanda,* 1188–93; id., *Physische,* 53–58, 81. Nahimana, *Le Rwanda,* 71–81, remarks that the same clans were not *abasangwa butaka* everywhere. Each region had its own.

102. Newbury, "Clans," is right in its critique of Nyagahene, *Histoire et peuplement,* and Lugan, *Histoire du Rwanda,* 65–75, on this point.

103. The remark of Delmas, *Généalogies,* 57, concerning the Abene draws attention to this fact. An examination of other genealogies reveals similar cases (thus he links a whole group of Yambwa to the Kono clan [139]). There are no doubt also many cases of incomplete genealogies.

104. Nyagahene, *Histoire et peuplement,* 662, and passim. Moreover, the economic specialization he attributes to each clan is illusory in many cases.

105. See Newbury, "Clans," for a conclusive demonstration involving the eighteenth and nineteenth centuries.

106. The presence of several autochthon clans, as in central Rwanda where there are three (Singa, Zigaba and Gesera), could be the result of the successive superposition of several "dynasties" of immigrants.

107. Besides Rwanda, only Nkore had a small number of clans in the nineteenth century and ones as large as those of Rwanda. Elsewhere, there were many more of them—Burundi, for instance, even then sported a hundred different ones at least.

108. For the ancient Renge, see Pagès, *Royaume hamite,* 543–44; see Schumacher, *Physische,* 37, 68–70, which is partly according to Makobe. See also id., *Ruanda,* 120–21, 149, as well as 156, where he notes that according to Sekarama, they would have ruled Nduga, Buberuka, Murera, Bugoyi, Bwisha, Bufumbira, Gishari, Bushi, Busanza, Bufundu, and Bunanyambiri, and Hiernaux, "Note sur une ancienne population du Ruanda-Urundi" (according to Kayijuka). The ancient Renge are thus associated with the northwest part of modern Rwanda and with Gihanga, as well as with Nduga and Bungwe. Today Renge are still found in Kigezi (P. Ngologoza, *Kigezi and its People,* 3, 6; Géraud," Settlement," 27; M. M. R. Rwankwenda, "The History of Kayonza," 124). The new ethnonym "Banyamulenge" has the same meaning as "Abarenge."

109. *"-anda,"* "to scatter," in Rwanda and Rundi. Derived from that is *"umwanda,"* "sweepings," in Rwanda, Rundi, and Ha, and *"urwanda,"* "the space occupied by a scattering or spreading out." Kagame, *Abrégé* 1, 47–49, unwittingly demonstrates the use of this qualifier.

110. *"uRwaanda rwaa Nzira"* (*Ibitéekerezo,* Ndori file, H, nos. 11, 12).

111. For nineteenth-century Twa, see Schumacher, *Kivu-Pygmäen,* and id., *Physische.*

112. The original language and the etymology of the word "Tutsi" are unknown, contra Kagame, *Les Organisations,* 21–22, and Kanyamachumbi, *Société, culture et pouvoir politique en Afrique interlacustre,* 57, 67–69. The term was used in Rwanda, Rundi, Ha, Sumbwa, Sukuma, Nyamwezi, southern Haya, and apparently Karagwe. The linguistic distribution of the term is of little use for the word could easily have spread rapidly along with a population movement. The term is used in all the genres of Rwandan traditions, poetry included, but that by itself does not absolutely prove great antiquity. Still one observes that after the conquest by Ndori, who was a Hima, the royal line let itself be labeled "Tutsi." So the word existed at that time and enjoyed high prestige either at the time of the conquest itself or a little later.

113. Burton, *Lake Regions,* 1:396; 2:185, notes its use in the Swahilized form "Watosi."

114. Hurel, *Dictionnaire,* 317. And yes, in the language of certain historical

narratives the ethnonym "Hima" is sometimes applied in a patronizing manner to the "small Tutsi." See *Ibitéekerezo*, Rwogera file, T, no. 1.

115. Burton, *Lake Regions*, 2:115, underlined this in the case of all the southern Tutsi.

116. These categories are not to be confounded with castes, despite the pronounced endogamy within each group, for the division did not rest on a religious ideology, it was neither ancient nor old, and the link between birth and specific occupation was not absolute (C. Newbury, *The Cohesion of Oppression*, 11–12). Thus, for instance, metalworkers did not constitute a separate "caste." If a foreign label must be used to designate these categories one would rather speak of "social estates."

117. J. Hiernaux, *Analyse de la variation des caractèrs physiques humains en une région d'Afrique centrale*, remains essential for the physical anthropology. See A. Froment, "Le peuplement de Afrique Centrale," 33, 44, 49 (a and b), 56–57 (lactase), and J. Cl. Desmarais "Le Rwanda des anthropologues," who outlines a theory of an artificial selection by Tutsi. Even if the sampling has been defective as claimed by certain social scientists still the results remain valid. At present the data allow for several equally plausible interpretations. Only further more advanced genetic studies will allow to choose among them. That the practice of cross-cousin marriage has been quite common for a long time is attested to by the fact that *"umubyaára," "cross cousin,"* derives from *"kubyaára," "to engender."* For details, see Schoenbrun, *Historical Reconstruction,* nos. 94, 95.

118. All these terms are quite old. See Schoenbrun, *Historical Reconstruction,* nos. 118, 163, 261.

119. *"Umwiru,"* is "ritualist," in Rwanda, Rundi, and Ha, but also in Kiga/Nkore where *"abairu"* designated the bulk of the farming population and *"umwiru"* was one of them. At first, then, ritualists would have been farmers.

120. An *umuganuro* or *umuganura* ritual is found everywhere from Bunyoro to Kivu and as far as Burundi. D. Newbury, "What Role Has Kingship?"; id., *Kings and Clans*, 200–26, and index. Schoenbrun, *Historical Reconstruction*, no. 175. The word and the essential rituals are certainly quite old.

121. Hence the praise name *"umuhinza"* given to kings in this context. *"Umuhínza"* is derived from *"guhinga," "to dig, to cultivate,"* and hence means "master of the farms," and not from *"guhinda," "to thunder."* Eventually the term came to be used scornfully by the Nyiginya court. See Nahimana, *Le Rwanda*, 202–4, and Kagame, *Abrégé* 1, 32. The derogatory use of this term was particularly frequent in the tales of conquests attributed to Ndori and is certainly older than the date of publication of *Inganji Karinga* in 1943.

122. War magic is included in the dynastic rituals, but would not yet have been standardized in the seventeenth century. See d'Hertefelt and Coupez, *Royauté*, 155–69 (ch. 10, "The Path of War").

123. Kagame, *Inganji Karinga* 1:30; Nahimana, *Le Rwanda*, 204–5.

124. The most celebrated one was Mashira, but he was far from being unique. This is what Kagame labeled "the magico-social function" (*Abrégé* 1, 32).

125. Newbury, "Role."

126. The cult stemmed from Bunyoro and Nkore. See Berger, *Religion and Resistance*, 57–66. Some of the spirits of its officers are Nyoro spirits. But, once in Rwanda, the cult also incorporated local heroes such as Mashira, the last king of the Banda dynasty in Nduga.

127. But in the nineteenth century wealthier persons as well as the elite of the kingdom met in separate congregations. Was this already the case during the seventeenth century?

128. Despite the fact that this assertion stems only from ethnographic observation, such a continuity in this type of belief is quite plausible as a parallel case shows among the Ambundu of central Angola. Here a territorial cult led by a *nganga nzumbi* with the help of a wooden statue whose aim was to oblige the ancestors to stop tormenting the living is documented in writing from c. 1650 to 1965! See G. A. Cavazzi, *Descrição histórica dos três reinos do Congo, Matamba e Angola*, 2:48, 58, 64 (data from 1650–60) and documents in the Sebestyén collection from Samba Cajú during the nineteenth century. I would like to thank E. Sebestyén for also telling me that the cult still existed in 1965.

129. On this topic the literature is quite abundant ever since A. Arnoux, "Le culte de la société secrète des Imandwa au Rwanda." See d'Hertefelt and de Lame, *Société, culture et histoire du Rwanda*, 2:1791, and index under "kubandwa."

130. Czekanowski, *Forschungen*, 245–46, did notice this and established a logical sequence from lineage governance without kingship (in certain parts of northwestern Rwanda and Kigezi) to a principality by an intermediary lineage-monarchy. We call a principality a territory ruled by a lord.

131. Nahimana, *Le Rwanda*, 121, describes the case of Bukonya.

132. *"Igitaka,"* "arable land." But certain families of herders also cleared land for pastures. Their rights were also *ubukonde*.

133. For Murinda, see Kagame, *Abrégé* 1, 67–68; *Ibitéekerezo*, Rugwe and Mukobanya files, but also Ndori file, H, no. 43 (in Kinyaga!); Coupez and Kamanzi, *Récits*, 124–27, but further on they confuse Murinda with Nzira!; Schumacher, *Ruanda*, 165 (Nyamuheshera!); for the Bugara of King Nzira, see Kagame, *Abrégé* 1, 80, 83–84, 104; Pagès, *Royaume hamite*, 278; Nahimana, *Le Rwanda*, 79–80, who accepts Kagame's argument; *Ibitéekerezo*, Ndori file, H, nos. 23, 30, 35, 46, 54, 70, 72, 93; other location, no. 31:3 (Kinyaga). "Gara" is mentioned in one of the praise poems *(icyivugo)* of Ndori (no. 15:6 derived from no. 17:6). Schumacher, *Ruanda*, 164, places Nzira in Bukamba. Note, however, that the place where Nzira lived is not important for the tale and often no place is mentioned at all. See Coupez and Kamanzi, *Récits*, 232–53, and many of the tales in *Ibitéekerezo*, Ndori file, H.

134. From 51 to 199 square kilometers. This is an approximate calculation according to the number of vassals cited by Kagame, *Abrégé* 1, 94–96. One

obtains the numbers by dividing the surface area in square kilometers of each part by the number of chiefs and then by the average surface area of a hill.

135. Their number is unknown. In later times great chiefs kept a guard of about one hundred men, but at this time the number was no doubt smaller. Just for comparison: in September 1902, von Parish saw two groups of *intore* dancers at Musinga's court of which the first counted about twenty-five men; the second must have been of the same size (F. R. von Parish, "Zwei Reisen durch Ruanda 1902 bis 1903").

136. The first of these teams was perhaps the so-called Abahiza corporation (Kagame, *Milices*, 18–20).

137. This estimate is derived from the average size of *intore* companies in the nineteenth century.

138. For example *Ibitéekerezo*, Ryangombe file, T and H. The model of royalty depicted in these myths and in the cult itself has naturally changed very much since its introduction and moreover has always been an ideal. Hence it is but prudent to avoid pressing on the data too hard. One must be content with a general outline without which neither the cult nor its myths would make any sense.

139. Schumacher, *Ruanda*, 436, 628, 678–79, is categorical on this point. One cannot speak about property without the king. This state of affairs has been presented as resulting from the arbitration by a herder among the various claims of farming families on a collective *ubukonde* domain (J. Maquet and X. Naigiziki, "Les droits fonciers dans le Rwanda ancien," 348–50). Schumacher, *Physische*, 40, is not deceived and underlines that the land was taken by force. The fact that this land tenure is called *isambu*, "fallow land," indicates the importance of such fields for herds. The *isambu* regime only makes sense within a context of a growing population when a family could no longer dispose of its own hill or its own portion of a hill, independently of all other families.

140. Adamantidis, *Monographie*, 30, 64–65. In 1954, the Hutu controlled 43.3 percent of all bovids and Tutsi 49.5 percent, and each head required on average from 0.8 to 2 hectares of pasture.

141. The exclusion of *imiryango* from the tenure of land is no doubt the main reason for their subsequent decline in central Rwanda among both farmers and herders, a decline that also benefited the Nyiginya court since it feared the potential power of these big lineages.

142. Reisdorff, *Enquêtes;* Maquet and Naigiziki, "Droits fonciers," 351–54; Schumacher, *Ruanda*, 436–38, and 678–79 (about the management of *ingobyi*). I suspect that in the seventeenth century there existed yet a third form of land tenure in Mayaga, according to which all herders had free access to huge tracts of pastures held in common. Reisdorff, *Enquêtes*, 136, cites the similar case of Rwamagana in Buganza. There everyone had access to the pastures, but all the herders lived in a single agglomeration so as to ensure their mutual and common safety.

Chapter 2. The Rwanda of Ndori

1. Pagès, *Royaume hamite*, 228–335; Kagame, *Abrégé* 1, 87–122, but see the original texts in Coupez and Kamanzi, *Récits*, 205–61, 270–81; Smith, *Récit*, 314–19, *Ibitéekerezo, Cyamatare, Ndori, Semugeshi*, and *Nyamuheshera* files (over one hundred tales and summaries), and even J. Vansina, *La Légende du passé*, 60–68.

2. *Ibitéekerezo*, Ndori file, H, no. 6:3.

3. Ibid., no. 10:1. The same expression used to refer to the "small kings" also appears in other tales.

4. Kagane, *Abrégé* 1, 108, finds the proof of his historicity in the fact that the Abaganzu family issued supposedly from his grandson as well as in the name of his armies, which survived after him. In truth these armies can only be traced back as far as Rujugira (id., *Milices*, 54–60) and the Abanganzu are the descendants of Semugeshi, Ndori's only son. This group, moreover, is the only one that did not adopt a personal name (Ndori), but a regnal one (RUGANZU), and their eponym is not the name of their ancestor, Nzuki. See Delmas, *Généalogies*, 54–55.

5. D. Henige, *The Chronology of Oral Tradition*, 34–36, gives many instances of "epoch rulers." Moreover, the references to some of Ndori's supposed conquests are anachronistic, such as, for example, one to the conquest of Bugesera, which occurred only between 1795 and 1801.

6. His regnal name RUGANZU ("the victor") was either posthumous or attributed to him toward the end of his life, not at his inauguration.

7. See Robertshaw and Taylor, "Environmental Change," 19 and n.158, on Bunyoro, Nkore, Buhaya, and Karagwe, J. Sutton, "The Antecedents of the Interlacustrine Kingdoms," 34–55, on Buganda and Karagwe, J. Freedman, "Three Muraris, Three Gahayas, and the Four Phases of Nyabingi," 186, on Ndorwa/Mpororo, and Wrigley, *Kingship and State*, 207–29, who argues that Mawanda would have been the first historical king of Buganda at the end of the sixth generation before 1856, i.e., around 1700.

8. Sutton, "Antecedents," 37.

9. D. Newbury, "Trick Cyclists?" 193–202. The oldest mentions of Burundi in the same sources are certainly anachronisms since the internal data of the kingdom do not allow for its emergence before c. 1700. See L. Ndoricimpa and C. Guillet, *L'Arbre-mémoire*, 11–93; Vansina, *Légende*, 69–117; A. d'Arianoff, *Histoire des Bagesera, souverains du Gisaka*.

10. These chronological gaps occur everywhere. But see n.8 for the supposed affinities among the various Hinda dynasties.

11. Robertshaw and Taylor, "Environmental Change," 19.

12. There are parallels to this phenomenon. Let us only cite, among others, the effects of the formation of the Zulu kingdom and the emergence of the Rundi, Kanyok, and Mutombo Mukulu kingdoms in central Africa.

13. See Robertshaw and Taylor, "Environmental Change," 27, for a summary of the state of this debate to date.

14. A. Kagame, *Poésie dynastique*, 101, 206, poem no. 171. But this poem was composed after November 1931.

15. Kagame, *Abrégé* 1, 98–99, and *Historique et chronologie*, 181. Gatsibo is associated not only with Gihanda; Mazimpaka would also have begun seizing power there. Has this seizure been attributed to Ndori even though in reality it happened under Mazimpaka?

16. Nearly all the tales mention Bumbogo. Hence the verse "the kings who come from Bumbogo" (Kagame, *Poésie dynastique*, 60, no. 71, verse 1 of *Ruhanga rucura inkumbi*, a poem that is thought to date to the time of Sentabyo [1796–1801]). Kagame, *Abrégé* 1, 99, is the only one to locate Byinshi's defeat at Bweramvura near Kabuye in Buriza. Since other traditions cite other localities, we do not regard any of them as historically accurate.

17. K. Oberg, "The Kingdom of Ankole in Uganda," 140.

18. The confusion between Sindi and Nyiginya would stem from this. See Nyagahene, *Histoire et peuplement*, 273–76, who underlines the case of RUGANZU Bwimba who claimed to be of the clan Musindi. See also *Ibitéekerezo*, Bwimba file.

19. Delmas, *Généalogies*, 152–55; d'Hertefelt, *Clans*, 5; Kagame, *Abrégé* 1, 99–100, on the queen mother. *Ibitéekerezo*, Ndori file, H, no. 15:27, records the case of a Singa woman who had hidden Ndori receiving thousands of cows, an act of bestowal that was later reenacted at each enthronement. See also d'Hertefelt and Coupez, *Royauté*, 245, 271, 310.

20. Pagès, *Royaume hamite*, 561, 573, declares that the spring and the sacred wood called Muhima near Kigari are given this name because they were the cradle of the Nyiginya. But Schumacher, *Ruanda*, 159–60, denies any identity between the name of the wood and the ethnonym Hima (different tones says he, but I find them identical). d'Hertefelt and Coupez, *Royauté*, 471, remark on the importance of the same spot in the ritual "path of the watering"; *Ibitéekerezo*, Ndori file, T, no. 4:4, makes this the spring where Ndori returning to Rwanda meets his enemies. Kagame, *Abrégé* 1, 112, 121, and id., *Poésie dynastique*, 72 n.112, mentions another Muhima on the northern flank of Mwurire in Busanza.

21. The list of "vassals" in Kagame, *Abrégé* 1, 94–96, is an amalgam that he cobbled together from various sources and is not to be trusted (Kagame, *Poésie dynastique*, 38 n.34). Most of these names come from tales that tell how Kavuna consulted these people before recalling Ndori from exile (many texts in *Ibitéekerezo*, Ndori file, H). The number of names varies between three and ten in different versions. Another part of the list of "vassals" consists of the main groups of ritualists and the name of the queen mother.

22. See Nkurikiyimfura, *"Gros bétail,"* 119–40, for the state of the question.

23. For a striking example, see *Ibitéekerezo*, Ndori file, T, no. 8:3, in which Katabirora demands Ndori's subjection and uses the verb *"guhakwa"* to express this demand.

24. The word *"ubuhake"* is unknown in Rundi where one would expect to find it if the term was ancient. Similarly *"musavyi"* is the proper Rundi term for "client," not *"mugaragu,"* although that word is known in northern Burundi.

25. See Schoenbrun, *Historical Reconstruction.* no. 185, *"-háka,"* and his no. 186:14, *"-háka,"* and the Rwanda/Nkore substantives that derive from this root. See also I. Jacob, *Dictionnaire rwandais-français, "guhaka,"* meaning 2. From this also comes "to contain in oneself."

26. Thus *ubuhake vaguely* recalls the feudal relationship between lord and vassal that was founded on the soil. In reality, this remains rather a spurious parallel though (Lugan, *Histoire du Rwanda,* 12–29).

27. In Nkore this word is *"abagaragwa,"* "relatives of the king," and it was applied to his pages (Oberg, "Kingdom," 138–41). Its use in Rwanda is a loan from Nkore, since the word is unknown in Ha and one only finds it in the north of Burundi and even there only as a synonym for the Rundi *"umusavyi."* This loanword clearly shows that the earliest *ubuhake* contracts were initiated by the king and his close followers.

28. Kagame, *L'Histoire des armées bovines,* 27–28.

29. d'Hertefelt and Coupez, *Royauté,* 51–52; E. Gasarabwe, *Le Geste rwanda,* 61–62. At issue is path nine, which was elaborated under Rujugira's reign. The division did not exist earlier than Ndori, for predynastic tales opposed a northern whole *plus Rukoma* to the southern regions called "Nduga."

30. *Ibiteekerezo,* Ndori file, H, no. 38:3, but in this case that did not prevent Ndori from killing his interlocutor.

31. Kagame, *Abrégé* 1, 87–88, 94–95, and see n.21; d'Hertefelt and Coupez, *Royauté,* 468, under KONO, 477, under NKIMA. For the Singa, see Delmas, *Généalogies,* 161–65. *Ibiteekerezo,* Ndori file, H, no. 15:22–27, mentions a major gift of cattle to Nyirarumaga and a Singa woman who had hidden him. According to Kagame, ibid., 99, she became his queen mother.

32. *"Byinshi,"* "the rich one" or "many things," is merely a backward formation of an eponym from *"abanyabyinshi,"* "those who own many things."

33. *"Karíinga"* is also found all around Lake Kivu. Cf. In Shi *"aakalinga"* means "royal drum," in Ijwi *"Kalinga"* means "dynastic drum" (Newbury, *Kings and Clans,* 202), and in Tembo *"bilingi"* means "rhythm of the drum during circumcision ceremonies." Schoenbrun, *Historical Reconstruction,* no. 221, *"-línga,"* adds Haavu to these. Did this word spread outward from the Nyiginya kingdom or from the lands around Lake Kivu?

34. One of these, also known in northern Burundi, tells how a man cutting vines found its hideout. A second one, which is very widespread in Rwanda, narrates how Karinga miraculously climbed by itself on top of the other official drums and thus was shown to be the dynastic drum.

35. Kagame, *Abrégé* 1, 101–2; *Ibiteekerezo,* Ndori file, H, nos. 4:5, 80.

36. *Ibiteekerezo,* Cyamatare and Ndori files; Kagame, *Abrégé* 1, 88–91; Coupez and Kamanzi, *Récits,* 204–21; Pagès, *Royaume hamite,* 127, 232–51.

37. This realm, the kingdom of Mashira, was supposedly taken over by a predynastic Rwandan lord called MIBAMBWE Mutabazi. Cyamatare ruled there and after his death the kingdom broke up. Pagès, *Royaume hamite,* 80–81, 577–85; Kagame, *Abrégé* 1, 75–77, 79–80; Delmas, *Généalogies,* 123; Schumacher, *Ruanda,* 161–62; Coupez and Kamanzi, *Récits,* 136–70; *Ibiteekerezo,* Mashira, Mutabazi, and Cyamatare files.

38. See A. Kagame, "Le code ésotérique de la dynastie du Ruanda," 367–72, for the prominent ritualists (Tsobe of Rukoma and Bumbogo with a ritual kingship in the first position, Tandura of Buringa in Marangara in the sixth place. The Tege of Remera in Kabagari came in second place but did not have a ritual kingship). Their genealogies suggest that although these families were of independent origin, they linked themselves to those of the Nyiginya (Delmas, *Généalogies,* 106–7 [on Tsobe] and 28–33 [on Tandura and Tege]). I believe that the two first ones were there before the arrival of Ndori but that the Tege immigrated with him. That is the reason why their genealogy makes them direct descendants of Gihanga. See also d'Hertefelt and Coupez, *Royauté,* 480, under Nyabirungu, 492–93.

39. Pagès, *Royaume hamite,* 293–94, 343, but this locality was also one of Rwogera's capitals and Rwabugiri resided there; Kagame *Abrégé* 1, 102.

40. Kagame, *Abrégé* 1, 106–7; *Ibitéekerezo,* Ndori file, H, nos. 4:5–6, 58; T, no. 4; Pagès, *Royaume hamite,* 325–28. The places that are associated with his demise are located in Rusenyi and near the upper Nyabarongo (Matyazo, Rusenge, Butantsinda).

41. *Ibitéekerezo,* Ndori file, H, no. 15:13. They are Nyamagana, Mwima, Giseke, Buhimba, and Mwurire. Giseke was famous at the time of Rwogera and Rwabugiri. Other storytellers mention other capitals that are equally famous for their association with later kings such as the Kamonyi of Mazimpaka or the Rubengera of Rwabugiri.

42. See Kagame, *Poésie dynastique,* 70 n.108, and 71, where he also notes that this is the Nyundo located near Bunyogombe; id., *Abrégé* 1, 112; see also d'Hertefelt and Coupez, *Royauté,* 484 and 99, who discuss the capital of the cattle king, which here is associated with Ndori's son, MUTARA Semugeshi.

43. The Rundi traditions speak of "Nduga of RUGANZU."

44. Pagès, *Royaume hamite,* 87, 339–40, 343–44, lists five principalities to the east of the upper Nyabarongo, which at that time did not belong to the kingdom, including Marangara as it was then known.

45. *Ibitéekerezo,* Semugeshi file, H, nos. 2, 4, 5, 5.6; T, nos. 1–6, 8; Pagès *Royaume hamite,* 129–36; Kagame, *Abrégé* 1, 109–14. The summary of *Ibitéekerezo,* Semugeshi file, H, no. 5 claims that he was educated at Mukarambo, a place unknown to the enemies of the king. But clearly this constitutes a confusion with the well known tale concerning the young Gahima, who was also hidden at Karambo.

46. Kagame, *Poésie dynastique,* 71, no. 90, 154–55, no. 43–45; id., *Abrégé* 1,

118–22; id., *Introduction*, 206–7; Schumacher, *Ruanda*, 165, but Pagès, *Royaume hamite*, 136, speaks of a "lazy" king about whom nothing is known. In *Ibitéekerezo* one finds only a single tale that relates to him (Nyamuheshera and Gisanura files, T, no. 2) about a victory at Rweru near Kageyo, but the the names of the armies mentioned makes clear that the reference is anachronistic. Mweru, the name of the conquered leader, is associated with Buberuka (Kagame, *Abrégé* I, 119). I believe that the whole refers to either to the reign of Rujugira or Ndabarasa.

47. A dynastic poem that probably was composed in the middle of the nineteenth century (during Rwogera's reign) and was reworked later on certifies that he as a military hero. Yet he did not create any new army (Kagame, *Milices*, 61).

48. D. Newbury, "Trick Cyclists?" 204–7, was the first to demonstrate this. The suicide of a queen mother is a cliché and the cause of her suicide is the same as that which provoked the murder of Rwabugiri's mother. The variants relating to her rise and her clan cited in the literature from Pagès to Kagame lead one to suspect that this is a fabrication (and that other ancient Ega queens are well, such as in J-N Nkuriyimfura, "La révision d'une chronologie," 151, 153, 169). The version Sekarama gave to Schumacher, *Ruanda*, 131, and to Kagame became the standard.

49. Kagame, *Poésie dynastique*, no. 49, 157–58, and id., *Abrégé* I, 124–25. In the same poem the great deeds of MIBAMBWE Gisanura were flagrantly transferred to MIBAMBWE Mutabazi (id., *Introduction*, 279–80).

50. I. Jacob, *Dictionnaire*, under *"-tsínda"* and *"-ganza"* with their derivations.

51. For the nineteenth-century Rwandan conceptualization of the process of conquest, see Schumacher, *Ruanda*, 716, 745–47.

52. Pagès, *Royaume hamite*, 230.

53. Ibid., 314–15; *Ibitékerezo*, file *Ndori*, H, nos. 10:4–5, 19:18–19, 39:53–73.

54. *Ibitéekerezo*, Ndori file, T, no. 2 (Forongo), and perhaps no. 3; Kagame, *Armées bovines*, 17, attributes the tale of Forongo to MIBAMBWE Mutabazi, but this should be MIBAMBWE Sentabyo—in any case, not Ndori. In tale no. 3 the mention of Burundi at least is an anachronism (contra Kagame, *Abrégé* I, 105–6, who accepts a slightly different version).

55. Kagame, *Abrégé* I, 112, 121. Kigari was acquired before Mazimpaka's reign but after Ndori's.

56. For all the military operations, see Schumacher, *Ruanda*, 163–65; Pagès, *Royaume hamite*, 276–310; Kagame *Abrégé* I, 103–6, 109–10, 119–21; Coupez and Kamanzi, *Récits*, 233–61, and *Ibitéekerezo*, Ndori, Semugeshi, and Nyamuheshera files.

57. *Ibitéekerezo*, Ndori file, T, no. 5, but this conquest is not attributed to any specific king. Pagès, *Royaume hamite*, 29–94, 343–44, underlines the autonomy of this "magician king" and is just as vague about his incorporation into the kingdom.

58. It is striking to observe that nearly all the tales about Burwi and Bungwe underline Muyenzi's role. For Bunyambiriri, see the tales about Gisurere, Suriri of Suti, and Mbebirimabya in *Ibitéekerezo*, Ndori file, H, nos. 1, 19, 38, 47, 52, 53, 59, 81. Schumacher, *Ruanda*, 164, locates the Mbebirimabya at Buhande near Kirinda just to the west of the Nyabarongo and in ibid., 165, the conquest of the Singa, who had refused to pay tribute, at Kinihira near Kirinda is attributed to Semugeshi.

59. The history of the agreements reached at Utwicara-bwami with Burundi suggests they must be attributed to Mazimpaka and Rujugira.

60. The conquest of Cyubaka, a descendant of Murinda, who supposedly reigned in the regions north of the volcanoes, in Bugoyi, in Nyantango, and in Budaha (Schumacher, *Ruanda*, 165), is also attributed to Nyamuheshera. But other traditions claim that Gisanura or Mutabazi conquered Cyubaka (Kagame, *Introduction*, 280). The campaigns attributed to Nyamuheshera in Kinyaga, Bugoyi, and north Kivu probably date from the reigns of Gahindiro, Rwogera, and Rwabugiri (Newbury, "Trick Cyclists?" 205–6). His conquests in Bwishaza, Nyantango, and Budaha west of the upper Nyabarongo all date to the time of Ndabarasa, and the same holds for Buberuka.

61. Kagame, *Abrégé* 1, 110, and *Ibitéekerezo*, Semugeshi file, T, nos. 4:10–11, 5:14–16, 6:11–13, and, above all, 9, for no. 4–6 were all told by the same storyteller, Mugina.

62. Kagame, *Abrégé* 1, 110; cf. 128–29.

63. *Ibitéekerezo*, Ndori file, H, no. 38:1 details the expedition against the giant Nyangara.

64. In historical narratives this placename can designate any area west of the upper Nyabarongo.

65. Kagame, *Armées bovines*, 18, 20–21; see *Ibitéekerezo*, Ndori file, H, nos. 41, 48:3, for the stories of Indorero and "the bull Rugondo who lowed at Kamonyi," 54; T, no. 1:5. Ibid., H, also mentions the Insanga herd from Nzira which would have been the one that became Indorero later on).

66. *Ibitéekerezo*, Ndori file, H, no. 35.

67. This is the standard tale of the "conquest" of Mpandahande at Ruhande near Butare.

68. Indeed all the best-known of Ndori's raids are either located on the main road from central Rwanda to the shores of Lake Kivu via the mountain pass of Rugabano, or on the road from central Rwanda to the north along the valley of the Mukungwa.

69. Delmas, *Généalogies*, 138, says that the Kono herders occupied the region from the time of the mythical Gihanga onward. But according to *Historique et chronologie*, 123, their ancestor Bigirimana had immigrated along with Mucocori, son of Cyamatare and brother of Ndori. See also Schumacher, *Physische*, 74, Reisdorff, *Enquêtes*, 110 (on Mucocori and Bigirimana), and Delmas, *Généalogies*, 52 (on Mucocori), and 138–39 (on Bigirmana). Mucocori's prestigious genealogy

is probably a late invention while his group actually probably inhabited Bigogwe long before the arrival of Ndori.

70. As late as 1899, Kirima, who claimed the kingship in Burundi, passed himself off as son of "Ntare," the father and the predecessor of Mwezi Gisabo, the then-ruling king.

71. The Rwanda word *"umwîru"* (plural *"abîru"*), meaning "ritualist," and "queen of bees," also occurs in Rundi and Ha. These ritualists were therefore well known in central Rwanda before Ndori. Note, however, that *"omwîru"* (plural *"baîru"*) in Nkore/Kiga, meaning "agriculturalist, farmer," would be derived from the Rwandan word, which implies rather that this type of ritualist would have been linked to kingdoms of farmers.

72. Kagame, *Milices*, 15, 20–23, 24, 33–35; id., "Code ésotérique," 368, 370–71; d'Hertefelt and Coupez, *Royauté*, 462 (Insanga), 468 (Kono), 480 (Nyabirungu), 492 (Tandura).

73. For *igicurasi* and *umuganura*, see d'Hertefelt and Coupez, *Royauté*, 49–51, 68–93, and Newbury, "Role"; id., *Kings and Clans*, 200–26, offers a comparison with other kingdoms. The Gakondo corporation was in charge of the preparation for *umuganura*, according to Kagame, *Milices*, 26–29.

74. Hence Muhanga in Kigezi (Ngologoza, *Kigezi*, 43) and Ruhanga in Bunyoro (J. Roscoe, *The Bakitara*, 21, 22, 23). These persons were considered to be gods, not kings.

75. Still, Kagame, *Abrégé* 1, 41, claims "this cannot be doubted" and Delmas, *Généalogies*, 7–8, 11, twice cites as proof of his existence the saying *"Gihanga, niwe wahanze Urwanda"* ("It is Gihanga who made Rwanda")!

76. Delmas, *Généalogies*, 12–15, details objects, fire, and places associated with Gihanga; Pagès, *Royaume hamite*, 358–59, discusses fire; Kagame, *Abrégé* 1, 42, also discusses fire, and associated places (43–44; id., *Milices*, 15–18, covers his herd *abanyasanga*).

77. Delmas, *Généalogies*, 29, 30; Kagame, *Abrégé* 1, 39–40.

78. Later the rainmaking kings of Bukunzi were to become famous. Pagès, *Royaume hamite*, 338 (Busigi), 344 (Bukunzi); *Historique et chronologie*, 174–75 (Busigi), 98–100 (Bukunzi). For rain rituals in the nineteenth century, see d'Hertefelt and Coupez, *Royauté*, 17–31.

79. Delmas, *Généalogies*, 49; Kagame, *Poésie dynastique*, 83 n.137; Pagès, *Royaume hamite*, 127–28; d'Hertefelt and Coupez, *Royauté*, 452, under Bweramvura. For the subordinate role of Kibogo in historical tales, see Smith, *Récit*, 307, 309–10, and *Ibitéekerezo*, Cyamatare file, T, no. 1; H, nos. 3, 8, 9; Semugeshi file, T, nos. 1:15–17, 4:9, 5:13–14, no. 6, p. 10–12, H, no. 2, p. 3.

80. Nahimana, *Le Rwanda*, 204–5, and Kagame, *Inganji Karinga*, I:30. Magicians who protected against calamities were called *abavumyi*.

81. See description by Mazina, who was Musinga's main diviner, in Schumacher, *Ruanda*, 1111–13, 1158–59, 1193–226. For a good example of the

diviner's importance, see *Ibitéekerezo,* Ndori file, T, no. 4, which tells the story of a contradictory divination that leads to Ndori's death).

82. Pagès, *Royaume hamite,* 29–94.

83. Ibid., 129–32; d'Hertefelt and Coupez, *Royauté,* 327 n.about lines 816–17 and line 452 under Bweramvura; Coupez and Kamanzi, *Récits,* 271–75; *Ibitéekerezo,* Semugeshi file, T, nos. 1–6, 8–9; H, no. 4. For this storyteller the tale relates to the inauguration of Ndori; id., Ndori file, H, nos. 52:11–13, 63. Kagame, *Abrégé* 1, 111–12 and 117, strongly distorts the historical narratives.

84. A great deal of confusion reigns in the interpretation of the traditions that inform us of this ritual innovation. First, interpreters attribute CYIRIMA Rujugira's reforms to the royal ideology to MUTARA Semugeshi (see Kagame, *Abrégé* 1, 111–16, and his *Milices,* 62). Then they mix up the tale of Mpande and Semugeshi (see n.83) with the introduction of the Ryangombe cult. The tie between both stories is suggested by the name MUTARA, an observation I owe to A. Coupez. MUTARA was certainly initiated himself and only under Rujugira did the king delegate this task to a specialized officer. The mix of both traditions and the attribution of the reforms to the ideology to different personages is therefore not entirely accidental as we shall see when we discuss the reign of Rujugira.

85. Contra Kagame, *Abrégé* 1, 117, and most traditions. Rujugira will use the fact that Rwaka had been initiated into this cult as a justification for his coup and he introduced the dogma that no king can be initiated in to it. For part of the detailed justification used, see Schumacher, *Ruanda,* 1088.

86. Kagame, *Milices,* 18–20.

87. Ibid., 41–42. This one probably took shape during Rujugira's reign.

88. Ibid., 26–30. Gakondo was under Tsobe control. Ndori probably created Inyanga kugoma.

89. Ibid., 20–26; 29–30.

90. Ibid., 33–35.

91. Ibid., 37–38.

92. Id., *Armées bovines,* 12–15.

93. Ibid., 15–22. The four different cattle corporations of the Kono ritualist might be successors of herds the Kono leader already had before he became Ndori's ally.

94. Ibid., 20–21.

95. The same word was also used in Nkore/Kiga and Nyoro but not in Rundi or Ha.

96. Mpande ya Rusanga was a foundling but considered to be a member of the Turagara lineage. Kagame, *Milices,* 55, 57, 59; *Ibitéekerezo,* Ndori file, H, no. 93.

97. For Kagame *Milices,* 54, there were six companies, but his *Abrégé* 1, 103–4, mentions eight of them, which is obviously exaggerated. A supplementary

company has the name of one of Rwabugiri's armies and another one's name is the same as that of another company but with different prefixes. In this way one arrives at eight, the lucky number in Rwanda. Is this an accident? Whether it is or not, the case supplies a cautionary tale us about the fragility of lists either in the oral discourse itself or, as in this case, in its compilation by an author.

98. *Ibitéekerezo*, Ndori file, T, no. 4; Kagame, *Abrégé* 1, 207, and id., *Milices*, 55.

99. Schumacher, *Ruanda*, 621.

100. Coupez and Kamanzi, *Littérature*; Kagame, *Introduction*. Thus most pastoral poems, such as Kagame's "eclogues," far from being idyllic, only celebrated combat (Kagame, *Introduction*, 90, 92–149, with examples). Today this literary glorification of violence persists, and is a particularly nefarious legacy of the ancestral heritage.

101. Kagame, *Milices*, 57–60 (i.e., the Abaruhije, Nyakare, and Nyantango). Rujugira created all of them and also created a new Ibisumizi army. As to Semugeshi, Abaganda was his only army since Impara was a creation of Rujugira.

102. d'Hertefelt and Coupez, *Royauté*, 452. "Bwanacyambwe" is opposed to "Nduga" (476) in the wide meaning but each term also possessed a narrow meaning. Bwanamukari was also a natural region that encompassed several political units but unlike Bwanacyambwe and Nduga, the word never seems to have been used to label a political unit. See Kagame, *Abrégé* 1, 104–5.

103. Kagame, *Le Code des institutions politiques du Rwanda précolonial*, 120, cites a technical term for the "capital of a district," namely, *"ururembo,"* "gate of the outside enclosure," a term also found in Nkore/Kiga. But the traditions talk mainly about *"umurwa,"* "capital, residence." That word also designates the hill on which a residence was built in Rwanda, a hill slope in Rundi and Ha, and an inhabited hill in Rundi, where *"ikirwa,"* "place of the king's couch," designated the residence. The toponym "Kirwa" is found in both Rwanda and Burundi. All this leaves the impression that the semantic link with a political residence and the practice of having such residences were internal Rwandan innovations.

104. d'Hertefelt, *Rwanda*, 62; Kagame, *Code*, 124–25, and n.77, for the twenty-one districts at the time of Rwabugiri, seven of which were overseen by maids.

105. Data about the emplacements occupied by the kings are found in tales and on the ground, but they are often contradictory. I only trust the places used in the royal rituals. See d'Hertefelt and Coupez, *Royauté*, 99, verses 1–4 and 35 regarding Bumbogo and Nyundo near Bunyogombe. According to the text of the ritual liturgy both places were founded by the first MUTARA, i.e., Semugeshi. Elsewhere Nyundo is always associated with Ndori (thus Kagame, *Poésie dynastique*, 70 n.108) as is Ruganda in Bumbogo but far less often (ibid., 64 n.92).

106. The famous Indorero herd raided at Nzira was taken to Muyira (Kagame, *Armées bovines*, 21).

107. But these lands have changed hands. Thus the Tsobe ended up by extending their hold over nearly all of Bumbogo and beyond, starting from a few

domains in central Bumbogo (*Historique et chronologie*, 56, suggests the dynamics involved). But the Kono were less lucky and the Tege could only maintain the small domain they had at the outset. For these "enclaved districts," see Kagame, *Code*, 121–24.

108. At the time these lands included Busigi, Suti, Nzaratsi, Kabuye in Kibari, Buhanga, the Buriba of Ndiza, Ntonde-Karama-Kabogwe, and Muhanga-Nyabitare (Pagès, *Royaume hamite*, 340, 599). Among the places of asylum in case of vendetta, those in Bumbogo, Busigi, Buhanga, Gaseke, and Bukunzi were all exempt of royal authority during the nineteenth century. Only Mwurire near Save was not (Schumacher, *Ruanda*, 732–33).

109. Pagès, *Royaume hamite*, 389–90.

110. Homosexuality was widespread among the *intore* and the king's "favorite" was therefore often also his lover. Thus when Ntare of Burundi felt that he was dying, he killed his favorite, Gikori, with the words "those who love each other do not leave each other" or "a favorite dies with his lover" (*Ibitéekerezo*, Mazimpaka file, T, nos. 1:3–4, 4:3–4). It is said that Gahenda "lived with the king under Muyenzi" (Coupez and Kamanzi, *Récits*, 271).

111. For Gahenda, see Pagès, *Royaume hamite*, 129; Coupez and Kamanzi, *Récits*, 271–72. He does not appear in the *Ibitéekerezo*, however. Kagame does not mention him either, but his silence is ambiguous. In *Milices*, 55, Kagame merely says that Mpande lost the favor of the queen mother. Yet the role of Gahenda appears in his *Abrégé* 1, 111–13, and in *Ibitéekerezo*, Semugeshi file, T, nos. 3–6, all narrated by Mugina, who often closely follows Kagame, this role is attributed to a certain Nyamwonda. But this person seems to have lived at the time of Rujugira and to have been involved with the refashioning of the ideology of kingship.

Chapter 3. Toward the Centralization of Power

1. Gisanura is the nickname of Sekarongoro Mutabazi (Kagame, *Abrégé* 1, 272).

2. Ibid., 126. A good description can be found in *Ibitéekerezo*, Mazimpaka file, T, no. 5.

3. *Ibitéekerezo*, Mazimpaka file, T, no. 7 (in prose), contrasts with H, no. 8 (martial poem), which opens "I am the king of peace."

4. Ibid., H, nos. 11:2–3 ("Is Yuhi the only drunkard?") and 3:3–4 (his intoxication caused the arrival of the Europeans).

5. For a portrait, see *Ibitéekerezo*, Mazimpaka file, T, no. 7. For his reign, see ibid., *Mazimpaka* file; Schumacher, *Ruanda*, 165–70; Kayijuka, "Lebensgeschichte," 131–33; Kagame, *Abrégé* 1, 125–33; Pagès, *Royaume hamite*, 136–41.

6. Schumacher, *Ruanda*, 165. It is strange that not even the names of these chiefs are to be found in any other source. One suspects that this tradition stems from the great Nyiginya lords, which would include Kayijuka, for example, but was not acceptable to the court.

7. Kagame, *Poésie dynastique*, 129–35.

8. Kagame, *Armées bovines*, 25–36, and *Ibitéekerezo*, Mazimpaka file, H, no. 11, which describes Akaganda with pastures at Kagina in Rukoma.

9. Kagame, *Armées bovines*, 22–115. The table in Nkurikiyimfura, *Gros bétail*, 56–57, does not completely correspond to these calculations for he accepts Kagame's attribution uncritically and does not distinguish between herds for cattle breeders and others. For that distinction, see A. Desforges, "Court and Corporations in the Development of the Rwandan State," 4–5. In this translation some errors in the original of this work have been corrected.

10. Kagame, ibid., 68, 73.

11. Ibid., 45, 71, for examples of herds created with animals pertaining to the royal booty stemming from raids in Burundi and Ndorwa.

12. Kagame, *Poésie dynastique*, 134, no. 10, *"Nigire imana nanoga."*

13. Kagame, *Armées bovines*, 22.

14. Ibid., 34–36. The source of this tale is a ballad for zither. Even if this story is the fiction I believe it to be, still it remains quite revealing.

15. Ibid., 63. For these parades in general, see Schumacher, *Ruanda*, 915–16; for *"kurundisha,"* meaning "to make a census of cattle" and a tax in head of cattle levied on owners of two hundred cattle or more, 601–2. That custom had already become obsolete by Rwabugiri's time.

16. Kagame, ibid., 72–73.

17. Schumacher, *Ruanda*, 620, 859, *"intore,"* "selected cattle." This practice differed from *kuzitura* according to which each army commander constituted a new herd each year with the issue of the official herd of the army (Kagame, *Code*, 88–89).

18. For a snapshot of Sentama fleeing Burundi, see *Ibitéekerezo*, Mazimpaka file, T, no. 11:2 ("I am accompanied by my relatives. They are about a hundred. I am also accompanied by our one thousand cows. We are fleeing . . ."); a shorter version can be found in H, no. 3, p:2–3.

19. Rugamba, *Poésie*, 70.

20. Kagame, *Armées bovines*, 70.

21. No systematic list of the residences founded by each king and kept up afterward exists. Moreover, as time went by the location of certain residences changed. Kagame, followed by Kanyamachumbi, estimates that there were twenty-one of these at the death of Rwabugiri, of which fifteen dated to before his reign. Around 1796 there would have been twelve and seven c. 1720. See maps in Kanyamachumbi, *Société*, 338, and in Kagame, *Abrégé* 2, endmap.

22. It is called "the heart of Rwanda." Kagame, *Poésie dynastique*, 55 n.61, and Rugamba, *Poésie*, 341 n.183.

23. Kagame, *Armées bovines*, 23, 34, 71, mentions Buganza for one of Gisanura's herds, Buberuka for one of Mazimpaka's herds, and Bugesera for a herd of Ndabarasa, but these regions lay outside the kingdom during the reigns mentioned.

24. Kagame, *Abrégé* 1, 107; *Ibitéekerezo*, Ndori file, H, no. 4:7. Louis Nturo, a great chief, drew this conclusion: "Mutára Sémugéshi did not have a single Igisuumizi soldier; they had all committed suicide."

25. Kagame, *Milices*, 66, 80. This actually was the only army of this king, as the others that are mentioned are in fact corporations of menials, with the exception of Inyangakurushwa (but then that one was founded by Rwogera).

26. This is glaringly evident in the cases of Burundi and Gisaka.

27. Kagame, ibid., 72–75.

28. The most famous case of this tendency will be the faithfulness of Semugaza's army, which followed him into exile (Kagame, *Abrégé* 1, 172, 176–81).

29. *Ibitéekerezo*, Mazimpaka file, T, no. 11; H, nos. 1, 3, 5, 6, 12, 13; see also Kagame, *Milices*, 78, 80, who notes that the Inkora–Maraso army founded by Mukungu.

30. The numbers in Nkurikiyimfura, *Gros bétail*, 56–57, differ from ours because not all the corporations listed in Kagame, *Milices*, 72–125, are armies and because certain armies were set up by other kings than those to whom Kagame has attributed their formation.

31. Desforges, "Court," 72 n.65, and Schumacher, *Ruanda*, 424–25, 621, claim that there were "usually" four companies who relayed each other during combat (a tactic perfectly described in *Ibitéekerezo*, Rujugira file, H, no. 1:9, 13–17). According to Schumacher—and his collaborator Kayijuka belonged to it—Musinga's army counted five of these, including a Twa company; Kagame, *Code*, 22–23, followed by Rugamba, *Poésie*, 182 n.25, cites the number eight, on claiming that Rwabugiri had eight and Musinga nine, including a Twa company in each, but the comparison with Schumacher shows that the number for Musinga really is five. As to Ndori's army, Kagame cites six companies in *Milices*, 54, but eight in his *Abrégé* 1, 103–4. Yet the two additional names in *Abrégé* are obviously derived from two earlier names.

32. The number of combatants per company would have been of 150 "at least" or from "150 to 200" for Kagame, *Code*, 22, and later *Milices*, 9, approved by Rugamba, *Poésie*, 182 n.25, but Kagame tends to inflate all his numbers. Desforges' collaborators estimated fifty soldiers per company ("Court," 22) but their estimate is probably derived from that of the number of Musinga's *intore* dancers. In 1902 there were about fifty according to von Paris ("Zwei Reisen," 9). But this number seems too low. Unfortunately Schumacher, the best-informed thanks to Kayijuka and Sekarama, gives no number at all. The only indication that we have, and it is a feeble one, comes from the ruins of the military camp of the Mvejuru army described by Reisdorff, *Enquêtes*, 43–44. During the reign of Rwabugiri a space three hundred-meter-long space had served to house one company. If one allots about three meters per person that yields about one hundred recruits.

33. All the sources underline that all the combatants were Tutsi at least

until Rwabugiri's reign when one mentions the presence of some Hutu warriors as exceptional. The Twa section of the royal army existed in Rwabugiri and Musinga's time, and both kings used it as a personal guard (Schumacher, *Ruanda*, 424–25, 621).

34. Reisdorff, *Enquêtes*, 43–44, found a proportion of two to one or better with respect to the linear surface of Tutsi to Hutu lodgings in the military camp of the Mvejuru, without counting a space of six hundred by five hundred meters, which, according to him, corresponds to Rwabugiri's own camp.

35. Kagame, *Milices*, 73, 77. This section was later separated from Indara by Rwogera. Kagame commits an anachronism when he asserts that the Hutu sections were part of the army at this time.

36. The data at our disposal are only directly valid for the practice of war at the end of the nineteenth century. Those of Schumacher, *Ruanda*, 425–28, 433, 453–54, 606, 621–28, 713–16, 730–31, 745–49, are most reliable, for they stem from the army commander Kayijuka and from Sekarama, men who had fought in Rwabugiri's armies. *Ibitéekerezo*, Mazimpaka file, H, no. 11 and Rujugira file, H, no. 1, vividly describe a military campaign. Despite their literary character both tales give us a concrete idea of what a military campaign was like.

37. For instance, Coupez and Kamanzi, *Récits*, 285–89 (Bwami); *Ibitéekerezo*, Mazimpaka file, T, no. 19:2.

38. Rugamba, *Poésie*, 268–69, 297, rightly underscores their importance.

39. For the nineteenth century, see d'Hertefelt and Coupez, *Royauté*, 155–69, 187–91.

40. Schumacher, *Ruanda*, 713.

41. *Ibitéekerezo*, Mazimpaka file, H, no. 1:2. For an analogous passage by another narrator, see ibid., T, no. 11: 4.

42. Schumacher, *Ruanda*, 608. This description certainly stems from an eyewitness, probably Sekarama.

43. *Ibitéekerezo*, Mazimpaka file, H, no. 11:4–5, relates that about eight thousand cows were involved, but the truce broke down when the Rundi chief refused to hand over his favorite cow. Multiple truces are described in ibid., file *Rujugira*, H, no. 1.

44. The many references in Schumacher to all aspects of war contradict themselves only on one point—that small boys were killed in Rwanda (416), and that they were spared (427, 748). For the ritual of testicles to be offered to Karinga, see d'Hertefelt and Coupez, *Royauté*, 170–85.

45. Thus "they rustled the cattle on the Ntáaga plateaus, they took the girls, they ravaged the country" (*Ibitéekerezo*, Mazimpaka file, T, no. 11:6).

46. A quarrel between the king and his son over booty is a cliché in the tales about Nyarwaya Karuretwa. In one version Nyarwaya even tells the king that as he had conducted an unauthorized raid, he does not owe him any part of the booty! (*Ibitéekerezo*, Mazimpaka file, H, no. 6:1). Nkoronko's malice toward

Murorunkwere is attributed to the fact that he did not receive anything from the booty taken in Ndorwa (Kagame, *Abrégé* 2, 30).

47. Kagame, *Armées bovines,* 71–72.

48. The total number of men and the number of people administered by a standard army can be estimated by extrapolation. Despite the fact that such an exercise always remains suspect, it may still be useful to give an idea of the order of magnitude involved. An army on the warpath counted about 1,620 people of which 500 were herders (four companies of combatants plus one company of rustlers), and 1,100 foragers. Schumacher, *Ruanda,* 713, states that two thirds of the men involved did not go in the field at the time of Rwabugiri, which we interpret as referring to the 1,200 noncombatants (foragers and rustlers). In that case there would have been 4,000 (3,600 + 400 combatants) men per army. At the rate of one adult male per five dependents (wife, children, elders), which was the number used in colonial times, one arrives at a total of 20,000 people directed by an army However, Desforges, "Court," 48, arrives at ten to fifteen thousand men in total for the *average* per army by the end of the nineteenth century when many armies had lost a good deal of their men. Moreover, she starts from different numbers (fifty per company rather than one hundred, three fourths of men in reserve rather than two thirds).

49. They were afforded protection in principle, according to Kagame, *Code,* 37–39, but Desforges, "Court," 27, 50–51, is more nuanced. Reisdorff, *Enquêtes,* 148, notes that around 1900 army commanders only protected their favorites. For Czekanowski, *Forschungen,* 262, the warriors were privileged and formed a special social class. Schumacher, *Ruanda,* 623, speaks of limited protection.

50. Schumacher, *Ruanda,* 440.

51. Kagame *Abrégé* 1, 13–38, and maps 5, 8; id., *Code,* 52–54; id., *Milices,* 10. For their functioning, see Schumacher, *Ruanda,* 426, 433, 454, 621; Reisdorff, *Enquêtes,* 43–44, notes that around 1900, such a camp comprised one thousand men among whom three hundred were Tutsi men.

52. Kagame, *Milices,* 73, describes the creation of their first camp at Kirarambogo.

53. Rugamba, *Poésie,* 264. Sekarama, the main collaborator of Schumacher and Kagame, composed these verses between 1931 and 1936.

54. Kagame, *Abrégé* 1, 122–23; Rugamba, *Poésie,* 208, uses the phrase "distribute things like Gisanura did." The milk came from the "household" cows of the chiefs who resided at court.

55. Schumacher, *Ruanda,* 707–9. Cf. Pagès, *Royaume hamite,* 355–456, who is more descriptive but perhaps less correct. The description is summarized in Lugan, *Histoire du Rwanda,* 203–15.

56. Thus von Parish, "Zwei Reisen," 9; Ramsay, "Über seine Expeditionen," 314, and his "Uha, Urundi und Ruanda," 179–80, mention one thousand or more men (warriors?) surrounding the king, but Ramsay labels the brand new capital a "village" while the former one, Giseke, was a "town."

57. Lugan, *Histoire du Rwanda,* 200, and id., "Nyanza, une capitale royale du Rwanda ancien," 98–112.

58. R. Kandt, *Caput Nili,* 258–61, on Mkingo. For a description of the capital and plan of the royal complex, see Lugan, *Histoire du Rwanda,* 196–203.

59. Schumacher, *Ruanda,* 708–9. Among the twelve manufacturing specializations the tanners and the hunters were especially distinguished from all other artisans; Pagès, *Royaume hamite,* 456–57, speaks of "the suppliers of his majesty" and adds mat makers, tailors, providers of perfumes, veterinaries, specialists in bleeding cattle, butchers, and even "rat catchers."

60. The exact number of times each king moved the capital is unknown except for Mazimpaka (Kayijuka, "Lebensgeschichte," 131), with the numbers cited tending to be a minimum. But it is sometimes difficult to distinguish between a residence, a temporary halting place of stay, or even a place of passage. Thus nineteen places are associated with Ndabarasa who moved much more often than Rujugira, but there are only five certain residences. According to Kagame, the total number of all the former royal residences *(ibigabiro)* was about 120. (Lugan, *Histoire du Rwanda,* 196 n.1).

61. Kayijuka, "Lebensgeschichte," 136–37; Schumacher, *Ruanda,* 169–70; *Ibiteekerezo,* Mazimpaka file, T, no. 1, adds: "He found the young men busy with jumping and with doing their hair, archers, and others who competed in high jumps or who were exercising" and a variant in T, no. 6.

62. Kagame, *Milices,* 68–71. It's possible, though, that the Abangongo corporation was only created under Gahindiro. In Gisanura's time only the western banks of the Nyabarongo in Cyingogo were part of the realm.

63. Ibid., 72–125; id., *Armées bovines,* 22–74.

64. Id., *Milices,* 101.

65. Id., *Poésie dynastique,* 53–56, 166–67. *Umwami si umuntu* is the title of two poems (nos. 65, 66) composed for Sentabyo during the civil war of 1796–1801. The French translation of no. 65 on which our quotations are based is that of Kagame, who does not provide the original.

66. Ibid., 53, verse 17.

67. d'Hertefelt and Coupez, *Royauté,* 460–61.

68. Newbury "Role?" The text and the practice of the royal rituals as known date to the nineteenth century, but the gist of the practice of *umuganura* is quite old, as comparative ethnographic data show. See Newbury, *Kings and Clans,* 200–26; Schoenbrun, *A Green Place,* 254–60.

69. Schoenbrun, *A Green Place,* 5, 12–14 (and index), shows that the distinction between "creative power" and "instrumental power" is very old in the whole Great Lakes region.

70. Kagame, *Abrégé* 1, 131–32, and also in Rundi (Rodegem, *Dictionnaire,* under *indira,* 9/10).

71. Ndabarasa was to add the drum Rugiramasango used during rituals for the hunt (d'Hertefelt and Coupez, *Royauté,* 488).

72. Mazimpaka's beauty is the motive cited for the murder of his half-brother twins and for that of his treacherous spouses. See Kayijuka, "Lebensgeschichte," 132–35; Kagame, *Abrégé* 1, 10, 126–27; *Ibitéekerezo*, Mazimpaka file, T, especially no. 5:2. For the king's beauty in general, ibid., Ndabarasa file, T, no. 14:4: "He found the child to be very handsome, by far more beautiful than the others. He was truly superior because he was the king of Rwaanda!" The appreciation of male beauty becomes even more significant when one remembers the prevalence of homosexuality at the court.

73. *Ibitéekerezo*, Mazimpaka file, H, no. 11, identical to ibid., Ndori file, H, no. 65; Bourgeois, *Banyarwanda et Barundi*, 315–17, who claims the cows are "genuine historical monuments"; Adamantidis, *Monographie*, 18–20, provides a list of their characteristics, and, 42–45, their breeding details and origins. See also *Ibitéekerezo*, Ndabarasa file, T, nos. 9:5, 5:7, 17:18 ("*Inyambo* cattle were led along with the grass they would eat along the way, the grass being carried by people").

74. Kagame, *Armées bovines*, 27–29. The first Inyambo herd was Akaganda and its first overseer a Twa from the court.

75. Nyakahoza was also the name of the royal drum of Kayonza and of other drums in Kigezi (Rwankwenda, "History," 131–32; Ngologoza, *Kigezi*, 19–20). Is this just happenstance or did the saying come from Kigezi to be reinterpreted later on in Rwanda?

76. Kayijuka, "Lebensgeschichte," 131–32. Being forced to perform corvée labor as a punishment for having eaten the favored cow or bull of a king recurs in other tales about Ndori and Rwabugiri, among others. See Pagès, *Royaume hamite*, 294–96. For Budaha, see Kagame, *Milices*, 101, 106.

77. Schumacher, *Ruanda*, 605.

78. *Ibitéekerezo*, Mazimpaka file, T, no. 2; Kayijuka, "Lebensgeschichte," 135; Kagame, *Abrégé* 1, 126.

79. Desforges, "Court," 31; Kagame, *Poésie dynastique*, 145–48. The tension between ritualists and king Ndabarasa in Ndorwa resulted from this struggle for influence.

80. *Ibitéekerezo*, Ndabarasa file, H, nos. 2:4, 13:4; Kagame, *Milices*, 97. Rubona was a Tsobe chief.

81. Kagame, "Code ésotérique," 366. The most important ones around 1900 were the chiefs of the Tsobe, the Tege, the Heka, the Kobwa, and the Kono.

82. Id., *Armées bovines*, 34.

83. According to *Ibitéekerezo*, Mazimpaka file, T, no. 10, and indirectly Rujugira file, T, no. 16:2–3. In the nineteenth century the Tsobe ritualist was crucial to guaranteeing the legitimacy of a new king, for it was he who announced his name to the people (Delmas, *Généalogies*, 107; d'Hertefelt and Coupez, *Royauté*, 232–35.)

84. Kagame,"Code ésotérique," 370, attributes this to CYIRIMA Rugwe

but in fact it was CYIRIMA Rujugira. These matridynastic lineages included another Kono lineage.

85. According to Delmas, *Généalogies*, 57, the genealogies of the Nyiginya nobility become precise only starting with Mazimpaka's sons.

86. On Makara, see Kagame, *Milices*, 64, 115. Id., "La documentation du Rwanda sur l'Afrique interlacustre des temps anciens," 306. Makara's son is said to have tried to assassinate Rujugira.

87. Kagame, *Poésie dynastique*, 139–41; id., *Abrégé* 1, 127, Rugamba, *Poésie*, 255–56, notes that this pasture was at the "head of a hill." As the domain of this person bordered on Bugesera he gave refuge to Nsoro, king of Bugesera, who was fleeing the Rundi. Kagame calls him "subchief," a flagrant anachronism, for the administrative structure of chiefs and subchiefs did not exist at the time (the person in question here would best be described as a lesser, direct client of the king).

88. *Ibitéekerezo*, Rujugira file T, no. 16; H, no. 9. Delmas, *Généalogies*, 187–91; Kagame, *Abrégé* 1, 130, 136. It seems doubtful whether this man was of Twa descent. Some local historians think that he was an emigrant from Gisaka or Bugesera.

89. The tradition about Rurinda perhaps offers the best example of an expatriation provoked by a fight. See *Ibitéekerezo*, Rujugira file, T, nos. 2, 6, 11, 14; H, nos. 6, 10, 13, 15, 27, in which Bugondo advises her husband to flee. For an example of expatriation to pursue a better career elsewhere, see ibid., no. 8:1–2 ("if we find that the king of Ndorwa treats the people who serve him better, he will accept us in his employ . . ." and the same comments about Burundi and Bunyabungo).

90. Schumacher, *Ruanda*, 478, 607.

91. Kagame, *Milices*, 84 n.1.

92. See Rugamba, *Poésie*, 253–54, on defectors in general, and Kagame, *Milices*, for examples of defectors from Burundi: Bashana and his warriors arrived under Rujugira (58) and Kamari received a defector from Gisaka with his guard (18).

93. See Kagame, *Abrégé* 1, 130, 133, on Rujugira in general and *Ibitéekerezo*, Rujugira file, H, no. 11, on his battling Karagwe.

94. For instance, *Ibitéekerezo*, Rujugira file, T, nos. 1:5–9, 22; H, no. 1:17–21.

95. A case is described in Kagame, *Poésie dynastique*, 139, no. 16.

96. For a good example of such rivalries, see ibid., 158–59, no. 51, which recounts a story where the king threatens a hostile family during a vendetta.

97. See Jacob, *Dictionnaire*, under *"ijabiro," "kugaba,"* and *"iteka."* For Schumacher, *Ruanda*, 586, *"ijabiro"* is "the place where justice was dispensed."

98. *Ibitéekerezo*, Mazimpaka file, T, no. 2:2.

99. The procedure as described was still common well after 1900 (Kayijuka, "Lebensgeschichte," 154–57; Mazina, "Nachtrag," 164–65.) There is no reason to believe that matters were different during the eighteenth or nineteenth centuries.

100. Kagame, *Abrégé* 1, 123. He secretly informed himself about the parties to the dispute. The only concrete knowledge of court cases we have stems from dynastic poems. They deal with a dispute about an order to a smith for a spear (Kagame, *Poésie dynastique*, 145–48), a quarrel over a zebra skin coveted by the queen mother (ibid., 131), and pleas for defense by poets (ibid., 131, 139–41).

101. Pagès, *Royaume hamite*, 136: "He always had the last word and witticism."

102. Kagame, *Abrégé* 1, 123. But the execution on an incandescent rock is a cliché (ibid., 127, 157). *Ibitéekerezo*, Mazimpaka file, T, no. 2:6 attributes it to Mazimpaka, while Pagès, *Royaume hamite*, 148, and Van Overschelde, *Bij de reuzen*, 92, ascribe it to Gahindiro.

103. Kagame, *Milices*, 70–71.

104. For Rujugira's argument, see Delmas, *Généalogies*, 48. *Ibitéekerezo*, Mazimpaka file, H, no. 7, is the only story about Rwaka that mentions *mandwa*.

105. For this "king of the *imandwa*," see Kagame, *Abrégé* 1, 117, and id., *Milices*, 62–66, where this action is erroneously attributed to Semugeshi. See also Delmas, *Généalogies*, 67, 93–94, 95–96; Schumacher, *Ruanda*, 1113–16.

106. Kagame, *Poésie dynastique*, 149, no. 32.

107. d'Hertefelt and Coupez, *Royauté*, 51–53, 98–163; Kagame, "Le code ésotérique," 377–85, and id., *Abrégé* 1, 111–16.

108. Kagame, *Poésie dynastique*, 152, no. 40. Contra Kagame we accept that the poem would have been the oldest one composed during Rujugira's reign.

109. Van Noten, *Tombes*.

110. Kagame, *Armées bovines*, 55. The ritual is path 9, called "of the watering."

111. Kagame, *Milices*, 57, 59.

112. d'Hertefelt and Coupez, *Royauté*, 49, 54–67, on path 6 called "of the fire."

113. Ibid., 51–53, 98–153, on path 9 and commentaries; Kagame, "Code ésotérique," 377–85.

114. Kagame, *Abrégé* 1, 208–9.

115. Kagame, "Code ésotérique," 386. The Ryangombe cult is an elaboration on the ancestor cult.

116. d'Hertefelt and Coupez, *Royauté*, 459.

117. Delmas, *Généalogies*, 6–8, 18.

118. d'Hertefelt and Coupez, *Royauté*, 514.

119. One may wonder from where this notion of a dynastic cycle comes, since one finds cycles with three or four names in some *biru* families and in the dynasties of the small Hutu kingdoms in the Mukungwa region, as well as in the surrounding kingdoms. Are they an eighteenth century innovation in the whole western Great Lakes region?

120. The idea that throne really had to pass from biological father to son was no doubt not relevant from the point of view of esoteric ritual. Whomever happened to be ruling was automatically presented as the son of his predecessor.

121. Newbury, "Trick Cyclists?" 204–10; J. Vansina, "Historical Tales." Thus toward the end of the nineteenth century the so-called military campaigns of Nyamuheshera were invented to act as precedents for those of Ndabarasa and above all those of Rwabugiri.

122. Contra Kagame, *Abrégé* 1, 127, and *Poésie dynastique*, 140, where the mention of Mazimpaka's "subchief" is an anachronism. He probably was just a lesser client of the king.

123. *Ibitéekerezo*, Mazimpaka file, T, no. 4 *(Binama)*; Kagame, *Poésie dynastique*, 158–59.

124. This was already the case in Mazimpaka's day with the private campaigns of Nyarwaya Karuretwa. (*Ibitéekerezo*, Mazimpaka file, T, no. 11; H, nos. 1, 3, 5, 6, 12, 13). One observes that the booty of these expeditions was not shared with the court!

125. Desforges, "Court," 23 (*"ngabo* fought each other for control of men, land, and cattle").

126. This rate of reproduction is hard to establish. The factors involved are the age of maturity, the frequency of births, the length of the fertile period, and mortality.

127. *Ibitéekerezo*, Rujugira file, T, no. 8, is a good example. Rujugira is obliged to give armies and herds to every one of his four sons and his two daughters, but there remained one son to endow. This passage is not unique, for all the variants of the story of the Abatangana start with the distribution of goods.

128. Kayijuka, "Lebensgeschichte,"131, speaks of the one hundred sons of Mazimpaka. The cliché "909 boys and 909 girls" is used for the many children of Rujugira (*Ibitéekerezo*, Rujugira file, T, no. 17:6 and Ndabarasa file, T, no. 4:3. Ibid., Ndabarasa file, T, no. 15:1, claims that this king had twenty-seven sons).

129. Schumacher, *Ruanda*, 601–2.

130. The number of members of the elite rapidly increased through natural growth and through the incorporation of small royal clients and "subclients" but the territory of the kingdom did not grow apace, at least not until the conquest of Buganza and Ndabarasa's attempt to take all of Ndorwa, Mpororo included. It follows that the imposition of dues per unit of land (not necessarily per *inzu*) must have increased considerably before the expansion of the 1780s.

Chapter 4. Government in the Eighteenth Century

1. Even though this episode is only found in Schumacher, *Ruanda*, 165, I believe that the information is reliable, given the competence of his collaborators. Yet Kagame's silence in this regard remains mysterious. Was this a tradition among the "great chiefs" but denied at the court?

2. For Gisanura's reign, see Kagame, *Abrégé* 1, 122–25, and *Ibitéekerezo*, Gisanura file, T, no. 1; H, no. 1.

3. *Historique et chronologie*, 181 ("Thereafter Mazimpaka, fleeing his brothers, established himself there and is said to have raised the army there that allowed him to seize royal power").

4. Delmas, *Généalogies*, 57. This is the earliest mention of the practice of exterminating people only because they belonged to a descent group. The history of the Kono that follows is another, better example of this. The case of some decimated families such as the Abagareka became notorious. In 1907, Musinga ordered the extermination of a large Twa family for letting the fire of Gihanga be extinguished (Classe, *Organisation politique*, 7). It is by the extension of this principle that the extermination of all the members of a social category, as happened in 1994, becomes conceivable.

5. *Ibitéekerezo*, Mazimpaka file, T, no. 2; Kagame, *Abrégé* 1, 126.

6. See Vansina, "Historical Tales," for the sources and variants of this tale.

7. *Ibitéekerezo*, Mazimpaka file, T, no. 8b (Mazimpaka's Cyaba wives accused Musigwa of adultery with them). Elsewhere one is given to understand that the magic of his wives was responsible for his killing his own son. Mazimpaka is thought to have composed a poem relating to this incident.(Kagame, *Poésie dynastique*, 143, no. 22).

8. Kayijuka, "Lebensgeschichte," 131, for the number of sons only, since: moreover, he "engendered many girls."

9. This is the version found in Kagame, *Abrégé* 1, 130–31. A variant in Desforges, *Court*, 19, speaks of a Putsch carried out by the Imitari army, which chose Rwaka, an usurper from abroad as ruler. This is not very credible, for if it was, it certainly would have become the received version at court, since it delegitimized Rwaka to the point of turning him into a stranger. Moreover, Mazimpaka's main army was no longer called Imitari but Intaremba (Kagame, *Milices*, 80).

10. Delmas, *Généalogies*, 189. Citation from *Ibitéekerezo*, Mazimpaka file, T, no. 10. For Rwaka in general, see *Ibitéekerezo*, Mazimpaka file, T, nos. 9, 10, H, no. 7, and Kagame, *Abrégé* 1, 130–31, 133–34; Schumacher, *Ruanda*, 166; Kayijuka, "Lebensgeschichte," 132, Delmas *Généalogies*, 58.

11. According to Delmas, Rwaka ruled about fifteen years in all but according to Kagame, he ruled sixteen. Schumacher claims he ruled on his own for four years after Mazimpaka's death. It is likely that Rwaka died either before the coup d état or at least was dying at the time (from yaws?), for he played no role at all in it.

12. For Rujugira's reign in general, see *Ibitéekerezo*, Rujugira and Ndabarasa files, H, nos. 1–3; Coupez and Kamanzi, *Récits*, 282–91; Kagame, *Abrégé* 1, 135–53; Schumacher, *Ruanda*, 166–67, 170–71; Delmas, *Généalogies*, 67.

13. The executioner who hides his victim is a classical motif in stories. This motif is linked to Busyete because he had to testify that the person chosen as queen mother by Rujugira truly was his birth mother. As to his Twa identity, see *Ibitéekerezo*, Rujugira file, H, no. 11:2, "You are no longer Twa, you are a person,"

and H, no. 9; Kagame, *Abrégé* 1, 130; Schumacher, *Physische*, 96. For *Ibitéekerezo*, *Rujugira file*, T, no. 16; H, no. 9, Busyete was a ritualist and not a Twa. Delmas, *Généalogies*, 188–89, cites versions who label him "Twa" and others that deny this. Therefore this case cannot be used to argue that the rigidity between the social categories "Twa" and "Tutsi" was only relative, as some twentieth century authors have done.

14. Delmas, *Généalogies*, 58. In the late nineteenth century make-believe kings were appointed to combat disasters and supposedly created kings to fool the fates. For another account of the KAREMERA regnal name, see Kagame, *Abrégé* 1, 131. For links between Rujugira and the seduction of Mazimpaka's wives, see *Ibitéekerezo*, Rujugira file, T, no. 11, and Kayijuka, "Lebensgeschichte," 132–33.

15. Desforges, "Court," 19, labels him "another stranger from the east." *Ibitéekerezo*, Mazimpaka file, T, no. 10, stresses that a coup took place. According to Kagame, *Poésie dynastique*, 155, no. 45, the king of Gisaka considered Rujugira to be a usurper of Rwaka's throne. Given the extraordinary efforts Rujugira made to establish legitimacy it seems to me that the official version is a fabrication and that Rujugira was a usurper from Gisaka.

16. For his role in the war between Gisaka and Karagwe, see *Ibitéekerezo*, file *Rujugira*, H, no. 11:2, in which it is related that he supposedly captured the king of Karagwe but then accompanied him back to his country.

17. Delmas, *Généalogies*, 58, 159. For Kayijuka, "Lebensgeschichte," 132–33, Nsigaye was the son of Gakombe (Gakomba) who was Mazimpaka's son. Nama would have been one of his brothers and a son of Mazimpaka but he is not mentioned by Delmas. Given his failure, however, Gakombe's name was probably suppressed and his descendants likely joined another lineage.

18. Armies as cited by Kayijuka, "Lebensgeschichte," 138. See also Kagame, *Milices*, 66–67, 80.

19. Delmas, *Généalogies*, 58. See also Kagame, *Abrégé* 1, 135–36, which describes Nama's suicide and the battle on the Bakokwe River; Kayijuka, "Lebensgeschichte," 131–32, 138–39, which relates how Nama was killed by Nsigaye on the Hogwe battlefield; *Ibitéekerezo*, Mazimpaka file, T, nos. 10, which details intrigues between ritualists and Ndabarasa; 14; on Ndabarasa; ibid., file *Rujugira*, H, nos. 2, 9, which have Rwaka being assisted by his mother's brother Rukoni and the capital at Bisagata of Muganza where the battle occurred; ibid., H, nos. 11, 16, on the role of Busyete. Other versions have carefully hidden the whole conflict. According to these, either Rwaka could not lift the drum or his illness proved that he was not legitimate. At that point, he resigned and went to live in Budaha (ibid., Mazimpaka file, T, nos. 9, 10, 14, and Rujugira file, H, no. 2).

20. Nkurikiyimfura, "Révision," 152–53, states that Kirongoro, daughter of Kagoro of Nyamuhenda, was an Ega woman.

21. Kagame, *Abrégé* 1, 169; *Ibitéekerezo*, Gahindiro file, T, nos. 7, 11, 20; H, nos. 6, 8, 23, 25. Nyiratunga, Gihana's wife and then widow, later became Gahindiro's queen mother.

22. Arguments summarized in Delmas, *Généalogies*, 58, Kagame, *Abrégé* 1, 131. As to the *imandwa*, see also *Ibitéekerezo*, Mazimpaka file, H, no. 7, where it is claimed that Rwaka had his mother killed because she refused to accept meat from cattle killed at his own initiation.

23. See d'Hertefelt and Coupez, *Royauté*, 217, verse 56–57, which is addressed to the spirit of Rujugira. See also verse 44–45 and 60–61. On matridynastic lineages in general, see ibid., 5, 200, 334.

24. Kagame, *Abrégé* 1, 115; d'Hertefelt and Coupez, *Royauté*, 5, 334. It is possible that the rule that requires all mothers of YUHI to be Ega was only formulated during Gahindiro's reign.

25. Delmas, *Généalogies*, 6–7, 18.

26. d'Hertefelt and Coupez, *Royauté*, 514; Delmas, *Généalogies*, 117, 118, notes that Makara and his son Bukuba were killed in Mutara probably by Ndabarasa's warriors. Kagame, *Milices*, 64, 115; id., "Documentation," 306, points out that they were killed very soon after their flight and id., *Abrégé* 1, 148, suggests that their flight would date to Mazimpaka's reign and their execution to a point during Rujugira's rule. Their flight to Ndorwa occurred before Ndabarasa's campaigns against that country, which places the assassination attempt before c. 1780. If this attempt had been perpetrated against Mazimpaka it is not very evident why Rujugira wanted to avenge it.

27. Delmas, *Généalogies*, 189; Kagame, *Milices*, 41, notes the army given to Semakamba.

28. Kagame, *Milices*, 97–98, on the Abadahemuka army.

29. Contra ibid., 114–15, who attributes this merger to Kimanuka, son of Ndabarasa. According to Kayijuka, "Lebensgeschichte," 139, Nsigaye fell into disgrace during Ndabarasa's rule and lost command of both the army and the herds.

30. Kayijuka, "Lebensgeschichte," 138–39.

31. Kagame, *Milices*, 24–25. Semahamba, the carver of the audience drum, was sacked.

32. *Ibitéekerezo*, Mazimpaka file, T, no. 10; Delmas, *Généalogies*, 590–61, notes that Rwaka supposedly died in neighboring Kabagari; d'Hertefelt and Coupez, *Royauté*, 447. Later the family regained some importance and around 1950 it counted chiefs and subchiefs everywhere in the country but especially in Bwishaza. See Delmas, ibid., 198, 206, 208, 212, 224, 228, 232.

33. See *Historique et chronologie*, 112, 114, and R. Vanwalle, "Aspecten van staatsvorming in West-Rwanda," 69–70, for the Abazimya, and *Ibitéekerezo*, Rujugira file, T, nos. 8:3, 10. Kagame, *Milices*, 101, for Budaha. *Historique et chronologie*, 122–24, Newbury, *Kings and Clans*, 92–93, and Pagès, *Royaume hamite*, 607–9, 638, for Bugoyi. For the northern regions, see Nahimana, *Le Rwanda*, 235–39. The situation with regard to Bufumbira, Jomba, and Bwisha still remains obscure.

34. See Kagame, *Poésie dynastique*, 158–59, no. 51, for a struggle between two families of lesser importance.

35. Ibid., 144–48, nos. 25–31, 47, 156–57; Desforges, "Court," 30–32.

36. Kagame, *Armées bovines*, 37–57; *Ibitéekerezo*, Rujugira file, T, no. 8, most explicitly but also nos. 10, 15; H, nos. 12, 13, 27.

37. Kagame, *Abrégé* 1, 138, 148, and id., *Milices*, 113–19.

38. Ibid., 153, and *Ibitéekerezo*, Ndabarasa file, T, no. 4:16–17, where he is described as "a very tall, bad-tempered child"; see also no. 11; H, nos. 17, 19.

39. For Ndabarasa, see *Ibitéekerezo*, Ndabarasa file, and Kagame, *Abrégé* 1, 153–59.

40. Kagame, *Poésie dynastique*, 160–62, nos. 54–46, and id., *Abrégé* 1, 157. According to some storytellers Ndabarasa declared himself king of Ndorwa as successor to Gahaya, who died without leaving a son, and his stay there finally fostered two attempts at insurrection in central Rwanda, which he put down in a ruthless manner. See especially Mugina in *Ibitéekerezo*, Ndabarasa file, T, no. 5:17, on the insurrection in "Nduga" but also H, no. 22.

41. Kagame, *Armées bovines*, 58–74. The ritualist Heka received one official herd, the *ibibanda* lineages four, his Ega son-in-law one, his Gesera kin two, a Ha warrior one, and a grandson of Mazimpaka one. The elites were given six of the fifteen new herds, his sons five, people of lesser status two, and Rukari, his favorite two.

42. Id., *Abrégé* 1, 163; id., *Armées bovines*, 68; id., *Milices*, 114, for Abantaguha, the army taken from Kamari with its marcher camp at Nyabwunyu in Mutara, and 125, on Rukari setting up his own army called Abanyoro; id., *Poésie dynastique*, 162–64, nos. 57–59.

43. Id., *Armées bovines*, 58–74, for the less focused attribution of the new official herds, namely one for a ritualist, two for favorites, five for his sons, four for the *ibibanda*: two for other relatives, one for a small client labeled a "Hutu" and one for an unknown person.

44. Id., *Milices*, 108, 114, 120, 121–22.

45. Id., *Abrégé* 1, 159.

46. Newbury, "Lake Kivu Regional Trade"; Lugan, *Histoire du Rwanda*, 163–80.

47. For a description of this "Kivu culture," see D. Newbury, "'Bunyabungo,'" and id., *Kings and Clans*, 43–64. With regard to food production one will observe that neither beans nor bananas grow in the high mountains. They were replaced by other crops, especially by peas. Moreover, the landscape was dominated by forests and the settlement on the hills was less dispersed than further east. In Bushiru, people actually lived in well-defined villages. The rains were more abundant and more regular there than in the savannas to the east. Communication took place in part by canoe all along Lake Kivu and in part across the volcanic plains, and the inhabitants crossed the high mountain ranges by lower passes such as the Rugabano pass and the valley of the Mukungwa. The political style of the region is also found in Kigezi and even in Buberuka further east.

48. Rwandan traditions referring to ancient times do not mention them but a few glass beads, cowries, and bits of copper from c. 1100 onward have been found in southern Uganda. See Robertshaw and Taylor, "Environmental Change," 15.

49. One of its capitals was located at Ryamurari in the north of Mutara. See Tshihiluka, "Ryamurari." Ugandans gave the name "Mpororo" to this kingdom.

50. Burundi took first shape far to the south in the Nkoma range and in connection with one of the kingdoms that the sources call "Buha." Its emergence was not *directly* influenced by the rupture in the balance of power provoked by the creation of Bunyoro.

51. I. Katoke, The *Karagwe Kingdom*, 44–47, on Karagwe, Buha; d'Arianoff, *Histoire des Bagesera*, 55–58, on Gisaka, Mubari, and Ndorwa; *Ibitéekerezo*, Mazimpaka file, H, no. 10; Kagame, *Abrégé* 1, 28, 80, 85, 96–97, 110, 120–21, 149, on the enclave of Gasura, Kigari, and the lands of the abane Ngwe.

52. Kagame, ibid., 121, 149. His chronology is inferred from a tradition that tells of a hostile relationship between the Nyiginya and Gisaka during Gisanura's rule which is unacceptable. The region of Mount Kigari was of such political importance that all the adjacent kingdoms (Ndorwa, Gisaka, Bugesera, and central Rwanda) strove to control it. This importance was due to its ecological situation as a refuge, especially during the dry season, for herds from the east, the south, and the southeast. Kigari was later turned into a sacred mountain because of this.

53. Ibid., 123–24. This derives partly from the tradition that relates the exchange of insults between Gisaka and Gisanura and partly from the fact that there seems to have been a "liberator" fighting against Gisaka during his reign and that a there is no "liberator" without war.

54. For the Ngwe (Abene Ngwe) Kagame, see *Abrégé* 1, 124–25. These people were called Abene Rwamba in Burundi. See J. Vansina, *Légende*, 123–24, for a tradition and doubts about the existence of this "kingdom."

55. The traditions about Nsoro, Ntare, and Mazimpaka in *Ibitéekerezo*, Mazimpaka file, fall into three groups: the block that deals with Mazimpaka's wives (T, no. 2; H, no. 9, replaces the actor Nsoro by "a Rundi"), a block that narrates the whole from the attack against Nsoro to the death of Ntare (T, nos. 1, 5, 6, and Gisanura file, T, no. 11), and a tale about a prophecy by Mazimpaka portraying Ntare as the king's friend (T, no. 3). Kagame, *Abrégé* 1, 126–29, brings it all together but leaves Ntare out of the prophecy and Kayijuka, "Lebensgeschichte," gives the two first blocks separately: "wives of the king" (133–35) and "war and Ntare's death" (136–38). Ntare's death is claimed as a victory in Kagame, *Poésie dynastique*, 136–39, nos. 13–15. For Rundi traditions about Nyabarega and their fairy tale atmosphere, see Vansina, *Légende*, 133–36. But here we deal with a second Ntare and the events that occurred between 1797 and 1800.

Accounts of the other earlier and later relationships between the Nyiginya kings and Burundi include a series of confusions. First about the blood pact at Utwicara-bwami, which Kagame, *Abrégé* 1, 111, and *Ibitéekerezo*, Semugeshi file, H, no. 3, T, no. 7, mistakenly attribute to Semugeshi, but that in fact was made by Rujugira (see also file *Rujugira*, T, nos. 1, 2, H, no. 23). Then the war with Ntare is confused with the war in Bungwe. Thus the camp established at Mujye-juru (Rusatira) would also have been Mazimpaka's during his campaign against Ntare and not Semugeshi's during his war in Bungwe (cf. Kagame, ibid., 109, 129) and the campaign of Binama (*Ibitéekerezo*, Mazimpaka file, T, no. 4) would have been directed against Bungwe and not the Rundi. Finally, for the episode or episodes of Rugaju and/or Foronko, herder of the Nyiginya king, raided by a foreign king of Bugesera or Burundi who was either not hurt or mutilated, see Kagame, *Abrégé* 1, 124–25, who places this under Gisanura (Rugaju) but which the fairly confused storyteller of *Ibitéekerezo*, Mazimpaka file, T, no. 13:2–3, places under Mazimpaka (Foronko) and in Bugesera, not Burundi. The main value of this tale is as a reminder of the frequency of cattle rustling on the borders.

56. *Ibitéekerezo*, Mazimpaka file, H, nos. 3, 5, 6; T, no. 11; Kagame, *Milices*, 78–79. Two storytellers (H, no. 6) speak of Nyarwaya's partial defeat and a third (Rujugira file, T, 20) speaks of a total defeat whilst the others underline that the fortunes of war changed sides several times before Nyarwaya won the battle.

57. Kayijuka, "Lebensgeschichte," 138. He is also said to have raided the region of Kabale. The Banyoni on Kigezi remember incursions by Gisanura and Mazimpaka according to Géraud, "Settlement," 30.

58. Kagame, *Abrégé* 1, 131–32, according to information received from the curator of the royal treasury. The words for "copper" and "glass bead" are regional innovations. Schoenbrun, *Historical Reconstruction*, has "**-lingá,*" "metal or copper," an innovation from "**-dingá,* 3/4," "ring," a meaning that one finds along with that of "copper" for these forms in the whole region of the Great Lakes and even in Gikuyu. The archaic meaning of "*ururíra*," "glass bead," seems derived from one meaning "coveted object," the plural of which *("indíra")* also occurs in Rundi. Perhaps the value of such beads then was comparable to that of diamonds today. The form "*-simbi,*" "cowry," stems from Swahili and is also found in the languages between Rwanda and the East African coast, as is also the case for the word that designates the jewel fashioned from a conus. As to the goods given in return, one probably must add to the ivory suggested by Kagame female slaves, cows, and goats.

59. Pagès, *Royaume hamite*, 138–40; *Ibitéekerezo*, Mazimpaka file, T, nos. 3, 7, 8a; H, no. 2; Kagame, *Abrégé* 1, 132–33.

60. We are here at the very limit of the memories that have been retained in these regions. Hence one speaks a good deal about the emergence of micro-kingdoms at this time, although several among these may well be older. See, for

instance, Géraud, "Settlement" and Rwandusya, "The Origins and Settlement of People of Bufumbira"; Nahimana, *Le Rwanda*, 139–52; *Historique et chronologie*, 96–102, 111–14, 121–23, 149–68, 174–78; Pagès, *Royaume hamite*, 338–45; Vanwalle, "Aspecten"; Newbury, *Kings and Clans*, 285–86 n.23. The only earlier kingdom would have been Bugara, which Ndori destroyed.

61. Kagame, *Milices*, 7–71; *Ibitéekerezo*, Gisanura file, H, no. 1.

62. Kagame, ibid., 68–69, but the first known chief of this corporation dates only from Gahindiro.

63. Kagame, *Armées bovines*, 3–31, locates these pastures in Nyantango at Nyakabuye, probably along the Nyabarongo and not far from Bunyambiriri. But the attribution of those pastures may well be more recent. That is very likely the case for a vague mention of a cattle-breeding domain in Buberuka (ibid., 34); Kayijuka, "Lebensgeschichte," 131–32 (Budaha).

64. Kagame, *Abrégé* 1, 135.

65. Schumacher, *Physische*, 17–18. For variants, see Newbury, *Kings and Clans*, 92–93, 105–6, 279 n.34, 280–82 nn.40–42; Reisdorff, *Enquêtes*, 81–84; *Historique et chronologie*, 121–22; Pagès *Royaume hamite*, 142, 598–607. Pagès observes (598 n.1) that he translates as "Ndorwa" what is labeled "Buhima," the Hima country from whence also came the first chief of Bwisha, north of the volcanoes. To these a set of immigrants into Kigezi can be added.

66. Macumu's genealogy in Schumacher, *Physische*, 17, does not completely tally with that of Reisdorff, *Enquêtes*, 81 (though it does for a number of generations after Macumu), nor with that of Pagès, *Royaume hamite*, 606, 607, 609, who counts Migwabiro and Makombe/Nyamakombe among his predecessors. Reisdorff does not cite any ascendants of Macumu, and Pagès lists two generations after Suti but he locates them in Kinyaga! Moreover, I wonder if the Suti in this tradition is the Suti of Bunyambiriri (rather than the Suti of Buberuka, which is on the road that goes directly from Ndorwa [called Buhima] to Bugoyi).

67. The lower number represent the smallest size a herd could be and still be efficient (and three to four men would have been required to tend to such a herd), whereas the higher number comes from the description of the flight of Sentama, a Rundi who fled "with a hundred relatives and a thousand cows," according to *Ibitéekerezo*, Mazimpaka file, T, no. 11:2 (see also ibid., Rujugira file, T, no. 13:5; H, no. 1:23).

68. Kagame, *Abrégé* 1, 136–39.

69. *Umutabaazi* meant "the helper," from *"gutabaara,"* "to help, to assist," an old word also known in Ha and Rundi (from which also derives *"umutabaazi,"* "defender, warrior, auxiliary"). See Schoenbrun, *Historical Reconstruction*, no. 243, in nearly all the languages of the Great Lakes region.

70. *Ibitéekerezo*, Mazimpaka file, T, no. 11; id., Rujugira file, T, nos. 1–6, 10, 11, 13–15, 19, 22; H, nos. 1, 5, 7–8, 10, 12–13, 15, 18–22, 24–27; id., Ndabarasa file, T, no. 10, 14; H, nos. 1–3, 9, 13; Kagame, *Abrégé* 1, 140–44; Vansina, *Légende*, 124–32.

71. Kagame, *Milices*, 97–98; see also *Historique et chronologie*, 83–84, on Bufundu. *Ibitéekerezo*, Ndabarasa file, H, nos. 2:4, 13:4, speak of Bunyambiriri and Buyenzi. But Buyenzi remained in Burundi. Its incorporation, hill by hill, by the Nyaruguru army was only completed after Rwogera's death (*Historique et chronologie*, 86, and *Ibitéekerezo*, Rwogera file, H, no. 1) in Rwabugiri's time. Schumacher, *Ruanda*, 478, 716, 745–46, describes the process according to Kayijuka who was commander of this army.

72. Kagame, *Abrégé* 1, 141–43, and *Ibitéekerezo* (preceding note) explain the need to send liberators in order to overcome famine. According to some, this one broke out after Gihana's second campaign and lasted, in Burundi at any rate, until well after Mutaga's death. See Vansina, *Légende*, 129–33.

73. Schumacher, *Ruanda*, 433–34, 453–54, 600–601; Reisdorff, *Enquêtes*, 43–44. The camps are shown in Kagame, *Abrégé* 1, map 5 (but the map does not document the older existence of at least one camp in Bufundu) and in Newbury, *Kings and Clans*, 88 (but one should ignore the camps in Kinyaga and on the upper Nyabarongo where the sources do not mention camps and also bear in mind that in the east all the camps were evacuated after Ndabarasa's death, except for the great camp of Munyaga facing Gisaka). Hence permanent military districts were mainly created facing the Akanyaru River and Burundi.

74. *Ibitéekerezo*, Rujugira file, T, no. 9, 17; H, nos. 3–4, 12, 13a; Kagame, *Abrégé* 1, 144–47; d'Arianoff, *Histoire des Bagesera*, 59–63.

75. *Ibitéekerezo*, Rujugira file, T, no. 18; H, no. 14; Kagame, *Abrégé* 1, 147–52. For Sendakize, see also id., *Milices*, 84 n.1.

76. Reisdorff, *Enquêtes*, 139, 142, 145. But the attribution of this conquest to Gahindiro is incorrect.

77. *Ibitéekerezo*, Ndabarasa file, T, nos. 4, 13–14, 16; H, nos. 1, 4, 15, 35. This action is also significant in the context of Ndabarasa's invasion of Mubari and his hostile attitude toward Karagwe which had raided Gisaka shortly before these events.

78. *Ibitéekerezo*, Ndabarasa file, T, nos. 5, 9, 12; H, nos. 4, 6, 22; *Historique et chronologie*, 178; J. Rwabukumba and V. Mudandagizi "Les formes historiques de la dépendance personnelle dans l'État rwandais," 7–10. See Géraud, "Settlement," 30, 32, 38, for his extraordinary notion that henceforth he was king of Ndorwa rather than king of central Rwanda and Ndorwa was therefore more his "home" than central Rwanda was. Kagame, *Poésie dynastique*, 59, 90, 103–104, 170; Karugire, *A History of the Kingdom of Nkore in Western Uganda to 1896*, 190–94; Schumacher, *Physische*, 141. It probably is from Ndorwa that he conducted a large-scale raid on the highlands of Buberuka (*Ibitéekerezo*, Nyamuheshera file, T, no. 2) but according to *Historique et chronologie*, 177, eastern Buberuka was only incorporated into the realm from Rwogera's time onward.

79. *Ibitéekerezo*, Ndabarasa file, T, no. 5:17; Kagame, *Poésie dynastique*, 160–62.

80. Kagame, *Introduction*, 194, 271 n.200.

81. These prophecies are amongst the most celebrated ones in the whole corpus of oral tradition. See *Ibitéekerezo,* Ndabarasa file, T, nos. 5, 15; H, nos. 5, 8, 10, 14–17, 20–21, 24–25, 27–28, 32, 36–38; Kagame, *Abrégé* 1, 154–56, plus his maps 7 and 8.

82. *Historique et chronologie,* 57.

83. Van Noten, *Tombes,* 7–8. Digs at Nyansenge, Rurembo, and Rambura have yielded some early Iron Age shards.

84. Kagame, *Milices,* 56–57, 59. These detachments were given the names of the most glorious armies of yore.

85. Kagame, *Armées bovines,* 61, 65, 67, 68, 69, 73. For the dates of the Inyambo, id., *Milices,* 82, 90. Sentabyo was inaugurated in 1796 at Nkuzuzu (id., *Abrégé* 1, 162) and Ndabarasa himself had already been at Bumbogo near Nkuzuzu, a hill in Bwanacyambwe on the very border of Buganza (*Ibitéekerezo,* Ndabarasa file, H, no. 11).

86. Kagame, *Abrégé* 1, 137: *"Urwanda ruratera, ntiruterwa."*

87. The civil war was succeeded by fighting between Semugaza's army and units faithful to the court. There were also clashes between Rwogera's armies (*Ibitéekerezo,* Rwogera file, T, nos. 7, 9; H, no. 30). During Rwabugiri's rule, open warfare erupted in Bugoyi between the Abashakamba and the Abakemba (Schumacher, *Physische,* 65).

88. Newbury, *Kings and Clans,* 92–93, 105–106 n.34, 280–82, n.40–42; Reisdorff, *Enquêtes,* 51, 81–84, and no. 27 (not paginated); C. Newbury, *Cohesion,* 27–219; Schumacher, *Physische,* 17–18. For variants, see Pagès, *Royaume hamite,* 598, who observes that he translates "Buhima," the Hima country as "Ndorwa." From there also came the first chief of Bwisha, north of the Mikeno volcano, and many immigrants into Kigezi. For the north Nahimana, *Le Rwanda,* 145, 150, shows that Bugambe and Kiganda, two subregions in Cyingogo and Bushiru were allegedly governed by Gesera (the ruling clan in Gisaka) dynasties.

89. Schumacher, *Physische,* 17–18, 63–64; Vanwalle, "Aspecten," 66–70. The Abazimya supposedly emigrated at least in part along the lake from Kinyaga toward Kibuye thus indicating that cattle breeders did not exclusively move from central Rwanda toward the west."

90. Nahimana, *Le Rwanda,* 235–37. This conviction was applied to the situation that obtained from 1990–94, and played a significant role in the preparation of the genocide as well as afterward in its justification.

91. *Historique et chronologie,* 122, on the Abashara.

92. Nahimana, *Le Rwanda,* 237; *Historique et chronologie,* 138; Pagès, *Royaume hamite,* 607–8. The appointment at a later date of Sharangabo, son of Rujugira, has remained entirely theoretical since Sharangabo apparently never went to Bugoyi.

93. Nahimana, *Le Rwanda,* 238–39; *Historique et chronologie,* 237–38.

94. Géraud, "Settlement," 32. This did not occur under Mazimpaka but under Rujugira or Ndabarasa.

95. Kagame, *Milices,* 89, on North Kivu; Schumacher, *Physische,* 63–64, *Historique et chronologie,* 122; Pagès, *Royaume hamite,* 607–8.

96. Pagès, *Royaume hamite,* 597–606; *Historique et chronologie,* 121–22. Recently the Yaka language, which is probably what the language of "the mute" refers to, was still spoken on some hills.

97. Kayijuka, "Lebensgeschichte," 140. The mythical king Gihanga is said to have been allied to a Singa-Renge. This "marriage" demonstrates once more how important the royal cult was at the eighteenth-century Nyiginya court. "Gishari" is a term that refers vaguely to a region beyond the volcanoes, probably just west of Bwisha and north of the Nyiragongo volcano.

98. Schumacher, *Physische,* 195–97.

Chapter 5. Social Transformations in the Nineteenth Century

1. From c. 1800 onward the sources become more abundant. The text of the liturgy of the rituals of kingship becomes fixed to a considerable extent and is learned by rote; different genealogies, especially those of the aristocratic families, become more abundant and more credible and the number of historical accounts of all sorts greatly increases. The synthesis presented in this chapter is therefore rooted in a much greater mass of detail than is the case for the eighteenth century.

2. For the first mention of smallpox, which dates to before Rujugira's coup, see Kayijuka, "Lebensgeschichte," 138. Kayijuka also mentions the quarantine of patients suffering from yaws (135). Botte, "Rwanda and Burundi," 56–57, underlines the epidemic nature of yaws. For a severe epidemic at court during Gahindiro's reign, see Kagame, "Code ésotérique," 366. We think that the codification of the liturgy for the "path of fire," which was supposed to conjure epidemics, dates from his reign. See d'Hertefelt and Coupez, *Royauté,* 49–67.

3. *Ibitéekerezo,* Rujugira file, T, no. 15:1, 4. See also Ndabarasa file, H, no. 11, which details how when Ndabarasa was being inaugurated, "bronchitis had killed off the cows" and hence "he went to Ndorwa to choose cows among the herds of his subjects."

4. *Ibitéekerezo,* Rwabugiri file, H, no. 62, speaks of "countless famines under Rwogera," as does H, no. 92. But is this because one remembers these better than the earlier ones? With the exception of Gikoko, these droughts seem to have been more localized and less devastating than those at the outset of the century.

5. Kagame, *Poésie dynastique,* 63–78. Kagame's translation has only been altered in the next-to-last line. The adoption of small girls captured in raids or of orphans of either sex taken in by unrelated families was common during the nineteenth century and is an expression of the same pronatalist mentality.

6. Kagame, *Abrégé* 1, 175, recounts the abundant harvest of these beans in 1801–2 after the end of the famine. Schumacher, *Ruanda,* 95, notes that,

according to Sekarama, there was an increase in bean yield and that the *igishyimbo* were introduced from Buyungu and Buzi, northwest of Lake Kivu (153), or, more vaguely, from Bushi (935). Sekarama probably confused the introduction of these beans with their success in putting an end to the famine.

7. No one remembers when tobacco was introduced but the plant was probably acquired from the east around or after 1750. Everaerts, *Monographie*, 90. Schumacher, *Physische*, notes the season in which tobacco was planted (23), and discusses how it was traded (30–31); Kagame, *Abrégé* 1, 176, notes that Gahindiro's mother smoked "like a man." But the mortuary ensemble of Rujugira, who died c. 1786, did not contain any pipes. The form *"itabi,"* "tobacco," is commonly used in the southern Great Lakes region and in Nyamwezi so tobacco is likely to have spread from the east coast, perhaps during the eighteenth century. More precisely, the form *"itabi"* is probably derived from the translation of the Portuguese *"tabaco"* into Swahili *("tumbako")* through Arabic, Persian, or Hindi, for *"*-tab"* is attested to in the languages of the western Great Lakes region and further west such as Lebeo, Komo/Bira, Tembo, Shi, Hunde, Nande, Rungongo, Ganda, Gisu, Nkore/Kiga Rwanda, Rundi, Ha, Haya, Nyamwezi, Nilamba, Sinza, Ziba, Hanga (Kavirondo), and Nyara.

8. Czekanowski, *Forschungen*, 109–15. His estimates are especially useful as an indicator of differences between the densities of various regions.

9. *Ibitéekerezo*, Ndabarasa file, H, nos. 2, 10, 15:4, represent it as having been introduced after Ndabarasa, probably under Rwogera. For Schumacher, *Ruanda*, 835, and Kagame, *Abrégé* 2, 55–56, the modern sweet potato was only introduced under Rwabugiri, coming from Ndorwa or Gikore in eastern Kigezi. Kagame insists on the fact that before the Gikore campaign only *agafuma* was known, which produced only one tuber at a time and was only harvested once a year. Yet Everaerts, *Monographie*, 66, cites at least two other varieties besides *kafume* as "known for a long time." It is quite likely that new, far more productive varieties were introduced during the Gikore campaign. According to Ntabwoba (*Ibitéekerezo*, Rwabugiri file), H, no. 77, the *akandore* variety of Murera, which is not mentioned anywhere else, was introduced at that time. Still, despite the fact that the older varieties were only harvested once a year, the population had figured out how to preserve them so that they were available during the dry season.

10. *Ibitéekerezo*, Ndabarasa file, H, no. 15:4 (Nyirabiyoro's prophecy about dry season farming).

11. Czekanowski, *Forschungen*, 135–36. But see Bourgeois, *Banyarwanda et Barundi*, 394, who argues that they "rarely" irrigated there at this time.

12. Bethe, "Bericht über einen Zug nach Ruanda," 11; Czekanowski, *Forschungen*, 136.

13. For its origin in Buberuka and Bushi, see Schumacher, *Ruanda*, 153, 935, in Butembo, Kagame, *Abrégé* 2, 46, and in Murera, Ntabwoba in *Ibitéekerezo*, Rwabugiri file, H, no. 77.

14. There seems to exist a link between the quantity of protein in the diet and the level of fecundity, but scientists still need to demonstrate that this link is specifically valid for vegetable proteins and obtain a measure of its effect on fecundity.

15. Czekanowski, *Forschungen*, notes the density of the population and many recent clearings in 1907 (112) and that an approximate calculation dates the immigration to around 1810–1820 (294), but Pagès, *Royaume hamite*, 600, 638, and Reisdorff, *Enquêtes*, 81, indicate a much older settlement and the survival of the Yaka language strengthens their case.

16. For recent clearing in Bushiru, see Reisdorff, *Enquêtes*, 103. For an estimate of the speed of clearing after 1910, compare Schumacher, *Physische*, 14 (one kilometer per year) and id., *Ruanda*, 110, 250–51 (one kilometer per year in western Budaha in the western part of Butare prefecture) with Reisdorff, ibid., 50 (250 meters per year in Bufundu). But all the clearings do not date from the end of the eighteenth century. Clearings had been made, albeit at a much slower rate, so far back in time that the first ones were often older than genealogical memory and hence were telescoped in genealogies. For ancient cases in Ndiza, Bumbogo, and Buriza, see Reisdorff, ibid., 17, 19, who notes that at Muhondo, clearing began "more than two hundred years ago" (Reisdorff was writing in 1950) and that it took generations to strip the whole hill. He also observes that vestiges of forests could still be found around 1900 (22). See also Nahimana, *Le Rwanda*, 118–32, on the northwest, and Rwabukumba and Mudandagizi "Formes historiques," 10–12, who erroneously generalized for all of Rwanda what was the case only at Nyaruhengeri, which was apparently cleared between c. 1786 and 1801 (from the reign of Ndabarasa to that of Gahindiro). Unfortunately, Moniot, "Nouvelles recherches sur l'histoire sociale du Rwanda," 338 and 341, got hold of this information and declared in magisterial tones, but alas completely erroneously, that the great clearings began around 1800 and resulted (only then!) in "settlement on the soil that accompanies a settlement of the lineage frameworks. Power as well as the armies became territorial." For him the whole socio-political organization of Rwanda c. 1900 is derived from these clearings and took shape between 1830 and 1885. See also the reservations of Nkurikiyimfura, *Gros bétail*, 79.

17. Classe, *Organisation*, 7–8. The void in the center struck the first European travelers. Thus Beringe, "Bericht," 296, has the population of Nduga/Marangara as "fairly dense"—not as dense as it was in the north but denser than around the capital itself. The contrast between the environs of Nyanza and Save speaks volumes. Compare Kandt, *Caput Nili*, which was published in 1898, 259, and Heremans, Bart and Bart, "Agriculture," 8–9, which provides a summary of the observations of missionaries in 1901 and 1911.

18. Maquet and Naigiziki, "Droits fonciers," 352, L. Meschi, "Evolution des structures foncières au Rwanda," 40–41; for the meaning of the word, see Schumacher, *Ruanda*, 609, and ibid., 682, for delimitation.

19. *Ibitéekerezo*, Rwogera file, T, no. 6:3.

20. See C. Vidal, "Économie de la société féódale rwandaise," for the situation around 1900 (62–67) and on day laborers and even poorer navvies without hoes (69).

21. Schumacher, *Ruanda*, 194, on Buriza; Classe, *Organisation*, 3–4, on Marangara and the whole center.

22. This reserved area is called *igikingi*, as are the herding domains to which all herders have access, especially those in charge of official herds. But the different uses of this word have generated much confusion. Hence I will not use the term *"igikingi"* in this work. C. Vidal, "Le Rwanda des anthropologues ou le fétichisme de la vache," was the first scholar to underline the importance of the seizure of land and not only of cattle, a seizure that derives from cattle through the allocation of pastures. This is a point that had remained implicit, for instance, in Schumacher's studies. But contrary to Vidal's assertion (397), this seizure had been accomplished long before the creation of *ibikingi* reserved domains. See also Rwabukumba and Mudandagizi, "Formes historiques," 13; Nkurikiyimfura, *Gros bétail*, 73–99; Kagame, *Code*, 95, art. 248; Schumacher, *Ruanda*, 400, 436–38, 626. For Kinyaga, see Newbury, *Cohesion*, 79–81. For a very different sort of *igikingi*, see Reisdorff, *Enquêtes*, 32.

23. According to Nkurikiyimfura, *Gros bétail*, 87, following Reisdorff, *Enquêtes*, 1–3, who argues that the *igikingi* were created by Marara, 99, 136, 140. Rugaju is said to have created such a domain in Buganza and a second one was given to one of his clients by Marara, who was quite powerful during the first years of Nyiramongi's government, after which he fell out of favor. Kagame, *Poésie dynastique*, 182, mentions one of these *ibikingi* under Rwogera. See also the two preceding notes.

24. *Ibitéekerezo*, Gahindiro file, H, nos. 4, 10. For a variant in which Rugaju asked for a sod of turf that he had put on his head, which I also heard before 1960, see Nkurikiyimfura, *Gros Bétail*, 89.

25. Schumacher, *Ruanda*, 422. This saying supposedly came from Sharangabo, Rujugira's son.

26. As attested to by several complaints of dynastic poets who were dispossessed of their herds (Rugamba, *Poésie*, 202–3, and Kagame, *Poésie dynastique*, 182, no. 103, and especially, 108–10).

27. See n.22 and map 10 for the extent of the breakup.

28. Schumacher, *Ruanda*, 429–30, 443, 455, 473, 625, notes that the *intara* chief of the province differed from the commander of an army, except in the border marchers, and that in his province he named the chiefs of the land and of the long grass; Newbury, *Cohesion*, 43–45, explains that the army commander was the chief of the province in Biru and Impara but later Rwabugiri installed a different governor in Impara only; Kagame, *Milices*, 65, points out that in Impara, the first chiefs of the land emerge in Rwabugiri's time. But it is evident that the existence of this function was solely a consequence of the appointment

of chiefs of the long grass. It was merely a new title given to the provincial chiefs in regions where chiefs of the long grass had been appointed.

29. See Newbury, *Cohesion,* 44 (and table), for Kinyaga; Nkurikiyimfura, *Gros bétail,* 99 (table), and Rugamba, *Poésie,* 28–29 (table), for the center. For the south, Schumacher, *Ruanda,* 451–53, 625–26, reflects the opinion of the great chiefs who dealt with the end of Rwabugiri's reign. They continued to underline the importance of the provincial governor *(umutware w'intara)* whom they distinguished from the army commander, the chief of the land, and the chief of the long grass. According to them, four different chiefs intervened at the level of the hill. This perception seems to strongly contrast with that of Rwabukumba and Mudandagizi, "Formes historiques," 20–21, but only superficially so.

30. Schumacher, *Ruanda,* 401.

31. According to Nkurikiyimfura, *Gros bétail,* 91, corroborated by Pagès, *Royaume hamite,* 157, 532 n.2, and *Historique et chronologie,* 132, he had been appointed to Cyingogo by the queen mother Mururunkwere and introduced *uburetwa* between 1867 and 1877. In Kinyaga this new custom was introduced from Budaha, a province adjacent to Cyingogo, by Ntizimira a few years before 1887 (Newbury, *Cohesion,* 82). But elsewhere the progression of this innovation was slow. It spread across the central plateau only between 1906 and 1908 (Classe, *Organisation,* 4–5) and is described as "very recent" in Bwisha (but before 1912) by Schumacher, *Physische,* 162. It is not mentioned in Bufumbira and may never have been introduced there. This does not, however, mean that Mworoha, *Peuples et rois de l'Afrique des lacs,* 232–33, is right in arguing that this institution was introduced into the region by caravans from the east coast and that it is essentially a colonial one, for the colonial authorities only began to act at this level after 1920. Contrary to his opinion also, the term *"uburetwa"* is Rwandan and derives by metaphor from the passive form of *"ukureeta,"* "to bring milk into the nipples." The "milk" was the product of the imposed corvée labor.

32. Reisdorff, *Enquêtes,* 17–19, discussing Bumbogo, is categorical and contradicts Nkurikiyimfura, *Gros bétail,* 91, according to whom this referred to collective labor due by the members of a lineage to their headman.

33. Czekanowski, *Forschungen,* 270–71, does underline the considerable variation in levels of exploitation that fell under the name of *uburetwa.* In 1907 this obligation was the greatest in Marangara. According to Classe, *Organisation,* 4–5, *uburetwa* spread mainly between 1906 and 1908, except in Bugoyi, Bushiru, Cyingogo, and Murera; see also C. Newbury *"Ubureetwa* and *Thangata,"* 100–107, 110. Kagame, *Code,* 125–26, remains vague as to the duration of corvée labor but establishes a list of "theoretical" payments. See also Vidal, " Rwanda des anthropologues," 393–94, 398, and her "Économie," 54–56, 67. Rwabukumba and Mudandagizi, "Formes historiques," 21, underline how hated and humiliating *ukureeta* was; Reisdorff, *Enquêtes,* 38, notes that it was also practiced among farmers in Bwanamukari. See Schumacher, *Ruanda,* 460, 605, 614, and d'Hertefelt, "Le Rwanda," 35, and the references cited there.

34. Classe, *Organisation*, 5. These abuses were believed to have been most widespread in Nduga and Marangara. In 1907 Czekanowski also underscored Marangara in this regard.

35. The term "Hutu" corresponds to French "rustre" or "manant" and the English "boor" or the now obsolete "villain." It was also used in Burundi with this connotation (Rodegem, *Dictionnaire*, "Hutu") but not in Buha where the word does not seem to have been much used. Nkurikiyimfura, *Gros bétail*, 77, dates the institutional opposition of Hutu and Tutsi to the sixteenth century, since he sees the usage of the names as flowing from differences in tenure status between herder and farmer. But I don't' believe that Hutu was already synonymous with "agriculturalist" at that time. Also contra Desforges, "Court," 24. Moreover, Hutu was not an objective term such as "lower-status person," but an insult and used with that connotation in the poem composed for Rujugira that she cites.

36. Kagame, *Milices*, 26–30 (on Gakondo), 101–2 (on Abadaha); Kayijuka, "Lebensgeschichte," 131–32 (on Budaha); Desforges, "Court," 5 (on Gakondo), and 14 (on Abangogo).

37. Schumacher, *Ruanda*, 459–78, 581. This work reports on a debate between aristocrats concerning the opposition Hutu/Tutsi that dates to between 1928 and 1936.

38. For the use of "Tutsi" with the meaning "not-chief," see *Ibitéekerezo*, Rwabugiri file, T, no. 2:4, and id., *Rutarindwa* file, T, no. 11:1. The opposition between "his Tutsi name" and "his regnal name" applied to kings is quite usual and related to the meaning of Tutsi as "not-chief." The Tutsi/Hutu opposition in the army is well reflected in the image of the Tutsi combatant and the Hutu carrying his weapons (Schumacher, *Ruanda*, 621).

39. See Kagame, *Milices*, 101–3, for the oldest known distinctions between companies of Tutsi combatants and Hutu companies, which date from Rujugira's reign.

40. Still crucial around 1935. See Schumacher, *Ruanda*, 469–71, for a discussion of the impact being a herder had on the physical appearance of the Tutsi by representatives of the high aristocracy, which concluded with *"inka zigir ubantu,"* "cattle cause civilization" (or "the essence of humanity").

41. Newbury, *Cohesion*, 86, 90, 111–13, and her *"Uburetwa and Thangata,"* 100–102; Schumacher, *Ruanda*, 400, notes poor Tutsi and some wealthy Hutu were exempt, but ibid., 428, describes some *uburetwa* tasks assigned to Tutsi; ibid., 405 and 428, confirm that Hutu were obligated to work for the chief two out of every four working days (the fifth day was one during which work on the farm was forbidden). In addition to this corvée labor, the taxpayer still had to pay such a large part of his harvest that he was sometimes obliged to offer his services elsewhere as a day laborer.

42. This thesis developed by Newbury in *Cohesion* for Kinyaga turns out to be valid for all of Rwanda with a few reservations. According to Schumacher

the term *"uburetwa"* was used to describe work performed by Tutsi, but the only tasks that were required of them were "noble," not "degrading" (Schumacher, *Ruanda*, 426, 605, 622–24). Also the Hutu farmers enrolled in an army were not subject to *uburetwa* in 1907, at least not in Bugoyi and Murera, but they did serve in separate companies according to Czekanowski, *Forschungen*, 262 (cf. Schumacher, *Ruanda*, 605, who argues that poor Tutsi and wealthy Hutu did not have to render humiliating *uburetwa* service). It was *uburetwa* added to the military distinction between Tutsi and Hutu, then, that in fact provoked the new awareness of the whole population. The administrative standardization of *uburetwa* by the Belgian authorities then institutionalized this practice and its nefarious consequences.

43. *Ibitéekerezo*, miscellaneous file, H, no. 62. In this "Nyirabiyoro" tale, Shongoka and her husband then received the military domain of the Imvejuru army because they had refused to order Tutsi to carry out a task for Hutu.

44. Vidal, "Économie," 56–62; see also Schumacher, *Ruanda*, 681, who notes that rich Hutu were those who hired day laborers with hoes.

45. Schumacher, *Ruanda*, 473–74, notes that "rebellions were continually breaking out" in the northern country and recounts the theft of a goat and the insurrection of the farmers of Save (474); *Ibitéekerezo*, *Rwabugiri* file, H, no. 3, on Save; Kagame, *Milices*, 166, on Save; A. Butare, "Les transformations politiques au Rwanda sous le règne de Kigeli IV Rwabugili," on Marangara shortly before 1889 (28), and on Save (67); Van Overschelde, *Bij de reuzen*, 109–10, on Bugoyi and Marangara. The bloody repression inflicted on Cyingogo by Rwabugiri in 1894 is not one of these cases for it was directed against Tutsi who refused to let the king take their cattle (Butare, "Transformations," 58).

46. We refer here to the episodes about Nkiramacumu and Mbanzabugabo (aka Bikotwa) which are discussed in chapter 7, note 111.

47. See von Ramsay, "Über seine Expeditionen," on the pillage of Gisaka (310), and the reception of him as if he was a savior king (311); id., "Uha," 179; G. A. von Götzen, *Durch Afrika von Ost nach West*, 155; W. Langheld, *Zwanzig Jahren in Deutschen Kolonien*, 195–96. Around the same time Baumann (1892) and Kandt (1898) mention appearances of the same ilk in Bugufi and in eastern Burundi adjacent to Gisaka.

48. See Langheld, *Zwanzig Jahren*, 196, on Mutara; von Beringe, "Aus den Berichten des Herrn. v. Beringe über seine Reisen im Gebiet der Kirungavulkane," 22, on Muhumuza and Nyabingi in 1899. J. Freedman, "Nyabingi" *passim;* id. "Three Muraris," *passim;* notes that in Mutara the cult began around 1820. Elsewhere in Rwanda her cult diffused after Rwabugiri's expedition to Gikore (1883–1884). See *Ibitéekerezo*, miscellaneous file, H, nos. 11, 14, 31, 34; Rwabugiri file, T, no. 42; H, no. 82. For the meaning of "Nyabingi" in Kigezi, see Ngologoza, *Kigezi*, 41–43; Z. Rwandusya, "The Origin and Settlement of People of Bufumbira," 65–66; Baitwababo, "Foundations of Rujumbura Society," 84; Géraud, "Settlement," 49, 51–52; id., "Traditional Religion" 165–66;

Yowana Ssebalijja, "Memories of Rukiga and Other Places," 183, notes that Muhumuza was supposedly possessed by Nyabingi; Schumacher, *Physische*, 130–32, 141–43. In addition, see d'Hertefelt and de Lame, *Société*, 2:1807, under "Nyabingi."

49. Schumacher, *Ruanda*, 176. In Bwisha and in Jomba, a revolt against Rwabugiri under the aegis of a male Nyabingi promised to liberate the Hutu from Tutsi domination.

50. Schumacher, *Ruanda*, 163–64. In view of the region where this happened the story probably comes from Kayijuka who commanded the region as of 1899 or 1900. See also *Ibitéekerezo*, Rwabugiri file, H, no. 16, which associates the arrival of Nyirafugi with the jiggers epidemic that broke out in 1892.

51. A. Desforges, "Defeat is the Only Bad News," 25–27, 68–72, 75–76, 150–95.

52. See chapter 7, n.111.

53. Bethe, "Bericht," 8.

54. See Czekanowski, *Forschungen*, 128–29, for the regional cultural differences among Hutu. For the label "Rundi," see O. Baumann, "Durch Deutsch Massai-Land zur Quelle des Kagera-Nil," 281 ("where the inhabitants are Warundi dominated by Watusi"). Between 1928 and 1936 the aristocratic collaborators of Schumacher still designated the northern Hutu "Kiga" to distinguish them from those of the south, for they portrayed them in a very different manner. See Schumacher, *Ruanda*, on Mu Nkiga (473) and Bakiga (474). This opposition between Kiga and Banyanduga (southerners) was to reappear after 1962 during the first Republic.

Chapter 6. The Triumph of the Great Families and Its Consequences

1. For a tale about his career, see Rwabukumba and Mudandagizi, "Formes historiques," 7–10.

2. Kagame, *Milices*, 75, 78, 108–9, 114, 120, 121.

3. It is probably at this moment that the Nkebya set became affiliated with the dynastic lineage. Kagame, *Abrégé* 1, 125, links it to a supposed ancestor called Gahindiro, which is more than suspect. Delmas, *Généalogies*, 57, cites neither Gahindiro nor Abakebya.

4. Kagame, *Milices*, 82, 114, 125.

5. *Ibitéekerezo*, Gahindiro file, T, no. 11; Kagame, *Poésie dynastique*, 164, no. 60.

6. He was short of warriors to the point that he had to ask the ritualists and the adherents of the Ryangombe cult at court to raise two armies (Kagame, *Milices*, 63, 129–31). For his other armies, see ibid., 125–29.

7. Rugamba, *Poésie*, 287.

8. Kagame, *Poésie dynastique*, 166–68, nos. 65, 66, 67. See also 162–66, nos. 57–63. For Gahindiro's reign, 88, 172–74, 176–77, nos. 78–83 and 176–77; Rugamba, *Poésie*, 238, 260–62, 264, 276, 286–87, 289.

9. Like Sentabyo's mother who thus was Barinyonza's "aunt." See Nkuri-kiyimfura, "Révision," 152, 168.

10. At the time a drought accompanied by famine was ravaging central Rwanda, which proved the supernatural failure of Sentabyo and favored the emergence of a new king. Gatarabuhura's success can be measured by the fact that even in the far west, which Kinyaga then was, the army commander Rwanteri chose his side. See Kagame, *Milices*, 64.

11. See *Ibitéekerezo*, Sentabyo file, H, nos. 4–5; Gahindiro file, T, nos. 7, 11, 20; H, nos. 6, 8, 23, 25; Kagame, *Abrégé* 1, 171; and, above all, Kayijuka, "Lebensgeschichte," 141–42, who notes that the role of Nyiramuhanda—the only woman who has ever been an *umwiru*—in the foiling of the plot accounts for her initiation as a ritualist.

12. Kagame, *Abrégé* 1, 172. The new queen mother was his aunt, the sister of his mother.

13. *Ibitéekerezo*, Gahindiro file, H, no. 8; T, no. 11, which relate that instead of being rewarded the traitor was condemned to death by Nyiratunga for having betrayed his *ubuhake* patron; Kagame, *Abrégé* 1, 169–74.

14. These calculations are based on Kagame, *Milices*, 72–131. The total excludes the three armies raised by the ritualists during the reign of Sentabyo. Still the calculation remains approximate because Kagame, just like us here, has been obliged to resolve several doubtful cases on his own.

15. The command of official herds that were not linked to armies was a far less important position although the job attracted clients because the cattle from such a herd could be entrusted to a client. In 1796 there were theoretically about forty such herds, but most of them were in the hands of army commanders. The chief of an official herd was in no position to compete with an army commander or with the foremost *ibibanda* lineages. Thus the observation that Mutimbo, the father of Rugaju, who was Gahindiro's great favorite, commanded a herd was only made to underscore that he was of negligible importance.

16. J. F. Saucier, "The Patron-Client Relationship in Traditional and Contemporary Southern Rwanda," 260–66, 273–75, notes that the decrease in new *ubuhake* contracts was linked to the increase in insecurity under Rwabugiri; Butare, *Transformations*, 73–74.

17. Kayijuka, "Lebensgeschichte," 103–6, recounts the history of this lineage in his biography, of which there exist two versions in the Rwanda language, one dictated by himself and one composed by Mazina ("Nachtrag"), both translated by P. Schumacher. The official Imikara herd is unrecorded elsewhere, except for *Ibitéekerezo*, Gahindiro file, T, no. 21, where the Imikara ya zeba are said to have been given by Gahindiro to Nyarwaya.

18. Kayijuka, "Lebensgeschichte," 138. This is the oldest case of smallpox known to date.

19. Kagame, *Milices*, 168. This corporation remained in the family until Nyantaba's disgrace in Rwabugiri's time.

20. Schumacher translates this relationship in Kayijuka, ibid., 144, as "particular friend."

21. Also Kagame, *Milices*, 45, and *Abrégé* 1, 208–9. He was believed to have been poisoned by the queen mother. For a mystical tie between them and the birth of Nyantaba, see *Ibitéekerezo*, Gahindiro file, H, no. 9.

22. Kagame, *Milices*, 45–47; *Abrégé* 2, 53.

23. Kayijuka in Mazina, "Nachtrag," 166–70.

24. See Nkurikiyimfura, "Révision," 151–52, for the forefathers on their father's side of the queen mothers discussed here.

25. Kagame, *Milices*, 94; *Armées bovines*, 110.

26. Delmas, *Généalogies*, 118, 122–23.

27. Kagame, *Milices*, 96–97; Rugamba, *Poésie*, 186–87 n.67. Thereafter this gift became a regular obligation for the Imvejuru army. The famine was perhaps Gikoko, the best-remembered of that period.

28. *Ibitéekerezo*, Rwogera file, T, nos. 3, 7, 9, 13; H, no. 11; Kagame, *Milices*, 94, 151. id., *Armées bovines*, 102–3, describes a herd offered by Rwogera on the occasion of his marriage to Shongoka and another one offered to her. Shongoka seems to have played an active role in the conflict with Nkusi.

29. See Kagame, *Abrégé* 2, 22–23, for the lawsuit he won against the commander of the Nyakare army.

30. *Ibitéekerezo*, Rwogera file, T, nos. 3, 13; H, no. 11, and Rwabugiri file, T, no. 35; H, nos. 6, 12, 72, 75; Kagame, *Abrégé* 2, 21–26; id., *Milices*, 95. Shongoka then committed suicide as well (Kagame, *Armées bovines*, 103). The collective and spectacular extermination of the Abagereka is an example of the nefarious principle of collective responsibility. This event caused a sensation because it affected one of the main families of the realm.

31. Reisdorff, *Enquêtes*, 18, on Bumbogo; *Historique et chronologie*, 56–59, 139, 155–56, 158, 159–60, 175, on the Tsobe expansion. As late as 1913 and even 1917 armed combat still occurred between Tsobe and Shambo in this region. See *Historique et chronologie*, 177, and *Ibitéekerezo*, Rwogera file, T, nos. 11 and 12, which actually refer to 1913.

32. A detailed analysis of Kagame's *Milices* as well as his *Armées bovines* allows one to follow the vicissitudes of many elite families, some ritualist families included. The content of both these works mostly derives from family histories.

33. Kagame, *Abrégé* 1, 174, recounts how Ruzamba, commander of the Abakemba army, fled to Burundi; see also id., *Poésie dynastique*, 174, no. 83, on Ruzamba, and, 176–77, no. 88, on his flight to Burundi; id., *Milices*, 64, on Rwanteri, and, 82–83, Ruzamba flees to Gisaka. For rewards to partisans, see id., *Armées bovines*, 83, 85–86.

34. *Ibitéekerezo*, Gahindiro file, T, no. 8; Kagame, *Abrégé* 1, 176–82, observes in passing that the name Abakotanyi appears here for the first time as a military formation that tried to stop Semugaza.

35. Nkurikiyimfura, "Révision," 172, dates this innovation to after Ndabarasa's reign.

36. Kagame, "Code ésotérique" 366.

37. About Rugaju, see Nkongori, "Les Abashakamba," 241; *Ibitéekerezo*, Gahindiro file, T, nos. 9, 14, 16, 19, 23, 27–29; H, nos. 1, 3, 4, 10, 13, 15, 16; id., Rwogera file, T, nos. 1, 3, 6, 24; H, 2, 3, 6, 24; Coupez and Kamanzi, *Récits*, 310–17.

38. Kagame, *Milices*, 131–50. We should not forget, however, that the older armies continued to exist although, although not with their full effectives.

39. Kagame, *Armées bovines*, 23, 56, 79, 90, discusses the investiture of four official herds, 87–88, herds that Rugaju raised himself, and, 164, a herd attributed to a diviner whom he protected. See also *Ibitéekerezo*, Gahindiro file, H, no. 13, which lists more than the five herds named here, and T, no. 16, which names four herds.

40. See *Ibitéekerezo*, Rwogera file, H, no. 6, and ibid., Gahindiro file, T, no. 9, for the case of one of Rugaju's clients.

41. Ibid., Gahindiro file, T, no. 9.

42. For the brother's murder, see *Ibitéekerezo*, Gahindiro file, T, nos. 14, 16, Rwogera file, H, nos. 2, 3, and Kagame, *Armées bovines*, 131.

43. Kagame, *Abrégé* 1, 183–84, and *Ibitéekerezo*, Gahindiro file, H, nos. 7, 14, on the hero called Rushenyi. When the Rundi attacked, the other troops supposedly abandoned his formation.

44. Nkongori, "Abashakamba," 247–50; *Ibitéekerezo*, Gahindiro file, T, nos. 19, 28, 29; H, no. 16, and Rwogera file, H, nos. 2, 3, 6; Kagame, *Milices*, 189.

45. For Rwogera, see *Ibitéekerezo*, the whole *Rwogera* file, and Kagame, *Abrégé* 1, 191–214.

46. According to information from Bigogwe, Rugaju seized all royal power after Gahindiro's death, including the prerogative of having young girls delivered to him (Schumacher, *Physische*, 74–75). Elsewhere his great power at the beginning of Rwogera's reign is stressed in *Ibitéekerezo*, Rwogera file, H, no. 3, and Gahindiro file, T, no. 16; Nkongori, "Abashakamba," 251, describes him as "the foremost chief of the realm"; Coupez and Kamanzi, *Récits*, 312–13.

47. *Ibitéekerezo*, Rwogera file, T, no. 1.

48. The fall of Rugaju is a favorite tale. Besides the *Ibitéekerezo* already cited, see, for example, Nkongori, "Abashakamba," 250–52, Kagame, *Abrégé* 1, 196, Coupez and Kamanzi, *Récits*, 312–17. One of Rugaju's sons was supposedly spared to attend to the worship of the spirit of one who had been so close to Gahindiro. The event happened around 1847.

49. *Ibitéekerezo*, Rwogera file, T, nos. 7, 9, 13; H, nos. 5, 13, 14, 30, and Kagame, *Abrégé* 1, 207–8, 210–14.

50. Pagès, *Royaume hamite*, 140–41, 535; Kagame, *Milices*, 67–68, 76–78, 79; id., *Armées bovines*, 186–87. It is said that a lugubrious voice emanating from the memorial fig tree of Mazimpaka at Kamonyi had demanded this worship. The new official herd that was dedicated to him included a cow named Nyagahoza in memory of his favorite cow.

51. Kagame, *Milices,* 113, 146–47, 151–60, and his *Abrégé* 1, 197–98, describe the situation toward the end of the reign. Marara, who had been disgraced a few years after Rugaju's fall, came back into favor and was reinstituted as the head of his army at the insistence of his soldiers. Moreover, his nephew on his father's side obtained the command of another army whose commander had been disgraced.

52. Ibid., 160–65. During the succession crisis after Rwogera's death, Kabaka, the second in command of Nyamwesa's army, betrayed him, along with his whole army. Later Kabaka was to prevail over all the Gisakan forces.

53. According to a dynastic poet (Kagame, *Poésie dynastique,* 180–81, no. 98), the king had to repress certain armed rebellions but the "rebellions" and the names of those involved in them who are cited are not reported in other sources, with the single exception of the Abayumbu. Hence, despite their relative abundance and the details in them given about the great clashes between parties, the narrative sources are far from giving us a complete picture of the state of the realm and, by their omissions, they underestimate the chaos that accompanied these struggles.

54. Ibid.; Rugamba, *Poésie,* 276. Kagame, *Armées bovines,* 74, merely says that their leader was deposed and replaced by a kinsman; id., *Abrégé* 1, 117; id., *Milices,* 63–66, 107.

55. After the Abagereka massacre, which followed Rwogera's demise by a few years, the court sent a band of initiates to chase their spirits away. An eyewitness from Nyakare on the border of Burundi recalls their depredations: "All the hills were covered by 'mandwa' at that time. I was about twelve years old. It is then that they killed our bull and ate it" (*Ibiteekerezo,* Rwogera file, H, no. 11:2). Ordinarily it is a serious crime to kill the lead bull of a herd.

56. For several cases of cattle robbery and an appeal to the court, see Kagame, *Poésie dynastique,* 184–85, nos. 108–11. Schumacher's generalizations, *Ruanda,* 895–96, concerning local turmoil are also valid for this period; however, *Ibiteekerezo,* Rwogera file, T, nos. 11 and 12, describe a fight over a hill in which vengeance was allowed by the court that is said to have occurred during his reign but that actually occurred in 1913.

57. Kagame, *Milices,* 146–47. One also recalls the rebellion of the Abashakamba in favor of Nkusi and against Rugaju.

58. *Ibiteekerezo,* Rwogera file, T, no. 7:2; H, no. 30:4. There were also clashes between the Abakemba and Abashakamba armies in Bugoyi although these may only date to the regency of Murorunkwere, Rwabugiri's mother (Schumacher, *Physische,* 65).

59. Kagame, *Abrégé* 1, 200.

60. *Ibiteekerezo,* Rwabugiri file, H, no. 62, and Rwogera file, H, no. 5:2, on Gikoko; Speke, *Journal of the Discovery of the Source of the Nile,* 196, mentions a famine that occurred "some time ago." Was this during the 1850s? Was it the Gikoko famine? See Schumacher, *Physische,* 61, for a severe famine caused by drought in Rwogera's time. Is it the same one?

61. Kagame, *Abrégé* 1, 208–9, 210.

62. *Ibitéekerezo,* Rwogera file, H, no. 12. For a lively description, see ibid., T, no. 3:4–6.

63. Name of a royal smith's hammer, an emblem of power. See d'Hertefelt and Coupez, *Royauté,* 291, 479.

64. Katoke, *The Karagwe Kingdom,* 64.

65. Examples: Rugaju's decision to send Ruyenzi "to be killed" in Burundi, the wager between Rugaju and Marara concerning a campaign in Ndorwa, and the wager of Nkusi and Nyarwaya of Byavu that provoked a campaign in Bushi. See Kagame, *Abrégé* 1, 184, 189, 207–8, and details in *Ibitéekerezo,* Gahindiro and Rwogera files.

66. d'Hertefelt and Coupez, *Royauté,* 155.

67. Ibid., 159, lines 1–3.

68. Ibid., 169 verse 244.

69. *Ibitéekerezo,* Sentabyo file, T, no. 2; H, no. 2.

70. Kagame, *Abrégé* 1, 166–67, and n.69 here. It seems to me that the popular version that underlines the role that the famine played in the invasion and the private character of the operation is preferable to that of Kagame who presents the data as if the court, prompted by strategic considerations, took the decision to invade itself.

71. Kagame, *Armées bovines,* 17.

72. Kagame, *Abrégé* 1, 166–68, on Sentabyo; d'Arianoff, *Histoire de Bagesera,* 66, 88–100; Coupez and Kamanzi, *Récits,* 292–309; *Ibitéekerezo, Gahindiro,* T, nos. 1, 12, 17, 22; H, nos. 2, 22. Kagame, *Milices,* 83, notes that the campaign of the Abakemba army was ordered by Nyiratunga, Gahindiro's mother.

73. Many detailed remembrances concerning the conquest of Gisaka have been recorded. See *Ibitéekerezo,* Gahindiro file, T, nos. 1, 12, 17, 22; H, nos. 2, 22; ibid., Rwogera file, T, nos. 2, 10, 14; H, nos. 7, 19–20, 22–23, 25–28; Kagame, *Abrégé* 1, 167–68, 187–89, 196–207; d'Arianoff, *Histoire des Bagesera,* 101–21; Schumacher, *Ruanda,* 174–75.

74. *Ibitéekerezo,* Gahindiro file, T, nos. 19, 28, 29; H, no. 16; ibid., Rwogera file, H, no. 6. Kagame, *Abrégé* 1, 181, 189, for the Marara affair; ibid., 207, 209–10, as well as perhaps *Ibitéekerezo,* Rwabugiri file, H, no. 19, and *Historique et chronologie,* 178–79, for the raids in Rwabugiri's time.

75. Kayijuka, "Lebensgeschichte," 143. See also Kagame, *Abrégé* 1, 185–86, who relates that among other measures to cope with the situation, a local military police was set up with the troops of a deserter from Gisaka whose orders were to kill any Nyiginya warrior fleeing the battle field; *Ibitéekerezo,* Gahindiro file, T, no. 25; H, nos. 13, 17.

76. Kagame, *Abrégé* 1, 186, 191–94; *Ibitéekerezo,* Rwogera file, H, nos. 14, 29.

77. *Ibitéekerezo,* Rwogera file, H, no. 1, describes the conquest of Buyenzi begun under Rwogera and completed under Rwabugiri; see Schumacher, *Ruanda,* for this conquest by corruption (478–79, 607, 623), and for daily life in the camps on the borders (478–79, 607, 623).

78. Van Noten, *Tombes*, 22–41, 55; see 48–50 for the dating of one object in wood.

79. Lugan, *Histoire du Rwanda*, 217–18; Chrétien, *Afrique*, 168–70; Katoke, *Karagwe*, 67–68; Burton, *Lake Regions*, 2:183.

80. Speke, *Journal*, 196. This drought occurred "some years before" 1861, thus certainly before 1860, but I think after 1855. He also speaks about "villages of extraordinary extent," thus documenting a high population density. One does not know if the famine was a pretext or if the sight of the armed men in the caravan and the memory of Rumanyika's accession frightened the court.

81. Kagame, *Poésie dynastique*, 181–82, nos. 100–101.

82. Gisaka also remained closed to foreign business, first because of internal strife and later because of its conquest by the Nyiginya.

83. Obviously considered to be taxes or dues by the court.

84. Schumacher, *Physische*, 63–66; *Historique et chronologie*, 122, 124.

85. Schumacher, *Physische*, relates that in Bigogwe, Rwogera only managed to recruit four men among them! (72), and that only four to five young girls had been levied in tribute in Bigogwe since Rugaju (74); *Historique et chronologie*, 123, notes that under Rwogera, Rwakagara enlisted the Abagogwe in the Uruyange army, i.e., the one commanded earlier by Rugaju; Nahimana, *Rwanda*, 239–40. The Abagogwe claim to be descendants of a child of NDAHIRO, without doubt to underline their former independence from the Nyiginya kingdom (Schumacher, ibid., 71, 72; *Historique et Chronologie*, 149; Nahimana, ibid., 239).

86. See Rwandusya, "Origin," 66–67, on the inhabitants of Bufumbira confusing Gahindiro with Mazimpaka. Gahindiro sent Mangabwoba who did not succeed in settling there. No chief managed to reside there until the arrival of Buki in Rwabugiri's time.

87. M. Ruriho, "Pour une révision profonde de l'histoire de la région des Grands Lacs," 184; Schumacher, *Physische*, 66, 159–61, mentions only Rutebuka and Buki as the first resident chiefs in Bwishya (and in Bufumbira).

88. Schumacher, *Physische*, 234–35; Kagame, *Abrégé* 1, 189–90. See also id., *Poésie dynastique*, 74, which notes that the chief of Buzi was Karinda.

89. *Ibitéekerezo*, Rwogera file, H, no. 18; *Historique et chronologie*, 112; Vanwalle, "Aspecten," 69–70; Kagame, *Milices*, 145–46.

90. Vanwalle, "Aspecten," 67–69. One of the two main local kings supposedly descended from an autochthonous group and the other from a group that would have migrated only at the time of Ndabarasa or Sentabyo. Is there any link between this migration and the great famine of the 1770s during Rujugira's reign? Among other autonomous leaders Nyirarumondo, mistress of the Kigeri forest near Kibuye, is worth mentioning (*Ibitéekerezo*, Rwabugiri file, T, no. 1:2).

91. Newbury, *Cohesion*, 24–26; Kagame, *Milices*, 63–64, 129–30. *Historique et chronologie*, 96, 103, probably attributes this mission to Ndabarasa by mistake.

92. Newbury, id., 24–37; Kagame, ibid., 22, 63–66, 129–31, describe the death of Rwanteri in Mutara;ibid., 129–31; id., *Armées bovines*, 77–78; *Historique et chronologie*, 94–97.

93. This occurred during the sixth generation before 1954 according to J. Hiernaux, *Notes sur les Tutsi de l'Itombwe,* cited by J. Mutambo, *Les Banyamulenge,* 21. Counting twenty-five years per generation we arrive at around 1800 at the earliest. It is quite likely that civil war and the famine between c. 1797 and c. 1802 led to their departure from central Rwanda. But one cannot wholly exclude the possibility that they then only migrated from Kinyaga where they would have arrived from the central plateau just thirty years or so earlier, having fled southern central Rwanda during a famine in the 1770s that devastated it.

94. The only available Shi source, and it is rather unsatisfactory, is P. Masson, *Trois Siècles chez les Bashi,* on Ngweshe (55–59) and on Makombe (60–63). For the sources at court, see Kagame, *Abrégé* 1, on Gahindiro's defeat (182), war in Rwogera's time, and the rivalry between Nkusi and Nyarwaya of Byavu, and war against Makombe (207–8); Kayijuka, "Lebensgeschichte," 143, describes three expeditions under Gahindiro but is vague as to the places involved. See also *Ibitéekerezo,* Rwogera, T, nos. 7, 9; H, no. 30, on Nkusi and Nyarwaya.

95. Newbury, *Kings and Clans,* 3, 149, 157, 160–62, 167–68, 180–81.

96. Kagame, *Abrégé* 1, 209.

97. *Historique et chronologie,* on Tsobe in Bukonya (139), on Murera, Bukamba (149–51), on Buki, Bufumbira, and Ndorwa (149–51), on Bukonya (159–60), on Buhoma, Buhanga but in the valley only (161), on Bugarura (164–66), and on Buberuka (177). Nahimana, *Le Rwanda,* 239–42, does not distinguish enough between local Tutsi initiatives or rivalries and the approval after the fact by the court. For him the court planned a colonization preliminary to a subsequent conquest. His conviction that "a fifth column" of Tutsi had deliberately been introduced by the kings was to have tragic consequences, for by analogy it "motivated" the genocide of 1994.

98. Nahimana, *Le Rwanda,* 239–42. For Bushiru, see Schumacher, *Physische,* 99–100, who notes that since Rugaju's time the local king gathered and paid a "tribute" and sent it to the chief designated by the court, for no representative of the court ever lived in the country, and *Historique et chronologie,* 126–28.

99. Kagame, *Milices,* 166.

100. *Historique et chronologie,* 157. On Mount Kabuye in Kibari was a spring of ritual water that in addition was also supposed to regulate the fertility of all bees, these being sources of honey mead at the court. (d'Hertefelt and Coupez, *Royauté,* 464).

Chapter 7. Nightmares: The Age of Rwabugiri (1867–1897)

1. Kagame, *Abrégé* 2, 13–128; Desforges, "Defeat," 12–19. Lugan, *Histoire du Rwanda,* 108, calls him "one of the greatest Rwandan monarchs."

2. For the German colonization, see Desforges, "Defeat," 22–235. The German presence was mainly felt in the support it gave to the court. Apart from this the colonial authorities did not interfere in the internal affairs of the country.

Notes to pages 165–166

3. Sources of all kinds abound for this period. Eyewitness accounts or accounts stemming from the children of contemporary witnesses have been gathered by the hundreds since about 1900, mostly covering the years after c. 1880. A feeling for the wealth of available data can be obtained by consulting the 151 tales, anecdotes, and poems gathered in *Ibiteekerezo* even though they are only a sample of what can be found elsewhere. And the ethnographic monographs and descriptions of the "traditional" or "precolonial" Rwanda found in social science studies in fact constitute a portrait of the country towards the end of Rwabugiri's reign. But despite the profusion of documentation, a genuine history of his age has still not been written. For a chronicle, see Kagame, *Abrégé* 2, 13–128, and, for a first historical sketch, Butare, "Transformations."

4. The only exception to this periodicity between 1877 and 1913 occurred when Nyirimigabo died, engendering a crisis at the court. As it took years to reach a new equilibrium after the turmoil and the realignments that accompanied each upheaval, the political situation was actually only rarely stable at court during this period.

5. For the internal chronology of the kingdom between 1867 and 1889, see Appendix I. The main dates are: 1867, Rwabugiri succeeds; 1873, his first marriages; 1877, death of the queen mother; early 1880, return from the Bumpaka expedition; 1883–84, birth of Musinga; December 1889, Rutarindwa appointed coruler; September 1895, death of Rwabugiri. Other dates are extrapolated by a dead reckoning from the above.

6. He only assumed the auspicious name of Rwabugiri several years later (Kagame, *Abrégé* 2, 21–22). This name means "about mastery" or "the boss, the lord," and derives from *"kugira"* "to do."

7. *Ibiteekerezo*, Rwabugiri file, T, nos. 6, 7; Rugamba, *Poésie*, 215; Butare, "Transformations," 12.

8. *Ibiteekerezo*, Rwabugiri file, H, no. 62. But is there no partial confusion here with the drought that occurred at the onset of Gahindiro's reign? There were many famines in Rwabugiri's time (*Historique et chronologie*, 12). For other references to famines, see Kagame, *Poésie dynastique*, 194, no. 138 (but is that the first one or one following Nkoronko's death?), 195–96, no. 141, for a famine that occurred after several attempts to conquer Bushi and might be linked to the uprising at Save (*Ibiteekerezo*, Rwabugiri file, T, no. 5:4–5), which would be the one of c. 1890 called Ruhatigicumuro, and not the Kijugunya famine of 1895. The information of ibid., T, no. 34, and H, no. 9, are mistaken in bestowing the name Rwagikoko on a great famine in Rwabugiri's time that would date from c. 1881. See T, no. 34, for a description of the measures taken against rainmakers or other responsible persons during a drought.

9. *Ibiteekerezo*, Rwogera file, T, nos. 3, 13; H, nos. 4, 11, 12; ibid., Rwabugiri file, H, nos. 72, 75; Kagame *Abrégé* 2, 21–26; Kayijuka, "Lebensgeschichte," 166–67 (Mazina's biography speaks of about two hundred partisans of

Rugereka being killed at Rwesero). For later repercussions, see *Ibitéekerezo*, Rwabugiri file, T, nos. 35, 38.

10. Kagame, *Milices*, 85–87, 170–71. The army rejected its commander. The court accepted this but the army was then gradually broken up into various groups. One of these was to become the new army entrusted to Bisangwa.

11. Kagame, *Abrégé* 2, 28–29.

12. For the Ndorwa expeditions, see *Ibitéekerezo*, Rwabugiri file, T, no. 1, and Kagame, *Abrégé* 2, 23, 29–30.

13. The excuse given for the attack on Ijwi was that its king had insulted the kingdom at the time of Rwogera's death by recalling a gift-giving mission. On Ijwi no one remembers anything at all about that. For the campaigns on Ijwi, see Newbury, "Rwabugiri and Ijwi," in *Kings and Clans*, 155–75, and compare with Pagès, *Royaume hamite*, 156, *Ibitéekerezo*, Rwabugiri file, T, nos. 1, 2, 5, 14, 20, 22, 25, 33, 38, 49; H, nos. 12, 16, 54, 55, 66, 71, 73, 91, Coupez and Kamanzi, *Récits*, 319–27, and Kagame, *Abrégé* 2, 26–28, 48–53, 64–67.

14. H. Stanley, *In Darkest Africa*, 2:360.

15. F. Stuhlmann, ed., *Die Tagebücher von dr. Emin Pascha*, 1:396: "But Rwanda also had been visited only once by Omer of Mervata. He was detained there for three years, and they married him to a daughter of King Kigeri, but later he is said to have returned from there." What can one believe of this hearsay information? But the note does contain the first written mention of the name KIGERI.

16. G. Schweinfurth et al., eds., *Emin Pasha in Central Africa*, 123, 285 (from 1878 and 1879–80).

17. Butare, "Transformations," 16; *Ibitéekerezo*, Rwabugiri file, T, no. 4; Pagès, *Royaume hamite*, 157–58, describes the massacre of hundreds of refugees in Cyingogo; Schumacher, *Ruanda*, 420, 598; Kagame *Abrégé* 2, 30, mentions a "Hutu tanner,"; id., *Armées bovines*, 30, 48, 95; *Historique et chronologie*, 132, notes the presence of Tsobe Tutsi in Cyingogo; Nahimana, *Le Rwanda*, 292. Seruteganya was a nephew on the mother' side of the lineage who was in charge of the tannery. He inherited two herds from members of this group who lacked direct descendants and received a third one from Murorunkwere who took it from a grandson of Gahindiro.

18. One may well doubt this point. Kagame, *Abrégé* 2, 33, asserts it, but *Ibitéekerezo*, Rwabugiri file, T, no. 39:4, has the king on the spot killing his mother himself. Be that as it may, later on the king was often accused of matricide. Thus, ibid., T, no. 37:4, in which Nyirigango asserts that "you have killed your mother Nyirakigeri, even though she was your own mother." But the same narrator also has it that he had approved of the execution of his mother at least after the fact for he did not even intend to mourn her until a sudden disease made him change his mind.

19. Kagame, *Milices*, 147.

20. Bisangwa was the son of a Shambo orphan who had been taken in at

Rwogera's court and had grown up there. He was known for his avoidance of quarrels and for the discreet aid he gave to those who had incurred the ire of Rwabugiri (*Ibitéekerezo*, Rwabugiri file, T, no. 54). They called him Hutu probably because of his modest condition. The antecedents of Mugugu are less well known.

21. Kagame, *Abrégé* 2, 35, and id., *Milices*, 169.

22. Kagame, *Milices*, 77, 114, 169–70. As a direct result of these events Kabare inherited the Abankungu army and the Mpawe herd while Kanjogera was given the personal army of the queen mother herself, although it remained under the command of Mugabwambere, with the exception of a section of it that went to Ruhinankiko. Ruhinankiko married a daughter of Rwogera who was his close cousin (Kagame, *Abrégé* 2, 38).

23. *Ibitéekerezo*, Rwabugiri file, T, nos. 8, 24, 45; H, nos. 42, 48, 58, 60–61, 78–80; Kagame *Abrégé* 2, 40–41.

24. Kagame, *Abrégé* 2, 42–43. According to *Ibitéekerezo*, Rwabugiri file, T, no. 34. Rwampembwe was executed at the request of Kanjogera, who accused him of having provoked a drought. We do not know why the suicides occurred. The suicide of Kabyaza, mother of Rwampembwe, made such an impression that it was linked to the apparition of the comet that appeared the next year (most likely in 1882) and that was called Rwakabyaza after her.

25. Kagame, *Milices*, 141, and id., *Abrégé* 2, 44; *Ibitéekerezo*, Rwabugiri file, H, nos. 13, 43, 65, 73. The expedition against Karinda is known as "Butembo."

26. Kagame *Milices*, 140, id., *Abrégé* 2, 45, and id., *Introduction*, 20–23.

27. This is plausible if one takes the following elements into account: the fact that the king went on an elephant hunt with the Abarashi c. 1883 (Kagame, *Abrégé* 2, 54), the existence of an ivory export market at the time (ibid., 93), the fact that there were merchants in the north, in Nduga (*Ibitéekerezo*, Rwabugiri file, H, no. 56), and especially the fact that the king allied himself with Sumbwa merchants from Tanzania to attack a Hima chief who refused to give goats to them (ibid, H, no. 64).

28. *Ibitéekerezo*, Rwogera file, H, nos. 19, 21; Rwabugiri file, T, nos. 1, 6, 39, 56–57; Kagame, *Abrégé* 2, 46–47.

29. In 1883–84, during the expedition in Gikore. See Kayijuka, "Lebensgeschichte," 147–48, 161–62, on death and prophecies; *Ibitéekerezo*, Rwabugiri file, T, nos. 1, 20, 22, 26, 33, 36, 39; H, nos. 60, 89; Kagame, *Milices*, 47, on the Gikore expedition. This was his second reversal of fortune. His first fall from favor occurred when Murorunkwere ruled, i.e., before 1877, but he regained favor in 1880 after the Bumpaka expedition (Kagame, *Milices*, 45–47, 166). Nyantaba's death mainly helped Nzigiye's career and, much later, that of Muhigirwa.

30. Kagame, *Milices*, 135, 157.

31. Kagame, *Poésie dynastique*, 191–92, nos. 129–33, and id., *Introduction*, 167–87.

32. Kagame, *Abrégé* 2, 39. It was directed by a prince from a Nyiginya lineage that issued from Ndabarasa. None of the leaders of the "war of the waters" took part in it.

33. Kagame, *Abrégé* 2, 38–39; see *Ibitéekerezo*, Rwogera file, H, 19, and Rwabugiri file, T, no. 39, which explain that the king took two head of cattle out of every five for his part and then again three out of six of the other booty, and H, nos. 83, 86, 91, which describe the Ndushabandi herd; see also Kagame, *Armées bovines*, 112, on Ndushabandi; id., *Milices*, 171–72. For Schumacher, *Ruanda*, 177, this is the same expedition as that of "the waters," whereas according to both Kagame and *Ibitéekerezo*, "the waters" expedition was a separate expedition that preceded it. The Nyiginya army went on to defeat Bugandan troops in December 1879 or early January 1880.

34. For these first two wars in Bushi, see *Ibitéekerezo*, Rwabugiri file, T, nos. 1, 26–27, 30, 32–33, 44; H, nos. 15–16, 57, 60, 68, 76; Kagame, *Poésie dynastique*, 195, nos. 139, 140; id., *Abrégé* 2, 56–64. Nyirimigabo probably died in late 1885.

35. Barring only Gacinya (a descendant of Gahindiro), who no longer was a chief of the first order, and especially Ndibyariye (descendant of Gihana of Rujugira) who still remained the overall general in command for several more years.

36. For their careers, *Ibitéekerezo*, Rwabugiri file, T, nos. 10, 25, 39, 48, 51, on all Nzigiye, no. 53, on Ntizimira; H, nos. 49, 52, on Nzigiye; Kagame, *Abrégé* 2, 68; id., *Milices*, 64, 147–49, on Ntizimira of the Abahenda; Newbury, *Cohesion*, 42–43, and index under "Ntizimira"; *Historique et chronologie*, 97, 111, on (Ntizimira), and 43–44, on Nzigiye.

37. For Nkundiye and this campaign, see *Ibitéekerezo*, Rwabugiri file, T, nos. 1–2, 5, 14, 49; H, nos. 12, 62, 66, and Kagame, *Abrégé* 2, 64–67.

38. These included two sons of Ndungutse, the Kobwa ritualist who was the guardian of Karinga.

39. For example, Kagame, *Milices*, 163.

40. He briefly clashed with Kanjogera at an unknown date (Kagame, *Milices*, 120), and died "about one year before Rwabugiri" (ibid., 88).

41. Schumacher, *Ruanda*, 44–41, 177–78, 390, 587. Kagame, *Milices*, 48–49, confirms that in 1896 Muhigirwa had the title of king and the regnal name of MUYENZI. See also *Ibitéekerezo*, *Rwabugiri*, H, nos. 9, 49.

42. Schumacher, *Ruanda*, 177, 703.

43. Ibid., 180, 199, and Kayijuka, "Lebensgeschichte," 148, on Nyantaba's predictions. See also *Ibitéekerezo*, Rwabugiri file, H, nos. 38, 58, which relates that Rwabugiri was jailed in a European-style house and that Kabare learned the secrets of Rutarindwa's destiny; T, no. 36.

44. Schumacher, *Ruanda*, 178.

45. Kagame, *Abrégé* 2, 75–79, and Schumacher, *Ruanda*, 124–25, 185, 440–41, 587–88, underline the procedural irregularities, but evaluate the decision from the vantage point of persons who knew about Rucunshu's coup d'état,

which resulted in Musinga's enthronement. The poet Ngurusi supposedly did warn Rwabugiri at the time to be wary of the Ega according to Kagame, *Poésie dynastique,* 200–201, nos. 155, 156, but the text of no. 155 was reshaped either before or after 1896.

46. Uvira was founded in 1860 and overtaken by the bellicose Rumaliza in 1885 (see E. Mworoha, *Histoire du Burundi,* 237, 240–42).

47. J. Iliffe, *A Modern History of Tanganyika,* 104–5.

48. *Ibitéekerezo,* Rwabugiri file, T, no. 54 (but is this an after-the-fact conclusion based on Bisangwa's defeat?); Kagame, *Abrégé* 2, 82–94, 112–13.

49. *Ibitéekerezo,* Rwabugiri file, H, no. 64, which notes that "the Abasuumbe are today called Abahaya."

50. Van Overschelde, *Bij de reuzen,* 115.

51. See Kagame, *Abrégé* 2, on the elephant hunt (54) and on the Ingangura-rugo camp at Minove (70).

52. Ibid., 82.

53. See Botte, "Rwanda," 53–57, for a general overview.

54. Ibid., 72; Nahimana, *Le Rwanda,* 268–69; Mworoha, *Histoire du Burundi,* 238; Kagame, *Abrégé* 2, 82; *Ibitéekerezo,* Rwabugiri file, H, no. 62, and maybe no. 92; *Historique et chronologie,* 12.

55. Kagame, *Abrégé* 2, 88; *Ibitéekerezo, Rwabugiri file,* T, no. 45; H, 16, 73, confirm that there were two epizootics; Botte, "Rwanda," 72–73; *Historique et chronologie,* 11.

56. C. Van Onselen, "Reactions to the Rinderpest in Southern Africa, 1896–97," no. 8, reports losses over 90 percent in Botswana (474) and 89.7 percent mortality for a district in Cape province (483).

57. Kagame, *Armées bovines,* 52. One herder was inspired to drive his herd of about forty head deep into the forest to isolate it. This herd, called "Akabira" ("the great forest"), survived.

58. On quarter (ten head) of the Akabira herd. Moreover, he forced the keeper of this herd to give another five head to his herder. In the case of Inyambo, the survivors of at least three herds were fused into a single one and entrusted to his favorite son. See also Newbury, *Cohesion,* 118–20. The author details the physical and political effects in Kinyaga. See also Kagame, *Armées bovines,* 74 and 90, which relates how some Inyambo herds were fused, and *Historique et chronologie,* 130–31, which notes that Cyingogo was plundered in 1894 because the inhabitants refused to yield the cattle demanded by the king for the reconstitution of his herds.

59. For a case, see Reisdorff, *Enquêtes,* 146–47, no. 54.

60. Schumacher, *Ruanda,* 182, 390–91, 587–88.

61. W. Langheld, *Zwanzig Jahren,* 209–10. The outbreak seems to have begun in March.

62. *Ibitéekerezo,* Rwabugiri file, T, no. 46; Botte, "Rwanda," 72, reports locust invasions in Burundi in 1890 (72), in 1897 (77), and in 1900 (69).

63. Mworoha, *Histoire du Burundi*, 242, reports the defeat at Kivu in December 1891; G. Von Götzen, *Durch Afrika*, 3, 146, notes that according to Tofik a first clash on land was followed by a naval engagement on Lake Kivu but see Lugan, *Histoire du Rwanda*, 228, who relates that the White Fathers reported on 26 February 1890 that Rumaliza headed toward Rwanda where he had already been beaten twice. Is there confusion here with Burundi?

64. Kagame, *Abrégé* 2, 80–81; *Ibitéekerezo*, Rwabugiri file, T, no. 52; H, nos. 37, 93. The specific illness remains unknown but it was probably not the well known smallpox.

65. Kagame, *Abrégé* 2, 81, and id., *Poésie dynastique*, 197, no. 144. The illness is unknown. If he really lost all his skin, as is alleged, he would have died.

66. Id., *Abrégé* 2, 80–82; Schumacher, *Ruanda*, 175; *Ibitéekerezo*, Rwabugiri file, T, no. 52; H, no. 93. This was not the only illness of the king or the only time that he followed the advice of his diviners by carrying out spectacular acts of vengeance or reconciliation to pacify the spirits. Thus *Ibitéekerezo*, Rwabugiri file, T, nos. 4, 26, 45; H, no. 82.

67. Kagame, *Abrégé* 2, 91–92; Schumacher, *Ruanda*, 479. But according to Von Götzen, *Durch Afrika*, 139, Kasasura considered Rwabugiri to be his enemy, far stronger than he was, and he complained about having been attacked again recently. Kasasura ruled between 1886 and 1928 according to R. Austen, *Northwest Tanzania under German and British Rule*, 264.

68. A clash with Rumaliza's forces in December 1891 probably occurred during this first campaign, known as "the war of ku-Kidogoro" (Kagame, *Abrégé* 2, 92–93). The story about an encounter between Rwabugiri and mutineering soldiers from the Free Congo State is not true. Rwabugiri died well before their arrival in the region.

69. For the wars in Bushi, see *Ibitéekerezo*, Rwabugiri file, T, nos. 2, 26, 32–33; H, nos. 36, 52, 59–60, 76, and Kagame, *Abrégé* 2, 83–91.

70. For the Nkore campaign, see *Ibitéekerezo*, Rwabugiri file, T, nos. 1, 10, 17, 21, 25, 38, 52; H, nos. 1, 9, 44, 52, 67, 74, 81, 85–88, 95; Langheld, *Zwanzig Jahren*, 194, 206, 209–10, 212; Kagame, *Abrégé* 2, 97–102.

71. Ntare died of pneumonia in July 1885 (Botte, "Rwanda," 56, no. 12).

72. Desforges, "Defeat," 19. R. Kandt, "Ein Marsch am Ostufer des Kivu," 247, saw the remains of the boat that brought him back dying or dead to Rwanda. His death was followed by a severe famine, mainly in the region of Butare. See Botte, "Rwanda," 74, and Nahimana, *Le Rwanda*, 208.

73. *Ibitéekerezo*, Rwabugiri file, T, no. 33:3.

74. For Rutarindwa's reign, see Desforges, "Defeat," 19–22; Pagès, *Royaume hamite*, 195–201; *Ibitéekerezo*, Rutarindwa file, T, no. 5; H, nos. 5, 7, 11, 13, 18, 20, 40; Kagame, *Abrégé* 2, 105–28.

75. In the historiography, this post was supposedly founded by Long and Deffense if not by Sandrart (Kagame, *Abrégé* 2, 113). It seems to me, however, that this is more likely the post called Kabamba, which was founded on August

27, 1896, by lieutenant Evrard-Louis Dubois. (A. Croix, "Dubois [Evrard-Louis]," 268–69).

76. For Musinga's reign, see Desforges, "Defeat."

77. Rugamba, *Poésie*, 295.

78. Reisdorff, *Enquêtes*, 148.

79. The first great massacres of the age, in which hundreds of persons were murdered, were the extermination of the Abagereka at court around 1869 and that of the inhabitants of Cyingogo by Seruteganya before 1877 (Pagès, *Royaume hamite*, 157).

80. Rugaju had already provided a model of how to achieve a huge concentration of wealth and power.

81. In *Ibiteekerezo*, Rwabugiri file, T, no. 34, Rwampembwe declares "if he shall be hated by his subjects," adding that "we have long since known that he hates us. He hates the nobles and all of us hate him. His subjects support him, but if one excited them against him and if they were starving, would they not hate him?"

82. Newbury, "Les campagnes de Rwabugiri." In the case of failure, the king could employ the motif of "aveng[ing] an insult" and in case of too easy a success, that of "conquest." *Ibiteekerezo*, Rwabugiri file, H, no. 65, is candid even if its chronology is wrong: "The warriors had not succeeded in enriching King Rwabugiri with war booty in Butembo. That was the reason they then declared an unjust war on Burundi."

83. Kagame, *Abrégé* 2, 23.

84. Butare, "Transformations," 66; *Ibiteekerezo*, Rwabugiri file, T, no. 39 (two head out of five or three out of six).

85. Kagame, *Armées bovines*, 107–15. Three spoliated herds, of which two were of an exceptional size, came from disgraced chiefs. In a fourth case, the herd was entrusted to the same chief from whom he had taken it.

86. Toward the end of the reign, two of the herds were designated for the service of the ritualists, one was given to one of his sons, and one was left to the chief whose herd he had confiscated. Kanjogera controlled the residences of Giseke (with a small domain) and Sakara (governing all of Gisaka). The residence of Rubengera governed the whole western slope of the Congo-Nile divide, from Bwishaza northward to Bwisha and Jomba.

87. Pagès, *Royaume hamite*, 178–79. He reports that some families lost almost all their men in one war after the other.

88. For example, the capture of Gisaka's dynastic drum. See Kagame, *Abrégé* 2, 36.

89. Kagame, *Milices*, 165–75. Murorunkwere raised two of them over ten years. Of Rwabugiri's eight, three were managed by chiefs, including one each by Ntizimira and Nzigiye, and five of them were raised by the king himself for his sons, his brother, and Bisangwa.

90. Toward the end of the reign, Nyaruguru became the most powerful

army when Muhigirwa managed to incorporate no less than four other ones that were near his military domain (Kagame, *Milices*, 47–48).

91. Ibid., 86.

92. Ibid., 170–71. For the breakup of Abakemba, see 85–87. First they lost their official herd, which was divided into three sections. Then the army was divided into four territorialized parts.

93. Unfortunately, there is no list of companies for these great expeditionary forces, but only a list of the armies that participated without any indication of their relative contributions. Thus Kagame, *Abrégé* 2, 61, 113, 115, signals that there were twelve armies for the expedition of Kanywiriri and twelve "commanders" for the one sent to Shangi. In this last case, only four companies, or about six hundred warriors, attacked. That is comparable to the number of combatants of a single army, but in this case the army was composed of elements from two armies. Nyaruguru only contributed a single company, but its elite one. Each of the ten other commanders contributed less than a full company each.

94. To my mind, these were the only objectives of this policy, but Butare speaks of a formal will to create a national army ("Transformations," 79).

95. Ibid., 65–66.

96. Nyirimigabo (Abagina army) against Abashakamba and Buki (Abashakamba) against Abakemba. See Schumacher, *Physische*, 64–65, and Kagame, *Abrégé* 2, 55. The border region in Kigezi was then divided into four marches that were given to four armies. Or again the Butare region Biyenzi's Imvejuru against Inzirabwoba. (*Ibitéekerezo*, Rwabugiri file, T, no. 3, and Kagame, *Milices*, 95–96). Moreover, this last battle directly opposed Hutu to Tutsi. Later Imvejuru fought the Nyakare army (*Ibitéekerezo*, Rutarindwa file, T, no. 11:1). Quarrels over the division of loot as occurred, for example, during a campaign to Ndorwa were more ephemeral (id., Rwabugiri file, T, no. 1:1).

97. Ibid., T, no. 54:1.

98. Ibid., T, no. 53, notes that he had "the ambition to kill" and one story attributes the cliché of wanting to kill a pregnant woman out of curiosity to him; see also Newbury, *Cohesion*, 49–59.

99. Thus in the end Nzigiye himself protected Gacinya.

100. Soon after her marriage Kanjogera began to intervene often and was successful thanks to her hold over the king (thus ibid., T, no. 34, about Rwampembwe, even though the details are not correct). Even so, one time she failed to protect Kabare who supposedly fell out of favor and was emasculated by the king's orders. But soon thereafter she managed to have him restored to favor.

101. Kagame, *Armées bovines*, 114; for other cases, such as a condemnation by Nzigiye who then seized the herd of the convict and the disgrace of "super-rich" Abaha of Murama, see ibid., 107–9.

102. Still the motive for some of the accusations made after the genocide.

103. See Kagame, *Milices*, and id., *Armées bovines*.

104. For those carried out under Rutarindwa and Musinga, see *Ibitéekerezo*,

Rwabugiri file, H, no. 43, and, for those carried out in general, T, no. 12; id., *Rutarindwa*, H, no. 7:3–6, lists by name the important men who were executed; see also H, nos. 17, 23–24, 26–27, 43; T, nos. 1, 3–4, 12, 14; Kayijuka, "Lebensgeschichte," 153, 162–64, in part covers massacres that occurred after 1906; Pagès, *Royaume hamite*, 201–6. These massacres were still remembered in 1960 since they are recounted in these tales.

105. Thus *Ibiteekerezo*, Rwabugiri file, T, nos. 26, 58; H, no. 53, and ibid., Imandwa file, nos. 68, 72. One was not supposed to wreak vengeance on a king but nevertheless Rwabugiri remained on his guard (ibid., Rwabugiri file, T, no. 1; cf. H, no. 34).

106. The most complex case known was the appointment of one descendant each of Rugereka, Nyantaba, and Nkoronko as the heads of various armies around 1888–89 (*Ibiteekerezo*, Rwabugiri file, T, no. 26). For the execution of Kabaka so as to heal the king from a sickness sent by the vindictive spirit of the king of Bushubi, see Kagame, *Abrégé* 2, 81–82.

107. Kayijuka, "Lebensgeschichte," 162–63, cites two tragic cases. Torture was so widespread that to be executed by a spear thrust was a favor (e.g., Rwanyonga captured by the enemy in Coupez and Kamanzi, *Récits*, 326–27). One impaled, skinned, and mutilated the living to see them devoured by dogs, and so on. For torture as a judicial punishment, see Schumacher, *Ruanda*, 732, 734–35. See also Pagès, *Royaume hamite*, 179, 201–3, and for cases of torture among the executions he mentions, 190–93; Van Overschelde, *Bij de reuzen*, 112–13.

108. *Ibiteekerezo*, Rwabugiri file, T, no. 58; H, no. 68.

109. Unfortunately Delmas, *Généalogies*, only lists the direct forebears of the chiefs and subchiefs living in his time, which eliminates the possibility of calculating losses within the ranks of the high nobility.

110. For a detailed case, *Ibiteekerezo*, Rwabugiri file, T, nos. 2, and especially 38, regarding his protégé Nyamurinda.

111. For two cases, see *Ibiteekerezo*, Rwabugiri file, T, no. 3, and Kagame, *Milices*, 95–96, 157, regarding Bikotwa, aka Mbanzabugabo. The first incident occurred between 1888 and 1895. Nkiramacumu had supposedly insulted an old man of high rank. The latter then called on all the Tutsi in the region for help and thus provoked armed clashes between the Inzirabwoba and the Imvejuru during which Nkiramacumu died. As to Bikotwa, in 1897 he insulted the corpse of Muhigirwa, the brother of Rutarindwa. Another brother of the deceased, Cyitatire, wanted revenge and organized a private expedition that included all the remaining Nyiginya of aristocratic extraction in the region and the impertinent upstart was killed. Contrary to Kagame's opinion this vengeance was private and not officially sanctioned. Both cases are also good examples of local disruptions occurring beyond the reach of central authority.

112. For local turmoil under Rwabugiri, see *Ibiteekerezo*, Rwabugiri file, T, nos. 2, 3, 5b, 38, 50; H, nos. 3, 8, 53, 68, 72. These cases include battles for hills and cattle. For clashes between armies, see nn.96 and 111 above. Butare's generalization about the causes of local turmoil in "Transformations," 78, is correct.

113. For the new residences se *Ibitéekerezo, Rwabugiri,* T, no. 39, H, nos. 37, 81, 85, 93, 96; Kagame, *Milices,* 157, 170 (Rubengera), his *Armées bovines,* 50 (Rubengera), 109 (Sakara), and his *Abrégé* 2, 36 (Sakara). In general see Butare, "Transformations," 61.

114. This is evident from an examination of Kagame's *Milices* and *Armées bovines.*

115. Contra the conclusions of Butare, "Transformations," 79.

116. *Ibitéekerezo,* Rwabugiri file, T, no. 14; H, no. 9.

117. Reisdorff, *Enquêtes,* 148.

118. Butare, "Transformations," 73, and this despite an extension of the system into Gisaka and other new regions. See Saucier, "Patron-Client Relationship," 261–66, for the decreasing number of contracts and their political characteristics. For the prophecy, see *Ibitéekerezo,* Rwabugiri file, H, no. 38. Reisdorff, *Enquêtes,* 147, cites a case of a patron in ill repute at court being abandoned by his clients.

119. Schumacher, *Physische,* 104, and id., *Ruanda,* 177–78.

120. Kagame, *Abrégé* 2, 29, 31; *Ibitéekerezo,* Rwabugiri file, T, no. 4.

121. Kagame, *Abrégé* 2, 35, notes that Karamira was a Tsobe.

122. For Giharamagara, see *Ibitéekerezo,* Rwabugiri file, H, nos. 5, 41, 46, which makes an explicit accusation; Kagame, *Abrégé* 2, 45, does not mention this accusation; Pagès, *Royaume hamite,* 165–7, speaks of a plot, places the action at Nyamasheke, and gives no role to Kanjogera, but follows the storytellers (mainly H, no. 46) in describing how she killed Rwakageyo who was wrestling with her husband.

123. *Ibitéekerezo,* Rwabugiri file, T, no. 37:4, and in particular no. 58.

124. Ibid., T, nos. 4, 26, 46, 52; H, no. 82. For a case in which a male member of a lineage was spared to take care of the ancestor worship of the victims, see T, no. 26:2. H, no. 53, shows the Imandwa in action while chasing the spirits of the Abagereka away.

125. Biyenzi was appointed around 1888 and fled to Burundi in 1892 after another local clash that followed this one by a few years (Kagame, *Milices,* 96; Kayijuka, "Lebensgeschichte," 167).

126. Scission is not identical to "racial hatred" as Bethe believed in 1898 ("Bericht," 8). That is but a projection of his own ideas, For "racial ideas," which were nothing of the sort, see Schumacher, *Ruanda,* 146, 469–71, and the difference between his views and those of his collaborators as late as 1928–36.

127. *Ibitéekerezo,* Rwabugiri file, T, no. 48:3–4. Should one understand that *uburetwa* only became officially sanctioned at this time?

128. Newbury, *Cohesion,* 82–83, 85. Ntizimira was chief in Kinyaga during the second Ijwi expedition in 1882–83 and was executed c. 1887 (Kagame, *Abrégé* 2, 51, 71).

129. Schumacher, *Ruanda,* 706, admits the killing of civilians in wartime and concludes that "although one disapproved of the violent killing of these defenseless creatures, such actions went unpunished."

130. This operation followed the refusal of the people of Cyingogo to hand over the cattle claimed by the king to reconstitute his herds after the epizootic epidemic (*Historique et chronologie,* 130; Butare, "Transformations," 58).

131. Von Götzen, *Durch Afrika,* 171.

132. Schumacher, *Ruanda,* 425–26, under his description of the word *gutsimba.*

133. Citation from Schumacher, *Ruanda,* 474. The three regions were Save (two or three suppressions), Marangara, and Bugoyi. See *Ibitéekerezo,* Rwabugiri file, T, no. 5b; H, nos. 3, 44, all of which cover Save; Van Overschelde, *Bij de reuzen,* 110, on Bugoyi and Marangara; Pagès, *Royaume hamite,* 172–73, on Marangara; Nahimana, *Le Rwanda,* 247–50, on Bugoyi in 1894 and the rebellion of 1898.

134. Schumacher, *Ruanda,* 474.

135. *Ibitéekerezo,* Rwabugiri file, T, no. 5b; H, nos. 3, 44.

136. Langheld, *Zwanzig Jahren,* 196–98; Von Götzen, *Durch Afrika,* 155. For nearby Burundi, see J-P. Chrétien, "Le passage de l'expédition Oscar Baumann au Burundi."

137. Nahimana, *Le Rwanda,* 247–50; Pagès, *Royaume hamite,* 210–13, notes uprisings from Busigi to Bugoyi; Schumacher, *Ruanda,* cites ones in Cyingogo, Buriza, Bugoyi (182–83) and "Bakiga" (473–74). Desforges, "Defeat," 25–27, mentions the insurrections but not their millenarian and anti-Tutsi context.

138. Butare, "Transformations," 78–80.

139. Vidal, "Rwanda des anthropologues," 394–95, is right to deny the existence of any real administrative structure, even that of the residences. For the territorial situation, see Butare, "Transformations," 39–61, who presents the information district by district.

140. *Ibitéekerezo,* Rwabugiri file, H, no. 6. This curse aptly summarizes the popular perception of the cause of all the nightmares experienced during his rule. It resembles the curse that the wives of Mazimpaka had heaped on him.

In Conclusion: History and the Present

1. Most of the following propositions have a long pedigree in the historiography of Rwanda and are even found in the most recent works, such as, for example S. Sebasoni's, *Les Origines du Rwanda,* published in 2000, or C. M. Overdulve, *Rwanda: Un peuple avec une histoire,* published in 1997.

2. Sebasoni, *Les Origines,* 61.

Appendix 1: Chronology

1. All the calculations start with the dynastic genealogy *(ubucurabwenge).* For this and the chronologies proposed before 2001, see de Briey "Musinga, 9, note; Pagès, *Royaume hamite,* 95–96; Delmas, *Généalogies,* 24–25; Vansina, *Évolution* (1962); ibid. (2000); J. K. Rennie, "The Precolonial Kingdom of Rwanda,"

25–29; and especially Schumacher, *Ruanda*, 121–43, who gives three slightly different lists. See also Kagame, *Notion*, 14–27, 87, and *passim;* Nkurikiyimfura, "Révision"; Newbury "Trick Cyclists?" As I recently came across some further information I have further fine-tuned dates in this translation for the years between 1876 and 1885.

2. Kagame, *Abrégé* 1, 37.

3. Wrigley, *Kingship and State*, 200–29, for Bunyoro and Buganda; Mworoha, *Histoire du Burundi*, 125, and J. Vansina, "Note sur la chronologie du Burundi ancien," 429–44, for Burundi c. 1700.

4. First elaborated by Kagame, *Notion*.

5. As was the case in preindustrial Europe.

6. Newbury, "Trick Cyclists?" 204–7. The paucity of data about this king and his lack of descendants confirm this point of view. See Vansina, "Historical Tales."

7. For BICUBA, see Kagame, *Poésie dynastique*, 53 n.54 (poem no. 65); id., *Abrégé* 1, 109, 112–13; *Ibiteekerezo*, Mutara file, T, nos. 3:7, 4:4, 5:0, 6:6, 8:1; H, no. 2.

8. Reported by Kagame, *Abrégé* 1, 162, 165, who is the only source for this topic.

9. Ibid., 169. According to the ritualist in charge of the annual first fruit rituals, he only celebrated five of these and he died when he was twenty-five or thirty-years-old. According to Schumacher's collaborators, *Ruanda*, 131, 171, he died young, just after Gahindiro was born. According to Pagès, *Royaume hamite*, 146, he only ruled for a short time.

10. R. Gray, "Annular Eclipse Maps," 151–52.

11. D. Henige, "Day Was of Sudden Turned into Night," 576–601. In general an eclipse only becomes truly evident to all when it has a magnitude of over 0.95 percent.

12. Gray, "Annular Eclipse Maps," 153, citing Kagame, *Notion*, 75.

13. Vansina, *Évolution* (2000), 49.

14. Schumacher, *Ruanda*, 130–33. The list of kings was elaborated on with the help of Sekarama in 1933–34. It differs from the earlier lists by Mazina in 1928 and of Kayijuka, Mazina, and Ruzigaminturo in 1933. It is the only one to give estimates of longevity, which were probably elicited by Schumacher. They are: Gisanura: died young; Mazimpaka: fifty years; Rujugira: longer lived than Ndabarasa; Ndabarasa: longer lived than Gahindiro; Sentabyo: died young and had only one son; Gahindiro: gray hair, sixty years; Rwogera, fifty years; Rwabugiri, fifty years.

15. Newbury, "Trick Cyclists?" 193–200. The case of Burundi has become famous and can serve as an example. Schumacher and his collaborators visited the Rundi Chief Baranyanka several times in 1936 to establish a synchronic list of the Nyiginya and Rundi kings (Schumacher, *Ruanda*, 137–43). Later Sekarama, Kagame's teacher in 1936, informed the latter of the results, which led Kagame to contact Baranyanka again and to obtain statements from him in

1949 and in 1957 (Kagame, *Notion*, 98 n.1, and id., *Poésie dynastique*, 42). For comparisons involving Kyamutwara, Buganda, and Nkore, see id., "Documentation," 309–13).

16. Kagame, *Abrégé* 2, 96, 103 (September), 112–16.

17. J. M. Dricot and C. Dricot-d'Ans, "Description du squelette de Kigeri Rwabugiri" 102. Schumacher's collaborators overestimated (as they seem to have done in general) his lifespan by about ten years and Kagame's interlocutors even more. The description of the king by Von Götzen in his *Durch Afrika*, 179, stresses his physical weakness, probably a sign of illness. Rwabugiri found it difficult to move and could almost not walk at all.

18. Kagame, *Abrégé* 2, 21, but in his *Notion*, 69, he has "at the age of ten to fourteen years."

19. *Historique et chronologie*, 10, gives 1865 without any further explanation. (Did the author get the date from Delmas? See below.) Indirect support for this approximate date stems from the estimated lifespan of Sekarama. According to this chronology he was born shortly before 1867 and not a few years before 1853 as Kagame implies in his *Abrégé* 2, 39, and see id., *Abrégé* 1, photograph 6. He died in 1946 at about eighty-five-years-old by our calculation, which is more likely than the ninety-six years of Kagame's calculation. His first military expedition is reported to have been the war of Bumpaka dated by Kagame to 1867–68 but that, as we shall see below, actually occurred in 1879–80, twelve years later than Kagame's estimate.

20. Kagame, *Abrégé* 2, 15–21, and id., *Notion*, 62–70, build his case on a list he solicited concerning the places where Rwabugiri celebrated his first-fruit rituals. Such a request was obviously unusual and Sezibera could not remember the number and even less the sequence of the sites involved.

21. According to Delmas, *Généalogies* 88 n.1, Rwabugiri became king in 1858 but his mother remained regent until 1865, that is for seven years. That explains the date of 1865 in his table on p. 24. But it is not clear by which calculations he arrived at this date. Rwabugiri's mother was probably not assassinated before late 1876, and in fact was more likely assassinated in 1877 (see below). Using seven years adduced by Delmas, we can deduce that the king would have been installed in 1869–70.

22. Van Overschelde, *Bij de reuzen*, 105, without explanation. But if Murorunkwere's regency really lasted only seven years, the date would be correct.

23. Kagame, *Abrégé* 2, 75, dated by the annular eclipse of 22 December 1889 (Gray, "Annular Eclipse Maps," 153).

24. The 1861 date for her death in Kagame, *Abrégé* 2, 35, must be rejected because it derives from his list of the places where the celebration of the first-fruit rituals were held, which is valueless.

25. According to Hamed Ibrahim in Stanley, *Through the Dark Continent*, 288–89. But one also find mention there of the suicide of her son, "the prince,"

several years earlier. Rwandan traditions do not speak of any event of this sort and the "prince" was certainly not the heir to the throne. Moreover, as Stanley's text is written in the past tense, one cannot be absolutely certain that the queen mother was still living in March 1876. But it is, however, extremely likely she was for otherwise her dramatic assassination would also certainly have been mentioned in Kafurro.

26. Pearson to Wright, letters from Rubaga dated to 7 January 1880, 23, 26, and dated to 5 March 1880, 5–6, CA6/019/18. Henri Médard, in a personal communication, drew my attention to a reference to an expedition to Usagara (Nkore) in March 1880 in the diary of the White Fathers of Rubaga and to the relevant passage in A. Kagwa's *Kings of Buganda*, 175. He concludes that there has been enough cross-checking of information to date the Ganda intervention to January–March 1880.

27. Kagame, *Abrégé* 2, 36, 38–39, 97–102.

28. The campaign against Ndorwa mentioned by Pagès, *Royaume hamite*, 174, during which guns were seized, pointing to possible Ganda involvement, may be the one that occurred in Bumpaka in 1895, although Kagame, *Abrégé* 2, 100–102, only speaks of gun involvement during the last campaign of 1895.

29. Kagame, *Notion*, 68, and id., *Abrégé* 2, 20, 43.

30. Kagame does not mention these except in *Abrégé* 2, probably because the year at the court ran, it seems, from June to June. If the comet appeared late in 1882 it is possible that the suicide dated from early in the same year.

31. R. Kandt, "Bericht der Forschungsreisenden," 115, suggests he was twenty-years-old in 1900, and id., *Caput Nili*, 269, 272, that he was barely eighteen in August 1900, photo 1900; von Beringe, "Bericht," 265, puts him at twenty-years-old in 1902, suggesting a birth date of between mid-1882 and mid-1883.

32. As reconstructed by Kagame, *Abrégé* 2, 13–15, 21–103, but remember that the chronology based on the list of localities where first-fruit rituals were celebrated is useless, and that the year as counted at court seems to have run from June to June so that of two events in year A, one might be remembered as having occurred in year A if it happened before June and the other in year B if it happened after June.

33. Ibid., 169, suggests he ruled for five years; *Ibitéekerezo*, Mazimpaka file, T, no. 3:, states that he ruled between three and five years. In this case Kagame seems to be better informed, so we accept five years as more probable.

34. Katoke, *The Karagwe Kingdom*, 67; J. A. Grant, *A Walk across Africa*, 137–38.

35. Katoke, *The Karagwe Kingdom*, 83–88; Burton, *Lake Regions*, 2:83, discusses the Arab role, but confuses the names.

36. Wrigley, *Kingship and State*, 228–29.

37. Kagame, *Abrégé* 1, 180; Schumacher, *Ruanda*, 130; *Ibitéekerezo*, Mazimpaka file, T, no. 3:5, by Mugina.

38. Kayijuka, "Lebensgeschichte," 140–43.

39. Katoke, *The Karagwe Kingdom*, 64. We observe, though, that a somewhat later date would be indicated by the case of Muhinjishi, one of Schumacher's collaborators, who was "well over" sixty-years-old around 1930 and who was supposedly already a strapping young man when Gahindiro died. If that had occurred in 1845, Muhinjishi would have been eighty-five in 1930 (Schumacher, *Physische*, 95).

40. Kagame, *Abrégé* 1, 191; *Ibitéekerezo*, Rwogera file, H, 25.

41. Kagame, *Abrégé* 1, 191 (fifty to sixty-years-old); Schumacher, *Ruanda*, 130, 175 (fifty-years-old). But *Ibitéekerezo*, Mazimpaka file, T, no. 3: states that he was young, and Bourgeois, *Banyarwanda et Barundi*, 145, claims he was very young.

42. *Ibitéekerezo*, Rwogera file, T, nos. 1:11, and 3:2, both by Mugina.

43. Ibid., T, no. 1.

44. Ibid., T, no. 13:1, is more affirmative than Kagame, *Abrégé* 1, 207–8.

45. J. Hiernaux, "Les restes osseux trouvés dans la tombe de Cyirima II," 63. His age was estimated according to the synosteoses (the union of bones) of the cranial sutures (seams). This examination indicated an age between twenty-five- and forty-five-years-old except for the start of a synosteosis of the temporal seam that most often occurs in people who are sixty-five and older. I deduce an age of about sixty years from this. For the dating, Van Noten, *Histoire*, 42, accepts 1700 +/- 90 AD on the basis of a single, uncorrected carbon-14 dating, which would mean that his having died in 1790 is just as likely as his having died in 1610. An earlier "corrected" dating in Van Noten, ibid., 56–61, had led Nkurikiyimfura in "Révision," 166, and Chrétien in *Afrique*, 339 n.47, to conclude erroneously that the body was not that of Cyirima Rujugira.

46. Apart from the almost unanimous opinion that Rujugira was very old, the estimates remain rather vague. For Schumacher, *Ruanda*, 190, he lived longer than Ndabarasa and the latter longer than Gahindiro. See also n.14. According to Kagame, *Abrégé* 1, 153, 158–59, Rujugira was "very old" and Ndabarasa "already old" when he died as the result from surgery. According to *Ibitéekerezo*, Mazimpaka file, T, no. 3:5, Rujugira and Ndabarasa both lived long but the storyteller Mugina has a tendency to confuse length of life and length of reign.

47. Desforges, "Court," 33, does not believe in this maternity.

48. The date of his death had already been estimated before I saw the chronology for Ndorwa proposed by Freedman in "Three Muraris," 186. He dates the death of Gahaya II to 1787. When we discussed Ndabarasa's plans we saw that Gahaya's death preceded Rujugira's by very little and is therefore quite close to the date proposed here.

49. Kayijuka, "Lebensgeschichte," 132, cites a four-year-rule; Kagame, *Abrégé* 1, 134, states that Rwaka celebrated first-fruit rituals sixteen times as coruler and as king. Delmas, *Généalogies*, 58, speaks of his having ruled for some fifteen years after the death of Mazimpaka, a number probably derived from Kagame.

We accept Kagame's figure for the combined corule and rule and Kayijuka's for the amount of time he was sole ruler, although one may well doubt how exact these figures are, and in particular that of the highest number, considering the errors which have beset a similar computation for the length of Rwabugiri's reign. See n.20.

50. Schumacher, *Ruanda*, 131, suggests he was fifty-years-old), 137 (*"Mannes-alter,"* he writes, meaning the same age attributed here to Rwogera and Rwabugiri); Kayijuka, "Lebensgeschichte" 131, on the number of capitals and sons; Delmas, *Généalogies*, 58–66, on the number of sons.

51. Desforges, "Court," 19, states the grandson was commander of the Intaremba army; Kayijuka "Lebensgeschichte," 138–39.

52. This is assuming that Rujugira was not his son. Otherwise, he would have to have been at least fifty-eight when he died, for Rujugira was at least thirty-eight in 1766.

53. According to Schumacher's collaborators he died young but I suspect that this declaration is an estimate informed by the observation that Gisanura left no known issue except for these two sons and that little is known about his reign. However, as we reach here the very limit of credible data both for traditions concerning the court and family histories, that argument can be put aside.

54. Delmas, *Généalogies*, 57.

55. This mean of seven generations of 22.85 years between 1735 and 1895 is short in relation to computations done over large numbers. Yet twenty-three years is the figure obtained by Nkurikiyimfura, "Révision," 172. He thought that he would obtain a higher number by including generational averages for noble families. This procedure is not acceptable, though, for these lineages did not encounter the rivalries that beset royal successions. The twenty-seven year figure historians of the Great Lakes find "reasonable" was adopted by Rennie "Precolonial," 27, for the Nyiginya dynasty. But that figure relates to a majority of cases in which succession was fraternal, which lengthens each dynastic generation. Henige, *Chronology*, 72–73, does not give any case of less than 27.3 years for father-son successions attested to in Europe during at least ten generations. But our case includes two quite irregular successions (Rujugira, Gahindiro) and two where the king was not the biological father of the successor (Rwabugiri, Rutarindwa). All in all, we believe then that the figure we obtained is credible.

56. Delmas, *Généalogies*, suggests Tege (40), Ganzu (55), Kono (138), and Ega (118); see also Nkurikiyimfura, "Révision," 167–72. Kagame, "Documentation," cites Tege and Ganzu (305–6) genealogies. We observe that correspondences between the Tege and the Nyiginya are suspect and that the intercalation of Mutabazi (whose name means "liberator") to align the royal generations and those of Ndori's supposed descendents is a blatant expedient.

57. Which shortens the chronology according to received wisdom. For Ndori's accession, see Kagame *Abrégé* 1, 38 (1510), Nkurikiyimfura, *Gros Bétail*, 13 (1600), Vansina, *Évolution* (1962), 56 (1624), and Rennie, "Precolonial," 25 (1603).

Appendix 2: Predynastic Fairy Tales: Central Rwanda before Ndori

1. Wrigley, *Kingship and State*, 137, is the only exception. Otherwise, even very recent authors, although of secondary importance on this point, such as Lugan, *Histoire du Rwanda*, 82–95 (with maps to boot) and Chrétien, *Afrique*, 134–35, still believe in the historicity of this pre-Ndori epoch.

2. According to Nahimana, *Le Rwanda*, 50 (map), 97, and 122–25, a certain Bwimba, son of Nkuzo, founded the little kingdom of Bukonya. Kagame, *Abrégé* 1, 87, 97, cites another Bwimba as the brother of Juru, King of Bumbogo and Buriza.

3. These are the words with which Kagame, *Abrégé* 1, 57, begins his discussion of the period from Bwimba to Cyamatare.

4. Pagès, *Royaume hamite*, 79–86, 114–28, 541–85; Schumacher, *Ruanda*, 158–63; Delmas, *Généalogies*, 32–53; Kagame, *Abrégé* 1, 57–92; Coupez and Kamanzi, *Récits*, 86–221; *Ibitéekerezo*, Bwimba, Cyamatare, and Mashira files; Smith, *Récit*, 75–76, 290–313.

5. Vansina, "Historical Tales," for more detail.

6. Smith, *Récit*, 75–76.

7. Kagame, *Introduction*, 279–81, while discussing a dynastic poem (n. 217) speaks of a stylistic device that created a confusion. But if that were the case, this confusion would already have existed in Rujugira's day, for the poem is dedicated to him. Since such confusion did not exist at the time, is this not rather a flagrant clue to the way an ancient king was made from a more recent one?

8. The literary genre of cryptic prophecies, related to riddles, seems to have been as much liked by the common people as detective stories are today.

9. See Pagès, *Royaume hamite*, 555–84, for three different tales. In the first one (577–79), a wholly fictitious "capital of the charms" plays a central role. Yet this expression has been cited as proving that a capital once did exist at Nzaratsi (*"nzaratsi"* means "charms") at the time of the so-called king YUHI Gahima.

10. This regnal name stems from *"indahiro,"* meaning "oath," and *"kurahira,"* meaning "to swear an oath," in Rwanda as well as in Rundi. According to F. Géraud, "Settlement," 24–25, *"endahiro,"* from *"okuharira,"* meaning "to promise, to swear an oath" in Nkore /Kiga refers, refers in this language to a type of oath that mentions a common place of origin. It is proof of an alliance among lineages or clans and might point to a common origin.

11. A subgenre of dynastic poetry, the *impakanizi*, dedicated a paragraph to each king preceding the one in honor of whom the poem was composed. It would then seem to be an easy task to figure out at what time each of the predynastic kings shows up in them. According to Kagame, *Poésie dynastique*, 127–28, the oldest known fragment, his no. 1, already includes paragraphs for Bwimba, Rugwe, and Sekarongoro. It is said to have been composed by Ndori's queen mother. Alas, things are not that simple. The attribution to a given composer is

not always credible, subsequent interpolations into older poems are facilitated by the very structure of this genre, and the relevant passages obscure almost all proper names, including those of kings, by periphrases and allusions that are so cryptic that only explanatory commentary can recover their meaning, as is apparent in the only two older examples published by Kagame (his nos. 24 and 90). Given these exigencies, one simply cannot rely on such texts to document the process by which the odds and ends were fitted together. Let us add for future reference that Kagame attributes poems or fragments of this type as follows: nos. 10, 11, 14, 15 to Gisanura and Mazimpaka's times, nos. 24, 34, 36, 48, 49 to that of Rujugira, no. 55 to Ndabarasa's, no. 61 to that of Sentabyo, nos. 79, 84 to Gahindiro's, nos. 90, 94, 97, 118 to that of Rwogera, and nos. 128, 131, 139, 142, 147, 148, 154 to Rwabugiri's.

12. The poem no. 24, *Bantumye kubaz' umuhigo,* composed for Rujugira includes sections for all the kings since Bwimba, but only directly mentions the names "Bwimba" (in his section) and "Rugwe" (in Gahima's section) without listing a single dynastic name. Therefore it does not prove much. See Kagame, *Introduction,* 190–205.

13. Nkurikiyimfura, "Révision," 172.

14. Reisdorff, *Enquêtes,* 142, notes that this repopulation was completed during Gahindiro's reign.

15. Kagame, *Milices,* notes that Ababito was set up under Rujugira (108) and that Abanyoro was raised by Rukari (125).

16. Schumacher, *Ruanda,* 161, believed that the invaders came from Karagwe or Bushubi.

17. For the toponyms are archaic. "Ishinjaniro" means "land of victory" (but the modern form is "Itsindaniro") and the word for the commemorative tree "Umuganzacyaro" means "Victor over the foreigner" but *"cyaro,"* a word that commonly means "land" in other languages, no longer exists in Rwanda. Kagame, *Abrégé* 1, 73, d'Hertefelt and Coupez, *Royauté,* 470–71. Umuganzacyaro was the official residence of the head ritualist in charge of the herds. Is it possible that neither name is archaic at all but that they both are just loan words from Nyambo or Nkore?

18. The uncertainty concerning this "king" is evident when Gakanyisha speaks of two contemporary MIBAMBWE who were brothers, one of whom was a liberator *(mutabazi)* and the other king. See Coupez and Kamanzi, *Récit,* 138 and 139, sentence 12.

19. Kagame, *Abrégé* 1, 79–80. But see *Ibitéekerezo, Mashira* files, which deal with Mashira's magical defeat and death, nothing more. In the last sentence of T, no. 2 only, the teller adds *"Mibáambw' araambuka, abuumb I Ndúga,"* "MIBAMBWE crossed the border and took Nduga," more as a logical conclusion to the tale than as a reference to a specific tradition! The historical sequence Kagame adopts includes a series of improbabilities such as that the Nyoro left Mashira in peace, but not the king of Bugesera whose lands lay

beyond those of Mashira, and that MIBAMBWE, who had taken refuge on the banks of the distant Rusizi, could return from so far away to defeat the Nyoro and Mashira without any difficulty.

20. Kagame, *Abrégé* 1, 87–88, 99. He also mentions two other brothers, Mutezi (88) and Bwimba (97), the homonym of RUGANZU Bwimba.

21. Wamara in Uganda. See Wrigley, *Kingship and State*, 39–40; Berger, *Religion and Resistance*, 27, 47, 51–52.

WORKS CITED

Adamantidis, D. "Monographie pastorale du Ruanda-Urundi." *Bulletin Agricole du Congo Belge* 47 (1956): 632–35.

"Alexis Kagame: l'homme et son oeuvre." *Uburezi Ubuhanga N'Umuco* 20 (1988): 13–318.

Arianoff, A. d'. *Histoire des Bagesera, souverains du Gisaka.* Royal Academy of Overseas Sciences, Moral and Political Sciences Section, no. 24. Brussels: Belgian Royal Colonial Institute, 1952.

Arnoux, A. "Le culte de la société secrète des Imandwa au Rwanda." *Anthropos* 7 (1912): 273–95, 529–58, 840–74; 8 (1913): 110–34, 754–74.

Austen, R. *Northwest Tanzania under German and British Rule: Colonial and Tribal Politics, 1889–1929.* New Haven, Conn.: Yale University Press, 1968.

Baitwababo, S. R. "Foundations of Rujumbura Society." In *A History of Kigezi in South-West Uganda,* edited by D. Denoon, 70–91. Kampala, Uganda: The National Trust, 1971.

Baumann, O. "Durch Deutsch Massai-Land zur Quelle des Kagera-Nil." *Verhandlungen der Gesellschaft für Erdkunde zu Berlin* 20 (1893): 277–83.

Berger, I., *Religion and Resistance: East African Kingdoms in the Precolonial Period.* Royal Museum for Central Africa Annals, no. 105. Tervuren, Belgium, 1981.

Beringe, R. von. "Aus den Berichten des Herrn. v. Beringe über seine Reisen im Gebiet der Kirungavulkane." *Mittheilungen von Forschungreisenden und Gelehrten aus den Deutschen Schutzgebieten* 14 (1901): 20–39.

———. "Bericht über seine Expedition nach Ruanda." *Deutsches Kolonialblatt* 14 (1903): 234–35, 264–66, 296–98, 317–19.

Bethe, H. von [Hauptmann]. "Bericht über einen Zug nach Ruanda." *Deutsches Kolonialblatt* 10 (1899): 6–12.

Botte, R. "Rwanda and Burundi, 1889–1930: Chronology of a Slow Assassination." Part 1. *International Journal of African Historical Studies* 18 (1985): 53–91.

Bourgeois, R. *Banyarwanda et Barundi: Ethnographie.* Royal Academy of Overseas Sciences, Moral and Political Sciences Section, n.s., no. 15, vol. 1. Brussels: Belgian Royal Colonial Institute, 1957.

Brásio, A., ed. *Monumenta Missionaria Africana Africa Ocidental.* Vol. 13. Lisbon: Portuguese Academy of History, 1982.

Briey, R. de "Musinga." *Congo* 1/2 (1920): 1–13.

Burton, R. *The Lake Regions of Central Africa: A Picture of Exploration.* 1860. Reprint, New York: Horizon Press, 1961. 2 vols.

Butare, A. "Les transformations politiques au Rwanda sous le règne de Kigeli IV Rwabugili (1853–1895)." Mémoire de licence, National University of Zaire, 1972.

Cavazzi, J. A. *Descrição histórica dos três reinos do Congo, Matamba e Angola.* 1687. Portuguese translation by G. M. de Leguzzano. 2 vols. Lisbon: Department of Overseas Investigations, 1965.

Célis, G. R. "La métallurgie traditionelle au Burundi, au Rwanda et au Buha: essai de synthèse." *Anthropos* 84 (1989): 25–46.

Chrétien, J. P. *L'Afrique des Grands Lacs: deux mille ans d'histoire.* Paris: Aubier-Historique, 2000.

—————. "Le passage de l'expédition Oscar Baumann au Burundi (septembre-octobre 1892)." *Cahiers d'études africaines* 29 (1968): 48–95.

Classe, L. *L'Organisation politique du Rwanda au début de l'occupation belge (1916). Notes rédigées par le R. P. Classe des Pères Blancs, Mission de Kabgayi, à la demande de l'Administration Belge. 28 août, 1916.* Manuscript, R. Lemarchand Collection.

Clist, B. "A Critical Reappraisal of the Chronological Framework of the Early Urewe Iron Age Industry." *Muntu* 6 (1987): 35–62.

Cochet, H. "Burundi: quelques questions sur l'origine et la différentiation d'un système agraire." *African Economic History* 16 (1988): 15–62.

Coupez, A., and Th. Kamanzi. *Littérature de cour au Rwanda.* Oxford, U.K.: Clarendon Press, 1970.

—————. *Récits historiques Rwanda dans la version de C. Gakaniisha.* Royal Museum for Central Africa Annals, no. 43. Tervuren, Belgium, 1962.

Czekanowski, J. *Forschungen im Nil-Kongo-Zwischengebiet. Ethnographie, Uele—Ituri—Nil-länder. Zwischenseengebiet. Mpororo, Ruanda.* Vol. 2. Leipzig, Germany: Klinkhardt and Biermann, 1917.

Delmas, L. *Généalogies de la noblesse (les Batutsi) du Ruanda.* Kabgayi, Rwanda, n.d. [1950].

Desforges, A. "Court and Corporations in the Development of the Rwandan State." Manuscript, 1984.

—————. "Defeat Is the Only Bad News: Rwanda under Musinga, 1896–1931." Ph.D. diss., Yale University, 1972.

Desmarais, J-Cl. "Le Rwanda des anthropologues: l'archéologie de l'idéologie raciale." *Anthropologie et Sociétés* 2 (1978): 71–93.

Desmedt, C. "Poteries anciennes décorées à la roulette dans la région des Grands Lacs." *African Archaeological Review* 9 (1991): 161–96.

d'Hertefelt, M. *Les Clans du Rwanda ancien: Eléments d'ethnosociologie et d'ethnohistoire.* Royal Museum for Central Africa Annals, no. 70. Tervuren, Belgium, 1971.

—————. "Mythes et idéologies dans le Rwanda ancien et contemporain." In

The Historian in Tropical Africa: Studies Presented and Discussed, edited by J. Vansina, R. Mauny, and L. V. Thomas, 219–38. London: Published for the International African Institute by the Oxford University Press, 1964.

———. "Le Rwanda." In *Les Anciens royaumes de la zone interlacustre méridionale: Rwanda, Burundi, Buha,* edited by M. d'Hertefelt, A. A. Trouwborst, and J. H. Scherer, 9–112. Tervuren, Belgium: Royal Museum for Central Africa, 1962.

d'Hertefelt, M., and A. Coupez. *La Royauté sacrée de l'ancien Rwanda: Texte, traduction et commentaire de son rituel.* Royal Museum for Central Africa Annals, no. 52. Tervuren, Belgium, 1964.

d'Hertefelt, M., and D. de Lame. *Société, culture et histoire du Rwanda: Encyclopédie bibliographique, 1863–1980/87.* 2 vols. Tervuren, Belgium: Royal Museum for Central Africa, 1987.

Dricot, J. M., and C. Dricot-d'Ans. "Description du squelette de Kigeri Rwabugiri." In *Histoire archéologique du Rwanda,* edited by F. Van Noten, 95–103. Tervuren, Belgium: Royal Museum for Central Africa, 1983.

Everaerts, E. *Monographie agricole du Ruanda-Urundi.* Brussels: Ministère des Colonies. Direction de l'agriculture et de l'elevage, 1947.

Freedman, J. *Nyabingi: The Social History of an African Divinity.* Royal Museum for Central Africa Annals, no. 115. Tervuren, Belgium, 1984.

———. "Three Muraris, Three Gahayas, and the Four Phases of Nyabingi." In *Chronology, Migration and Drought in Interlacustrine Africa,* edited by J. B. Webster, 175–87. London: Longman, 1978.

Froment, A. "Le peuplement de l'Afrique centrale: contribution de l'anthropobiologie." In *Paléo-Anthropologie en Afrique centrale. Un Bilan de l'archéologie au Cameroun,* edited by M. Delneuf, J.-M. Essomba, and A. Froment. Paris: Harmattan, 1998.

Gasarabwe, Laroche E. *Le geste rwanda.* Paris: Union Generale d'Editions, 1978.

Gautier, A. "Les restes osseux des sites d'Akameru et de Cyinkomane (Ruhengeri, Rwanda)." In *Histoire archéologique du Rwanda,* edited by F. Van Noten, 104–20. Tervuren, Belgium: Royal Museum for Central Africa, 1983.

———. "The Settlement of the Bakiga." In *A History of Kigezi in South-West Uganda,* edited by D. Denoon, 23–55. Kampala, Uganda: The National Trust, 1971.

Géraud, F. "Traditional Religion." In *A History of Kigezi in South-West Uganda,* edited by D. Denoon, 163–68. Kampala, Uganda: The National Trust, 1971.

Götzen, G. A. von. *Durch Afrika von Ost nach West: Resultate und Begebenheiten einer Reise von der deutsch-ostafrikanischen Küste bis zur Kongomündung in den Jahren 1893/94.* 2nd ed. Berlin: D. Reimer, 1899.

Grant, J. A. *A Walk across Africa; or, Domestic Scenes from My Nile Journal.* Edinburgh: W. Blackwood and Sons, 1864.

Gray, R. "Annular Eclipse Maps." *Journal of African History* 9 (1968): 147–57.

Grunderbeek, M-C. van. "The Iron Age of Rwanda and Burundi." *Nyame Akuma* 18 (1981): 26–31.

Grunderbeek, M-C. van., and H. Doutrelepont, "Étude de charbons de bois provenant de sites métallurgiques de l'âge du fer ancien au Rwanda et au Burundi." In *Bois et archéologie: Actes du symposium européen tenu à Louvain-la-Neuve, octobre 1987,* edited by T. Hackens, A. V. Munaut, and C. Till. Strasburg: Council of Europe, 1988.

Henige, D. *The Chronology of Oral Tradition: Quest for a Chimera.* Oxford, U.K.: Clarendon Press, 1974.

————. "Day Was of Sudden Turned into Night: The Use of Eclipses in Dating Oral History." *Comparative Studies in Society and History* 18 (1976): 576–601.

Heremans, R., A. Bart, and F. Bart. "Agriculture et paysages rwandais à travers les sources missionnaires." *Cultures et développement* 14 (1982): 3–39.

Hiernaux, J. *Analyse de la variation des caractères physiques humains en une région d'Afrique centrale.* Royal Museum for the Belgian Congo Annals, no. 3 (Anthropology). Tervuren, Belgium, 1956.

————. *Les Caractères physiques des populations du Ruanda et de l'Urundi.* Royal Academy of Overseas Sciences, Moral and Political Sciences Section, n.s., no. 52. Brussels: Belgian Royal Colonial Institute, 1954.

————. "Note sur une ancienne population du Ruanda-Urundi: les Renge." *Zaïre* 10 (1956): 351–60.

————. "Notes sur les Tutsi de l'Itombwe." *Bulletin and Records of the Anthropological Society of Paris,* no. 7. Brussels, 1965.

————. "Les restes osseux trouvés dans la tombe de Cyirima II." In *Les Tombes du roi Cyirima Rujugira et de la reine-mère Nyirayuhi Kanjogera,* edited by F. Van Noten, 63–73. Royal Museum for Central Africa Annals, no. 77. Tervuren, Belgium, 1972.

Hiernaux, J., and E. Maquet. *Cultures préhistoriques de l'âge des métaux au Ruanda-Urundi et au Kivu (Congo belge).* Part 2. Royal Academy of Overseas Sciences, Moral and Political Sciences Section, n.s., no. 10. Brussels: Belgian Royal Colonial Institute, 1960.

Historique et chronologie du Rwanda. N.p., n.d. [Kigali, Rwanda, 1954].

Hurel, E. *Dictionnaire français-runyarwanda et runyarwanda-français.* Kabgayi, Rwanda: Vicariat apostolique du Ruanda, 1926.

Iliffe, J. *A Modern History of Tanganyika.* Cambridge, U.K.: Cambridge University Press, 1979.

Jacob, I. *Dictionnaire rwandais-français.* 3 vols. Butare, Rwanda: National Institute of Scientific Research, 1984–85.

Johanssen, E. *Ruanda: Kleine Anfänge-Grosse Aufgaben der Evangelischen Mission in Zwischenseengebiet Deutsch-Ostafrikas.* Bielefeld, Germany: Bethel, 1912.

Kagame, A. *Un Abrégé de l'ethno-histoire du Rwanda.* Butare, Rwanda: Éditions universitaires du Rwanda, 1972.

————. *Un Abrégé de l'histoire du Rwanda de 1853 à 1972.* Vol. 2. Butare, Rwanda: Éditions universitaires du Rwanda, 1975.

————. "Le code ésotérique de la dynastie du Rwanda." *Zaïre* 1 (1947): 363–86.

————. *Le Code des institutions politiques du Rwanda précolonial.* Royal Academy of Overseas Sciences, Moral and Political Sciences Section, no. 26. Brussels: Belgian Royal Colonial Institute, 1952.

————. "La documentation du Rwanda sur l'Afrique interlacustre des temps anciens." In *La Civilisation ancienne des peuples des Grands Lacs,* 300–330. Paris: Editions Karthala, 1981.

————. "Étude critique d'un vieux poème historique du Rwanda." *Perspectives of Contemporary African Studies: Symposium Leo Frobenius,* 151–95. Cologne: K. G. Saur, 1974.

————. *L'Histoire des armées bovines dans l'ancien Rwanda.* Royal Academy of Overseas Sciences, Moral and Political Sciences Section, no. 25. Brussels: Belgian Royal Colonial Institute, 1961.

————. *Inganji Karinga.* 2 vols. Kabgayi, Rwanda: Editions Royales, 1943–47.

————. *Introduction aux grands genres lyriques de l'ancien Rwanda.* Butare, Rwanda: Editions universitaires du Rwanda, 1969.

————. *Les Milices du Rwanda précolonial.* Royal Academy of Overseas Sciences, Moral and Political Sciences Section, no. 28. Brussels: Belgian Royal Colonial Institute, 1963.

————. *La Notion de génération appliquée à la généalogie dynastique et à l'histoire du Rwanda des Xe–XIe siècles à nos jours.* Royal Academy of Overseas Sciences, Moral and Political Sciences Section, n.s., no. 9. Brussels: Belgian Royal Colonial Institute, 1959.

————. *Les Organisations socio-familiales de l'ancien Rwanda.* Royal Academy of Overseas Sciences, Moral and Political Sciences Section, no. 38. Brussels: Belgian Royal Colonial Institute, 1954.

————. *La Poésie dynastique du Rwanda.* Royal Academy of Overseas Sciences, Moral and Political Sciences Section, no. 22. Brussels: Belgian Royal Colonial Institute, 1951.

Kagwa, Sir Apolo. *The Kings of Buganda.* Translated and edited by M. S. M. Kiwanuka. Nairobi, Kenya: East African Publishing House, 1971. Originally published as *Basekabaka be Buganda* (1900).

Kandt, R. "Bericht der Forschungsreisenden Dr Richard Kandt aus Ruanda." *Mittheilungen von Forschungreisenden und Gelehrten aus den Deutschen Schutzgebieten* 14 (1901): 114–24.

————. "Bericht über meine Reisen und gesammte Thätigkeit in Deutsch Ost-Afrika." *Mittheilungen von Forschungreisenden und Gelehrten aus den Deutschen Schutzgebieten* 13 (1900): 240–64.

————. *Caput Nili Eine empfindsame Reise zu den Quellen des Nils.* 2nd ed. Berlin: D Reimer, 1905.

————. "Gewerbe in Ruanda." *Zeitschrift für Ethnologie* 36 (1904): 329-72.

————. "Ein Marsch am Ostufer des Kiwu." *Globus* 86 (1904): 209-14, 245-49.

Kanyamachumbi, P. *Société, culture et pouvoir politique en Afrique interlacustre: Hutu et Tutsi de l' ancien Rwanda.* Kinshasa, Democratic Republic of the Congo: Editions Select, 1995.

Karugire, S. *A History of the Kingdom of Nkore in Western Uganda to 1896.* Oxford, U.K.: Clarendon Press, 1971.

Katoke, I. K. *The Karagwe Kingdom: A History of the Abanyambo North Western Tanzania, c. 1400-1915.* Nairobi, Kenya: East African Publishing House, 1975.

Kayijuka. "Lebensgeschichte des Grossfürsten Kayijuka und seiner Ahnen seit Sultan Yuhi Mazimpaka, König von Ruanda. Von Ihm selbst erzählt." Translated by Dr Peter Schumacher, M. A. In *Mitteilungen der Ausland-Hochschule an der Universität Berlin 41 (Afrikanische Studien)* (1938): 103-61. Original in Kinyarwanda included.

Kopytoff, I. *The African Frontier: The Reproduction of Traditional African Societies.* Bloomington: Indiana University Press, 1987.

Lacroix, A. "Dubois (Evrard-Louis)." *Biographie coloniale belge* 3 (1952): 268-69.

Lame, D. de. "Instants retrouvés. Rwanda, regards neufs au fil du temps." In *Cahiers africains*, ed. P. Wymeersch, 115-31. 1993.

Langheld, W. *Zwanzig Jahren in Deutschen Kolonien.* Berlin: W. Weicher, 1909.

Loupias, P. "Tradition et légende des Batutsi sur la création du monde et leur établissement au Ruanda." *Anthropos* 3 (1908): 1-13.

Lugan, B. "Famines et disettes au Rwanda." *Cahiers d'Outre-mer* 38 (1975): 151-74.

————. *Histoire du Rwanda: De la Préhistoire à nos jours.* Paris: Bartillat, 1997.

————. "Nyanza, une capitale royale du Rwanda ancien." *Africa-Tervuren* 26 (1980): 98-112.

Maquet, J. *Le Système des relations sociales dans le Ruanda ancien.* Royal Museum for Central Africa Annals, no. 1. Tervuren, Belgium, 1954.

Maquet, J., and S. Naigiziki. "Les droits fonciers dans le Ruanda ancien." *Zaïre* 10 (1975): 339-59.

Masson, P. *Trois siècles chez les Bashi.* Royal Museum for Central Africa Ethnographic Archives, no. 1. Tervuren, Belgium, 1960.

Mazina, D. "Nachtrag zur Lebensbeschreibung des Kayijuka." In Kayijuka, "Lebensgeschichte des Grossfürsten Kayijuka und seiner Ahnen seit Sultan Yuhi Mazimpaka, König von Ruanda. Von Ihm selbst erzählt." Translated by Dr Peter Schumacher, M. A. In *Mitteilungen der Ausland-Hochschule an der Universität Berlin 41 (Afrikanische Studien)* (1938): 161-70.

Meschi, Lydia. "Évolution des structures foncières au Rwanda: le cas d'un lignage hutu." *Cahiers d'études africaines* 53 (1974): 39-51.

Moniot, H. "Nouvelles recherches sur l'histoire sociale du Rwanda." *Annales ESC* 32 (1977): 337-45.

Mutambo, J. *Les Banyamulenge*. Kinshasa, Democratic Republic of the Congo: Imprimerie Saint-Paul, 1997.

Mworoha, E. *Peuples et rois de l'Afrique des lacs: Le Burundi et les royaumes voisins au XIX siècle*. Dakar, Senegal: Les Nouvelles éditions africaines, 1977.

———, ed. *Histoire du Burundi: Des Origines à la fin du XIXe siècle*. Paris: Hatier, 1987.

Nahimana, F. *Le Rwanda, emergence d'un état*. Paris: Harmattan, 1993.

Ndoricimpa, L., and C. Guillet. *L'Arbre-mémoire: Traditions orales du Burundi*. Paris: Editions Karthala, 1984.

Nenquin, J. *Contributions to the Study of the Prehistoric Cultures of Rwanda and Burundi*. Royal Museum for Central Africa Annals, no. 59. Tervuren, Belgium, 1967.

Newbury, C. *The Cohesion of Oppression: Clientship and Ethnicity in Rwanda, 1860–1960*. New York: Columbia University Press, 1988.

———. "*Ubureetwa* and *Thangata:* Catalysts to Peasant Political Consciousness in Rwanda and Malawi." *Canadian Journal of African Studies* 14 (1980): 97–111.

Newbury, D. "'Bunyabungo': The Western Rwandan Frontier, c. 1750–1850." In *The African Frontier: The Reproduction of Traditional African Societies*, edited by I. Kopytoff, 164–92. Bloomington: Indiana University Press, 1987.

———. "Les campagnes de Rwabugiri: chronologie et bibliographie." *Cahiers d'études africaines* 53 (1974): 181–92.

———. "The Clans of Rwanda: An Historical Hypothesis." *Africa* 50 (1980): 389–403.

———. *Kings and Clans: Ijwi Island and the Lake Kivu Rift, 1700–1840*. Madison: University of Wisconsin Press, 1991.

———. "Lake Kivu Regional Trade in the Nineteenth Century." *Journal des Africanistes* 50 (1980): 26–30.

———. "Rwabugiri and Ijwi." *Etudes d'histoire africaine* 7 (1975): 155–75.

———. "Precolonial Burundi and Rwanda: Local Loyalties, Regional Royalties." *International Journal of African Historical Studies* 34 (2001): 255–314.

———. "Trick Cyclists? Recontextualizing Rwandan Dynastic Chronology." *History in Africa* 21 (1994): 191–217.

———. "What Role Has Kingship? An Analysis of the *Umuganura* Ritual of Rwanda." *Africa-Tervuren* 27 (1981): 89–101.

Ngologoza, P. *Kigezi and Its People*. Dar es Salaam, Tanzania: East African Literature Bureau, 1969.

Nkongori, L. "Les Abashakamba (ou l'histoire d'un corps de guerriers au pays du 'Royaume hamite')." In *Die Wiener Schule der Völkerkunde*, edited by J. Haekel, A. Hohenwart-Gerlachstein, and A. Slawik, 237–52. Vienna: F. Berger, 1956.

Nkurikiyimfura, J-N. *Le Gros bétail et la société rwandaise: Évolution historique des XIIe-XIVe siècles à 1958*. Paris: Harmattan, 1994.

———. "La révision d'une chronologie: le cas du royaume du Rwanda."

Sources orales de l'histoire de l' Afrique, edited by C. H. Perrot, 149–80. Paris: Publications of the National Center for Scientific Research, 1989.

Nkusi, L. "Quelques remarques de toponymie rwandaise." *Rencontres* 4 (1979): 9–26.

Noten, F. Van. *Histoire archéologique du Rwanda.* Royal Museum for Central Africa Annals, no. 112. Tervuren, Belgium, 1983.

———, ed. *Les Tombes du roi Cyirima Rujugira et de la reine-mère Nyirayuhi Kanjogera.* Royal Museum for Central Africa Annals, no. 77. Tervuren, Belgium, 1972.

Nyagahene, A. "Histoire et peuplement. Ethnies, clans et lignages dans le Rwanda ancien et contemporain." Ph.D. diss., University of Paris–VII, Septentrion, 1997.

Oberg, K. "The Kingdom of Ankole in Uganda." In *African Political Systems,* edited by M. Fortes and E. E. Evans-Pritchard, 121–62. London: Publications for the International Institute of African Languages and Cultures by the Oxford University Press, 1940.

Onselen, C. Van. "Reaction to Rinderpest in Southern Africa, 1896–7." *Journal of African History* 13 (1972): 473–88.

Overdulve, C. M. *Rwanda: Un peuple avec une histoire.* Paris: Harmattan, 1997.

Overschelde, G. Van. *Bij de Reuzen en dwergen van Ruanda.* Tielt, Belgium: Lannoo, 1947.

Pagès, A. *Un Royaume hamite au centre de l'Afrique: Au Ruanda sur les bords du lac Kivu (Congo belge).* Royal Academy of Overseas Sciences, Moral and Political Sciences Section, no. 1. Brussels: Belgian Royal Colonial Institute, 1933.

———. "Au Ruanda. À la cour du Mwami. Ordonnance méticuleuse des obsèques royales." *Zaïre* 4 (1950): 471–87.

———. "Au Ruanda sur les bords du lac Kivu. Congo belge." *Congo* 8 (1927): 377–404, 566–80, 723–53.

Parish, F. R. von. "Zwei Reisen durch Ruanda 1902 bis 1903." *Globus* 86 (1904): 5–13, 73–79.

Pearson-Wright Correspondence. Microfilm CA6/019/18, Christian Missionary Society, Statesboro, GA.

Phillipson, D. W. *African Archaeology.* 2nd ed. Cambridge, U.K.: Cambridge University Press, 1993.

Prioul, C., and P. Sirven, eds. *Atlas du Rwanda.* Kigali, Rwanda: The French Ministry for Cooperation on behalf of the University of Kigali-Rwanda, 1981.

Ramsay, H. von. "Über seine Expeditionen nach Ruanda und dem Rikwa-See (Vortrag 4.6.1898)." *Verhandlungen der Gesellschaft für Erdkunde zu Berlin* 25 (1898): 303–23.

———. "Uha, Urundi und Ruanda." *Mittheilungen von Forschungreisenden und Gelehrten aus den Deutschen Schutzgebieten* 10 (1897): 177–81.

Reid, A., and P. Robertshaw. "A New Look at Ankole Capital Sites." *Azania* 22 (1987): 83–88.

Reisdorff, I. *Enquêtes foncières au Ruanda*. N.p., n.d. [Kigali, Rwanda, 1952]. Mimeograph.

Rennie, J. K. "The Precolonial Kingdom of Rwanda: A Reinterpretation." *Transafrican Journal of History* 2 (1972): 11–53.

Robertshaw, P., and D. Taylor. "Clima te Change and the Rise of Political Complexity in Western Uganda." *Journal of African History* 41 (2000): 1–28.

Roche, E. "Apports de la palynologie à la connaissance du Quaternaire supérieur au Rwanda." In *Exposition sur le thème recherche scientifique au Rwanda par le Musée de Tervuren*, by D. Thys van den Audenaerde. Tervuren, Belgium, 1987.

Rodegem, F. *Dictionnaire rundi-français*. Royal Museum for Central Africa Annals, no. 69. Tervuren, Belgium, 1970.

Roscoe, J. *The Bakitara or Banyoro: The First Part of the Report of the Mackie Ethnological Expedition to Central Africa*. Cambridge, U.K.: Cambridge University Press, 1923.

————. *The Banyankole: The Second Part of the Report of the Mackie Ethnological Expedition to Central Africa*. Cambridge, U.K.: Cambridge University Press, 1923.

Rossel, G. A. *Taxonomic-Linguistic Study of Plantain in Africa*. Leiden, Holland: Research School CNWS, School of Asian, African and Amerindian Studies, 1998.

Rugamba, C. *La Poésie face à l'histoire: Cas de la poésie dynastique rwandaise*. Butare, Rwanda: I. N. R. S., 1987.

Ruriho, M. "Pour une révision profonde de l'histoire de la région des Grands Lacs: le cas du Bwisha précolonial." In *La Civilisation ancienne des peuples des Grands Lacs*, 173–85. Paris: Editions Karthala, 1981.

Rwabukumba, J., and V. Mudandagizi. "Les formes historiques de la dépendance personnelle dans l'Etat rwandais." *Cahiers d'études africaines* 53 (1974): 6–25.

Rwandusya, Z. "The Origins and Settlement of People of Bufumbira." In *A History of Kigezi in South-West Uganda*, edited by D. Denoon, 56–69. Kampala, Uganda: The National Trust, 1971.

Rwankwenda, M. M. R. "The History of Kayonza." In *A History of Kigezi in South-West Uganda*, edited by D. Denoon, 124–33. Kampala, Uganda: The National Trust, 1971.

Saucier, J. F. "The Patron-Client Relationship in Traditional and Contemporary Southern Rwanda." Ph.D. diss., Columbia University, 1974.

Schebesta, P. "In Memoriam Peter Schumacher." *Anthropos* 53 (1958): 233–36.

Schoenbrun, D. "Great Lakes Bantu: Classification and Settlement Chronology." *Sprache und Geschichte in Afrika* 14 (1994): 1–62.

————. *A Green Place, a Good Place: Agrarian Change, Gender, and Social Identity in the Great Lakes Region to the Fifteenth Century*. Portsmouth, N. H.: Heinemann, 1998.

_____. *The Historical Reconstruction of Great Lakes Bantu Cultural Vocabulary: Etymologies and Distributions.* Cologne: Rüdiger Köppe Verlag, 1997.

Schumacher, P. *Dictionnaire phonétique Français-runyarwanda, runyarwanda-français.* Kabgayi, Rwanda: Vicariat apostolique, 1956.

_____. *Expedition zu den zentralafrikanischen Kivu-Pygmäen: Die Kivu-Pygmäen (Twiden).* Royal Academy of Overseas Sciences, Moral and Political Sciences Section, no. 5, vol. 2. Brussels: Belgian Royal Colonial Institute, 1950.

_____. *Expedition zu den zentralafrikanischen Kivu-Pygmäen: Die physische und soziale Umwelt der Kivu-Pygmäen (Twiden).* Royal Academy of Overseas Sciences, Moral and Political Sciences Section, no. 3, vol. 1. Brussels: Belgian Royal Colonial Institute, 1949.

_____. *Ruanda.* Micro-Bibliotheca Anthropos, vol. 28A. Posieux (Freiburg): Institut-Anthropos, 1958. Microfilm.

Schweinfurth, G., et al., eds. *Emin Pasha in Central Africa: Being a Collection of His Letters and Journals.* Translated by R. W. Felkin. London: G. Philip and Son, 1888.

Sebasoni, S. *Les Origines du Rwanda.* Paris: Harmattan, 2000.

Smith, P. "Entretien avec l'Abbé Alexis Kagame." *Recherche, pédagogie et culture* 51 (1981): 48–54.

_____. *Le Récit populaire au Rwanda.* Paris: A. Colin, 1975.

Speke, J. H. *Journal of the Discovery of the Source of the Nile.* 1863. Reprint, London: Dent, 1906.

Ssebalijja, Y. "Memories of Rukiga and Other Places." In *A History of Kigezi in South-West Uganda,* edited by D. Denoon, 179–99. Kampala, Uganda: The National Trust, 1971.

Stanley, H. M. *In Darkest Africa, or, the Quest, Rescue, and Retreat of Emin Governor of Equatoria.* 2 vols. New York: Scribners, 1890.

_____. *Through the Dark Continent, or, the sources of the Nile around the Great Lakes of Equatorial Africa and down the Livingstone River to the Atlantic Ocean.* 1878. Reprint, London: Sampson Low, Marston, Seale and Livingston, 1890.

Stuhlmann, F., ed. *Die Tagebücher von dr. Emin Pascha.* Hamburg: G. Westermann, 1916–27.

Sutton, J. "The Antecedents of the Interlacustrine Kingdoms." *Journal of African History* 34 (1993): 33–64.

_____. "Archaeological Sites of East Africa: Four Studies." *Azania* 33 (1998): 1–169.

Taylor, C. *A Simplified Runyankore-Rukiga-English and English-Runyankore-Rukiga Dictionary: In the 1955 Revised Orthography with Tone-Markings and Full Entries under Prefixes.* Kampala, Uganda: Eagle Press, 1959.

Tshihiluka, T. "Ryamurari, capitale de l'ancien royaume du Ndorwa." In *Histoire archéologique du Rwanda,* edited by F. Van Noten, 149–53. Tervuren, Belgium: Royal Museum for Central Africa, 1983.

Van Sambeek. J. *Dictionary English-Kiha.* N.p., n.d. Mimeograph.

————. *Small Dictionary of Kiha for Beginners.* N.p., n.d. Mimeograph.

Vansina, J. *L'Évolution du royaume rwanda des origines à 1900.* Royal Academy of Overseas Sciences, Moral and Political Sciences Section, n.s., 26. Brussels: Belgian Royal Colonial Institute 1962. Second edition with *Supplément 1999.* Royal Academy of Overseas Sciences, Moral and Political Sciences Section, n.s., 52. Brussels: Belgian Royal Colonial Institute, 2000.

————. "Historical Tales (Ibitéekerezo) and the History of Rwanda." *History in Africa* 27 (2000): 375–514.

————. *La Légende du passé. Traditions orales du Burundi.* Royal Museum for Central Africa Anthropology Archives, no. 16. Tervuren, Belgium, 1972.

————. "Note sur la chronologie du Burundi ancien." *Bulletin des séances* 38 (1967): 429–44.

————. *Oral Tradition as History.* Madison: University of Wisconsin Press, 1985.

————. *Paths in the Rainforests: Toward a History of Political Tradition in Equatorial Africa.* Madison: University of Wisconsin Press, 1990.

————. "Useful Anachronisms." *History in Africa* 27 (2000): 415–21.

————, ed. *Ibitéekerezo.* 6 reels. Chicago: Center for Research Libraries, 1958–62.

Vanwalle, R. "Aspecten van staatsvorming in West-Rwanda." *Africa-Tervuren* 28 (1982): 64–78.

Vidal, C. "Économie de la société féodale rwandaise." *Cahiers d'études africaines* 53 (1974): 52–74.

————. "Le Rwanda des anthropologues ou le fétichisme de la vache." *Cahiers d'études africaines* 35 (1969): 384–401.

————. *Sociologie des Passions: Rwanda, Côte d'Ivoire.* Paris: Editions Karthala, 1991.

Webster, J. B., ed. *Chronology, Migration, and Drought in Interlacustrine Africa.* New York: Africana Publishing Company, 1979.

Wrigley, C. *Kingship and State: The Buganda Dynasty.* Cambridge, U.K.: Cambridge University Press, 1996.

INDEX

Note: Bold numbers refer to maps.